*About the author*

For nearly twenty years Graeme Donald has been tracking down the origins of thousands of phrases. Now a full-time writer and journalist, his broadcasting experience includes setting the questions for *Back to Square One*, a quiz programme broadcast on Radio 2, Radio 4 and the World Service and soon to be televised. He has written a column expounding his knowledge of etymology in *Today* newspaper for the last seven years, and published two books based on the column, *Things You Didn't Know You Didn't Know* and *More Things You Didn't Know You Didn't Know*.

# The Dictionary of Modern Phrase

*Graeme Donald*

SIMON & SCHUSTER

LONDON·SYDNEY·NEW YORK·TOKYO·SINGAPORE·TORONTO

First published in Great Britain by Simon & Schuster Ltd, 1994
A Paramount Communication Company



**Simon & Schuster Ltd**
**West Garden Place**
**Kendal Street**
**London W2 2AQ**

Simon & Schuster of Australia Pty Ltd
Sydney

A CIP catalogue record for this book is available from the British Library.

ISBN 0–671–71309–4

Typeset in Bembo by Hewer Text Composition Services, Edinburgh
Printed and bound in Great Britain by
Butler & Tanner Ltd, Frome and London

## Abbreviations

| | |
|---|---|
| b. | born |
| *c.* | *circa* |
| d. | died |
| OED | Oxford English Dictionary (first edition) |
| Partidge | *The Dictionary of Slang and Unconventional English*, Eric Partridge (eighth edition, 1984) |
| WW1 | World War One |
| WW2 | World War Two |

## Cross references

These are indicated in the text by SMALL CAPITALS.

To the memory of Vernon Noble, a tireless lexicographer and friend and correspondent of Eric Partridge. Also with special thanks to Sian Parkhouse for all her friendly help, support – and patience.

# A a

**A.1.:** *Of first class quality.*

Lloyd's Register of British and Foreign Shipping was launched in 1760 for the benefit of marine insurance companies and underwriters. In it each ship was classified by a letter and a number, the former indicating the sea-worthiness of the hull and the latter the state of the general equipment. Apart from its use in general speech, 'A.1.' is basically obsolete since it referred to ships with wooden hulls. The modern equivalent is '100-A.1.'.

**A GO-GO:** *In abundance.*

The French '*à go-go*' is the equivalent of our 'galore', and would appear to derive from the Old French '*en gogues*' – frolicsome, in merry mood – from the idea that revellers indulge every whim to excess. The trend of attaching it to a noun started in the 1960s when the Whisky A Go-Go, a night-club in Paris, became fashionable.

**A OK:** *Absolutely fine.*

This was the result of a mis-heard transmission from astronaut Alan Shephard to NASA Control in May 1961. Shephard denies ever having said any such thing, but acknowledges that he could well have mumbled: 'Er . . . OK' in reply to a mission control enquiry. In any case, the NASA Public Relations Officer, Colonel 'Shorty' Powers, was so impressed with what he thought he had heard that he used it in several press conferences, thus launching it on the world.

**ABANDON ALL HOPE YE WHO ENTER HERE**

Now used with mock severity of, for example, one's place of work, this is the popular rendition of 'All hope abandon ye who enter here.' It is taken from Verse 9, Canto 111 of *Inferno*, the first part of *The Divine Comedy* completed by Dante (1265–1321) in the year of his death.

**ABDERITAN LAUGHTER:** *Derisive laughter.*

The Thracian port of Abdera was the home of Democritus, dubbed the Laughing Philosopher because of his habit of laughing to scorn any theories other than his own. Additionally, the Abderitans were nationally reputed to be simple-minded to a man and such people frequently laugh hysterically at ideas they are unable to comprehend.

**ABOVE THE SALT:** *Of high social standing.*

The previously high cost of the condiment meant it was placed fairly high up the banqueting table near the more important guests, thus its position on the table dictated the seating arrangements and guests found themselves either above or below the salt cellar.

**ABOVE-BOARD:** *Without deception.*

This was originally a gambling term; a player whose hands were visible above the table was unlikely to be cheating. It first appeared in the sixteenth century as 'above bord' when 'bord' signified any plank or table.

**ABRACADABRA:** *Magicians' chant used to indicate dexterity or success.*

This is a very ancient word indeed, originally used in serious incantations. Its derivation is in some doubt; it could be a Latinized form of the Aramaic prayer used in cabalistic faith-healing rituals, '*Abhadda kedabrah*' (Disappear O Sickness). Alternatively it could be a distortion of the Hebrew '*Ab, Ben, Ruach Acadsch*' – Father, Son and Holy Ghost.

**ABSENCE MAKES THE HEART GROW FONDER**

This is a line taken from an extremely popular nineteenth-century song entitled *Isle of Beauty* by Thomas Haynes Bayly (1797–1839).

**AC/DC:** *Bi-sexual; hermaphrodite.*

In the terminology of electricity this means able to function on either Alternating Current or Direct Current, hence the analogy.

**ACE IN THE HOLE:** *Hidden reserves.*

In seven-card stud poker the first two cards are dealt face down and known as 'the hole'; the next five are dealt face up in rounds interspersed by betting, the highest up-turned card or best combination dictating the stakes. If a player knows that one of his first cards is an ace, he is in a strong position.

**ACEY-DEUCY:** *A mixture of extremes.*

In most card games the ace is the highest and the deuce, named from the French *deux* (two) the lowest. Acey-deucy is actually the name of a variant of backgammon in which the dice combination 1-2 holds great significance.

**ACHILLES' HEEL:** *Weak spot.*

Greek mythology recounts how Achilles' mother dipped him at birth in the River Styx in Hades to render him invulnerable. Unfortunately the magic water could not reach the heel by which she held him and when he was a man he was killed during the Trojan Wars by a poisoned arrow shot by Paris and guided to his foot by Apollo.

**ACID TEST:** *A stringent check.*

This derives from the testing of gold which remains invulnerable to most acids and will dissolve only in a 3–1 mixture of concentrated hydrochloric and nitric acid, known as *aqua regia* (royal water) since gold has always been regarded as the king of metals. If a sample should succumb to any weaker acid or mixture it would be suspect to say the least.

**ACK OVER TOCH:** *Euphemism for arse over tit.*

In radio communication even the spelling out of a word can be misheard so there is always a code of words to represent and confirm the letters of the alphabet. In WW2 British Army signals 'Ack' stood for 'A' and 'Toch' for 'T'. *See also:* DIM AS A TOC H LAMP.

**ACKNOWLEDGE THE CORN:** *Admit an error, especially a minor point in an argument, or a minor offence to avoid a graver charge.*

This expression, which arose in America in the early–mid 1800s, is probably a straightforward usage of 'corn', small particle, as in 'peppercorn'. There are several unconvincing tales pinning the saying to specific Congressional debates, and an equally unconvincing yarn of a man who, accused of stealing a horse and some corn with which to feed it, confessed only to the theft of the corn because horse-stealing was a capital offence.

**ACROSS THE BOARD:** *All inclusive.*

When the results of a race have been announced the betting shops list the first, second and third animals across the board, leading the expression to become synonymous with 'each way'.

**ADDLE-HEADED:** *Muddle-headed.*

The Greek for an egg which failed to hatch out was '*ourion oon*' – literally egg of wind. Because of the slight similarity in spelling, this was poorly translated into Latin as '*ovum urinae*', egg of urine. The medieval English for urine was '*adel*', hence addled eggs and addled brains.

**ADMIRABLE CRICHTON:** *One who excels in many fields.*

*The Admirable Crichton*, first produced in 1902, was written by J. M. Barrie (1860–1937). It popularized the epithet bestowed by John Johnson in his *Heroes Scoti* (1603) on one James Crichton, a Scottish scholar of prodigious ability. Already an MA at the age of fifteen, he went on to the Sorbonne where he astounded the Parisian intelligentsia. His dazzling career was cut ignominiously short in Italy where he was killed in a street brawl in 1585, ironically by Vincenzo di Gonzaga, a young Prince of Mantua, whose tutor he was at the time.

**ADONIS:** *An extremely handsome man.*

This is derived from the Phoenician '*adon*' – Lord. According to Greek mythology, Adonis, the issue of an incestuous relationship between the Syrian King Theias and his daughter Myrrha, was so handsome that he was pursued by both Aphrodite and Persephone. In the end he was killed during a boar-hunt and his spilt blood brought forth a new flower, the pheasant's eye. The most famous use of the word occurred in 1813 when Leigh Hunt

(1784–1859) attacked the Prince Regent in *The Examiner* by referring to him as a corpulent Adonis of fifty – he was jailed for his temerity.

**ADONIS GARDEN:** *An ephemeral or worthless object.*

In ancient Greece, mainly in Byblos, festivals were held in honour of Adonis and his re-birth as flowers. Small pots of flowers were forced to rapid growth for the ceremonies only to be flung into the sea along with representations of Adonis himself.

**AFFLUENT SOCIETY:** *A wealthy community.*

The economist John K. Galbraith (b. 1908) in his book *The Affluent Society* (1958) commented on how a glut of the trappings of affluence resulted in a corresponding reduction in the ability of the public sector to cope. For example, people who were better off than ever before tended to produce more children who lived longer, but the number of doctors and teachers available would find this situation hard to handle.

**AFTER THE LORD MAYOR'S SHOW:** *Failure following initial success.*

An expression common since the last century when the Lord Mayor of London's parade was exclusively made up of horse-drawn floats. After the Lord Mayor's Show . . . comes the man with the bucket and shovel to clean up after the animals.

**AID AND ABET:** *Assist in wrongful acts.*

Through misunderstanding of this precise legal term, the two words are frequently regarded as synonymous which is far from the case. The second word properly means to incite and is ultimately rooted in the Norse '*beita*', to bite, and progressed to its current meaning through the bear gardens of old whence it emerged a verb meaning to urge the dogs on to the attack. The full expression thus means to not only assist another in an unlawful act but also to encourage them to greater wrongdoing.

**AIN'T NOBODY HERE BUT US CHICKENS**

The expression was born in America in the mid–late nineteenth century and arose from a tale of a dim-witted farmer plagued by a cunning chicken thief. Awoken one night by a suspicious disturbance, the farmer went to the henhouse with his gun and demanded that the thief give himself up. The sly thief responded with the above and the farmer, his fears allayed, went back to bed.

**ALADDIN'S CAVE:** *A treasure trove.*

Something of a misnomer since the cave in question contained only a lamp. The lamp admittedly housed a genie who bestowed three wishes on Aladdin, one of which he had to invest in extricating himself from the cave. The name is derived from the Arabic '*Ala-ad-din*', the nobility of faith.

**ALADDIN'S WINDOW:** *An unfinished work begun by a master.*

Aladdin's genie built him a palace

with twenty-four windows, twenty three of which were set in precious stones. Later, a Sultan tried to complete the set and beggared himself in the attempt, the moral being that one competes with a master in vain.

**ALAR(U)MS AND EXCURSIONS:** *Confused, frantic activity.*

In Elizabethan days this stage direction called for the simulation of feverish skirmishing on the outskirts of a battle while the noise of warfare and trumpets sounded from the wings.

**ALBATROSS ABOUT THE NECK:** *A heavy burden of guilt.*

*The Rime of the Ancient Mariner* exemplifies the sailors' superstition that killing an albatross brings bad luck. When the title character of the poem brought doom upon his ship by doing just that, his shipmates hung the corpse around his neck to show the Fates who had so invited their anger.

**ALIBI IKE:** *A shirker with an ever-ready excuse.*

The original character was created by the American sports writer and features columnist Ring Lardner (1885–1933) who introduced him in a short story written in 1924. It was later built into a long-running cartoon strip.

**ALIVE AND KICKING:** *Fit and well.*

This was a seventeenth- and eighteenth-century London fish vendors' cry extolling the freshness of the wares.

**ALL AGOG:** *Excitedly eager.*

Like A GO-GO this is derived from the Old French '*en gogues*' meaning frolicsome or in merriment, a term which had heavy overtones of wantonness and hedonism, so there is perhaps a link with the excitement generated by scenes of revelry.

**ALL DRESSED UP AND NO PLACE/NOWHERE TO GO:** *Ready for action, but left on the sidelines.*

This was the title of an American song written by Gus Whiting in 1912 and popularised in 1913 by the comedian Raymond Hitchcock. Its currency owes much to its use in 1916 by the American writer–journalist William Allen White (1868-1944) who so described the Progressive Party after Theodore Roosevelt had refused their nomination to run for presidential office at their head.

**ALL I KNOW IS WHAT I READ IN THE NEWSPAPERS**

This can mean either 'Don't snow me with fancy talk because I already know the truth from the newspapers' or 'How should I know? My only source of information is the newspapers and they are notoriously inaccurate or untruthful.' The saying is invariably attributed to the American cowboy philosopher, Will Rogers, but, as is so often the case with famous quips, he had in fact 'borrowed' it from someone else. During one of his frequent visits to his contemporary Herbert Swope, Rogers asked him how he had acquired his diverse and enviable store of knowledge; Swope's response was: 'I only know what I read in the newspapers.' The response so impressed Rogers that he included it in his cracker-barrel philosophy act in Ziegfield's Follies and also in his *Letters of a Self-made Diplomat to his President* (1927). It was the opening line of a letter dated 21 May 1926, supposedly directed to President Calvin Coolidge.

**ALL AT SEA, TO BE:** *Completely lost.*

In the days before charts and navigational aids ships liked to keep the shore line in view. If blown about at the mercy of a storm in the night the ship was described as 'all at sea' if no land was in view the following morning and the crew were left unsure of which way to head.

**ALL IN:** *Exhausted.*

A nineteenth-century Stock Exchange expression describing a market that was depressed because cautious traders were holding *all* stock *in* until they could see the way ahead. *See also*: ALL OUT.

**ALL IN THE BEST POSSIBLE TASTE:** *In bad taste.*

Hollywood's response to the strict censorship rules imposed upon it in its so-called Golden Era was to portray any hint of eroticism 'in the best possible taste'. When defending *Tarzan the Ape Man* director John Derek told *Time* magazine: 'The sacrifice scene was done in the finest of all taste – taste the Pope would applaud.' Kenny Everett turned the cliché into a national catch-phrase when he lampooned it in his 1981 series of *The Kenny Everett Show* screened on BBC 1. In each episode he appeared garishly attired as the archetypal blonde Hollywood siren, 'Cupid Stunt', flaunting ample bosom and thighs and writhing ecstatically while she described some forthcoming lurid attraction; the punch line was always 'And in the best possible taste!'.

**ALL IN THE SAME BOAT:** *All subject to the same rigours.*

This was most probably prompted by the hardships shared by sailors adrift in a small boat when their mother ship had been sunk. The idea that the saying was an indictment of the atrocious conditions once suffered by the crews of British ships of the line is untenable; no sailor worth his salt would confuse 'boat' (a small, open craft without decking) with 'ship' (a sea-going vessel with decking).

**ALL MY EYE AND BETTY MARTIN:** *Nonsense.*

The first part of this Cockney expression is straightforward enough and refers to the age-old gesture of pulling down the lower eyelid to indicate disbelief. The addition of 'and Betty Martin' first appeared in the mid 1700s so it is highly probable that Betty Martin was a well-known character in London around that time and, indeed, Charles Lee Lewis refers in his memoirs, published in 1805, to a certain Betty Martin, a one-time actress who became a notorious woman about town. There are other theories that depend upon the fact that Latin was incomprehensible to the masses. One claims that the name is a anglicized version of '*O mihi beate Martine*' (O grant me, blessed St Martin), supposedly from a prayer to St Martin of Tour, but no record of any such prayer exists. Another sees the expression as a corruption of '*O mihi Britomartis*', a plea for help from the Cretan goddess Britomartis since the Phoenicians adopted her into their culture and could have introduced the phrase into Cornwall when trading for tin there. However, no explanation is given as to why the saying lay dormant for hundreds of years only to burst forth hundreds of miles away in eighteenth-century London. Perhaps this localized eruption of the expression in the complete form lends support to the conjecture perceiving the addition of the name to be but rhyming slang for 'fartin', as in the accused raconteur standing accused of emitting less than plausible hot air.

**ALL OUT:** *Strenuously.*

A piece of nineteenth-century British Stock Market jargon describing a trading floor in full swing with *all* manner of companies laying stocks *out* for dealing. *See also*: ALL IN.

**ALL OVER BAR THE SHOUTING:** *The matter is effectively settled.*

From boxing circles and descriptive of a conclusion to a match which will remain unchanged despite the inevitable bickering and appeals against the referee's decision.

**ALL ROADS LEAD TO ROME:** *No matter your course of action, the result will be the same.*

First noted in the twelfth century this was likely born of the passion for pilgrimages, Rome being the most important of all. Having embarked on such a trip the devoted tended to maximize piety by calling at all holy sites of interest *en route* – whichever route they picked, they all ended up in Rome. Incidentally, this circuitous rambling produced 'roam' as a varient of the city's name.

**ALL SET?:** *Are you ready to go?*

Prior to departing the harbour a sailing ship must set her sails to take the wind.

**ALL SHIP-SHAPE AND BRISTOL FASHION:** *Extremely smart.*

In the eighteenth/nineteenth centuries the port of Bristol's reputation for efficiency went unchallenged.

**ALL SORTS AND CONDITIONS OF MAN.**

This is taken from *A Prayer for All Conditions of Men* which is to be found in the Book of Common Prayer: 'O God, the creator and preserver of all mankind, we humbly beseech thee for all sorts and conditions of men, that thou wouldst be pleased to make thy ways known unto them, thy saving grace unto all nations.' In the mid-1500s when this was written, 'condition' in this context meant status or social position.

**ALL THE GO:** *The height of fashion.*

In the eighteenth century, this was drapers' terminology for material that was so popular that it would sell furiously, i.e. *go* rapidly out of the shop.

**ALL TO THE GOOD:** *Very positive.*

A rather antiquated accountancy

term referring to the profit and loss sheet on which the benefit side was known as the good.

**ALL YOUR CHICKENS WILL COME HOME TO ROOST:** *The consequences of your actions will rebound on you.*

This is an ellipsis of the older 'Curses are like young chickens; they always come home to roost.'

**ALLEY UP:** *Pay up.*

Top quality playing marbles were made out of either marble or alabaster, the latter leading to the nickname 'alleys'. When a player lost a game, he had to hand over the marbles used or 'alley up'. Although the game was often played in alleys, this has no bearing on the saying.

**ALLEY UP/OOP:** *Get to it.*

This 'alley' is derived from the French '*aller*', to go, which is ultimately rooted in the Latin '*ambulare*' – to walk. Partridge holds that the dramatic reduction of the word would have been occasioned by its use in military commands to get troops marching.

**ALMA MATER:** *Name given to a school or university by its alumni.*

This is Latin for 'bounteous mother', a title bestowed by the Romans on Ceres (goddess of tillage and corn), Cybele (mother goddess) and other goddesses. The source of one's education is here personified as a foster mother who has bestowed the gifts of knowledge and learning.

**ALMIGHTY DOLLAR**

As early as the seventeenth century Ben Jonson had used the expression 'almightie gold' to disparage the blind pursuit of wealth. Washington Irving, (1783–1859) the American essayist, up-dated this to 'almighty dollar' and used it in his essay 'The Creole Village' published in 1836 in the *Knickerbocker* magazine, in which he said of settlements along the Mississippi: '. . . the almighty dollar, that great object of universal devotion throughout the land, seems to have no genuine devotees in these peculiar villages'. This was taken as a slur implying that his fellow Americans were mere money-grubbers and brought forth such a barrage of criticism that Irving was obliged to issue a statement that he had not intended any such insult and that he, as much as anyone, regarded the dollar as a venerable institution. Probably as a result of his close friendship with Irving, Dickens used the expression in 1843 in *Martin Chuzzlewit* and this popularized it in Britain, where it is always used in disparagement.

**ALNASCHER'S DREAM:** *A grossly over-optimistic aspiration doomed to failure.*

Alnascher was the deaf fifth brother of the Barber in *The Arabian Nights*. He invested all his money in a basketful of fine glassware which he planned to sell off at enormous profit and repeat the process until he became wealthy enough to marry the Vizier's daughter. With his basket at his side, he lay down to sleep, dreamed that he kicked out at his intended bride during a quarrel and, alas, actually did kick out, overturning the basket and smashing its contents. The derivation of the name is the Arabic '*al naschar*' – the lawyer.

**ALPHA AND OMEGA:** *The be-all and end-all.*

From the Revelation of St John in which God underlines his omnipotence with the words: 'I am alpha and omega, the first and the last.' Although 'alpha' ('a') and 'omega' ('o') have been the first and last letters of the Greek alphabet for some time now, 'tau' ('t') used to be the last and ancient references to 'alpha and tau' are common.

**ALPHONSE AND GASTON:** *Conflicting good intentions.*

These two strip-cartoon characters, created in 1902 by the American Frederick Burr Opper (1857–1937) and extremely popular in the first few years of this century, were constantly trying to out-do each other in courtesy. Each episode ended with the words: 'After you, my dear Alphonse.' 'No, no. After you my dear Gaston.'

**ALSO-RAN:** *A mediocre performer, a loser.*

When a racing commentator calls out the names and places of the winning horses, he continues with: '. . . *also running were* . . .'

**ALTHAEA'S BRAND:** *A dark force which will assert itself in the end.*

In Greek mythology Althaea overheard the Fates whispering that her new-born son Meleager would live only as long as the log – or brand – on the fire in front of her, so she snatched it from the flames and locked it away. In later life Meleager killed his maternal uncles in a brawl and, to avenge them, Althaea threw the brand back on the fire.

**ALTMARK:** *A harsh regime.*

When the Germans decided to scuttle their pocket-battleship *Admiral Graf Spee* in 1939, there were 299 captured British seamen on board who were then transferred to the *Altmark*, which lay in Jossing Fjord, Norway, until the British destroyer HMS *Cossack*, under the command of Philip Vian, later Admiral of the Fleet, effected their release. Their tales of hardship endured aboard the *Altmark* launched the name into current usage.

**AMASIS'/POLYCRATES' RING:** *Misfortune from which one cannot escape.*

When Amasis, King of Egypt, was on a good-will visit to Polycrates, the Tyrant of Samos (*c.* 535–515 BC), he became worried about his friend's only too apparent wealth and good fortune and advised him to throw his most valuable ring into the sea lest the gods became jealous and vengeful. Polycrates did so and held a banquet to celebrate his salvation. Alas, when he cut open his fish, he found the ring in its belly. This was indeed an ill omen which was fulfilled when he was lured a short time later to the mainland by his old enemy Draetes, the Persian Governor of Lydia, and crucified upon landing.

**AMAZON:** *A strong, statuesque woman.*

The Amazons were a tribe of female warriors said to have lived near the Euxine (now the Black) Sea. Tolerating no man in their midst, they ensured the continuance of their race by mating with the men of the near-by Gargareans; male children were killed or returned to the fathers. As for the origin of the name, there seems little need to look further than the Old Persian '*hamazan*', a warrior, but this has not stemmed lurid speculation. Folk etymology claims that Amazons had their right breast cauterized at birth to facilitate the drawing of a bow in later life and links the word with the Greek '*a mezos*', without a breast, but there has never been a single representation of an Amazon so mutilated; neither is there any foundation to the suggestion that, because the Amazons were meat-eating huntresses, the Greek '*a maza*', no cereal, was involved. The name of the river is derived from its native nick-name '*Amassona*', the boat-destroyer, and not from any fanciful tales of Spanish explorers encountering female warriors along its banks.

**AMBROSIA:** *Delicious food or drink.*

Originally the food of the gods of Olympus and reputed to confer on them their immorality, this is most probably based on the Greek '*a brotos*' (not mortal). Some believe there is also a connection with '*ambar*', the Semitic for ambergris, since that too was thought in the East to have magic properties.

**AMEN CORNER:** *American term for slavish followers of 'yes men'.*

Derived from association with Evangelical or Hot Gospel meetings where the dedicated faithful sit in pews near the pulpit muttering fervent 'amens' throughout the sermon, this expression gained wide currency when James Baldwin's play *Amen Corner,* written in 1953, was produced on Broadway in 1965.

**AMYCLAEAN SILENCE:** *A silence which no one dares to break.*

To the south of Sparta lay Amyclaea, a town plagued by panics resulting from repeated false alarms of Spartan invasion. Finally, the city elders proclaimed a penalty of death for spreading such rumours with the result that, when the Spartans *did* invade it, the town fell because nobody dared to raise the alarm.

**ANANIAS:** *A liar.*

A gesture of faith demanded of early Christians was that they should sell a proportion of their possessions and donate the money to a central fund administered by the Apostles. In Acts 5:1–10, Ananias sold the required proportion of his chattels but withheld part of the proceeds. When questioned, he lied, whereupon he fell down dead at the feet of Peter; when his wife arrived, she told the same lie and suffered the same fate. The use of the word was popularized by Theodore Roosevelt (1858–1919) who coined 'The Ananias Club' as a slur on certain sectors of the Yellow Press who persistently breached confidence or printed deliberate falsehoods.

**ANCIENT MARINER:** *A crashing bore.*

This was the 'hero' of Samuel Taylor Coleridge's *The Rime of the Ancient Mariner* (1798), who button-holed a guest on his way to a wedding and proceeded to regale him with an interminable tale of woe.

**AND SO TO BED:** *It is time to finish.*

Although the Irish dramatist James Bernard Fagan (1873–1933) staged a highly successful play of this title in 1926, the expression was already famous through its repeated use by Pepys to close entries in his *Diary* .

**ANDREW, THE:** *The Royal Navy.*

It is said that in the 1760s the main Portsmouth Press Gang operated under the leadership of one Andrew Miller, a gentleman unequalled in zeal and success. So many men were 'andrewed' that the Navy itself acquired the nickname, and warships are still referred to as Andrew Millers.

**ANDROMEDA STRAIN:** *A previously unknown virus.*

Specifically a virus that has escaped from an experimental establishment, this was the title of a successful American sci-fi chiller published in 1971 by Michael Crichton, which tells of a contaminated space probe returning from the constellation of Andromeda bearing a terrible infection.

**ANGEL:** *One who finances a theatrical production.*

The usage probably came about quite simply by association with 'guardian angel'. The suggestion that it is derived from Luis de Santangel (*c.* 1451–1506), the Keeper of the Privy Purse for Ferdinand of Spain and the man who personally raised most of the money required to finance Columbus's voyage to the New World, seems an over-complication.

**ANGRY YOUNG MAN:** *A young man alienated by conventional mores.*

George Fearon bestowed this title on John Osborne, whose controversial play of 1956 *Look Back in Anger* placed him firmly among a group of disaffected writers and dramatists which included such luminaries as Colin Wilson and Kingsley Amis. The epithet became immediately fashionable. It had however been in use in the same context for years, even figuring as the title in 1951 of an autobiography by Leslie Paul, an English social philosopher.

**ANIMAL MAGNETISM:** *A pseudo-scientific term for physical attraction.*

This rather misleading term was coined by Anton Mesmer (1734–1815) who carried out experimental work on patients suffering from hysteria and similar disorders. Having begun by stroking the patients with magnets, he realized that the 'cure' was effected by some power emanating from himself and labelled it 'animal magnetism'. His work laid the foundations for modern hypnosis.

**ANNIE OAKLEY:** *Any free ticket, but especially one for the theatre; a spinnaker.*

Although modern free tickets are stamped with a red stripe or the word 'complimentary', they were originally standard tickets punched with holes to prevent their being surrendered for cash at the Box Office. The allusion to Annie Oakley, the cowgirl show-woman who specialized in shooting the spots out of playing cards, is obvious. Similarly, a ventilated spinnaker in sailing circles is referred to as an Annie Oakley.

**ANOTHER DAY, ANOTHER DOLLAR:** *A routine day at work.*

This comes from the American cattle ranches of the nineteenth century when the average wage of a cowboy was one dollar a day plus keep.

**ANTE UP:** *Pay up.*

'*Ante*' is Latin for 'before' and the rules of many card games stipulate that the deal cannot begin *before* the players have placed the agreed minimum stake, also known as the 'ante', on the table.

**ANVIL CHORUS:** *A rowdy scene.*

This is a reference to 'The Gypsy Song' in Act II of Verdi's *Il Trovatore* in which numerous anvils are used to create the impression of a busy blacksmith's workshop. The anvils are rarely, if ever, the real thing; instead, rather robust xylophone-type instruments are used.

**APICIAN:** *Luxurious and expensive, usually applied to food.*

This is derived from the name of Marcus Gavius Apicius who lived in the time of Tiberius and was the second of three great Roman epicures to bear that surname. He squandered his fortune on high living and committed suicide rather than suffer the indignity of existing on plain fare. There is extant a collection of recipes published in the third century by Caelius Apicius under the title *Apicius* better known by its sub-title *De Re Coquinaria* – of culinary matters.

**APPEAL FROM PHILIP DRUNK TO PHILIP SOBER:** *To make a second approach at a more appropriate time.*

This is derived from an apocryphal tale of a woman who approached Philip of Macedon for a judgment. Unfortunately, Philip was extremely drunk at the time and gave a totally irrational verdict. The dissatisfied plaintiff infuriated the king by calmly announcing her intention of appealing. Philip, the supreme power in the land, demanded to know to whom she thought she could appeal, only to be told: 'To Philip sober'.

**APPEASE YOUR MANES:** *To carry on the traditions of your ancestors.*

The Romans, in common with many other ancient cultures, believed that the 'manes' (spirits of the departed) could not rest in peace in the other world unless their last wishes had been carried out to the letter in this one.

**APPLE OF DISCORD:** *A cause of envy and contention.*

In Greek mythology, Peleus, King of the Myrmidons, and his bride Thetis, leader of the Nereids, understandably did not invite Eris, the Goddess of Discord, to their wedding feast. Enraged by this slight, Eris turned up anyway, determined to ruin the occasion. She placed a golden apple on the table, pronouncing it to be the prize for the most beautiful woman present and, having elected the luckless Paris judge, sat back to watch gleefully as the three vain goddesses present tried to affect his choice by bribing him. Hera offered him wealth and power, Athene, glory in war, but Aphrodite triumphed by offering him Helen of Troy and his acceptance led to the Trojan Wars.

**APPLE OF YOUR EYE:** *One favoured above all others.*

In medieval times the pupil of the eye was believed to be round and solid like an apple, and the Middle English '*apel*' meant both 'pupil' and 'apple'. The expression arose because the pupil is the central and most important part of the eye.

**APPLE POLISHERS:** *Sycophants.*

The reference is to school-children who curried favour by bringing polished apples to their teachers.

**APPLE-PIE BED:** *A bed specially prepared as a joke.*

The old schoolboy joke of folding the bottom sheet of a bed up and over the top so that nobody can get into it reinforces the '*nappes pliées*' origin in APPLE-PIE ORDER.

**APPLE-PIE ORDER:** *Perfect neatness.*

This could have come about simply by association with an apple-pie with precisely crimped edges, but the most likely source is the French '*nappes pliées*', folded linen, hence neat as a pile of freshly ironed laundry. It has been suggested that the Old French '*cap à pie*' which meant armed to the teeth was the source, but as pointed out by the OED, a transitional stage of '*cap à pie* order' would be required before complete metamorphosis and no such examples are to be found anywhere in print. Furthermore, 'apple-pie order' did not emerge until the early eighteenth century when '*cap à pie*' was teetering on the brink of obsolesence and the normal French equivalents of 'from head to toe/foot', were '*de la tête aux pieds*', or '*de pied en cap*'.

**APPLE SAUCE:** *Words meant to deceive.*

This was coined in nineteenth-century America where mean boarding-house keepers cheated their lodgers by camouflaging poor portions of pork with lashings of apple sauce.

**APRES MOI, LE DELUGE (After me, the flood):** *When I am gone chaos will ensue.*

The meaning of this has changed since it was first uttered by Jeanne Antoinette (1721–64), Marquise de Pompadour and mistress of Louis XV of France. It was Frederick the Great's (1712–86) astonishment at her prodigious personal extravagance, presumably meaning that she would live out her life as she wished after which the flood could return for all she cared. Metternich (1773–1859) employed the saying in the 1850s in its now accepted sense to imply that when his hand was removed from the tiller of Austria trouble would ensue. As it happened, he was right.

**ARCADIA:** *An idyllic place of rustic simplicity.*

Once a district of Greece, Arcadia

was the traditional home of Pan, the Greek god of pastures, flocks and woods; Virgil cited it as the seat of pastoral bliss, hence its accepted meaning. Sir Philip Sidney (1554–86) reinforced this in 1580 when he used *Arcadia* as the title of his famous pastoral poem. However strange this must seem, the actual inhabitants of Arcadia were by no means tranquil rustics and were despised for their brutal savagery by the rest of their nation with whom they were in complete contrast.

**ARCHIE BUNKER:** *A fractious reactionary.*

Applied especially to a right-wing, working-class reactionary, the source is the star character of the TV show *All in the Family*, the American version of the British programme *Till Death Do Us Part* in which Warren Mitchell played the main character, Alf Garnet.

**ARGOSY:** *A great merchant ship.*

From the close of the thirteenth century until the seventeenth century large merchantmen were built in the Dalmatian port of Raguas, better known today as Dubrovnik. These ships were called '*ragusyes*' a word that underwent many changes in spelling on its way to the English 'argosy'. Argosy is also used to describe a collection of various works; this comes about by association with the varied nature of the precious cargoes carried by such ships.

**ARGUE THE TOSS:** *Argue in vain.*

Once the coin has been tossed and the result is there for all to see, it is futile to dispute it.

**ARGUS-EYED:** *Vigilant or all-seeing.*

This comes from the classical legend of Argus, a giant with a hundred eyes no more than fifty of which slept at any one time. His end came when Zeus had changed his mistress into a cow to protect her from his wife Hera's wrath. Not to be outdone, Hera set Argus to guard the cow so that Zeus could not get near enough to reverse the spell. However, Hermes, at Zeus' behest, lulled the giant to sleep with sweet music and managed to kill him, after which his eyes were used to decorate the tail-feathers of peacocks.

**ARMAGEDDON:** *A great war or battle between nations.*

This was the name chosen to describe the final, decisive conflict between good and evil as foretold in the Revelation of St John the Divine. The name was based on an actual plain, the site of many battles fought in ancient times. The plain was overlooked by Har Megiddo (Hill of Megiddo) on which stood an ancient city of great strategic value which commanded the pass through the Mount Carmel Ridge as well as the trade and military routes connecting Egypt and Palestine with Syria and Mesopotamia. In modern Israel, that city is now called Tel Megiddo whilst the plain is called the Plain of Esdraelon. Theodore Roosevelt made much use of the word in his speeches prior to WW1 and its consequent association with that terrible conflict sealed its fate with all its grim connotations.

**ARMED TO THE TEETH:** *Fully equipped with weapons.*

In the days when sailors had to clamber aboard an enemy ship for the final man-to-man fight, their hands had to be free and their weapons slung about them. They carried a fighting knife between their teeth.

**AS THE ACTRESS SAID TO THE BISHOP:** *A response to an unintentional* double entendre.

Mainly used in Britain and Australia, this was born in the heyday of music hall when 'actress and bishop' jokes abounded in stand-up comedy. The punch-lines always rested on the radically different interpretations the characters placed on a statement or situation, these being dictated by the nature of their background.

**ASLEEP AT THE SWITCH:** *In gross dereliction of duty.*

This is an American rail-road expression concerning the man in charge of the operation of points that switch trains from one track to another.

**AT LOGGERHEADS:** *In violent dispute.*

This has a naval origin, although which particular loggerhead is responsible is not clear. Based on the old, well-established 'logger', any thing or person that was stupid, clumsy, heavy or awkward, a 'loggerhead' on board could denote either a long pole topped by a heavy ball which was heated to melt pitch for deck maintenance, or a bar-shot with a cannon-ball at each end. Since the former made a formidable weapon with which sailors were prone to sort out their differences, and the latter was fired in close-quarters battles, whirled about like a lethal weight-lifting bar to sweep clear the enemy's decks, either one could have inspired the saying.

**AT SIXES AND SEVENS, TO BE:** *To be wholly confused.*

A long-established expression originating in gaming with dice, most games placing significance on the appearance of either six or seven which create junctures in play with various options as to how to continue. Should all the players be making sixes and sevens then there would be confusion indeed.

**AT THE END OF YOUR TETHER:** *Extremely angry or beset by problems.*

A snarling dog is at is most frustrated and aggressive when reared up at the end of its leash or tether with the reason for its ill-humour just out of reach.

**ATTIC SALT:** *Delicate refined wit.*

The most important city in Attica was Athens which was widely famed for its philosophers and its masters of polished discourse. In both Greek and Latin, 'salt' and 'wit' were interchangeable.

**AUNT SALLY:** *A target of collective anger.*

This derives from the old fairground stall housing the effigy of an old woman smoking a clay pipe which the punters had to break off by throwing balls from a certain distance. Why 'Sally' is not certain but it could have a connection with 'sally forth' to the attack.

**AUNTIE:** *The BBC.*

This popular name was coined in 1954 after the advent of British commercial television when the BBC seemed a trifle conventional by comparison. Some say the broadcaster Gilbert Harding was responsible but comedian Arthur Askey claimed that he had coined it on his radio show *Bandwaggon*. In any case, the BBC, quite unruffled, welcomed the tag as a compliment saying that an Auntie was a 'much-loved member of the family'. Just to remove any hint that they might be offended, the corporation instructed its vintners to start labelling the house Burgundy '*Tantine*' – French for 'Auntie'.

**AVANT-GARDE:** *Those in the vanguard of new ideas or techniques.*

This was originally a security guard who scouted ahead of the main French army and thus was always breaking new ground.

**AXE TO GRIND:** *An ulterior motive.*

Usually attributed to Benjamin Franklin (1706-90) the origin actually post-dated him, first appearing in a column written by Charles Miner for the *Wilkes-Barre Gleaner* in 1811. Recalling his childhood, he wrote of a stranger who wished to use the grindstone in the Miner backyard. He invited the stranger in and was rewarded with a barrage of compliments on his fine physique, whereupon completely duped, he worked the grindstone with all his might while the visitor simply held his axe in place. Having recounted this tale, Miner's column went on to say: 'When I see a merchant over-polite to his customers, begging them to taste a little brandy and throwing half his goods on the counter – thinks I, that man has an axe to grind.'

# B

**BABBITT:** *A materialistic Philistine.*

The original Babbitt was the eponymous hero of a novel by Sinclair Lewis (1885–1951), the first American author to win the Nobel Prize for Literature. Published in 1922, the book satirized the provincialism of the Mid-West and its dull, small-town mentality. It has been alleged that one or other of several well-known Americans actually called Babbitt was the inspiration for the character but this is not so.

**BABES IN THE WOOD:** *The excessively naive.*

First noted in 1601 and later featured in Percy's *Reliques* (1765) is the now-hackneyed tale of the Children in the Woods. This told how the Master of Wayland, Norfolk, died entrusting his cherubic offspring and their inheritance to the ubiquitous wicked uncle who would inherit all should something befall the mites. Naturally, he hired a couple of thugs to do away with the children but they relented and simply abandoned them in the woods. This is the point where along should happen a maternal mama bear, wolf or kindly peasant – but not in this case for the children perished and became part of the spirit of the forest. After this nothing went right for the nasty old uncle who lost all and perished in jail after one of the hired assassins confessed.

**BABYLON:** *Police.*

Primarily employed by West Indians, this rather strange reference is to a city that was corrupt and depraved, as the police are in the eyes of some West Indians.

**BACK A HUNCH:** *To follow up an intuitive feeling of luck.*

In medieval England it was believed that touching the lump on the back of a deformed person would ward off evil and bring good luck – a reason why many monarchs kept dwarfs or hunchbacks as jesters. Gradually, touching a hunchback became 'backing a hunch', now sometimes rendered as 'playing a hunch'.

**BACK AND EDGE:** *Force and might.*

This expression came from the

strenuous work involved in log-splitting, which was accomplished by driving a wedge – or *edge* – into the wood with the flat *back* of an axe.

**BACK AND FILL:** *To vacillate.*

When the old square-riggers were allowed to ride along with the tide or roadstream of a river, the sails were so braced as to be easily turned to bring the wind against their forward surface. This manoeuvre, known as backing and filling, acted as an air-brake which could stop the vessel in her tracks. The ship could thus be shuffled to and fro at will, hence the present meaning.

**BACK DROP:** *Contemporaneous events in the background.*

The back drop, or back cloth, hung at the rear of the stage, is painted to represent the scene against which the actors play out the story. Now dangerously close to becoming a CLICHÉ, events are frequently said to take place against the back drop of one political climate or another.

**BACK NUMBER:** *A spent force.*

Old, out-of-date issues of magazines and periodicals are referred to as 'back numbers'.

**BACK OF BOURKE:** *Utterly remote from any centre of civilization.*

In the nineteenth century, Bourke, located in the far north-west corner of New South Wales, was the most isolated of all the Australian mining towns. 'The back of beyond' is the more familiar British and American version.

**BACK PEDALLING:** *Putting a brake on your enthusiasm.*

Around the turn of the century the fixed rear wheel of the bicycle gave way to the freewheel which not only allowed the pedals to disengage but also incorporated a braking system operated by rotating the pedals backwards.

**BACK TO SQUARE ONE:** *Start all over again.*

In pre-television days, British radio did its best to provide comprehensible coverage of football matches. To this end, the *Radio Times* and the newspapers published alongside the list of programmes a diagrammatic football pitch divided into squares. In 1927 when the system was implemented, the layout showed 'square 1' over the kick-off point at the centre. After each goal the commentator would describe the players as moving 'back to square one'. The phrase caught on and has no doubt been reinforced by games like Snakes and Ladders in which players are frequently sent back to the first square.

**BACK TO THE DRAWING BOARD:** *The necessity to review a plan from its inception.*

One of America's most famous cartoonists and satirists of the early part of this century was Peter Arno (1904–68) – real name Curtis Arnoux Peters. In the 1920s he produced a great many cartoons for *New Yorker* magazine, one of which, published in 1928, showed two boffins clutching BLUEPRINTS and imperturbably watching an experimental plane explode on impact. The caption read: 'Ah well, back to the drawing board.'

**BACK TO THE SALT MINES:** *Humorously, let's get back to the task in hand.*

The salt mines of Siberia have long been the destination of criminals and political dissidents, this holding equally true of Tzarist and Communist Russia. The regime was harsh in the extreme and survival a rarity. It seems the expression was introduced to colloquial English through the popularity of an 1890s play called *Siberia* which, according to Henry Collins Brown's *In The Golden Nineties* was publicized by a poster showing such slave labour at their toil 'under the lash of the Cossack'.

**BACKBITE:** *To speak ill of someone behind his back.*

In the bearpits and beargardens of medieval England the younger dogs attacked their quarry from the front, but the older, more experienced, not to say sneaky hounds harassed it by snapping at it from the rear.

**BACKCHAT:** *Rude, abusive talk.*

Backchat, or more properly backslang, was a Cockney code far more complicated than rhyming slang but devised for the same purpose, namely to make a conversation incomprehensible to outsiders, for the uninitiated could not hope to understand this exchange in which all the major words were reversed. One example which has passed into general use is 'YOB', another is 'ecilop' which shortened to 'slop'. Both of these have become debased, but particularly 'slop' which probably gave rise to 'the filth' – if this is not just a straightforward, insulting epithet for the police. Since the need for such a code seemed to indicate criminal, immoral, or at best anti-social tendencies, the word became overlaid with its present meaning.

**BACKHANDER:** *A tip or bribe.*

Drinking from a glass involves bringing the back of the hand towards the mouth and a backhander originally meant a quick drink. In the Royal Navy the term altered slightly to mean an *extra* drink obtained either by stealing it from a messmate behind his back or by having the bottle passed back instead of forward at the table. By the 1900s it was used to denote extra money given to a tradesman with which to buy himself a drink, not only to reward him for services rendered but also to guarantee good service in the future, hence its extension to 'bribe'.

**BACKLOG:** *An accumulation of stock or unfinished business.*

In late colonial America the back of the hearth was filled by a large section of tree-trunk against which the smaller logs burned merrily away. The backlog, being more durable, survived and was replaced when it too eventually burned away.

**BACKROOM BOYS:** *Those doing important work behind the scenes.*

This phrase has been in currency throughout North America since before the middle of the nineteenth century but it was made popular by the Canadian-born Max Aitken (1879–1964) who, as Lord Beaverbrook, was appointed Minister of Aircraft Production by Churchill in WW2. Speaking on BBC radio on 19 March 1941, he sang the praises of his ministry's research staff: 'Let me say that the credit belongs to the boys in the backrooms. It isn't the man who sits in the limelight like me who should have the praise. It is not the men who sit in prominent places. It is the men in the backrooms.' His adoption of the phrase was apparently prompted by his admiration for the film star Marlene Dietrich. In the 1939 film *Destry Rides Again* she played the tart-with-a-heart owner of the Last Chance Saloon, which was the setting for her famous rendition of *The Boys in the Back Room*. This was, according to Beaverbrook, '. . . a greater work of art than the Mona Lisa'.

**BACKSTAIRS INFLUENCE:** *The power exercised by an unseen presence in the background.*

The servants' staircase in a castle or palace served as a useful secret avenue of approach for clandestine meetings between influential noblemen or ministers.

**BACKWATER:** *A tranquil spot.*

This metaphor is taken from what is literally a pool or side-stretch of water, fed by the back-flow of a river and out of the mainstream. Oarsmen are said to backwater when they reverse their strokes in order to slow down or stop their craft.

**BAD BLOOD:** *Lasting animosity.*

This was originally said to exist between families who had fought and literally spilt each other's blood, though only in a feud and not in a fair duel of honour.

**BAD CESS:** *Ill luck.*

To wish bad cess on another was originally to invoke his financial ruin. It is an Irish expression: '*cess*' is Irish for land dues and taxes.

**BAD COUNT:** *A raw deal or a fraud.*

This is an American expression with its roots in the sport of boxing. A referee can fail to start his count until a contender has already been down for several seconds, thus affording him an unfair advantage; alternatively he can favour the opponent by rattling off the count too quickly.

**BAD DAY AT BLACK ROCK:** *Any unpleasant experience.*

From the title of a highly acclaimed film of 1955 starring Spencer Tracy as a one-armed stranger who arrives in the hamlet of Black Rock and stirs up all the guilty secrets.

**BAD PENNY:** *One whose constant reappearances are unwelcome.*

It is notoriously difficult to rid oneself of a dud or foreign coin that has been unwittingly accepted. It is invariably handed back again.

**BADGER, TO:** *To harass persistently.*

One medieval blood-sport involved imprisoning a badger in an up-turned barrel and then setting on a number of dogs to drive it out. Each time the dogs achieved their objective they were pulled off their quarry so that the whole process could be repeated until, finally, they were allowed to rip the badger to pieces. We have inherited the expression along with a regrettable dearth of badgers.

**BAG/BAGGAGE:** *A woman of loose morals.*

Originating in British Army slang of the 1800s, this epithet referred to a prostitute or female camp-follower who tagged onto armies on the move. Considered to be the lowest of the low, such women tramped along with the baggage train at the rear of the column.

**BAG AND BAGGAGE:** *Entirely.*

Seemingly a tautology, this was first an army expression meaning the quitting of a barracks never to return. If only leaving for a short while a simple bag would suffice but when the regiment moved the officers had to load up all the personal belongings as well and leave them to the tender mercies of the baggage train.

**BAKER'S DOZEN:** *Thirteen.*

In thirteenth-century England a strict code of weights and measures was imposed upon bakers in an attempt to curb their notorious cheating, and the penalties for infringement were severe. It was not as easy then as it is now to guarantee the cooked weight of a loaf so bakers added to their deliveries an extra loaf, known as the vantage loaf, rather than risk a swingeing fine.

**BAKSHEESH:** *Unearned money.*

'*Bakhshish*', the Persian for a gift or a tip, was the standard cry of street beggars in the Middle East. By the 1800s it had been introduced into England by British troops returning from that area.

**BALAAM:** *A false prophet, a turncoat.*

When the Israelites arrived from Egypt, they presented a significant immigration problem to Balek, King of Moab, who appealed to Balaam, the seer and prophet, to come and lay a curse upon them. Balaam, however, sought guidance from God and was instructed to bless the Israelites rather than curse them, so he rejected Balek's appeal. Later, he changed his mind, and was *en route* with Balek's ambassadors to Moab when the Lord sent an angel, only visible to Balaam's ass, to block his road. Driven to fury by the animal's refusal to proceed, Balaam beat it relentlessly until God permitted him also to see the angel and, speaking to him through the mouth of the donkey, explained that the angel would have slain him had it not been for the observance of his ass. Balaam then continued to Moab but, instead of cursing the Israelites, he made sacrifice to their blessing, thereby enraging Balek. The term is also used to describe press articles held in reserve in the 'Balaam Box' to be used as fillers in the silly season. Such articles were named after Balaam's talking ass because the bulk of them concerned mutant animals born in the deep countryside and other amazing 'facts'.

**BALD AS A COOT:** *Completely devoid of hair.*

The European coot's bill is overlaid by a frontal shield, or bare, white callus, which extends well up the forehead.

**BALDERDASH:** *Senseless talk.*

In the sixteenth century this meant froth or scum and later any incongruous mixture of alcohol like gin and brandy. The ramblings of anyone drunk on balderdash prompted the change in meaning.

**BALL THE JACK:** *To travel rapidly, even recklessly.*

When a player in a game of bowls is faced with a no-win situation and his opponent's bowls are gathered tightly about the jack, he usually hurls the last wood directly at the pack in the hope of picking up some points by a fluke.

**BALLED UP:** *Completely bungled.*

In snow, horses build up balls of impact snow and ice in their hooves which effectively places them on skates. In the days of horse-drawn transport, many a balled-up horse fell, overturning its cart and causing total chaos. An alternative theory suggests that the source is a flag packed incorrectly so that it does not fly out when unfurled but remains in a tight ball.

**BALLOON GOES UP:** *There is trouble ahead.*

This was coined in the Allied trenches during WW1. Before an infantry attack, the artillery softened up the target area and, to give aim to the batteries, manned observation balloons were raised, thus alerting both sides that a bombardment was about to commence.

**BALLYHOO:** *Noisy propaganda.*

By the late 1800s this word was firmly established in America for a fairground barker's spiel, no doubt in allusion to Ballyhooly, a village in County Cork, Ireland, which was famed for its colourful annual fair. There is no evidence to suggest that the inhabitants of Ballyhooly were conspicuously rowdy, but the Irish immigrants in America did have that reputation, and the word's raucous overtones were fixed forever when it was adopted to describe the razzle and hype of Madison Avenue advertising.

**BAMBOOZLE:** *To cheat or confound.*

This is based on 'bombace', the seventeenth-century word for raw cotton used as padding for clothes or furniture, and consisting of a confused mass of fibre.

**BAND OF HOPE:** *A small group with unduly high aspirations.*

This was formerly the name of a children's temperance movement founded in Leeds in 1847. By 1855 the group had grown into the Band of Hope Union by which name it is known today. Like so many other well-intentioned organizations, it attracted connotations of do-gooding which accounts for the rather sneering use currently made of the expression.

**BANDBOX NEAT:** *Beautifully turned out.*

Clerical vestments and fine lace ruffs or collars used to be stored in bandboxes to keep them in an immaculate condition ready for formal wear.

**BANDY WORDS:** *To indulge in verbal exchanges.*

'Bandy' in this sense derives from the Old French 'bander' to knock a ball to and fro in a casual manner.

The word also produced the name of the game bandy as played in Ireland and resembling a fairly lethal brand of hockey. The curved sticks employed in turn produced talk of people being 'bandy legged'.

**BANE OF YOUR EXISTENCE:** *The scourge of your life.*

Bane actually means death or destruction and is derived from the Old English '*bana*', a murderer. 'Bane' suffixed to the name of a plant indicated its use as a poison, e.g. wolfsbane, once used to poison wolves.

**BANG ON:** *Exactly right.*

This is a shortened version of 'bang on target', WW2 RAF slang for bombs that exploded exactly where they were aimed.

**BANNED IN BOSTON:** *Censored.*

In the early 1920s the regime of censorship in Boston determinedly rooted out the slightest hint of obscenity. All of Eugene O'Neill's plays were banned on principle as was much of G.B. Shaw's work; even some Shakespeare was branded as lewd, which, to be fair, it is. Several authors and playwrights deliberately set out to fall foul of the Boston Watch and Ward Committee in the sure knowledge that a billing of 'Banned in Boston' would boost sales throughout the rest of the country. In 1925, the American satirist H.L. Mencken (1880–1956), who was a noted friend and champion of both Shaw and O'Neill, was appointed editor of the magazine *American Mercury*. He deliberately included in its pages a story centred on a prostitute and then publicly challenged the Rev. J.F. Chase, the Watch Committee's Secretary, to meet him at noon on Boston Common and buy a copy from him personally. The transaction completed, Mencken was duly arrested, but the Court threw out the case, which heralded the decline of the Committee's power.

**BANSHEE:** *A wailing woman.*

Built on the Irish '*bean sidhe*' – woman of the fairies – this was the spirit who, in Irish folklore, wailed and shrieked to warn mortals of impending death. Although the banshee was traditionally held to be of great beauty, the word is now usually applied insultingly to denote a nag or harridan.

**BAPTISM OF FIRE:** *One's first experience of an ordeal.*

This originally applied to martyrdom achieved by being burnt at the stake *auto-da-fé* after one's faith had been affirmed by baptism. When the number of Christian martyrs dwindled, the expression transferred to a young soldier's first taste of active service, and was most notably used in this context by Napoleon III when, in 1871, he sent his fourteen-year-old son into battle during the Franco–Prussian war. The lad survived only to die, rather ironically, fighting in the British Army against the Zulus.

**BAR SINISTER:** *The symbol of illegitimacy in heraldry.*

This term is popularly but mistakenly used instead of the correct 'bend sinister' or 'baton sinister'.

Heraldry does not include such a term but it could have arisen because French heralds called a bend sinister, which denoted bastardy, '*un barre*'. The erroneous term was first noted in Sir Walter Scott's *Quentin Durward* (1823), which was set in fifteenth-century France. Scott's works were widely read, and many writers copied not only his style, but also the expressions he coined, e.g. FREELANCE. Actually, there has never been one specific symbol in heraldry denoting illegitimacy; many different ones have been used at different times, and, taken across the board, need not always have had the same significance. Apart from the baton sinister (a baton is always sinister) the bend sinister has signified bastardy from time to time. A bend sinister is a line drawn diagonally across a shield from the top left-hand corner as seen from the front; a baton sinister follows the same path but stops short of both edges.

**BARE-FACED CHEEK:** *Sheer impudence.*

The colloquialism 'cheek' arose because the cheek moves when the impertinence is uttered. The slang use of 'lip' for insolence came into being in the same way. 'Bare-faced' in this context alludes to the lack of beard growth on adolescents who are often criticized for their unconcealed rudeness.

**BARK UP THE WRONG TREE:** *To follow a false scent.*

The sport of raccoon-hunting in America takes place at night; coon-dogs are on hand to tree the quarry and bark at the base until the hunter comes along with torch and gun. Fortunately for the raccoons, they can sometimes leap onto the nearby branches of another tree, thus leaving the hound baying at the wrong one.

**BARMY:** *Mentally unsound.*

When malt liquor is fermenting, froth and scum continually rise to the surface and have to be removed. The less fastidious distillery workers were prone to consuming this 'barm', consequently becoming greatly intoxicated. Another derivation frequently postulated is that 'barmy' comes, by association, from a large lunatic asylum located at Barming Heath, near Maidstone, Kent, but the word according to the OED made its debut in 1535, whereas the lunatic asylum was not built until the beginning of the nineteenth century.

**BARNEY:** *A rowdy quarrel.*

The notorious hasty temper of the Irish has earned them a reputation for brawling and Barney is a common Irish forename.

**BARNSTORM:** *A* WHISTLE-STOP TOUR.

In nineteenth-century America and Britain, 'barnstormers' were strolling players who 'stormed' (ranted) in the countryside barns where they put on one-night stands. The term stayed a while with the American flying circuses whose stock stunt was flying a bi-plane through an open barn. Now in America, 'barnstorm' has moved into the political arena to describe the frantic rural itinerary undertaken by a candidate at election time.

**BARRACK:** *To interrupt by shouting hostile comments.*

It has been suggested that this usage arose from the rowdy nature of football matches played on the St Kilda Road pitch near the Victoria Barracks in Melbourne, but it would be unwise in the extreme to ignore the Aboriginal Australian '*borak*', to poke fun at or ridicule.

**BASH YOUR PAN IN, TO:** *To work until exhausted.*

In eighteenth/nineteenth century miners' slang 'to bash' meant to fill in and the 'pan' was the hopper taking coal to the surface. Then, as now, filling one's quota in a mine was arduous work.

**BASHI BAZOUKS:** *Thugs or hooligans.*

In the mid 1800s, the Turkish government employed irregular troops who wore no identifying uniform and who supplemented their equally irregular pay by robbery and extortion. They were nicknamed 'Bashi Bazouks' – literally meaning 'wrong-headed' but basically meaning 'insane' – because of their savage behaviour.

**BASKET:** *Euphemism for a bastard.*

This was born of the once common practice of abandoning an unwanted child by leaving it in a basket on the doorstep of the local vicarage or some charitable institute. The word is of course used as an insult, and this could have been reinforced in the fighting cockpits where it was the cry raised against a dishonoured gambler unable to meet his debts; his punishment was to be suspended in a basket above the pit, a target of ridicule and abuse.

**BASTARD:** *One born out of wedlock.*

In Old French '*bast*' described the sort of mule-driver's pack saddle which converted into a makeshift bed used for camping out on the trail. 'Bastard' was the spin-off produced by the assumption that any child conceived on a mule-driver's pack saddle during a one-night stop was unlikely to be the product of a sanctified union.

**BASTE:** *To beat; to moisten with fat.*

The first meaning derives from the Old Norse '*beysta*' which also means to beat. The second meaning derives from the Old French '*basser*'. There is no foundation to the notion that the long-handled spoon used in medieval kitchens to moisten down meat roasting on the spit was also recognized as the ideal instrument with which to ginger up idle scullery hands, and therefore became known as the 'basting' spoon from which its real function was named.

**BATTEN DOWN THE HATCHES:** *Prepare for serious trouble.*

When a storm loomed imminent at sea the crew would prepare to dress the ship accordingly and ensure the cargo hatches on the deck were properly clamped down. The hatch battens are strips of wood or steel wedged to the side of the hatch coming to allow the securing of tarpaulins for extra weatherproofing when things were going to get really rough.

**BATTER THE TAR OUT OF SOMEONE, TO:** *To batter them senseless.*

In all probability, 'tar' appears as a euphemism for 'shit' but there is another possibility. As explained in SPOIL THE SHIP FOR A HA'PORTH OF TAR, this substance and creosote were frequently applied to wounds on sheep and would obviously remain in dried lumps on the fleece. When the animal was slaughtered these fleeces received a severe pounding to remove the residual tar and dried-on dirt.

**BATTLE ROYAL:** *A fight to the finish.*

The origin of this is two-fold. In medieval days it was used to describe a friendly knock-about in which several knights took the field together, the last to remain mounted being the winner. Later it applied to an altogether more lethal contest in the cockpits where up to a dozen birds were pitted against each other to fight until only one remained alive.

**BATTLE-AXE:** *An overbearing harridan.*

Despite the antiquity of the weapon, this application dates only from the early 1900s and was in all likelihood derived from an American Women's Rights Movement magazine called *Battle-Axe*, this title being in turn derived from the activities of one Carry Nation (1846–1911), a suffragette and prohibitionist of Amazon stature and unusual strength who specialized in closing down saloons with an axe. Later women's associations did their best to distance themselves from her and her increasingly bizarre behaviour.

**BATTY:** *Slightly crazy.*

There is nothing to suggest that this is anything more than a logical development from 'bats in the belfry' which alludes to the wild wheeling and seemingly disorganized flight of bats that have been disturbed. Despite this there has been speculation that any one of several eccentrics may have been responsible, particularly Fitzherbert Batty, a deranged barrister of Jamaica in the 1830s. The OED records that the word meant 'belonging to a bat' as early as 1590, but places the slang usage at about 1920, as does Partridge.

**BEAK:** *A magistrate or schoolmaster.*

This colloquialism is based on the Celtic '*beachd*', judge.

**BEANFEAST:** *A jollification.*

This was formerly an annual dinner given by an employer to his workforce. The traditional fare was beans and a bean goose (so named because of a bean-shaped mark on its bill), which returned to Britain in May when these celebrations took place. One can go further back for the inspiration of this word to the ancient revels of Twelfth Night at which a cake containing a bean was divided up, the finder of the bean becoming the master of the revels in the same way as did the old king of the Saturnalia. The bean in the cake survives today as the coin in the Christmas pudding.

**BEANO:** *A jollification.*

This is basically a twentieth-century development from BEAN-FEAST which arose in the printing trade to describe their annual revel in August given originally to mark the end of summer and the beginning of work by candlelight. The printers' dinner was first called a 'wayzgoose' and the modern 'beano' was probably influenced by such terms as the Spanish '*bueno*', good.

**BEAR:** *A stockmarket trader who sells short.*

Originally known as a 'bearskin' jobber, from the old adage which cautions against selling the bearskin before catching the bear. A 'bear' anticipates a fall in values and sells stock he does not actually yet possess in the hope of buying it back at a lower price before accounting day, thus making a profit.

**BEAR UP:** *To face difficulties with fortitude.*

Possibly this alludes to the bearing rein which, when pulled in tight by a rider, forces the horse to tuck in its chin, arch its neck, and look altogether more spirited. Alternatively, the nautical command 'bear up', calling for a ship's head to be brought closer to the wind in order to pick up speed, could be the source.

**BEARD THE LION IN HIS DEN:** *To confront an adversary on his own territory.*

Before David confronted Goliath, Saul tried to dissuade him by cautioning that the Philistine was a much more experienced fighter. David then pointed out that, when a lion or a bear stole one of Saul's lambs, it was he who went after it and: 'smote him and delivered it [the lamb] out of his mouth; and, if he arose against me, I caught him by his beard, and smote and killed him'.

**BEARGARDEN:** *A place of total confusion.*

Fortunately for bears, these places where they were fought to the death by dogs no longer exist, but their reputation for rowdiness and lawlessness lives on.

**BEAR'S SERVICE:** *A well-intentioned ill-service.*

This refers back to the old tale of a lonely woodsman who became friends with a bear. While he was sleeping one day, a fly landed on his head. So that his friend should not be woken by it, the bear crushed it with a mighty blow.

**BEAT A HASTY RETREAT:** *To retire in confusion.*

This harks back to the particular drum roll once beaten to recall troops from action.

**BEAT ABOUT THE BUSH:** *To avoid the real issue.*

This is an allusion to the 'beaters' employed to put up birds for the hunters. They achieve little or nothing if they beat about – or around – the edge of the bush.

**BEAT IT:** *Go away.*

This slang has gained currency in Britain only because people remain unaware that it is an ellipsis of the American 'go away and beat your meat' – in other words, 'go play with yourself'.

**BEAUTY SPOT:** *Euphemism for a mole.*

In the days of powdered wigs it was also fashionable for both men and women to powder their faces white and stick on small black paper cut-outs of, for example, stars, to attract attention to what they considered to be their best features.

**BECAUSE IT WAS THERE**

When George Mallory (1886–1924) returned from the abortive British attempt on Everest, he was asked why he had wanted to climb it. Because it was there was his response. This is sometimes attributed instead to the New Zealander, Sir Edmund Hillary, but what he said when he came down with Sherpa Tensing in 1953 was, 'Well, we've knocked the bastard off.' Tensing confirmed this with his own vivid but never reported phrase 'We done the bugger good!' Hillary later said in his autobiography, *Nothing Venture, Nothing Win* (1975) that the remark was addressed to fellow team member, George Lowe, who greeted the assault party on their triumphal return, and that it was never intended for public consumption.

**BEDLAM:** *Total chaos.*

This is a corruption of Bethlehem and was the recognized name of old London's most infamous lunatic asylum. Founded in 1247 by Simon Fitzmary, Sheriff of London, the building was initially a priory for the Order of the Star of Bethlehem which became in the fourteenth century a hospital specializing in the care of the insane. By the seventeenth century Bedlam had become a meeting place for prostitutes, petty criminals and riff-raff, and was one of the great scandals of the city. The inmates were treated abominably by the staff who, for the price of a few pence, would admit members of the public to bait the unfortunate patients to the point of hysteria. In 1815 the hospital was moved from Moorfields to St George's Fields in south-east London, thence in 1930 to near Croydon, Surrey. There it still exists as the Bethlehem Royal and Maudsley Hospital.

**BEE:** *A gathering of people for a common purpose.*

This use of 'bee' as in sewing bee etc. was coined in America in the eighteenth century when it was applied to occasions when several families of settlers gathered together with the common aim of labouring for a neighbour in need or for a newcomer. The social structure of the bee hive was its inspiration.

**BEEF, TO:** *To complain.*

In nineteenth-century England, street urchins used to chant; 'Hot beef! Hot beef!' to drown out genuine cries of 'Stop thief!' from outraged shopkeepers or victims of muggings. Partridge notes that the expression 'to give hot beef', meaning to cry out, was obsolete by 1930, and, since 'beefing' emerged in the early 1900s, it may well be that its meaning had transferred to the *complaints* of the victims and that the current expression 'to beef' is in fact an ellipsis of the original street cry. Reinforcing this, Cockney rhyming slang 'stop thief' means 'beef', but only stolen beef.

**BEE'S KNEES:** *The last word in excellence.*

This alludes to the manifestly important nectar-gathering sacs located at the point on a bee's leg which equates to the human knee.

**BEHIND THE EIGHT BALL:** *In a tight spot.*

In American pool, a player's objective is to pot the black ball, but only after he has potted his seven other balls. If in so doing he hits the black directly he suffers two penalty strokes. A player who takes his turn when the cue ball has been left tucked away behind the black (eight) ball is in a difficult situation.

**BEHIND THE SCENES:** *Hidden influence, especially Machiavellian.*

Part of theatre jargon from perhaps medieval times, this points to the fact that few dark deeds were acted out before the audience; the condemned, for example, were led off-stage to their fate and dastardly deeds were reported to those on stage by breathless messengers. All foul play therefore took place behind the set scenes. Although the precise origins of 'obscene' are obscure, it is deemed highly likely that this, for the selfsame reasons, was born of Roman theatre and the Latin '*ob scaena*', against or away from the stage.

**BELL, BOOK AND CANDLE:** *With the greatest severity.*

In the Roman Catholic Church this still properly describes the major ritual of ex-communication, in which the presiding bishop leads the procession to a public place and rings a bell to attract the attention of all to witness the ceremony. He holds a book which represents the book of life and, after intoning the necessary words, formally closes the book. Next, the attendant priests who are holding lighted candles symbolic of the saving light of God in the soul of the subject, dash these into the dust to extinguish the flame, chanting '*Fiat. Fiat. Fiat*' – Let it be done.

**BELL THE CAT, TO:** *To undertake a dangerous or odious task to the benefit of others.*

An ancient parabolic tale concerning a colony of mice distressed by their ever-diminishing number due to the attentions of an overly jealous mouser. At the meeting held to decide a course of action a young mouse draws roars of approval with the suggestion that they simply hang a bell round the cat's neck so they can all hear it coming. Naturally, there was also present the ubiquitous wise old mouse who causes despondency by asking which of their number is going to place the bell in position.

**BELOW THE BELT:** *Unfair.*

This refers to the Marquess of Queensberry rules, drawn up in 1867 and enforced in 1872. They regularized the sport of boxing and outlawed blows below the waist.

**BENCH MARKS:** *Fixed standards.*

This can be traced to two sources. Firstly there is an obvious connection with marks and measurements cut into the benches of carpenters and engineers; secondly there is a more important, though less obvious, connection with surveyors' bench marks cut into rock to indicate the exact height above or depth below sea level. These are taken as control points in map-making and their name arises from the apparatus used to fix them. A vertical post is erected and an iron bar affixed horizontally to act as a support, or bench, for the levelling staff. A mark is then cut into the rock, consisting of a broad arrow surmounted by a horizontal line at the exact recorded height.

**BENDER:** *A concentrated drinking spree.*

The source of this is probably twofold. In the eighteenth century 'bender' was slang for the rather malleable sixpenny piece which, in those days, could buy a lot of ale. In addition, 'bender' was also slang for the elbow, which has an obvious connection with drinking still evident in the expression 'bending the elbow'.

**BERK (BURKE):** *Idiot.*

Still enjoying wide usage – even on prime time television – only because few are aware that it is crude rhyming slang – Berkshire Hunt = cunt. Not only is the Royal Berkshire Hunt one of the most prestigious fox-hunts but the county name – which should be pronounced Barkshire – is all too frequently rendered as spelt.

**BERSERK:** *In a violent frenzy.*

Berserk was the war hero of Scandinavian mythology who went into battle without armour or shield, naked or clad only in a bearskin, hence the etymology of his name from the Norse '*bjorn serkr*', bear-shirt, '*berr serce*', bare of mail, or [illegible]r serkr', bare of shirt – it is uncertain which. His human emulators, the Berserkers, were an élite warrior sect who went into battle howling and chewing their sword-blades to impress the enemy with their savagery. Their brutality was not however restricted to the battlefield, and it was common for them to rape and murder within their own community.

**BEST BIB AND TUCKER:** *One's most splendid outfit.*

The 'bib' was an item of seventeenth-century dress for men, infinitely more ornate than the modern baby's bib but much the same shape and designed for the same purpose, hence its Latin origin, '*bibere*', to drink. A 'tucker' was the lace counterpart for women, the word being a variant of 'tugger' which alludes to the method of removing it.

**BEST MAN:** *Attendant to the bridegroom.*

At the turn of the millennium a man would sometimes kidnap the object of his desire and he would be accompanied on the raid by his friends, the best swordsman among whom guarded his rear. This type of foray lived on for a while as a mock ritual accompanied by much skylarking, and in the modern wedding, the swordsman survives as 'the best man', the other members of the raiding party as wedding ushers.

**BET YOUR BOOTS ON IT:** *This is a certainty.*

This refers to the fact that a cowboy would never risk losing his boots on a hazardous bet; though sometimes a trifle fancy, they nevertheless constituted an extremely important part of his working gear. Snakes, scorpions and shrubs with thorns like steel needles abounded in his territory and his life often depended on the strength of his boots.

**BET YOUR BOTTOM DOLLAR:** *This is a certainty.*

Reference to the pile of dollar coins on an American poker table which the confident player will push to the centre – right down to the bottom of the stack.

**BETWEEN THE DEVIL AND THE DEEP BLUE SEA:** *In a desperate dilemma.*

There is no reference to Satan here: this devil was a seam which margined a ship's waterways, the outboard deck planks which projected beyond and at right angles to the hull. A man hanging underneath this would find it virtually impossible to regain access to the deck, and he would have nothing below him but the deep blue sea. Another seam near the keel was also known as the devil, and produced the saying DEVIL TO PAY.

**BETWEEN SCYLLA AND CHARYBDIS:** *In an invidious position.*

All ships using the Straits of Messina had to pass between Charybdis, a giant whirlpool off the coast of Sicily, and Scylla, a massive rock close by. Both were portrayed in Greek mythology of any sailor careless enough to come within grasp.

**BEYOND THE BLACK STUMP:** *Utterly remote.*

An Australianism designating tracts of land even more remote than the back of beyond, this refers to the deep interior where spontaneous brush fires are common.

**BEYOND THE PALE:** *Unacceptably offensive.*

This developed in the fourteenth century from an area of Ireland known as the English Pale, the etymon of which is the Latin '*palus*', a stake, although there was no actual fence. It embraced Dublin, Louth, Trim, Meath, Kilkenny, Waterford and Tipperary and was under the direct control and protection of the English Crown. The expression is a straight reference either to the uncivilized behaviour of those living outside the pale, or to the sort of conduct that might put one in danger of being exiled there.

**BIG APPLE:** *New York.*

This epithet arose in the 1930s at a time when the apple figured largely in American cooking and phraseology, e.g. as American as apple pie. it might have come about simply because the city was big and ripe with opportunity but it might also owe something to the Hispanic influence which was and still is very pronounced there. The Spanish '*manzana*' properly describes both an apple and a block or complex of buildings.

**BIG BERTHA:** *A woman of over-generous proportions.*

This nickname was originally bestowed by the Allied Press upon a massive gun used by the Germans in WWI to shell Paris from a distance of seventy-six miles. The 142-ton piece fired a 264-pound shell but its impact was mainly psychological since it was wildly inaccurate and needed a new barrel after every eleven rounds. The name was a dig at Frau Bertha Krupp in whose armament factory it was thought to be manufactured; in fact it was one of several produced by the Austro–Hungarian Skoda works.

**BIG BROTHER:** *A powerful restrictive government.*

This was the name chosen by George Orwell (1903–50) for the invisible state machinery in his book *Nineteen Eighty-Four.* The expression was greatly popularized by the BBC TV dramatisation in 1954 in which every episode showed the grey, sombre Head of State signing off one of his frequent broadcasts with the paternalistic, chillingly ominous words: *'And don't forget, Big Brother is watching you.'*

**BIG CHEESE:** *An important person.*

A nineteenth-century acquisition based on the Hindustani '*chiz*', thing, this has nothing to do with cheese.

**BIG SHOT:** *An influential person.*

Used of any major wheeler and dealer though sometimes with a derogatory edge. It is long-standing soldiers' slang for a large piece of artillery.

**BIG WHEEL:** *A prominent businessman.*

This refers to the massive water wheel at the side of the old cotton mills which operated all the smaller wheels inside.

**BIGWIG:** *A dignitary.*

Refers to the powdered wigs worn by the upper classes in the eighteenth and nineteenth centuries. The greater a man's importance, the bigger his wig.

**BILLY-O/BILLIO, LIKE:** *Vigorously.*

All eponymous explanations are spurious and the only likely possibility uncovered is the sixteenth to eighteenth-century use of 'billio' in the smelting and coin-striking business to describe the molten metal bubbling away in the pot. Naturally, this is a varient of the old 'billion' which ultimately produced 'bullion'.

**BIMBO:** *A girl.*

Stems from the Italian '*bambino*', baby and first arose in American usage through the Italian influence into the country.

**BINGE:** *A drunken spree.*

In the early-mid nineteenth century a ship's empty barrels were swilled round, or 'binged', to freshen them before refilling; rum casks too were binged but this was done with the minimum of water which the sailors retained and drank. Binging further ensured that the wood of the barrels did not shrink but remained swollen with liquid and this could well have contributed to the present meaning.

**BINGO:** *A cry indicating jubilation or sudden success.*

This word was used from the late seventeenth to the late nineteenth century for any strong liquor, but particularly brandy, and could have been constructed from 'brandy' and 'stingo' – a strong ale or beer of the time often used as a pick-me-up. BINGE could have had some influence as could 'bing-ale', a late seventeenth and eighteenth-century term for ale the Church distributed to farmers after they had gathered in the harvest and filled the tithe barns, all of these having some connection with rejoicing or stimulation. The game, as played in all good ex-cinemas, is almost certainly named for the cry of glee at winning.

**BINT:** *Pejoratively, any girl.*

This word is used of a female regarded as little more than an object of pleasure. The source is the Arabic '*bint*', daughter, and the word probably acquired its disrespectful overtones because so many British soldiers were offered the proverbial 'good, clean daughter' by Arab street pimps.

**BIRD OF ILL OMEN:** *A harbinger of doom.*

This refers back to the appearance of certain birds during the ancient practice of augury, in which the flight paths of birds were considered significant. Crows and ravens were regarded as bad omens because of their association with death and carrion.

**BIRD-DOG SOMEONE, TO:** *To follow persistently.*

A retriever keeps close to the heels of the hunter awaiting his commands.

**BIT OF HOW'S YOUR FATHER:** *Sexual activity.*

Harry Tate was a music hall entertainer of the same era as Harry Lauder. One of his favourite comic routines was to be seated with his girlfriend on a settee trying to win her sexual favours. Each time it seemed he was about to succeed, the girl's father appeared on the set whereupon Tate, pretending not to notice this, stretched back on the settee inquiring 'And how is your dear father?'

**BITE THE BULLET:** *To steel oneself.*

Surgery on eighteenth and nineteenth century battlefields was crude and performed without anaesthetic. The only solace offered to those about to go under the knife was a bullet on which to bite.

**BITER BIT, THE:** *Poetic justice.*

One of Aesop's fables tells of a viper which bit a file under the misapprehension that it was a tasty morsel. The file informed the snake in no uncertain fashion that its own *raison d'être* was to bite and not to be bitten.

**BITTER END, THE:** *The last extremity.*

The 'bitts' were a pair of stout oak posts or bollards fixed on the foredeck of an old square-rigger and used when the vessel was being moored. When the rope was paid out to the last loop around the bitt it was said to be 'at its bitter end'. No doubt the adjective 'bitter' has contributed to the current meaning.

**BLACK HOLE OF CALCUTTA:** *A dark and very crowded place.*

This refers to an act of brutality

perpetrated by Suraj-ud-Dawlah after he stormed Fort William, the East India Company garrison in Calcutta on 20 June 1756. He used the company jail, unventilated and measuring only 18 feet by 14 feet 10 inches, to incarcerate 146 British prisoners, some 123 of whom suffocated during the night. Indian historians dismiss these figures as ridiculous, placing them much lower. They point out, quite correctly, that the British prisoners were simply confined in their own jail in which several locals had also died because of over-crowding, claiming that the British had only themselves to blame for the appalling conditions.

**BLACK MARIA:** *A police van for prisoners.*

In nineteenth-century Boston, Massachusetts, Maria Lee, a negress of staggering proportions, ran a celebrated boarding house just round the corner from the Central Police Station whence she was wont bodily to deliver unruly customers by the simple expedient of tossing them over her shoulder and carrying them there. Naturally, she became something of a local character and a number of cartoons in the Boston newspapers showed the police having to send for Black Maria to cart off the criminals. (Incidentally, every country has its pet name for the van; in South America it is known as 'mother's heart' because there is always room inside for one more.)

**BLACK SHEEP:** *The disreputable member of a family.*

Black sheep have never been welcome. The long-standing superstition of sheep farmers that the arrival of black lambs augured a bad year was probably inspired by the fact that black fleece was of little value.

**BLACKBALL:** *To ostracise.*

This arises from an outmoded form of ballot, now used only in the election of members to exclusive private clubs, in which votes are cast by dropping into a box a white ball for 'yes' and a black ball for 'no'. Just one black ball is enough to cause a man's rejection.

**BLACKJACK:** *A leather-covered club.*

In medieval drinking haunts ale was dispensed from a stiff, thick-walled, leather jug additionally strengthened by an outside coating of tar and therefore called a blackjack. It made an effective tranquillizer for unruly customers.

**BLACKLEG:** *A strike-breaker.*

This started life on the racetracks of eighteenth-century England where the bookmakers and their runners were all easily identifiable by their customary tall, black leather riding boots. Since their honesty was not unquestionable the word moved into general currency as a synonym for a cheat and later into industrial disputes to describe one who cheats the union man of his traditional defence.

**BLARNEY:** *Gift of the gab.*

This owes its existence to an apocryphal yarn concerning the surrender of Blarney Castle in 1602 by Cormac Macarthy to the English forces under Sir George Crew who tried for days to settle the terms of surrender but always fell foul of the Irishman's silver tongue. To stop the rot, Queen Elizabeth I intervened by letter only to receive a procrastinating reply from Macarthy, which she allegedly dismissed as: 'More of the same damned Blarney'. The name of the castle certainly came to mean honeyed words and a particular stone in its parapets is still held to bestow the gift of the blarney on those who kiss it.

**BLATHERSKATE:** *A loquacious idiot.*

This word is compunded from the Scottish and Northern English dialect '*blate*' – prattle – and '*skyte*' – shit. 'Blatherskyte' became 'blatherskite' and subsequently 'blatherskate' perhaps by association with the fish. 'Bletherskate' is a variant.

**BLEACHERS:** *The cheap seats in a sports stadium.*

This American and Australian term makes reference to seats that are situated in the open where the wood becomes whitened by the sun.

**BLIGHTY:** *An affectionate term for Britain.*

This was originally used by British troops serving in India in the early years of the twentieth century. It is based on the Hindustani '*bilayati*', foreign, European.

**BLIND PIG/TIGER:** *An illegal drinking haunt.*

In common use in America since the early–mid 1800s, it appears to derive from a ruse employed by unlicensed saloons in order to circumvent the laws covering the sale of liquor. Claiming to be exhibiting some freak, such as a blind pig or tiger, the owner charged so much per peek and gave away 'free' whiskey.

**BLOCKBUSTER:** *A monumentally successful enterprise.*

This WW2 RAF slang for a bomb big enough to take out an entire city block became, logically, a superlative.

**BLOOMER:** *A minor error.*

This is a simple contraction of 'blooming error'.

**BLOW AWAY:** *To kill.*

In New Orleans jazz funerals, the cortege includes a band which 'plays' the coffin through the streets. Since it is predominantly a brass band, the procedure is known locally as 'blowing a friend away'. The term became a convenient euphemism among criminal elements, first in Louisiana and later throughout America.

**BLOW THE GAFF:** *To disclose a secret.*

This piece of carnival jargon used the word 'gaff', a hook for landing large fish, to describe any ruse that attracted and held a crowd. If the crowd saw through the trick, then the gaff was blown (away).

**BLOW YOUR OWN TRUMPET:** *To sing one's own praises.*

In days gone by, heralds literally trumpeted the arrival of a dignitary to draw attention to his importance.

**BLOW YOUR STACK:** *To erupt in anger.*

In America, where this expression was born, it was the custom of the

Mississippi flat boats periodically to direct a blast from the steam engine up the smoke stack to clean it out. The resultant noise and cloud of smoke and soot strongly suggested an eruption of black anger.

**BLOW YOUR TOP:** *To erupt in anger.*

An oil well which built up too much pressure 'blew its top'.

**BLOW THE WHISTLE ON:** *To expose and bring to a halt.*

This expression, which refers especially to uncovering illegal or forbidden practices, is linked to the policeman's erstwhile whistle and to the referee's.

**BLOWED-IN-THE-GLASS:** *The very best.*

In America, the premier brands of whiskey are marketed in bottles which have the name moulded into the glass.

**BLOWER:** *The telephone.*

Operators of earlier forms of communication devices such as talking-tubes had to blow down them to attract attention at the other end.

**BLOW HOT AND COLD, TO:** *To be unreliable.*

An old tale tells of a satyr who happened upon a frozen, exhausted traveller and took him home for food and shelter. He was astonished to see the man blow upon his hands to heat them up and, later, blow upon his soup to cool it down. Deeply distrustful of one who could blow hot and cold at will, the satyr threw the man back out into the night.

**BLUE:** *Risqué.*

The colour has been associated with sexual innuendo since the Middle Ages. This could have come about by association either with the licentiousness of a 'blue-blooded' nobility, or with the 'blue blazes' of the Devil. Whatever the ultimate origin, a number of examples can be cited. In England prostitutes locked up in houses of correction were obliged to wear blue gowns as a badge of their shame. In nineteenth-century France a collection of risqué novels was branded *La Bibliotheque Bleu*. In eighteenth-century America certain New England laws were nicknamed the 'BLUE LAWS', and in the 1920s any dubious sexually orientated passages were deleted by censors using a bright blue pencil.

**BLUE:** *A man.*

Eighteenth and nineteenth-century Australian hoboes carried their belongings rolled up in a blanket which was invariably dyed blue. Reinforcing this, 'Blue' or 'Bluey' was certainly used in Tasmania, and probably in mainland Australia too, for a convict who wore the standard issue smock-type garment made of heavy duty cotton dyed blue. Blue was a common colour for hard-wearing materials because it was the most durable.

**BLUE BLOODED:** *Aristocratic.*

The Castilian nobility of the seventeenth century conferred this accolade upon themselves because, having remained untainted by Moorish or Jewish blood, their skin was pale and their veins appeared blue against it.

**BLUE CHIP STOCK:** *The most reliable shares.*

At poker tables the blue gaming chips are always the highest in value so a player holding a number of these is obviously doing well.

**BLUE LAWS:** *Puritan laws.*

Although now used in America for the Sunday Trading Laws, this was originally the nickname for some extremely restrictive legislation imposed by Puritan settlers in the early-mid seventeenth century. Apart from curtailing business and entertainment on Sundays, the laws demanded the death penalty for adultery and heavy fines for any public display of affection even between man and wife. It is said that the nickname derived from the blue posters on which the laws were promulgated by the Elders of New Haven, Connecticut, but no doubt it was helped along by the fact that the laws prohibited activities considered to be Satanic, lewd, or blue. The term was introduced into England by the Rev. Samuel Peters, a haughty American cleric of well-known loyalist sympathies who deemed it wise to flee there after the American War of Independence. His *General History of Connecticut by a Gentleman of the Province* listed forty-five of these Draconian laws. These were labelled by colonists as vindictive invention, but they were substantiated by *The Report of the American Historical Association* of 1889 which showed that all but two of them were in operation somewhere in the Colonies at some time or other.

**BLUE MURDER:** *An unholy racket.*

This arrived when the French blasphemy '*Mordieu*', God's death, euphemized to '*Morbleu*', blue death, crossed the channel.

**BLUE PETER:** *A ship's flag denoting imminent departure.*

The name of this blue flag bearing a white rectangle seems to be a corruption of 'blue repeater' since its original use was to ask another ship to repeat a flag signal which had not been understood. Its purpose changed and it is not outside the bounds of possibility that the French '*partir*' exerted an influence.

**BLUEPRINT:** *Plan or guideline.*

Originally the name of a system of photoprint developed in 1840 by Sir John Herschel (1792–1871). The paper, sensitized with ferro-prussiate, was blue in colour and once much used to reproduce technical drawings.

**BLUE SKY LAWS:** *A group of American laws first enacted in Kansas in 1911 to protect the public from fraudulent stock and bond schemes.*

These laws, detested by the financial sector which lobbied and appealed against them in vain, acquired their name from one of the more prominent test cases, Hall *v.* Geiger-Jones during which the presiding judge referred to them as a defence for purchasers protecting them from share issues 'which have no more basis than so many feet of blue sky'.

**BLUE STOCKING:** *A rather pedantic learned woman.*

There were very obvious reasons

for this epithet, but the coining if it must be accredited to Edward Boscawen (1711–61) – coincidentally an Admiral of the Blue – whose wife was a prominent member of an association of savants founded by Elizabeth Vesey (1715–91) and dominated by women. According to one of its members, the novelist and diarist Fanny Burney, their association with blue stockings originated when the poet Benjamin Stillingfleet declined Mrs Vesey's invitation to one of her gatherings on the grounds that he possessed no formal attire and was bidden to come as he was, blue worsted stockings and all. In any event, in the 1750s Elizabeth Montague (1720–1800) became the leading light of the group, not only because of her intellectual prowess but also because her husband had bequeathed her a considerable fortune which enabled her to indulge her passion for the arts. She started to sport bright blue stockings and the rest of the club followed her lead.

**BLUENOSE:** *A strict moralist.*
This was first applied to the late eighteenth-century colonists of New England whose noses did show a pale blue tinge during the long, hard winters and whose traditional puritanical beliefs ran deep.

**BLUES, THE:** *A state of melancholy.*
In the nineteenth century the despondency induced by 'coming down' after a bout of drinking was called a 'fit of the blue devils'. This could have been inspired either by the creatures imagined in a fit of delirium tremens or by the bluish hue of a heavy drinker's face. The American Negro style of folk music called the blues came about by association since this music does concentrate on the more melancholy aspects of life.

**BLURB:** *A publisher's puff.*
This is now used also of brief explanatory notes or the text of an advertisement. The word was coined by the American author Gelett Burgess (1866–1951) as part of a spoof he organized during the launch of his 1907 publication *Are You A Bromide?* At the publisher's annual dinner that year the guests were to be presented with a commemorative copy and Burgess, a man who hated self-praise, decided to have special dust jackets printed for the occasion. They fulsomely sang the praises of the primping model pictured on the front who, borrowed from a cosmetics advertisement, had, of course no connection with the book. The fatuous name given to the vacuous model by the author was 'Miss Belinda Blurb' – the surname conjectured to be a blend of 'blurt' and 'burp'.

**BOB:** *A shilling or any unspecified amount of money.*
The coin is now redundant, but the word lingers on, usually in such expressions as 'that will cost you a bob or two' etc. The origin is obscure but it may be relevant that, in 1864, the British literary review *The Athenaeum* stated that the word was first used in this context in the time of Robert Walpole's political prominence when he was First Lord of the Treasury and Chancellor of the

Exchequer. In addition, 'bob' has since the fourteenth century denoted a small, round object, such as a drop earring or a clock's pendulum. There has also been an attempt to link the word with the '*bobe*', a coin of Old France worth about one and a half old pence, but no real connection has been established.

**BOB RULY:** *Burnt out woodland.*

Sometimes also used of deserted tracts of land, this mainly Western American expression is a corruption of the French '*bois brulé*', burnt forest.

**BOBBY:** *A policeman.*

One of the more affectionate names the British aim at their policemen, this refers to Sir Robert Peel who, as Home Secretary, founded the Metropolitan Police Force in 1829.

**BOBBY DAZZLER:** *A striking or showy person, especially a girl.*

At the turn of the century, rapidly burgeoning cycle clubs in Britain presented a considerable road hazard when returning after dark from day trips. Legislation was passed demanding that they equip their cycles with powerful acetylene lamps and it is said that the few members who did so rode at the outside of the group so that their bright lamps would blind any policeman (BOBBY) to the fact that the inner riders were unlit. The name of the lamps then transferred to equally bright, showy people.

**BOB'S YOUR UNCLE:** *Easily accomplished.*

Gaining wide currency in the 1880s, this could well be a product of the relationship between Robert Gasgoine-Cecil, 3rd Marquis of Salisbury (1830–1903) and his nephew Arthur Balfour (1848–1930). Salisbury served some fourteen years as Prime Minister and was suspected by many of nepotism in that Balfour had only to hint that he wanted a particular post and his Uncle Bob appointed him to it.

**BOCHE:** *A German.*

This appears to be an ellipsis of the French slang '*tête de caboche*', essentially bonehead, '*caboche*' describing things hard, round and solid which dates from the mid-late nineteenth century. It transferred to English through contact with the French during WW1. Of course, the English 'cabbage' comes from '*caboche*' and the Germans are notoriously fond of cabbage.

**BOFFIN:** *An eccentric scientist or specialist.*

Nicodemus Boffin was the name of the ingenious dustman featured in Dickens's *Our Mutual Friend* (1864/65). Described as 'a very odd-looking odd fellow indeed', he was nevertheless the one who resolved all the mysteries in the plot. In 1891, William Morris (1834–96) used the same name for his intelligent dustman with a deep interest in mathematics.

**BOHEMIAN COASTLINE:** *A literary anachronism or inaccuracy.*

This owes its existence to *The Winter's Tale* in which Shakespeare refers to a ship's being wrecked on the Bohemian coast. Bohemia is, of course, completely land-locked. There are other Shakespearean inaccuracies: he mentions striking clocks in *Julius Caesar* though such clocks were a fifteenth-century invention, and he refers to turkeys in *Henry IV Part I* though turkeys were introduced to Britain from America a full century after the time of Henry IV.

**BOLONEY (ALSO BALONEY):** *Nonsense.*

Although no connection has been firmly established, there is a strong assumption that this Americanism derived from the Italian immigrants' cheap Bologna sausage. Jack Conway, a long-time staffer of the magazine *Variety*, used it frequently in this sense, apparently inspired by a popular song from the 1870s 'I Ate the Boloney'. Later, Alfred E. Smith, governor of New York, spoke of the 'boloney dollar' after its devaluation in 1934, and in 1936, referring to some piece of political double-speak, said: 'No matter how thin you slice it, it's still boloney.' This said, and considering the Hispanic influence in America, especially in New York, it would be foolish to ignore the possibility of a connection with the Spanish/gypsy '*pelones*', balls.

**BOLSHY:** *Intransigent.*

This ellipsis of Bolshevik arose because most of the world regarded the revolutionaries as an irksome, troublesome lot.

**BOMB IN NEW HAVEN, TO:** *To fail completely.*

American theatre companies use New Haven, Connecticut, as a testing ground for material before committing themselves to the cost of a Broadway production and the potential embarrassment of failure there. A play that fails in New Haven is unlikely to succeed anywhere. It must be noted here that 'to bomb' or 'to go down like a bomb' in America means 'to be a failure' whereas in England the expression denotes great success.

**BOMBER CREW:** *A motley crew.*

In the American film industry this describes the sort of saga in which a number of dissimilar persons, each with his own dark secret or problem, are brought together in some form of transport which is then beset by danger. The first of such films featured a USAF bomber crew on active service over Germany during WW2.

**BONE TO PICK WITH SOMEONE, A:** *To have a score to settle with them.*

Plain allusion to two dogs with only one bone to pick at between them.

**BONE UP:** *To study.*

This celebrates the reputation of George Henry Bohn (1796–1884), a London publisher whose books came to be accepted as good, standard works. In all, his company issued 766 different volumes on a wide variety of subjects.

**BOONDOCKS or BOONIES:** *Any tract of desolate land.*

This is derived from the Filippino Tagalog '*bundok*', mountain, which entered English through the slang of Americans serving in the Spanish–American War of 1898, who corrupted its meaning. American civilians adopted the word after a press campaign exposed the brutal training methods employed to toughen up raw recruits. These included forced marches through decidedly inhospitable terrain and actually claimed some lives.

**BOONDOGGLE:** *Work deliberately contrived as a palliative.*

This emigrated to America with Scottish settlers and seems to be based on the Scottish '*boon doggle*', a playing marble given as a gift rather than won. Perhaps with the trivial nature of a game of marbles in mind, the word came to mean wasting time and, in the nineteenth century, cowboys used it to describe the saddle trappings which they constructed of braided leather to pass the time when they were not working the herd. The term appeared in print in 1925 when Walter Link, a Scoutmaster of Rochester, New York, so described the braided leather lanyard worn by American Scouts. All this came together to reinforce the meaning of work that was of little practical value and was applied in this way in the early 1930s, when President Franklin D. Roosevelt implemented his New Deal in which the 'manufacturing' of work for the unemployed played a major part.

**BOOT, TO:** *As well as, or, to the good.*

Surviving usage of the Anglo Saxon '*bot*', advantage or profit, and is wholly unconnected with footwear despite several attempts to force such a link. Incidentally, the car boot is derived from the French '*boite*', a box.

**BOOT IS ON THE OTHER FOOT, THE:** *A painful reversal has come about.*

Until the mid nineteenth century, boots and shoes for the mass market were not made to fit the left and right foot, but were identical, and it was up to the wearer to break them into the desired shape. Once this was done, putting a boot on the wrong foot would be painful. Shoes for the nobility, as you might expect, were tailored for the individual foot.

**BOOTLEGGER:** *A shady trader.*

Bootlegger originally applied to someone who dealt in illicit booze. The word was launched into prominence by the American Prohibition Era, 1920–33, but it had been widely used since the mid-1800s to describe the distillers' delivery boys who carried flat bottles inside their tall boots.

**BOOTSTRAPPER:** *A self motivated person who raises himself from poverty to riches.*

This originated in the nineteenth century and draws an analogy between succeeding by one's own efforts and hauling on one's own boots by the loops stitched on for that purpose.

**BORN AGAIN:** *Turned to Christ.*

This is taken from John 3:3 in which Jesus tells Nicodemus that he must be born again in the spiritual sense before he can hope to see the Kingdom of God. The expression has long been known and used in American Evangelist circles and was given its first major exposure outside this sphere when President Jimmy Carter so described himself during his successful election campaign.

**BORN IN THE PURPLE:** *Born to great riches and social advantages.*

In the Byzantine Empire, the Emperor's heir was delivered at birth in a special room swathed in purple; the title *Porphyrogenitus* (Greek '*porphyra*', purple and '*gennetos*') born was bestowed on all the Emperors after Constantine VII (905–59), who was the first to be born there. In both Ancient Greece and Rome, rank and position were always associated with this Tyrian dye which was extracted from the purpura shellfish and used to colour not only the robes of the emperor, but the ink with which he wrote.

**BORN ON THE WRONG SIDE OF THE BLANKET:** *Illegitimate.*

In all probability this is a reference to the way a child was conceived rather than born, suggesting that it was the result of a quick, casual mating on the top of a made bed rather than a sanctified union under the covers of the marriage bed.

**BORN WITH A SILVER SPOON IN THE MOUTH:** *High born.*

This refers to the Master Spoon in a set of silver Apostle Spoons, once a traditional christening gift, but one which only wealthy godparents could afford.

**BOSH:** *Foolish talk.*

This is derived from the Turkish '*bosh*', worthless, and was introduced into English by the Turkish-born British author James Morier (1780–1849). His first work to include the word was *Ayesha* (1834).

**BOSOM BUDDIES:** *Best friends.*

This common American expression originated in England in the form of 'bosom friends' and is recorded in print as early as the late sixteenth century. The inspiration lies in the Bible where several references are made to the closest of male friends reclining against each other's chest. St John is mentioned as sharing such a degree of intimacy with Jesus and is actually described as Christ's bosom friend in the New Testament. It is perhaps also possible that the expression was reinforced by the sharing of a wet nurse by boys from close families.

**BOTTLE:** *Courage.*

This is derived from the Cockney rhyming slang 'bottle and glass' = arse and could well have originated with 'losing one's bottle', a rather coarse reference to the effect of fear on the bowels. Its continuing popularity owes much to British television series such as *The Sweeney* and *Minder* which use a lot of rhyming slang in the script. The Milk Marketing Board also picked up on it in their 1982 on-going campaign to promote milk as having 'a lot of bottle'.

**BOTTOM DRAWER:** *Possessions stored in preparation for marriage.*

The necessity for this has now been circumvented by the Wedding Present List, but, in previous centuries when a woman was expected to enter married life with at least a full set of linen, she collected it while still a spinster and stored it in the largest drawer available. The style of the times dictated that this was the lowest in the chest.

**BOTTOM LINE, THE:** *The final deal.*

Simple reference to the accountants' balance sheet on which the figure at the bottom says it all.

**BOUGHT IT:** *Killed in action.*

This expression, which is a shortened form of 'bought the farm', has its origins in the talk of American soldiers at war, discussing what they will do when they get home. 'Buying that little farm' is a favourite dream, probably reinforced by repeated promises, made by American politicians since the Civil War, of rewarding the soldiers with 'homes fit for heroes' or 'forty acres and a mule'.

**BOW AND SCRAPE, TO:** *To act obsequiously.*

In times and cultures of more rigidly structured society, the downtrodden were required to demonstrate respect in the presence of their superiors by retreating from their presence in a fixed bow with one foot still extended well forward – this scraped across the floor as the other foot was used to propel the retreating underling in a series of undignified hops.

**BOWDLERIZE:** *To expurgate, especially over-prudishly.*

In 1807, a heavily expurgated version of Shakespeare called *The Family Shakespeare* was published. The name of the editor was unaccountably missing but the mystery was apparently solved by the second edition in 1818 which bore the name of one Dr Thomas Bowdler (1754-1825) of Ashley, near Bath. He publicly acknowledged the work and also a later expurgated version of Gibbon's *Decline and Fall of the Roman Empire*. There is, however, considerable evidence suggesting that Bowdler's sister actually did the work and that Thomas only took the credit to spare her blushes; a lady would not care to admit publicly that she could even recognize, for example, a sexual innuendo.

**BOX THE COMPASS:** *To reverse one's opinion completely.*

'Box' in this sense is derived from the Old Spanish '*bojar*', to sail either round an island or in circles pronounced rather like '*boxhar*'. In purely nautical terms, boxing the compass entails reciting all the points on the instrument in their proper order – and then backwards.

**BOYCOTT:** *To ostracize.*

In 1880, retired Army Captain Charles Cunningham Boycott (1832–97) was appointed land agent for the Earl of Erne's Irish estates in County Mayo. On the instructions of his employer, Boycott served several eviction notices for non-payment of rent, and this singled him out as the first target of Charles Parnell (1846-1891) and his Land League which sought to protect tenants from high-handed landlords. Adopting a policy of passive resistance, they simply refused all labour, supplies and, indeed, contact of any kind, and the estates were suddenly cut off from the outside world.

**BOZO:** *A man, particularly a stranger.*

Of nineteenth-century Spanish–American origin but its precise etymology is not clear. A probable source is the Spanish '*bozal*', an African or a person who speaks only broken Spanish, which emerged in America to mean a stupid or crude individual. Should this be the case, the derivation would have a lot in common with the Spanish American use of GRINGO, Spanish for gibberish. On the other hand, it could be taken directly from the Spanish '*bozo*', soft, downy facial hair, and therefore allusive to a young and inexperienced man. There is also the possibility that 'bozo' is an amalgam of the Spanish '*mozo*', a young man, and 'Bo' the American form of address for a man which is a contraction of 'HOBO'. Other possibilities include the Spanish 'bozal', young and inexperienced or the Spanish 'boso', 'you people!' – a shouted discourteous hailing to those who do not matter socially, rather like 'Hey, you!'

**BRAINSTORM:** *A sudden disturbance of the mind or a sudden inspiration.*

Initially this was a quasi medico–psychiatric term for a sudden burst of erratic impulse patterns in the brain resulting in fits and convulsions. Since the brain functions electrically, the impulse patterns recorded on an encephalograph resemble those of electrical storms recorded on meteorological instruments.

**BRAINWASH:** *To indoctrinate.*

This was unknown in English before the Korean War of the 1950s. It is the best possible translation of the Mandarin '*hsi nao*' by which the Chinese 'advisers' to the North Koreans described the process they used to 'cleanse' the stain of capitalism from the minds of American POWs. When the Chinese released film of twenty-one Americans who, after processing, elected to live in China, the massive media coverage guaranteed 'brainwash' a place in English.

**BRAINWAVE:** *A flash of inspired genius.*

The allusion is to the print-out of an encephalograph which peaks in waves when the brain is stimulated.

**BRAND NEW:** *Absolutely new.*

This originated in the branding of a slave with the mark of ownership. Later, trades and associations identified themselves by various marks and symbols, and then individual artisans started to use a personal symbol which was burned into his work as soon as it was completed.

**BRASS:** *A woman of easy virtue.*

The source is Cockney rhyming slang but whether it is from 'brass nail' = tail or more pointedly from 'brass hat' = twat is unclear.

**BRASS HAT/TOP BRASS:** *The superiors in an organization.*

This expression was born in military slang and refers to the gold embellishment on the hats and sleeves of higher ranks.

**BRASS MONKEY WEATHER:** *Extremely cold weather.*

This has its origin in the phrase 'cold enough to freeze the balls off a brass monkey'. From the sixteenth to the eighteenth century, 'monkey' was the nautical jargon for a cannon, or indeed, any one of its operators. For example, those responsible for loading the gun were called 'powder monkeys' and this peculiar designation survives today in the mining and lumber industries to denote those who work with explosives. Motor mechanics, too, in America are still called 'grease monkeys'. It is widely suggested that situated next to the cannon was a heavy brass square used as a collar to hold a stock of ammunition and this was affectionately nicknamed the 'brass monkey' as if it too were part of the team. In extremely cold weather, brass monkeys contracted more quickly than the iron cannon balls they contained and tended to shed them because of this and also because of the invariable swell that accompanied such weather. Unfortunately for this latter part of the theory, no one has ever found a 'brass monkey' on one of these old ships; until someone does the expression will remain an etymological mystery.

**BRASS RING:** *The ultimate goal.*

In the early twentieth century, American merry-go-rounds had brass rings hung on hooks that were placed around the perimeter of the ride, and any child who managed to unhook one was granted another free ride. This potentially lethal incentive disappeared with improved safety regulations.

**BRASSED OFF/BROWNED OFF:** *Bored and depressed.*

These two expressions have the same origin. In nineteenth-century London, the slang term for the heavy copper pre-decimal penny was a 'brown' or a 'brass' and it could be that bored, whining children were 'browned off' or 'brassed off', i.e. given a penny to go off and spend at the shops: a subsequent back-formation would have transferred the action to the mood that promoted it. It is also possible that 'brassed off' referred to the lack-lustre appearance of brass-coated items that had lost most of their veneer, and 'browned off' to the dirty, yellow-brown colour of neglected solid brass.

**BRAVE NEW WORLD:** *The nightmare of a society at the mercy of genetic engineering.*

Aldous Huxley's book described just such a terrible world, but, possibly tongue-in-cheek, he took its title from Shakespeare's *The Tempest* Act V Scene 1, wherein it was used quite differently: 'O, wonder!/How many goodly creatures are there here!/How beauteous mankind is! Oh, brave new world/That has such people in't!'

**BREAD:** *Money.*

This is from Cockney rhyming slang, 'bread and honey'. 'Dough' in the same context came about by extension.

**BREAD AND CIRCUSES:** *Entertainment cynically aimed to pander to the masses and distract them from important issues.*

'*Panem et circenses*' (bread and circuses) was one of the many aphorisms to flow from the pen of arch-misanthrope Decimus Junius Juvenalis (*c.* 60–135 AD), better known simply as Juvenal. In times of strife in ancient Rome, civil disobedience was speedily quelled by the announcement of free admission to hurriedly arranged gladiatorial games at which free food and wine were distributed.

**BREAK A LEG:** *Good luck!*

It is highly probable that this expression was spawned after the murder of President Lincoln in his private box at Ford's Theatre, Washington, on the night of 14 April 1865. His assassin, John Wilkes Booth (1838–65), a Shakespearean actor of some national repute, was unable to leave the scene of his most significant public appearance without playing to the gallery, and made good his escape by leaping down to the stage proclaiming: '*Sic semper tyrannis*' (Ever thus to tyrants), the motto of neighbouring Virginia where the first main battles of the Civil War (Bull Run and Lexington) had been fought, and whose capital, Richmond, became the capital of the Confederacy. Unfortunately, he botched his big scene by breaking his leg on landing, and was forced to exit at an undignified hobble. The assassination aroused a tidal wave of witch-hunting and a great deal of public aggression against the acting profession which, with black humour, thereupon used 'break a leg' as an expression of good will. Some are unhappy with this origin and try to establish a connection with the German '*Hals und Beinbruch*', May you break your neck and leg, a traditional way of wishing a friend luck with a venture which almost certainly originated amongst young blades about to embark on a steeplechase. German pilots in WW2 wished each other happy landings this way, but chronology certainly favours the Booth–Lincoln theory since the expression was well established even before WW1.

**BREAK THE MOULD:** *To render similar excellence impossible.*

In days gone by, when an artist was commissioned to cast an expensive artefact of high quality, the mould was broken to eliminate the possibility of replication by others.

**BRICK:** *A reliable character.*

This personification arose because of a housebrick's solidity, squareness and dependability.

**BRICKBAT:** *A missile or a hefty insult.*

Since the early sixteenth century this has properly described a third-part of a housebrick with one square end intact; this obviously served as a convenient missile.

**BRIDLE:** *To evince resentment by a movement of the head.*

This arose because the stance of a horse reined in on the bridle is similar to the posture of a person reacting haughtily to an insult.

**BRIGHT AS A BUTTON/BUTTONSTICK:** *Lively and intelligent.*

This harks back to the times when nearly all buttons were made of brass, or even silver. 'Bright as a buttonstick' was a nineteenth-century British Army development referring to the centre-cut brass plate which was used by a soldier to protect his tunic from polish stains when buffing his buttons and so received more polishings than any single button.

**BRING HOME THE BACON:** *To be successful.*

The most likely origin of this is the Dunmow Flitch, one of the most unusual trusts ever to be set up in Britain. It is alleged that, in the year 1111, a Lady Juga instituted a fund to encourage matrimonial harmony by offering a flitch of bacon to any man who could satisfy a panel of judges that he had not once wished himself unmarried or had a cross word with his wife for one year and a day. Although the reality of Lady Juga, or at any rate her name, is in some doubt, if only because her name bears a suspicious association with 'conjugal', from the Latin '*iugum*' or '*jugum*', a yoke, nevertheless, the custom is still enacted today, and has parallels of equal antiquity both at home and abroad. It is also possible that competitions to catch a greasy pig at the fairs of old had an effect, since the winner was allowed to keep the quarry.

**BRINKMANSHIP:** *The art of treading thin ice.*

This was first used in 1956 by Adlai Stevenson (1900–65) to describe the inflexibly anti-Communist policies of Secretary of State J. Foster Dulles which many believed were bringing America to the brink of war with Russia. In the sixties, when the word was on everybody's lips, Stevenson said in an interview with *Life* magazine: 'I cannot claim authorship of "brinkmanship" for I am not sure if I read it, heard it somewhere, or just dreamed it up. I am reasonably sure I did not invent it' – a statement which, in fine political tradition, was completely self-contradictory. Whoever was the originator, the word was in all probability a play on Stephen Potter's already established 'GAMESMANSHIP'.

**BRISTOLS:** *Breasts.*

This colloquialism, used mainly in Britain and Australia, is based on the Cockney rhyming slang Bristol City = titty. The reason that Bristol was chosen over other cities is attributable to a peculiarity of the local accent which tacks a rogue 'l' on to the end of certain words (the city was known originally as Bristowe) and also distorts the sound of 'i', so that 'Bristol' came to be pronounced 'Breastle'.

**BROACH A SUBJECT, TO:** *To open discussion on a matter.*

Derived from the Middle English 'broach', a spike, this was also used of the peg used to tap a wine or beer barrel to allow the contents to flow.

**BROAD:** *A woman.*

This piece of American slang appeared around the turn of this century at which time it really meant a woman of loose morals, so, although its origin is in some doubt, it could well have arisen through association with 'broad-minded' or, more earthily, 'broad-assed'. There have been attempts to link the term to 'bawd' but these are unconvincing if only because 'bawd' fell into disuse nearly two centuries before 'broad' put in its appearance.

**BROAD IN THE BEAM:** *Cumbersomely large, especially female hip measurements.*

In the construction of a ship's hull the beams are the transverse timbers upon which the decking is laid. Any ship too broad for her own length and draught presented steerage problems exacerbated to the point of danger in heavy weather.

**BROADSIDE:** *A very comprehensive reproof.*

This comes about by association with the Naval broadside in which all the guns positioned down one side of the vessel are discharged simultaneously.

**BROGUE:** *A stout, country shoe; a rural accent, especially an Irish one.*

The word derives from the Irish '*brog*', shoe and it is highly probable that both meanings are closely connected; brogues are worn in the countryside where speech is affected by a brogue. It is however believed by some that 'brogue', accent, derives from the Irish '*barrog*', wrestling hold or hindrance, which implies that the accent has a hold on the speaker and hinders his communication with strangers.

**BROMIDE:** *A platitude or a platitudinous person.*

Obviously based on the use of bromides in sedatives, this application was coined by American author Gelett Burgess (1866-1951) in his essay 'Bromidioms' in the April 1906 issue of *Smart Set.* He developed the idea into a book which appeared the following year under the title *Are You a Bromide? See also:* BLURB.

**BROODY:** *Preoccupied and slightly aloof.*

This originated in the farmyard where chickens become unusually quiet and withdrawn from the flock when hatching their brood.

**BROUGHT TO BOOK:** *Brought to account.*

Originally a bookmakers' term for a customer's being brought to account for his debts. It is first noted in print in 1804.

**BROUGHT UP ALL STANDING:** *Stopped in one's tracks, physically or metaphorically.*

This derives from the days of sail and describes a sort of nautical emergency stop in which the anchor was tossed over the side to bring the ship up dead. Under such conditions, there was no time to strike the sails which remained up, or 'standing'.

**BROUGHT UP SHORT:** *Stopped in one's tracks, physically or metaphorically.*

When a ship is riding at anchor and drifting with the current, she may reach the limit of slack. As soon as she does so, the anchor cable snatches up smartly, thwacks against the hull and she is brought up short.

**BROUGHT UP TO SPEED:** *Fully briefed for entry into a group.*

More commonly used in America, this expression most probably alludes to the synchromesh in gearboxes which, to facilitate a smooth change, grabs hold of the idle gear-cog and spins it at the same speed as the approaching engagement wheel. This seems far closer to the meaning of the phrase than the other suggested origin which supposes a link to the speed of gramophone records.

**BROUHAHA:** *An excited clamour.*
Taken directly from French where it means a confused hubbub of conversation.

**BROWBEAT:** *To cow or bully.*
This word reflects the metaphorical use of an angry, furrowed brow to beat or intimidate.

**BROWN AS A BERRY:** *Extremely suntanned.*
The expression is puzzling since no berry is actually brown, however, there are plenty of possible origins for the phrase. 'Berry' could be a corruption of 'Barbary' which was once used of any African (by association with the Barbary Coast). A coffee bean used to be called a coffee berry. As a now obsolete variant of 'barrow', 'berry' was often used of a rabbit burrow, which is, of course, dark. Lastly, until late in the eighteenth century, 'brown' meant not only the colour, but also 'dark' as in BROWN STUDY so the expression could once have meant 'dark as a berry'.

**BROWN STUDY:**
A sombre, contemplative mood. This expression uses 'brown' in its ancient meaning of 'dark' or 'gloomy'.

**BUBBLE SOMEONE, TO:** *To inform on someone, especially to the police.*
This is taken from the Cockney rhyming slang 'bubble and squeak', set to rhyme with both 'speak' and 'BEAK', magistrate. Bubble-and-squeak is a London dish of left-over cabbage and potato which, when fried, produces noises akin to its name.

**BUCK:** *The dollar.*
This almost certainly originated in the ubiquitous American poker game. In the West, in the eighteenth century, a small object was circulated at the poker table, being placed beside the player who was next in turn to deal. This came to be known as 'the buck', perhaps because it was usually a piece of heavy buckshot, or sometimes a knife with a buck-horn handle. The meaning transferred since they played with real money and it was the responsibility of each successive dealer – whose turn was marked by 'the buck'- to contribute the entire ante, the standard amount of which was a dollar. This connection was reinforced at the gambling tables of the East, where the players used poker chips instead of money and indicated the next deal with a silver dollar. It has been suggested that the term was born of buck skins which were at one time used as a medium of exchange but an expression like PASS THE BUCK (i.e. passing responsibility on to another) would seem to validate the gambling origin.

**BUCK STOPS HERE, THE:** *This is the point of ultimate responsibility.*
A natural development from 'PASS THE BUCK', this was coined by Harry S. Truman (1884–1972), America's poker-playing president, who, throughout his eight-year tenure

from 1945, kept a sign inscribed with that legend on his desk in the Oval Office. When Jimmy Carter became president in 1976, he ordered that the original sign be taken out of storage and replaced on the desk. The public became aware of the expression through the publication in 1962 of Alfred Steinberg's biography of Truman *The Man from Missouri.*

**BUCKET SHOP:** *An agency dealing in relatively small numbers of goods or services passed on to them by larger companies.*

In the nineteenth century, a bucket shop on both sides of the Atlantic was a low bar or an illegal drinking haunt where beer was sold by the bucketful to groups of drinkers. Then in post Civil War Chicago, establishments were set up which, ostensibly small traders in stocks and shares, were in reality nothing more than illegal gambling dens in which bets on the rise and fall of market prices were camouflaged as purchases of one or two shares – derisory quantities as far as regular speculators were concerned. These too became known as bucket shops, probably because the shares 'purchased' would buy only a bucketful of grain – the main commodity involved in Chicago dealings. Later, when legitimate operators began trading in batches of shares considered uneconomical by the major brokers, they inherited the term, which, eventually moved on to non-stockmarket-related enterprises.

**BUCKLE DOWN:** *Get down to serious endeavour.*

This originally meant to strap on armour in readiness for battle.

**BUCKRA:** *A white man.*

In both Ibibio and Efik, the two languages of Calabar where this word originated, '*buckra*' meant a devil or a powerful superior. It entered English when African slaves used it for a white master.

**BUCKSHEE:** *Absolutely free; a windfall or tip.*

This is one of the many terms brought back from the East by returning British troops, in this case a corruption of 'BAKSHEESH'.

**BUFF:** *A devotee or enthusiast.*

Born *c.* 1865 in New York when there was an unsuccessful attempt by Confederate sympathisers to burn down the city. This highlighted the inadequacies of the volunteer fire service which was then disbanded and replaced by a regular, paid force. Many of the old volunteers continued to turn out to fires, often being more of a hindrance than a help according to the regulars, who christened them 'The Buffs' because of the heavy, buffalo-skin coats they wore as a protection and as an unofficial uniform. They extended 'buffs' to embrace those members of the public who loved to hang around and watch the action, and their officials' use of the term in press interviews launched it into general speech.

**BUFFOON:** *An idiot or clown.*

Derived from the French '*bouffir*', to puff up, 'buffoon' was the name of the stock character of ridicule in medieval pantomime whose *pièce de resistance* was to puff himself up with an enormous breath which he released in the form of a protracted raspberry.

**BUG:** *A hidden microphone.*

From the American poker tables of the late nineteenth century where it was used of a card hidden by a cheat under the table, because insects lurked there too.

**BUG:** *To annoy.*

This is taken from black American slang and seems to be based on the West African '*bugu*', to infuriate, which was built into West African pidgin in the form of 'bug' and is still employed there in that context today. The irritation caused by body parasites must have helped to promote the expression.

**BUGBEAR:** *A cause of fear or annoyance.*

'*Bwg*' was Old Welsh for a ghost or evil spirit possessed of tremendous strength, and a bear was undoubtedly the most powerful creature to roam the medieval British countryside. The two terms came together to describe a sort of devil-bear that stalked the night, a notion not unlike the Yeti or the American Bigfoot.

**BUGGER:** *A general term of abuse, properly one who engages in sodomy.*

This is derived from the French '*bougre*', which was taken from the Latin '*Bulgarius*' and originally meant a Bulgarian. The debasement of the term started in twelfth-century France when it was applied to a member of the Albigenses, a religious sect which held Catharist beliefs and had associations with Bulgaria. The sect was denounced as heretical, persecuted, and finally eradicated, but the word persisted and acquired its present meaning because heretics were believed capable of any form of vice, such as sodomy.

**BULL:** (1) *Verbal rubbish.*

This is in fact based on the French '*boule*', false, bragging statement, and has been in use certainly since the sixteenth century. Ever anxious to improve matters, people in more recent times sometimes added 'shit', thus creating a misconception that the animal was involved.

(2) *A plainclothes policeman.*

This is derived from the Gypsy '*bul*', policeman, although, no doubt, the fact that a policeman's size is somewhat intimidating will have helped to reinforce the usage.

**BULL'S EYE:** *The centre of a target or a shot that hits it.*

When a bull is seen in profile, its large protruding eye is located in the centre of its massive head. The modern application did not emerge until the early nineteenth century, but the expression had been used before then for other centred items such as the boss in the middle of a shield and the central bulge that appears in the making of a sheet of blown glass.

**BULLY FOR YOU:** *Good for you! Well done!*

Originally a 'bully' was a fine or excellent fellow and derived from the

Dutch '*boele*', friend or lover. It came to mean also a hearty, swashbuckling type and it was not until the end of the eighteenth century that it started to drift towards its present meaning of a swaggering coward, possibly because of the aggressive tendencies of swashbucklers.

**BUM:** *An idler or tramp.*

No connection with the anatomical usage but derived instead from the German '*bummeln*', a leisurely stroll or to waste time. The usage arose in early 1800s America through the influx of German immigrants.

**BUM STEER:** *Unsound advice or deliberately misleading information.*

Originally sailors' jargon, this described incorrect navigational data which resulted in the ship's being steered in the wrong, or bum, direction.

**BUMF:** *Paperwork, disparagingly.*

Based on 'bum fodder', 'bumf' has been an English Public School term for lavatory paper since the nineteenth century.

**BUMPKIN:** *A clumsy rustic or a buffoon.*

The interminable squabbling between the English and the Dutch, which lasted until well into the eighteenth century, left several racially inspired marks in English, as indeed it did in Dutch. The Dutch '*boomkin*', small, stunted tree and therefore woodenhead, was adopted into English in the mid sixteenth century because its Dutch origin made it the more insulting.

**BUNCE:** *Unexpected or unearned benefit.*

This was born of schoolboy dog Latin, built on '*bonus*', good or beneficial.

**BUNG UP AND BILGE FREE:** *Absolutely as it should be.*

Every barrel stored on board ship had to be racked with the bung-hole showing at 'twelve o'clock' and well raised on laths to ensure that its bilge, or bulge, was not in contact with the deck. See also details regarding 'cuntline and bilge free' under CUNT.

**BUNK:** *Verbal clap-trap.*

In 1820, the American House of Representatives was wrestling with the highly complex hypocrisy known as the Missouri Compromise, whereby they were trying to find a way of admitting Missouri into the Union despite the fact that it was still operating as a slave state. In the middle of the debate, Felix 'Old Oil Jug' Walker, Congressman for Buncombe County, North Carolina, launched himself into an interminable, irrelevant speech which caused many to walk out in frustration. Others remained to jeer but Walker, who was quite simply drunk, refused to yield the floor, shouting that he was speaking for Buncombe and would be heard. That county's name was later corrupted to 'bunkum' and finally contracted to 'bunk'.

**BURIDAN'S ASS:** *One who cannot or will not make a decision.*

This sophism, erroneously attributed to Jean Buridan (*c.*1295–*c.*1358), French philosopher and theorist, maintained that a hungry ass positioned equidistant between two identical haystacks would starve to death since there was nothing to motivate it towards one rather than the other. In his commentary on Aristotle's *Caelo*), Buridan does illustrate an argument on motivation for decision taking using the concept of a *dog* between two equal amounts of meat, and he did not intend even this to be taken seriously.

**BURKE AN ISSUE:** *To attempt to hush up a political scandal.*

In the late 1820s in Edinburgh, Scotland, William Burke and William Hare together murdered at least fifteen people and sold their bodies to the city's leading anatomist, Dr Robert Knox. Undamaged bodies fetched a higher price, so they resorted to smothering sleeping victims.

**BURN THE CANDLE AT BOTH ENDS:** *Properly meaning to waste, but used loosely to mean to stay up late roistering.*

The allusion is to the once extravagant practice of cutting a candle in two and using both parts simultaneously to gain extra light – perhaps to carouse by. Candles were, in the Middle Ages, extremely expensive, and within the reach of only the Church or the nobility; the poor simply went to bed when it turned dark.

**BURN YOUR BOATS:** *To commit yourself to a course of action.*

In previous eras, an invading army indicated its intention of fighting to the bitter end by burning the boats in which it arrived. Not only did this intimidate the enemy, it also put resolve into the invading troops by scotching any ideas of mutiny or escape.

**BURY YOUR HEAD IN THE SAND:** *To ignore a glaring truth.*

The age-old myth that the ostrich buries its head in the sand was started by the creature's habit of standing for long periods with its head lowered to the ground.

**BURY THE HATCHET:** *Make peace.*

In America, when an Indian intertribal war was settled, each tribe would ceremoniously bury a war hatchet to symbolise the end of hostilities.

**BUSHED:** *Exhausted.*

The original Australian application was much more grave and meant being a victim of a serious mental condition characterized by acute depression and lethargy brought on by prolonged periods of solitude in the bush. It was common amongst trappers and station farmers' wives.

**BUSHWHACKER:** *A person who mounts a sneak attack from ambush.*

It has been suggested that this is a variant of the Dutch '*bosh wachter*' (forest keeper) or it could be just what it says – a whacker of bushes. Either way, the word was used originally of the men hired to clear tracts of land in late eighteenth-century America and acquired its present meaning because such men tended to be saddle-tramps who supplemented their pay by murdering and robbing any unforunate who crossed their path or wandered into their camp.

**BUSMAN'S HOLIDAY:** *A holiday spent in activities similar to one's work.*

In the years when London's transport was horse-drawn, drivers were wont to spend their rest days cruising the city by cadging rides from their on-duty mates. Some say the reason for this was that the drivers, being fond of their horses, wished to ensure they were well treated, but, though the British are notorious animal lovers, this was not the case. Basically, the men wanted to watch the world go by and pester any unattached female passengers. The practice became so scandalous that *Punch* carried some cartoons to highlight the abuse.

**BUTCH:** *Overtly masculine.*

This was born of the long-standing but false belief that butchers were full of health and vigour because they had all the fresh meat they wanted. In the early 1900s in America, Butch was a common nickname for a young man of physical prowess and for a large, aggressive dog, but this usage declined when the gay community adopted the term for the dominant partner in a relationship.

**BUTCHERS:** *A quick glimpse.*

This is from the Cockney rhyming slang, 'butcher's hook' = look.

**BUTT OF A JOKE:** *An object of ridicule.*

This comes from the French '*but*', archery target.

**BUTTER WOULDN'T MELT IN YOUR MOUTH:** *To look deceptively demure and innocent.*

This depends on the belief that emotional control and a cool, reserved manner indicate good breeding and, by extension, high moral standards.

**BUTTONS OFF THE FOILS:** *In deadly earnest.*

This refers to the balls (buttons) of waxed thread which used to be fitted to the points of practice fencing foils. After the seventeenth century, their points were permanently filed or otherwise blunted.

**BY A LONG CHALK:** *To beat very soundly.*

Early scoreboards were nothing more sophisticated than a piece of wood with several lines scored across, each player's chalk line being extended one division for each point gained.

**BY AND BY:** *In the fullness of time.*

In pre-Shakespearean days this was understood to mean physically side by side and in neat order; each by the other's side, if you like. As the designation spread to encompass a chain of events occuring one after the other, or side by side, the general meaning altered.

**BY AND LARGE:** *On the whole.*

It is a bad day at sea for the vessel confronted with headwinds forcing her to sail 'by' the wind, or close to the wind with her sheets (the rope used to trim the sails) hardened in. Conversely a good day's progress is made with a tail wind coming abaft the beam when the sails could be allowed to stand full. A voyage complete after a blend of such fortunes encompassed the rough with the smooth.

**BY HOOK OR BY CROOK:** *By any means, fair or foul.*

Although it cannot be proved beyond doubt, the most likely source for this would appear to be a feudal wood-gathering right afforded to serfs by their lord; they could take live wood from common land, but only that which could be pulled down within reach by a shepherd's crook, and cut through with a bill hook. *The Bodmin Register* of 1525 states: 'Dynmure Wood was ever open and common to the inhabitants of Bodmin, to bear away on their backs a burden of lop, crop, hook, crook and bag wood.'

**BY THE LEFT:** *A rejoinder indicating incredulity.*

This is a modern development of the British Victorian 'over the left (shoulder)'. For reasons now obscure, disbelief was then indicated by gesticulating over the left shoulder with the right thumb.

**BY THE SKIN OF YOUR TEETH:** *The narrowest of margins.*

The expression is a misunderstanding of Job 19:20 in which the eponymous hero of the book laments his situation thus: 'My bone cleaveth to my skin, and to my flesh, and I am escaped with (only) the skin of my teeth.' Feeling slightly picked upon by God at the time, Job is suffering nightmares, scabs that peel and turn black, disfigurement, anorexia and, to cap it all, breath so bad that his wife walks away – the above line is interpreted as meaning that even his teeth are gone, which makes the modern usage something of a nonsense.

**BYZANTINE:** *Intricate, tortuous; rigidly hierarchic.*

There are two influences here, Byzantine architecture which was elaborately ornamented, and the pre-Justinian (483–565) rulers of the Byzantine Empire who were rightly notorious for their political conniving and duplicity. In 1914, Theodore Roosevelt highlighted this application of the word when he described President Woodrow Wilson, who was holding America back from entering WWI, as a Byzantine Logothete (a highly placed official at the Byzantine court). His words were well remembered if only because most people had to consult a dictionary to discover what he meant.

# C

**CACK-HANDED:** *Clumsy and awkward.*

Originally a late nineteenth-century London term for 'left-handed', this literally means 'shit-handed', being derived from the Latin '*cacare*', to void excrement.

**CADGER:** *A scrounger.*

In the early fifteenth century, a 'cadge', variant of 'cage', was a large wicker hamper or basket, and a cadger was an itinerant vendor of farm produce who carried his wares in it; such hawkers had a reputation for pestering and begging. Oddly enough, in the early 1800s, a falconer's servant who carried hawks in cages or open frames was also called a cadger, but there is no connection between the two types of hawker.

**CAKEWALK:** *A task that presents no challenge.*

In the Southern States of nineteenth century America, blacks indulged in a form of competitive fashion show cum entertainment in which competitors, dressed to the nines in pairs, strutted and postured about in a circle around the judges. The couple deemed the most elegant were presented with a cake. White people, dismissing such a competition as a non-event, coined cakewalk, and also 'a piece of cake' with the same meaning.

**CALAMITY JANE:** *An accident-prone woman.*

The nickname of Martha Jane Cannary (1852–1903) who was part of the folklore of the American West. She was indeed accident-prone, but she also frequently threatened anybody who annoyed her with 'calamity'. Unlike the wholesome character portrayed by actresses such as Doris Day, the genuine article was an unprepossessing, unwashed, foul-mouthed transvestite prostitute whose behaviour often shocked even the bar-flies and saddle-tramps with whom she associated.

**CALL SOMEONE'S BLUFF:** *To challenge what could be an empty boast.*

In poker, a player sometimes bluffs by exaggerating the strength of his hand, betting large amounts on it hoping the others will withdraw but at some stage an opponent matching his stake has the right to call upon him to expose his hand.

**CALL THE SHOTS, TO:** *To have total control.*

The formal rules of pool demand the player nominates which ball is destined for which pocket, thus eliminating fluke scores. As ever round the pool or snooker table there is no shortage of advice as to which ball the player should attempt, but the one calling the shots has the final say.

**CALLED TO THE BAR:** *Admitted into the profession of barrister or advocate.*

In the days when courts of law were much less imposing places, justice was dispensed in any building on the circuit that was large enough to accommodate the proceedings. This was quite often for example a barn across which a rope was tied to separate the officials from the rabble. Anyone wishing to speak on his own or another's behalf was required to approach the rope and address the court. When courts became purpose-built, the rope was replaced by a wooden bar at which interested parties pleaded their cause, and when advocacy was drawn up into a formal, closed profession, those who spoke on behalf of their clients were called inside the bar and known as barristers.

**CAMELOT:** *The name given to the bright, youthful, hopeful administration of J.F. Kennedy (1917–63).*

JFK was inaugurated in January 1961, just before the Broadway opening of the hit musical *Camelot* by Lerner and Loewe. America liked the association and, in one of the first interviews she gave after the assassination, Jackie Kennedy said to *Life*: 'At night before we'd go to sleep, Jack liked to play some records and the song he loved most came at the very end of this record [*Camelot*]. The lines he loved to hear were: "Don't let it be forgot, that there was once a spot, for one brief shining moment that was known as Camelot." . . . There will be great residents again . . . but there'll never be another Camelot again.' America was delighted when in 1988 *Burke's Peerage*, undeterred by the scepticism of British experts, supported the claim of Professor Norma Goodrich of Claremont College, California, that the site of ancient Camelot lay in Ayrshire, Scotland, since generations of Kennedys dating back to Arthurian times had occupied a nearby castle, and were frequently visited by Kennedys from the Irish branch of the family.

**CAMP:** *Theatrical, affected, or characteristic of homosexuals.*

This application dates from the early 1900s and is somewhat obscure but there is a strong likelihood that it developed from a piece of stage terminology. 'Camping' in the early English theatre, and '*se camper*' in the French, described the dressing up of men in dresses for women's parts, the trailing skirts of which could also have produced DRAG. '*Se camper*' can also mean to posture in an exaggerated manner and an elaboration of this, '*se camper sur un pied*', can be used of the classic pose of the effeminate dandy. Two other suggestions are perhaps worthy of mention, but unlikely: (1) It is said that in the mid-nineteenth century, soldiers *camped* out in London's Regent's

Park clandestinely served as male prostitutes to the gay blades of town. (2) The word might be an acronym of 'Known As Male Prostitute' from New York police criminal records. Acronyms are, however, suspect for, no matter how apposite they seem, they invariably turn out to be spurious. For classic examples see FUCK and POSH.

**CANARD:** *A false rumour.*

Derived from the old French expression '*vendre un canard à moitié*', literally to half-sell a duck, understood as to cheat. The word would never have gained such currency in English had not Belgian journalist Egide Cornelissen set out in 1889 to test the public's gullibility by releasing a series of reports on a scientific research programme allegedly investigating the hitherto unrecognized voracity and killer instinct of the common duck. A new strain of killer duck had been produced by taking a batch of twenty ordinary ducks, killing one and feeding it to the others, and repeating the process until there was only one very well-fed but blood-crazed duck left. The European and the American press picked up on the story which inspired a deal of speculation as to how this awesome force could be directed. Charles-Eugene, Vicomte de Foucald (1858–1916), who was probably no more insane than any other contemporary military commander, proposed training squadrons of kamikaze ducks to fly, snapping viciously, into enemy cavalry and create havoc. There was much embarrassment in 1890 when Cornelissen announced it had all been a joke. That same year, Foucald went to Palestine to become a hermit.

**CANUCK:** *Any Canadian, or descriptive of anything from that country.*

It is possible that this is nothing more complicated than the first syllable of Canada suffixed with 'uck' which, along with 'ock' can be found capriciously attached to countless words e.g. ball – ballock. It has however been suggested that this slightly pejorative term is a corruption of 'Connaught', originally used by French Canadians of the Irish immigrants they saw as early nineteenth-century interlopers. Seemingly less plausible is the Hawaiian '*kanaka*' which means 'man' but can be used in a dismissory sense. This, the theory holds, was brought back to New England by returning whalers and sneeringly applied to those across the border to the north. It must be said that the earliest spelling found in 1835 does present the form 'Kanuk' and 'Kanak' has also been noted in the following decades.

**CANNON INTO:** *To collide with.*

The source of this is the Spanish '*carambola*' – a starfruit. The fruit's name was shortened to 'carom' and, for reasons now totally obscure, used of the shot in billiards when the cue ball is hit in such a way as to make contact with the other two balls on the table. No doubt the idea that the fieldpiece was somehow involved altered the spelling but in America where the Spanish influence is still significant the shot is still properly called a 'carom'.

**CARD:** *An eccentric; a wag.*

This probably arose in the textile industry in which a card, in this case derived from the Latin '*carduus*', a thistle, was an instrument for combing and teasing cloth to raise its nap, functions which fit metaphorically with the character of a wag. As early as the sixteenth century the textile card was incorporated into such sayings as 'a good carding', which, in allusion to its punishing action, (sometimes literally carried out), meant a good dressing down.

**CARD-CARRYING:** *Fully committed, usually to an unpopular or suspect cause.*

This arose during America's Communist witch-hunt, led by Senator Joseph Raymond McCarthy (1909–57). He leapt to prominence, as did the expression, when, in a speech made at Wheelong, West Virginia, he announced that he held conclusive proof of the existence of a large number of 'card-carrying Communists' in the State Department. The card in question was, of course, the official Communist Party Membership Card.

**CAREY STREET:** *Financial straits, bankruptcy.*

This thoroughfare is in the City of London, just off Chancery Lane where the bankruptcy courts are located.

**CAROUSE:** *To indulge in drunken, riotous behaviour.*

Derives from the German '*gar aus*', completely empty, the allusion being to a beer stein that is emptied too often.

**CARP:** *To indulge in fault-finding.*

This derives from the Old Norse '*karpa*', to boast, which emerged in Middle English as '*carpen*', to talk slanderously, probably modified in meaning by association with the Latin 'carpere', to pluck, deride.

**CARPETBAGGER:** *One moving into an area for self-serving or political ends.*

A derogatory Americanism originally aimed by post Civil War (1861–65) Southerners at the flood of get-rich-quick Northern speculators who swept south to snap up bankrupt businesses and plantations at rock-bottom prices. Intent on travelling fast and light, they were immediately recognizable by their outsize Gladstone bags made of strong carpet-like material. Feeling ran so high against them that they received constant death threats, several of them fulfilled, from the Ku Klux Klan, as did 'scalawags' – native Southerners who had retained enough money to indulge in similar acquisitive tactics. The Southern establishment felt equally strongly: in September 1868, the *Tuscaloosa Independent Monitor* ran a cartoon of a KKK lynching, claiming that this was the best way of dealing with: 'these great pests of Southern society, the carpetbagger and the scalawag. The scalawag is the local leper of the community. Unlike the carpetbagger, he is native, which is so much the worse.' Political connotations were assumed when the term was applied, again by disgruntled Southerners, to the Northern officials sent down to take control of local and regional government. In Britain, the word's only application is to a political candidate standing in one constituency whilst actually living in another.

**CARRY ON:** *A bout of unrestrained behaviour.*

This was originally British Naval parlance in which 'to carry' meant to come alongside a vessel with intent to board her, and 'carry on' denoted the actual boarding which carried the fight onto the decks of the enemy.

**CARRY THE CAN:** *Take the responsibility, or the blame.*

Originally in the form of 'carry the can back', this was first noted in the RAF slang of the early 1920s. It arose from the custom of electing one man from a hut to fetch a bucket of beer from the NAAFI and also carry back the empty can.

**CARSEY:** *Privy.*

A faithfully spelt rendition of the Cockney pronunciation of a distortion of 'case' as based on '*casa*', the Italian and Spanish for a house. All three terms served time as a synonym for 'brothel' but, by the mid nineteenth century, they had become more generally applied to any disorderly establishment such as low drinking dens. By extension, the term shifted to the privy.

**CARTE BLANCHE:** *Complete freedom of action.*

Literally meaning white card or paper, this French expression alludes to the practice of signing one's name a blank piece of paper on which someone else is free to write what he wishes. For example, the general of a defeated army might be forced to sign blank papers on which the victor unilaterally set down the conditions of peace.

**CASE A JOINT:** *To appraise an establishment with a view to burglary.*

This emerged in early twentieth-century American thieves' cant and could have been imported from England where, in the eighteenth and nineteenth centuries, the verb 'to case' meant 'to skin'. Apart from the fact that a skinned animal is laid bare for inspection, there is another connection with robbery in that, in the thieves' cant of the time, a 'skin' was a leather purse. The meaning of the two terms could have melded and transferred from the English underworld to the American. More directly, a case is an external structure, as indeed is an animal's skin, so the expression could simply refer to the way a burglar might stroll round the perimeter of a building looking for weak spots. The least likely derivation is the Spanish '*casa*', house; this is unsupported by any evidence.

**CASE-HARDENED:** *Rendered insensitive by the harsh realities of life.*

Since the mid-seventeenth century, which was long before the smiths understood the chemistry of the procedure, an iron artefact was 'case-hardened' in a blast-furnace by being brought into contact with incredibly hot charcoal which toughened the outer surface without altering the shape.

**CASH ON THE BARREL-HEAD:** *Immediate payment.*

In the American frontier era an up-turned barrel served as a counter in the general store where goods were sold on a cash only basis.

**CASSANDRA:** *An unheeded prophet of doom.*

In Greek mythology Cassandra, daughter of King Priam of Troy, was loved by Apollo who gave her the gift of prophesy by having serpents lick her ears as she lay asleep in his temple. Later, because she rejected his advances, he punished her by ensuring that, though her prophesies were true, nobody believed or heeded them.

**CAST NOT A CLOUT TILL MAY BE OUT:** *Proceed with caution.*

'Clout', a piece of cloth, here indicates any item of clothing, however inconsiderable it may seem, so this cautionary saying warns against discarding winter clothing during fluctuating spring temperatures. Some hold that 'May' means 'may-blossom' but the capital letter refutes this as does the early eighteenth-century Spanish equivalent '*Hasta passado mayo no te quites el sayo*', Do not leave off your smock till May be past. In Spanish, '*mayo*' means only the month of May. (The months of the year do not start with a capital letter in Spanish.)

**CAST PEARLS BEFORE SWINE:** *To waste fine things or lofty thoughts on those incapable of appreciating them.*

The source is Matthew 7:6 which reads: 'Give not that which is holy to dogs, neither cast ye your pearls before swine, lest they trample them under their feet, and turn again and rend you.'

**CAST YOUR BREAD UPON THE WATERS:** *To invest in the future.*

Today, this is used to express the idea that one must speculate to accumulate, a sentiment which is not in keeping with anything in the Bible. The full quotation, 'Cast your bread upon the waters for thou shalt find it after many days', Ecclesiastes 11:1, has been the subject of much conjecture and the meaning remains obscure. It could simply imply that one should not be afraid to give of oneself; sooner or later, life will repay the gift in some way.

**CASTLES IN SPAIN:** *Self-deluding fantasy.*

In use since the tenth century when Spain was regarded by the common man as a far-away country shrouded in Moorish mystery. It came to represent the epitome of the unattainable and the nebulous.

**CASTLES IN THE AIR:** *Pipe dreams.*

This probably has its origin in fairy tales in which exotic castles, occupied by either wicked witches or kindly wizards, floated magically in the air atop mist-shrouded mountains.

**CASTOR AND POLLUX:** *Inseparable.*

Greek mythology relates how these twins, otherwise known as the Dioscuri (Sons of Zeus), were born of Leda, Pollux having been fathered by Zeus and Castor by Leda's husband Tyndareus. So close were they that, when the mortal Castor died, the immortal Pollux petitioned Zeus to allow him to die also so that they could be together. Zeus placed them both in the heavens where today they are called the constellation of Gemini.

**CAT'S WHISKERS:** *Something of prime importance.*

Animals and things are frequently paired in this way, sometimes for no better reason than a pleasing contrast or rhyme. There is however, a practical reason for this one in that a cat's whiskers, being highly sensitive, enable it to negotiate narrow confines in total darkness.

**CATCH AS CATCH CAN:** *By any possible means, fair or foul.*

This was, (and still is in certain areas of Britain), a rough-house wrestling style with no holds barred, a participant being allowed to grip and twist whatever parts of his adversary came within grasp. The concept survives in wrestling as 'catch-weight contest' – a fight in which no weight limits are imposed.

**CATCH FLATFOOTED, TO:** *To catch off-guard.*

Boxers, and horses, dance on their toes to keep themselves supple and alert while waiting for a contest to begin.

**CATCH 22:** *A no-win, no-way-out predicament.*

The title of Joseph Heller's book about the lives of war-time USAF pilots, the central character in which, Yossarian, reported to the medical officer feigning insanity in order to work his ticket. The doctor hid behind the solve-all Catch 22, which stated a man: 'would be crazy to fly more missions and sane if he didn't, but, if he was sane, he had to fly them. If he flew them he was crazy, but if he didn't, he was sane and therefore had to.' Everything in the book had a catch, but this was the greatest catch of all, and even Yossarian had to admit its magnificence. There was no significance in the number 22, for the work was originally entitled 'Catch 18', but, during its proof-reading, Leon Uris brought out *Mila 18*, so the title was hurriedly changed.

**CATCHWORD/CATCHPHRASE:** *A slogan so closely associated with certain persons or organisations that it identifies them.*

Rooted in the printing trade in which, since the early eighteenth century, the 'catchword' appeared both at the beginning of the first line on a page and at the end of the last line on the preceding page, and acted as a follow-on point of reference for the typesetter. Later, the word encompassed a single word heading, in e.g. a dictionary, this being set in bold type for easy identification, hence 'catchword' and 'catchphrase' in the current sense.

**CAUCUS:** *In America, a group of leading politicians meeting to select candidates for a forthcoming election. In Britain, an elected committee responsible for concerted activity in a specific location or a group thought to be manipulating voting trends by suspect means.*

The word originated in America and it is almost certain that its source is Amerindian. As early as 1608, Captain John Smith, British pirate and mercenary of Pocahontas fame, wrote a pamphlet about the colonization of Virginia in which he mentioned meetings with the '*cawcawwassoughes*' – elders or advisers of the Indian tribes. This word was simplified to '*kaw-kaw-asu*' and adopted by the whites as 'caucus'. The adoption of Indian terms for political clubs and organisations is not rare.

The first direct reference to the word occurs in a diary entry of 3 February 1763 made by John Adams who became the second president of America. He wrote: 'The Caucus Club meet at certain times in the garret of Tom Dawes, the Adjutant of the Boston Regiment . . . there they smoke tobacco till you cannot see from one end of the garret to the other. There they drink flip I suppose, and choose a Moderator.' The word cropped up again in 1788 in a work published in Boston dealing with the American Revolution, in which its author, William Gordon stated: 'More than fifty years ago, Mr Samuel Adams' father and twenty-two others, one or two from the north end of town where all the ship business is carried on, used to meet, make a caucus, and lay their plans for introducing certain persons into places of trust and power.' Although Gordon went on to say that he had been unable to uncover the origin of the word despite exhaustive enquiries, there are those who believe that it derived from just such a political club known as The Caulkers (corrupted to Caucus), Club, either because they met in a caulk-house, or because so many of its members were in the shipping business.

The word appeared in the British political arena in 1878 when Disraeli (1804–81) used it as a dig at what he saw as the American-style organization of Joseph Chamberlain's (1836–1914) Liberal Associations which assembled for election management purposes.

**CAVE IN:** *To collapse inwards; to give way to outside pressure.*

Originally 'calve in', derived conversely from the Dutch '*uitkalven*', the falling out from its mother of a calf. This inspired '*inkalven*', to collapse inwards, a word which Dutch workmen used, for example, of a trench. A specialized Dutch labour force, imported into England in the mid-late eighteenth century to drain and secure the East Anglian Fens, brought the expression with them. Although 'calve', in this instance, changed later to 'cave', it is interesting to note that a glacier is still properly said to 'calve' a massive lump of ice when it sheds it. Also, the 'calf' of the leg is allied, being so-called because of its shape which is similar to the belly of a pregnant cow.

**CHAMP AT THE BIT:** *Aggressively impatient; keen to begin something.*

The reference here is to a horse opening and closing its mouth on the bit, anxious for the rider to move off.

**CHANCE YOUR ARM:** *To take risks.*

The most likely source is British Army jargon in which this would have meant to act in such a way as to risk demotion, thus losing the stripes off one's sleeve. An alternative theory suggests that the expression could have referred originally to a boxer who was inclined to strike out too freely, but this does not seem so apposite.

**CHARIVARI:** *A raucous cacophony.*

The final etymology of this remains obscure but it may be derived from the Latin '*caribaria*' – a headache. It was the name of an old French wedding custom which involved 'serenading' the bride and groom by beating together pots and pans or anything else calculated to create an unholy din. In the fifteenth century, charivaris were reserved for unpopular weddings and even used for disrupting actual marriage services and this led to their being banned by the Council of Tours in the early 1600s. Despite this move by the Church, the custom survived and, even today, French weddings include a charivari of sorts, created by the guests' driving slowly through the streets in convoy blowing their horns the while. In 1832 the term was adopted as a title by a satirical magazine published in Paris, and it was also used as a sub-title for the English magazine *Punch*. Because of the strong French influence which flowed into America and Canada, 'charivari' survives there as 'shivaree', though 'bull band' is equally common.

**CHARLATAN:** *A quack or a fraud.*

The ultimate source of this is the Italian town Cerreto, the inhabitants of which were previously held to be charlatans one and all. Using the placename as a foundation, the Italians built '*ciarlatano*', fast talker, which became '*charlatan*' in French and then in English.

**CHARLIE:** *An idiot.*

A fine example of the process whereby a name that suddenly becomes popular, usually through the monarchy, is later overshadowed by connotations of stupidity due to its very ubiquity. *See also:* DAGO, DICK.

**CHATTERBOX:** *One given to incessant prattle.*

This appeared in the eighteenth century and would appear to be an allusion to the noise created by the incessant shaking of a beggar's box, which always contained a couple of coins as bait. Before the eighteenth century, the preferred term was 'chatter-basket', in this case an allusion to the never-ending noise of a baby's wicker rattle. Even earlier, there was the now totally redundant 'clack-dish', a leper's begging bowl whose hinged lid the leper noisily flapped up and down to warn of his approach.

**CHAUVINISM:** *Fanatical attachment to a group, place, cause, etc.*

Nicholas Chauvin (the Bald One) from Rochefort in France, who was wounded while serving with Napoleon's army and pensioned off, never lost his fanatical devotion to his general. Even after Napoleon's defeat and exile, Chauvin continued singing his praises, in parks and on street corners, to such fulsome extent that he became the laughing stock of Paris. He was ridiculed in several plays including *Soldat Laboureur*, 1829, by Scribe, and *La Cocarde Tricolore*, 1831, by the Brothers Cogniard.

**CHEAP AT HALF THE PRICE:** *Extremely cheap.*

Widely used to indicate a fine bargain, this expression contains an apparent contradiction, for goods that are cheap at half the price would be dear at the one demanded. The only possible explanation is that we have had some peculiar reversal from 'cheap at *twice* the price'.

**CHEER UP, THE FIRST SEVEN YEARS ARE THE WORST:** *False comfort to those not enjoying a situation.*

Quite definitely an Army expression of the early twentieth century when the standard term of soldiering was seven years active service and five on reserve. Naturally, relaxing on reserve was preferable to being shot at.

**CHEESECAKE:** *Pictures of attractive women in erotic poses.*

Cheesecake, like honey, has long been deemed an irresistible food. Its application to 'pin-ups' originated in America, the most likely source being a comparison with the edible variety enticingly displayed in the windows of many New York and other city restaurants to stimulate trade. In the late twenties and thirties, theatre jargon adopted the term for the 'come-on' posters of vapid, leggy girls intended to stimulate *their* trade, and one can safely presume that cheesecake proper is a type of tart. This comparatively recent origin may seem to be questionable in view of seventeenth-century examples of the expression 'cheescake and tarts': Partridge points with concrete comment to a 1662 quotation from *Rump, or An Extract Collection of the Poems and Songs relating to the Late Times.* One poet, lamenting Cromwell's New Order that purged their town of prostitutes, says: 'But, ah, it goes against our hearts/To lose our cheesecake and our tarts', but 'cheesecake and tarts' was then simply a current way of describing the idle pleasures of life, like 'beer and skittles' or 'cakes and ale'. Later on in the same era, Nell Gwyn says in the epilogue of a tragedy included in Rosamond Gilder's *Theatre Library Association Broadside* 'Nay, what's worse, to kill me in the prime/Of Easter-time, in Tart and Cheesecake time!' As further proof of a recent origin, the OED records that the word, used in this sense, first appeared in Britain in print in 1934, when it was deemed necessary to place it in inverted commas and explain what it meant. Even more recently, the corollary 'beefcake' was adopted for titillating pictures of brawny men.

**CHEESED OFF:** *Fed up.*

The source is one of Dickens' most popular novels, *The Old Curiosity Shop*, in which Dick Swiveller, the clerk to the corrupt lawyer, is endowed with a turn of phrase that is colourful to the point of nausea. When he is deferentially asked how he, 'the cream of the clerkship' is, he replies despondently: 'Turning rather sour, I'm afraid, almost to cheesiness.'

**CHEESE-PARING:** *Stingy, parsimonious.*

The allusion is to making mouldy cheese presentable by paring off the infected surfaces.

**CHESTNUT:** *A stale joke.*

The ultimate source of this would appear to be a long-forgotten play by William Dimond, *The Broken Sword*, first performed in London's Covent Garden in 1816. In it, one of the characters, Captain Xavier, launching yet again on an oft-repeated account of an 'amusing' exploit, says: 'When suddenly, from the thick boughs of a cork-tree . . .' – and is interrupted by another character, Pablo, with: 'A chestnut, Captain . . . a chestnut. I should know as well as you, having heard you tell the tale these twenty-seven times.' It would appear, though, that the use of the word in this sense was started in America by an English actor, William Warren, who had gone there to live and work and who, on some apposite occasion, quoted the 'chestnut' line. Perhaps his fondness for it arose from the fact that his success blossomed after he became manager of the renowned Chestnut Street Theatre in Philadelphia.

**CHEW THE FAT:** *To talk idly.*

Whether one is talking or chewing through fat and gristle, the mouth seems to go through the same motions.

**CHEW THE RAG:** *To talk incessantly.*

The tongue has long been known as 'the red rag'.

**CHICANO:** *Pejoratively, any Mexican.*

If not a simple expansion of 'Chico', as a generic name for any Hispanic, there could be a play on the harsh native pronunciation of Mexican which sounds something like Meschikano.

**CHI-CHI:** *Overly prim and proper, affectedly well-bred.*

Taken from the French '*chichi*', false hairpiece, especially one dressed in a multitude of little curls, the allusion being to a false, fussy 'front'.

**CHIME IN:** *To interject a pertinent comment.*

Bell-ringers sometimes remain silent for much of the time, only pulling their rope occasionally to bring a variant note into the sequence.

**CHIN-CHIN:** *Popularly a drinking toast, or a valediction.*

From the Chinese '*ts'ing, ts'ing*', 'chin-chin' emerged in Anglo–Chinese Pidgin most probably with an implication of 'if it please you' or perhaps 'may it please you'.

**CHINAMAN'S CHANCE:** *No chance at all.*

Coined in the 1849 California Gold Rush when, like so many others, itinerant Chinese headed west in search of riches. The strcng discrimination against them, however, gave them little or no chance. They were kept away from prime diggings and, if they wandered away by themselves and struck gold in virgin land, the whites came and drove them off while the 'law' looked the other way.

**CHINESE WHISPERS:** *Mistakes caused by bad communication.*

This originates from the party game in which a message is passed in a whisper to all the participants in turn. The last player's version of the message is usually so distorted that it might as well be in Chinese.

**CHINK:** *A disrespectful slang term for a Chinese.*

Probably arose because the oriental's eyes look like slits, or chinks. There could also have been a certain amount of influence from that fact that 'chink' is derived from 'chine', to split open, which could have been punningly connected with 'Chinee', a long-standing synonym for Chinese. The suggestion that the original name of China, Chung-kua, might have been the source seems unlikely in view of the fact that 'Chink' only came into prominence in English in the early twentieth century.

**CHIP IN:** *To contribute to a conversation or to a central fund.*

This owes its existence to the use of gaming chips.

**CHIP OFF THE OLD BLOCK:** *A son with the same characteristics as his father.*

A piece of wood bears the character of the parent block from which it is chopped.

**CHIPPY:** *A prostitute.*

The origin of this, which is undeniably American, could lie in the low brothels of late nineteenth-century south-western America and Mexico in which the customers bought poker chips or other such similar tokens which were non-redeemable and could only be spent on the premises either at the bar or in the bedrooms. The second possibility rests on the short, 'chipped-off' skirts favoured by the New Orleans prostitutes of the same era. There could also have been some influence from the contemporary use of 'chippy' to denote a lively and brightly coloured cage-bird.

**CHIPS**

The following expressions are all based on gambling chips. **(1) THE CHIPS ARE DOWN:** *The scene is set and nothing can change it.* When gambling chips are placed on the table, they may not be withdrawn nor may their position be moved after the game is in train. **(2) TO CASH/HAND IN YOUR CHIPS:** *To die.* A gambler who has finished his session at the tables has the cashier convert his chips into currency and leaves the casino. **(3) TO HAVE HAD YOUR CHIPS:** *To have died, or had one's chance.* Once the chips have been staked and lost, there is no way of replacing them. **(4) LET THE CHIPS FALL WHERE THEY MAY:** *Let Fate do its worst.* An uncaring, or devil-may-care, gambler will simply toss his chips onto the roulette table and let luck dictate where they land.

**CHISELLER:** *A cheat.*

Reference to the chisel that was once used in trimming the precious metal from gold and silver coins before passing them on, a standard ruse that was eventually frustrated by the introduction of milling around the rims of coins.

**CHIVVY:** *To harass.*

In the late 1300s, the House of Percy in Northumberland and the

House of Douglas in Scotland constantly harassed each other by sending raiding parties across the Cheviot Hills which separated them. This gave rise to 'chevy' – to goad or annoy – otherwise spelt 'chivy', now normally 'chivvy'. The original 'chevying' escalated and culminated in the Battle of Otterburn in which both sides were all but annihilated.

**CHOCK-A-BLOCK:** *Absolutely full.*

Originally a Naval term describing the situation when all the available rope has been hauled through a block and tackle, leaving the chock hard up against the block.

**CHOCKS AWAY!:** *Let's go!*

When a WW2 fighter pilot was on board and ready to go, he gave this command to the ground crew who then removed the chocks that blocked the wheels of his aircraft.

**CHOKEY:** *Prison.*

The Hindustani '*chauki*', place surrounded by walls, was appropriated by troops in British India.

**CHOP AND CHANGE:** *To shift ground persistently.*

'Chop' here is a variant of 'cheap', both being connected with buying and selling, and the expression really means to strike a deal and then retract it, or, in barter, to change one's mind about an agreed exchange of goods.

**CHOP-CHOP:** *Quickly.*

Chinese Pidgin meaning the same and formed on '*k'wai-k'wai*', a phrase which also produced in English the term 'chopsticks' as based on '*k'wai-tse*', generally understood to mean 'the quick ones'.

**CHOP LOGIC:** *To bandy words.*

'Chop' is again used here in its meaning of to deal or barter, hence this extension which means to exchange arguments. There has been a recent tendency to use this expression as if it meant to MINCE WORDS or split hairs, which would seem to indicate a growing confusion about the meaning of 'chop' in this context.

**CHOW:** *Food.*

Early–mid nineteenth-century Chinese Pidgin, but it is unclear whether it was donated by English or Chinese. It certainly *sounds* Chinese, and much opinion goes along with this, seeing a logical derivation from the Mandarin '*ch'ao*', stir, fry or cook. However, the word *could* have come from the other side of the linguistic fence as a slighting allusion to the fact that the poorer Chinese, when in dire straits, ate Chow dog.

**CHUFFED:** *Highly delighted; severely disgruntled.*

The second usage is rarely heard these days but it is possible the two meanings are tenuously linked through disease. In the Middle Ages 'chuff' denoted facial swellings present in diseased men and beasts and it is therefore possible that it was a variant of 'puff' and has a connection to 'puffed up' with pride and contentment. Alternatively 'chuff' was used to describe a boor or surly fellow; in this, a connection between disease and a state of disgruntlement could have arisen as it did in HAVE THE PIP.

**CHUM:** *A friend.*

This has been in existence since the seventeenth century and is a corrupt contraction of 'chamber-mate'.

**CHUNDER:** *To vomit.*

Probably arose from Australian rhyming slang based on Chunder Loo (= spew), a cartoon character of long standing used nationally in the early part of the twentieth century to advertise Cobra shoe polish. It has been suggested too that the term goes further back to the days when sea-sick transportees might have shouted 'Watch under!' as a warning to those on lower decks to keep away from openings and scuttles, but this sounds rather contrived; sea-sickness normally leaves little time for courtesy to others.

**CHURN OUT:** *To produce continuously and tediously.*

This arose by association with the monotonous cranking required in churning butter.

**CINCH:** *A certainty, something upon which one can depend; something easy.*

Derived from the Spanish '*cincha*', saddle girth, upon which a rider's safety hangs. It applies to things easily accomplished, as the tightening of a saddle girth, whilst crucial, is not difficult. At times, this metaphor is mixed and emphasised by prefixing it with 'lead pipe' – which is easily bent.

**CLAP:** *Venereal disease, especially gonorrhoea.*

Taken from the Old French '*clapoire*', bubo or swelling.

**CLAPPED OUT:** *Extremely tired; no longer in working order.*

This description also aptly describes one riddled with the CLAP.

**CLAPTRAP:** *Rubbish, nonsense.*

The origin lies in the theatre where the word was used of any device or ploy calculated to make the audience applaud. For example, an audience will obediently applaud when a scantily clad magician's assistant postures with arms outspread after performing some relatively trivial task.

**CLEAN AS A WHISTLE:** *Really clean.*

All early whistles and flutes had to be carved and hollowed out by hand very carefully indeed. A flawed whistle would not produce a clean note.

**CLEAN BILL OF HEALTH:** *An assurance that one is free of disease.*

Properly this is the certificate, handed to the captain of a ship about to sail, stating that no one on board is infected with a notifiable disease. He is required to present this at his next port of call, and must obtain another before departing that location.

**CLEAN OUT:** *To strip of assets.*

It would appear that there is an analogy here with the way one guts a fish or removes the intestines of game. Such terminology, relating to the complete mastery of the hunter over his quarry, is of long standing; in *The Old Curiosity Shop*, Dickens wrote: 'He was plucked, pigeoned and cleaned out completely.'

**CLEAN SLATE:** *A fresh start.*

Possible reference to the slate on which a ship's watch recorded all details. At the end of the period of duty, the information was transferred to the log and the slate wiped clean ready for the next watch. Alternatively, the slate might have been that on which an inn-keeper kept tabs on accounts.

**CLEAN UP:** *To make a large profit.*

This could simply be an allusion to making money as easily as sweeping it up, but in the American gold fields 'cleaning up' described the washing of the pieces of gold sifted from silt and mud.

**CLEOPATRA'S NOSE:** *The potential effect of female sexuality and beauty on world events.*

The source of this expression is Blaise Pascal (1623–66). In his *Pensées*, viii, 29, he wrote: 'If the nose of Cleopatra had been shorter, the whole face of the earth would have changed.'

**CLEOPATRA'S PEARL:** *Anything of great value capriciously destroyed.*

Legend has it that, at a banquet in honour of Mark Antony, Cleopatra toasted his health with a glass of wine into which she had deliberately dropped, and let dissolve, a priceless pearl. Similar stories have been recounted throughout history, all of them, alas, resting on a myth. Pearls do not dissolve in wine; in fact, substances of much stronger acidity are widely used to clean them.

**CLIFFHANGER:** *Anything that induces tension and suspense.*

In the early days of cinema, each instalment of the traditional serial was designed to ensure that the audience returned for the next, the heroine often being left in a seemingly fatal predicament. The arch exponent of this was Pearl White who starred in *The Perils of Pauline* and was often seen dangling from the Palisades above the Hudson River.

**CLIMB ON THE SOAP BOX, TO:** *To pontificate or lecture.*

Every nineteenth-century Sunday afternoon, Speakers' Corner in London's Hyde Park was full of 'stump' orators harangueing the crowd on a variety of subjects. Their vantage point was achieved by standing on a soap-box brought for the purpose since this was one of the few products packed in wooden boxes strong enough to take a man's weight.

**CLINCH:** *To settle or confirm conclusively.*

This figurative usage derives from the ship-building term for a process very similar to dead-nailing (*See:* DEAD AS A DOOR NAIL). The nails used to secure clinker boards to the skeleton of a hull were long enough to pass through the board and the baton, and protrude by half an inch or so. They were then clinched by being beaten flat from the inside which made them absolutely fast.

**CLINK:** *Prison.*

A possible source is an actual Clink Prison that stood in London's Southwark until it was destroyed in the Gordon Riots of 1780. Undoubtedly, though, the ubiquitous clinking of keys in prisons would have reinforced the term.

**CLICHÉ:** *Anything that is hackneyed.*
From the French 'cliché', a printing plate which 'clicked' up and down churning out the same thing over and over again in a printing method called 'stereotype'.

**CLIP JOINT:** *A place of entertainment where the customers are cheated.*
Derived from the old use of 'clip', to rob, from the past habit of clipping gold and silver coins before passing them on. This also gave rise to 'clipper', rogue, which was common in Britain until the end of the nineteenth century. In the case of 'clip joint', the notion of sheep and other animals being clipped and shorn would have reinforced the usage.

**CLIP SOMEONE'S WINGS:** *To restrict his activities or ambitions.*
The custom of clipping the flight feathers of captive birds to stop them escaping.

**CLIQUE:** *Disapprovingly, an exclusive group.*
The ultimate source of this word is the French '*clique*', a battalion's drum and bugle band, but to understand why, it is necessary also to examine another word with which it became closely associated: 'claque', paid applauders at a theatre, from '*claquer*', to slap or bang together. The custom of employing people to attend first nights and ensure success by 'kindling' the audience goes back as far as Ancient Greece, but, in 1820, it was put on a proper business footing when Monsieur Sauton of Paris opened an agency supplying people who specialized in clapping, cheering, crying or laughing loudly at all the right moments. Originally known as '*claqueurs*', they were eventually dubbed 'Le Clique', not only because of the association with the loud band, but also because 'clique' made an ideal ricochet with 'claque'. Perhaps understandably, they were held in low esteem, even by the people who employed them, and forced to form their own little subculture on the fringe of the theatrical world.

**CLOBBER:** *Clothing, gear.*
Origin unclear, but there may be an association with 'clout', which can mean an item of clothing or, of course, to hit very hard, which is another meaning of 'clobber'.

**CLOCKING ON:** *Travelling fast, or ageing.*
Both allude to a car's speedometer that indicates the speed of travel, and also the cumulative total of miles 'on the clock'.

**CLODHOPPER:** *A rustic, a clumsy oaf, a dolt.*
No doubt originating in the city-dweller's contempt for his country cousin, this pictures him as a dull-witted ploughboy stumbling about among clods, lumps of muddy soil or turf.

**CLOSE SHAVE:** *A narrow escape.*
There is literally only a hair's-breadth between a good shave and a cut face.

**CLOSE YOUR EYES AND THINK OF ENGLAND!:** *Endure an odious situation with resignation, especially unwelcome sexual attentions.*

This began life among the ex-patriot British community in India, where it had a quite literal application; thoughts of a tranquil English scene could temporarily lighten the rigours of colonial life.

**CLOSE QUARTERS, AT :** *In very near proximity.*

Originally called 'close fights', close quarters were wooden barriers erected on the decks of large merchantmen. In the event of a raid, men would be stationed, or quartered, behind these with musket and shot to deliver a cross-fire at the enemy on the deck.

**CLOUD NO BIGGER THAN A MAN'S HAND:** *The first, small portent of change.*

I Kings, 18–19, tells of a confrontation before a crowd atop Mount Carmel between Ahab, representing Baal, the ancient god of storms and rain, and Elijah, representing the new God. The land was in drought and each man appealed to his god for rain. Ahab's prayers had no effect, but Elijah's sacrificial flames could not be quenched, and the people shouted that God was the only true god. Then, I Kings 19:44: 'there ariseth a little cloud out of the sea, like a man's hand.'

**CLOUD CUCKOO LAND:** *A dream land.*

In a work by Aristophanes (448–385 BC) entitled *The Birds*, the birds built between the gods and men a town whose name translates as Cloud Cuckoo Town. 'Town' was replaced in common usage by 'land'.

**CLOUD NINE:** *In a state of bliss.*

This started out as a real cloud classification used by the American Weather Bureau which categorized clouds in nine sections according to their normal altitude. Cumulo-nimbus was the ninth and therefore the highest, so the allusion is obvious.

**COACH:** *Tutor or crammer.*

Adopted into university slang in the mid nineteenth century in allusion to the way the vehicle of the same name speeds its passengers to the desired destination or objective. As for the ultimate origin, this lies in the name of the town of Kocs, just outside Budapest in Hungary. Here were made the vehicles for one of the earliest public transport systems in the fifteenth century – the waggons concerned being known as '*kocszekers*', which, perhaps mercifully, had been truncated and altered to 'coach' before it arrived in sixteenth-century English.

**COBBER:** *Friend or companion.*

The Yiddish '*chaber*', friend, pronounced 'kahber', gave rise to this Australian colloquialism.

**COBBLER SHOULD STICK TO HIS LAST:** *Stay with what you know best.*

The sentiment was aimed at a cobbler because of a possibly apocryphal story which tells that Apelles, the Ionian painter of the fourth century BC, was interrupted in mid-picture by a passing cobbler who pointed out that his portrayal of the subject's footwear was faulty. Bowing to the cobbler's expertise, Apelles amended the work, but when the emboldened cobbler criticized the ankles as well, he was told to 'stick to his last'.

**COBBLERS:** *Rubbish.*

The rhyming slang 'cobblers' awls' = balls gave rise to this, though the fact that 'cobs' has long been dialect slang for testicles doubtlessly helped the expression along.

**COCK A SNOOK:** *To indicate derision or defiance.*

Literally meaning to thumb one's nose, this is a combination of 'cock', to tilt up and 'snook', which became slang for the nose since it originally meant a narrow strip of land, especially one projecting into the sea.

**COCK AND BULL STORY:** *An incredible, rambling tale.*

Many ancient fables concerned animals that not only talked but were endowed with all the human vices and virtues. The cock and the bull were stock characters who usually finished off a cautionary story by endlessly discussing its salient points. The fact that both BULL and 'cock' have long meant verbal rubbish must have helped. The French too had a similar expression in their '*coq à l'ane*', cock to the donkey story, and 'cockalane' was picked up by English, appearing first in the late sixteenth century, but became obsolete by the seventeenth century, having been pushed out by 'cock and bull'. There is also a theory frequently cited that links the origin to two inns, The Cock and The Bull, which were next to each other on a famous coaching route, or at either end of it. In any event, the idea suggested is that a story told in the one was distorted when repeated in the other, but the expression is noted as early as 1660, long before the advent of coach travel.

**COCK LANE GHOST:** *A gruesome tale invented to frighten.*

The source of this is a particularly nasty confidence trick perpetrated in 1762 by Charles Parsons, a resident of Cock Lane, Smithfield. He claimed that his house was haunted by the spirit of a previous tenant, Mrs Kent, who had died two years earlier. The story caused quite a stir in London and several persons of note, such as Dr Johnson, went to Cock Lane from time to time to investigate the phenomenon, which was eventually revealed as a hoax executed by Parsons and his eleven-year old daughter to throw suspicion for Mrs Kent's death on her timid widower in order to blackmail him.

**COCK-A-HOOP:** *Exultant.*

That the expression is allied to the drinking of ale seems almost inescapable, but there is nevertheless confusion surrounding the original and precise application and meaning of the expression. The generally expressed view is that beer tap or stop cock was in times of extreme revelry knocked out of the barrel to allow the ale to flow unimpeded. For safekeeping it was placed on the top of the barrel on one of the hoops while everyone got well and truly 'cock a hooped'. This is all very well, but in the time it would take an openly breached barrel to empty into waiting jugs, why place the cock anywhere – especially on top of the barrel where it might roll off. Perhaps a more sensible assertion is that 'cock' referred to the spigot in the top of the barrel which served as a bleed valve as the fluid level dropped – but no reference to the spigot as a cock can be found. Having said all that, one of the earliest uses of the expression appears thus in 1529 'sett the cocke a hoope and fyll in all the cups at once'. There could be influence from the French '*houppe*', a tuft or raised mound, which might have produced a now obsolete and lost 'hoop' meaning raised up. Surely it would make more sense to simply lift the tap and leave the ale running. At least it could then be shut when all the jugs were full. Anyone who has ever tried to replace a removed beer tap from a barrel in full flow will appreciate the sagacity of this option.

**COCK-HORSE:** *A child's imaginary horse.*

A favourite game for children is to bounce up and down astride an adult's leg. The term could have arisen because, for this, the leg and the foot have to be bent or cocked.

**COCK-UP:** *Organizational chaos.*

This is most probably a simple allusion to the male genitals which seem to have become something of a whipping boy. It has been suggested though that the origin could be a British Naval expression describing a berthed vessel's yard-arms that have been left cocked up at all angles instead of being properly squared away after the sails have been furled. This may be so but the term seems to have developed after the heyday of sail.

**COCKAMAMIE:** *Crazy or eccentric.*

The Greek '*decalcomania*', a craze for transferring pictures from paper onto other items, was applied to a fashion in France in the 1860s for lift-off transfers which could be transposed onto everything, including the human skin. The craze hit America around the turn of the century and a corrupted form of its name came to describe things crazy and trivial.

**COCKNEY:** *A Londoner born within earshot of Bow Bells.*

'Cockney' is derived from the Middle English '*coken-ey*', cock's egg, a biological impossibility which was the countryman's term for a yolkless egg laid by a young hen. Since the egg was worthless, cokeney became common in rural areas as a term for simpletons and layabouts. The tag was inevitably hung on townsfolk who, ignorant of country ways, always appeared lost and out of place there. Some time in the early seventeenth century, the term narrowed to those born and living in London before becoming even more specific.

**COCKPIT:** *The control area of a ship or aircraft.*

In the old man-of-war, the space below the lower gun-deck always served as the surgeon's 'operating theatre' during battles. Given the times and the nature of the injuries likely to be sustained from a blast of grapeshot, it is not difficult to imagine how this area became known as the cockpit. When smaller vessels such as yachts came along, the term transferred to the corresponding space which now housed the steering-wheel and the navigational aids. From this development, it was short step to the flight 'deck' of a modern aircraft which served the same purpose.

**COCKSURE:** *Arrogantly confident, absolutely sure.*

It would be unwise to assume that the origin of this word is self-evident. Originally it most probably meant 'as sure as God' for, in medieval times, 'cock' was a euphemism for 'God'. In his *Actes and Monuments of these latter and perilous Days* (better known as *The Book of Martyrs*) published in 1563, the theologian and pre-eminent recorder of religious events, John Foxe (1516–87) wrote: 'and the help of the Lord shall be cocksure for ever more', and it seems highly unlikely that he would have drawn a comparison between God's help and the arrogant strutting of a cockerel. There are other theories that see the origin in, for example, the cocking of a fire-arm, the stopcock on a barrel which should never leak, the notch in the back of an arrow for the bow-string which was called the cock, and the Welsh '*coc*', gear or cog.

**COCKTAIL:** *A mixed alcoholic drink and by extension any imaginative melange.*

The origin is obscure but the author's theory is that it rests on 'cock tail' which was applied in the eighteenth and nineteenth centuries to a horse which had undoubted racing quality but whose pedigree could not be proved or even conjectured and was thus a spirited mixture of unknowns. This in turn arose from the fact that 'mongrel' horses used for general riding or for drawing coaches generally had cropped tails which 'cocked up'. The theory would seem to be supported by the fact that the first mention of the drink in America was in 1806, in *Balance and Colombian Repository* where it was certainly spelled 'cock tail', and other early examples were spelled the same way as 'cock-tail'. Another attributes the invention of the cocktail to Antoine Peychaud, a New Orleans restaurateur, who served it in a type of small glass called a '*coquetier*', French for 'egg-cup'. Peychaud's bitters are on sale to this day. France herself lays claim to the origin, citing a mixed drink from the Gironde, a '*coquetel*' which was all the rage during the revolution. Britain, too, claims that the origin was a vile brew concocted in cock-fighting circles to keep the birds in top form. Consisting of ale, gin, herbs, bread and flour, this was consumed even by the fancy themselves and rejoiced in the name of 'cock-bread ale' before shortening to 'cock-ale'.

**COD:** *To dupe, to fool.*

Although obscure, this could have arisen from the sixteenth-century use of 'cod's head' for a simpleton. It could also perhaps be a crude reference to testicles or lastly a simple distortion of 'kid'.

**CODGER:** *An old man, especially an eccentric one.*

It is not certain but this is most probably a variant of 'CADGER', since the two terms seem to have been interchangeable in rural areas where they both described a miserable old man. Attempts have been made, unsuccessfully, to link the term to 'cogitate' and give it a meaning of 'thoughtful old man'.

**CODSWALLOP:** *Utter nonsense.*

Although its origin is obscure, this word is probably a combination of 'cods', testicles and 'wallop', boiling or fizzing fluid. It has appeared in the form of 'cod's wallop', but this does not lend credence to the tale that it derives from a beer drinker's contemptuous name for lemonade, the connection being Hiram P. Codd, who, according to this theory, invented the first air-tight, marble-in-the-neck bottle in which lemonade was sold. Actually, there is no reference to Codd in the history of bottle manufacture and design, and this particular type of bottle was in wide use almost a century before the first recorded appearance of 'codswallop'.

**COIN A PHRASE, TO:** *To invent or generate a new catchphrase or expression.*

Inspired by the production methods in the early mints wherein the coins were stamped out using a wedge-shaped die originally called a coign, this allied to the French '*coin*', a wedge or corner.

**COLD AS CHARITY:** *Unfeeling and joyless.*

Since charity means universal love and benevolence, this simile is an apparent contradiction, but it can be attributed to the old 'charitable' institutions that rather grudgingly did their duty by the 'undeserving' poor without the warmth and compassion that underlies true Christian charity.

**COLD CASH:** *Reliable funds.*

This indicates the preference for gold or silver coinage that existed in the days of early paper money, which was always subject to devaluation or even collapse. 'Hard cash' carries a similar meaning.

**COLD-COCK:** *Literally or figuratively to stun from ambush.*

This is perhaps a variant of 'cold caulk', to hammer and stamp rope fibres into the seams in a ship, prior to sealing them with hot tar.

**COLD-DECK:** *To cheat.*

At the poker tables of America in the nineteenth century, this referred to substituting a new, rigged deck (pack) for the one in use which was 'warmed' by handling.

**COLD SHOULDER:** *Deliberate unfriendliness.*

The rules of chivalry dictated that no knight could refuse another hospitality and stabling facilities for as long as he needed them. Inevitably, there were those who played on this courtesy and had to be edged towards the portcullis. The strongest hint that a reluctant host could drop was to offer his guest a meal of cold shoulder of mutton, such food being normal fare for the menials of the household.

**COLD TURKEY:** *The plain, unvarnished truth.*

This is drug addicts' jargon for the painful withdrawal symptoms experienced by those who try to 'kick' their habit instantly, without medical help or substitute drugs that wean them slowly off the one they are abusing. One of these symptoms is that the skin becomes hypersensitive and covered with goose pimples, so that it resembles the plucked skin of a dead turkey.

**COLOUR OF YOUR MONEY, (LET'S SEE THE):** *A demand for proof of ability to pay.*

Born in the days before paper money, this was quite literally a demand to see if one's money was gold, silver or base copper.

**COLUMBUS'S EGG:** *Something apparently impossible to achieve until someone demonstrates the knack.*

At a banquet given in his honour, Columbus came under attack from other explorers present who tried to diminish his achievement saying that if he had not done so, someone else would have come across America sooner or later. In response, Columbus passed among them a hard-boiled egg, challenging them to stand it on end. When no one could he tapped the egg lightly on the table to flatten one end, thus demonstrating that everything is easy when someone shows the way.

**COME A CROPPER:** *To take a hard fall, literally or figuratively.*

The origin is unclear, but the most likely explanation is that this is a corrupt ellipsis of something like 'to come off neck and crop', alluding to complete downfall, as would be expected of a bird amputated at the neck with the axe cutting through the crop. Another suggestion is that 'neck and crop' was responsible but it referred to a rider at full gallop falling head-first over the neck of his mount with his crop still in his hand. Perhaps 'cropper' was simply a hunting expression indicating a fall so catastrophic that the rider cut a swathe through the crops in the field where he fell.

**COME OFF IT!:** *Stop exaggerating! Stop lying!*

This began life in America in the late nineteenth century as 'come off the side' which referred to the sidespin imparted a pool ball to produce sudden, deceptive and exaggerated swerves as it moved across the table. In general American usage this transmuted to 'come off the grass' which is found in verges at the side of the road and is also green, a colour associated with gullibility and youthful excess and exaggeration. By the opening of this century the expression had been truncated to either 'come off' or 'come off it'.

**COME OUT, TO:** *To proclaim a previously dark secret, especially one's homosexuality.*

Although debutantes were previously said to 'come out' when first admitted to the social whirl, this is derived from the previously used 'to come out of the closet' – clandestine homosexuals being referred to as closet-QUE(A)ENS – which in turn is a cryptic allusion to the SKELETON IN THE CLOSET.

**COME UP TO SCRATCH, TO:** *To meet expected standards.*

Before the Queensberry Rules of boxing a round only finished when one fighter was knocked to the ground. The prone man was dragged to his corner for a thirty-second rest after which he had a further eight seconds to make his way unaided to a line scratched in the middle of the dirt-floor ring. Inability to comply meant that the fight was lost.

**COMMON-OR-GARDEN:** *Ordinary, found everywhere.*

A reference to the type of plants to be found in any garden and growing wild on common land.

**COMMONPLACE:** *Hackneyed.*

An example of 'place' used in its obsolete meaning of a topic or a passage in a book. A book of common places, now commonplace book, was one in which were noted down the events of the day, or passing thoughts on common topics, some of which were decidedly mundane.

**COMSTOCKERY:** *Prudery.*

George Bernard Shaw (1856–1950) coined this word, which first appeared in print in the *New York Times* on 26 September 1905. Anthony Comstock (1844–1915), an American, had banned Shaw's plays in Boston where he was the moving spirit behind the famous/infamous Boston Watch and Ward Committee, and later used his influence against them as head of the New York Society for the Suppression of Vice. *See also:* BANNED IN BOSTON.

**CONFABULATION, CONFAB:** *Conversation but often confused and noisy chatter.*

From the Italian '*confabulare*', to talk or discuss, this was picked up by English blades visiting Italy on their Grand Tour of Europe in the eighteenth century. Given the Italian animated manner of talking, the extension was inevitable.

**CONK OUT:** *To break down or grind to a halt.*

This could simply be echoic, but, since the expression seems to have originated in aviators' slang, it could have arisen because the engine is mounted in the nose of an aircraft; if it fails, the aircraft nose-dives and crashes.

**COOK THE BOOKS:** *To falsify the accounts.*

Cooking food makes it more palatable.

**COOK YOUR GOOSE:** *To finish you off, to ruin your plans.*

The origin of this expression, not noted until the early-mid nineteenth century, is unknown and is perhaps nothing more complicated than an analogy with countless other sayings like 'to settle one's hash'. It could possibly have connections with 'making things hot for someone' being perhaps based on 'goose', which at one time signified a goose-neck handled smoothing iron that was heated on the fire. There are also tales of ancient cities that hoisted a goose, the symbol of stupidity, to taunt a besieging enemy, and were subsequently burnt to the ground in reprisal, but the expression can be dated back only to the middle of the nineteenth century.

**COOL YOUR HEELS:** *To be kept waiting.*

A horse, during a respite from a long journey, often actually stood in the stream from which it drank.

**COOLIE:** *A hired, non-European labourer.*

This is almost certainly based on the name of the Kuli tribe of Guzerat in the West of India, whose enslavement by the Portuguese was first mentioned in 1554, when they were referred to as 'coles'. Also postulated is the Tamil '*kuli*', hireling, but chronology favours the Kuli tribe. That the Chinese for 'bitter effort' is '*ku-li*' is pure coincidence.

**COON:** *Derogatory term for a Negro.*

This may have derived from an imagined similarity to the animal, the whites of whose eyes are highlighted by the dark rings around them. It enjoyed only very limited usage until 1896 when a black American singer, Ernest Hogan, came out with a song entitled *All Coons Look Alike to Me*. If he meant the song to be a wry comment on the white attitude to blacks, it misfired. The word caught on, and the song was whistled as an insult to passing Negroes in the street. Any intended satire was certainly lost on the blacks, who regarded Hogan as a traitor, especially as two more songs written by whites soon followed: *Every Race has a Flag but the Coon* and *Coon, Coon, Coon*. There is a theory that the word is derived from the Portuguese '*barracoe*', a stockade for holding freshly imported Negroes pending sale at auction, the end of which word was pronounced with a nasal 'n', but the time-lag between the influence of Portuguese traders and the emergence of the word is too long. As late as 18 May 1903, the *Western Gazette* placed it in inverted commas and felt the need to explain its being 'modern slang for a nigger'.

**COP OUT:** *To renege.*

This is seemingly an extension from 'cop a plea', criminal jargon meaning to inform on one's associates, when caught by the police, in exchange for a promise of leniency, or even immunity from prosecution. 'Cop' is used here in its meaning of 'grab' or 'catch hold of'.

**COPACETIC:** *Excellent.*

The origin of this piece of American slang is much debated. Various Yiddish and African sources have been postulated, as has the Chinook pidgin '*copasenee*' (everything is fine) but no one knows for sure.

**COPPER:** *Any policeman.*

Noted since the 1840s and probably nothing more than a simple development from the verb 'cop', to catch hold off or arrest, as noted since the 1820s. This in turn could be derived from the Scottish '*cap*', to lay hands on or the Dutch '*kapen*', to take. Both in turn likely owe existence to the Latin word '*capere*', to capture. There is no substance to the notion that it is an acronym of 'constable on patrol' or that it was reference to the buttons on the uniforms which were black horn, not copper.

**COPPER-BOTTOMED:** *Sound, especially financially.*

A fairly common expression that came to us from the world of marine insurance. Simple wooden hulls gradually gave way to hulls that were clad in copper, and the insurance companies then regarded a copper-bottomed ship as a much safer prospect against which to issue cover.

**COR BLIMEY:** *A typical Cockney exclamation of surprise.*

This is a corruption of 'God Blind Me!'.

**CORDON BLEU:** *A somewhat ill-defined level of attainment in the culinary arts.*

There is no issuing body to monitor the use of '*cordon bleu*' – French for blue ribbon – but not surprisingly, the story of its origin starts in France with the knights of the Holy Ghost who met regularly at lavish banquets that were the talk of the land; like our own Knights of the Garter, they wore round their neck a blue ribbon, a long-standing symbol of the supreme. Eventually, it became common in France to refer to a good meal as one fit for the knights of the blue ribbon and, in elevated circles, a tradition arose of presenting a chef who had excelled himself with a strip of blue ribbon in thanks.

**CORKER:** *Something considered excellent.*

The British Navy slang 'caulker', of which this is a corruption, referred to the job of sealing a ship's seams – the final, finishing touch. Thus, in a way, 'corker' is akin to 'topper' in an expression like 'What a topper!'.

**CORNY:** *Old-fashioned, hackneyed, over-sentimental.*

This developed on Broadway to describe plays that were unfit for city slickers and had to go on tour in the sticks where 'corn-fed', unsophisticated audiences were less discriminating. This same concept of rural standards gave a similar meaning to 'cornball', which is eaten in country areas.

**COTTON ON:** *Finally to understand.*

The allusion is to cotton fibres which 'latch on' to clothing and are the very devil to remove.

**COTTON TO:** *To come to like or admire.*

Again a reference to cotton fibres that attach themselves and stick close.

**COTTON-PICKING:** *Inferior or trivial.*

This originated in American Southern States slang in the eighteenth century when only Negroes and poor white people picked the cotton.

**COUP DE GRACE:** *The finishing touch or blow.*

This was originally a term of the torture chamber; when a victim had signed his 'confession', he was put out of his misery by a *coup de grâce*, blow of mercy.

**COVER YOUR ASS/ARSE:** *Take every step to protect yourself.*

American soldiers on active duty in Vietnam sat on their helmets when flying over jungle territory to avoid the risk of castration by ground-fire.

If this did not actually start the saying, it helped it along considerably.

**COWBOY:** *Any untalented tradesman reckless in his work.*

The disparaging overtones attached to 'cowboy' have been there since the term first arose long before the days of the big cattle drives; during the American War of Independence it denoted an American guerrilla loyal to the British Crown. This rather bizarre appellation is said to have been bestowed through their habit of tinkling cow bells in the brush to entice farmers loyal to the cause to their deaths in ambush. Thus, even in the days of the big herds, few cared to chance calling anyone else a cowboy, trailhand, drover or vaquero, for throughout most of the Western States it was generally accepted that 'cowboy' denoted a Texan rustler who specialized in raids across the border into Mexico. By the 1940s Americans were using the term of any inconsiderate driver – especially one in a lorry – and here came the most significant shift to the present meaning. With its associations with lorry driving the term was adopted here in the 1960s to attach itself specifically to the lorry drivers on the Middle East runs who paid scant regard to vehicle safety or loading restrictions and would run anything anywhere if the price was right. By the 1970s, the term had broadened to embrace a feckless worker more concerned with speed than efficiency.

**COXEY'S ARMY:** *A chaotic organization.*

This celebrates Jacob Sechler Coxey (1854–1951) who, in April 1894, organized a march of the unemployed from Massillon, Ohio, where he ran a sandstone quarry, to the Capitol in Washington. His so-called 'living petition' did not reach his predicted target figure of 100,000 minimum, and he was obliged to set out at the head of an 'army' numbering 500 at best. Most of these either deserted or were arrested for petty crime along the way, and, immediately he arrived at the Capitol, Coxey himself was promptly arrested for trespassing.

**CRABBED / CRABBY:** *Cantankerous and perverse.*

'Crabbed', of which the modern version is 'crabby', arose because the crab's sideways gait was regarded as symbolic of ill-humour, though its habit of snapping or pinching would have helped as would also the mean-mouthed, piggy-eyed appearance of its 'facial' features. The sour crab apple too could have had some influence. The most famous use of the word occurs in translations of Seneca, the Roman writer and statesman (*c.* 4 BC–65 AD) who, when discussing the life of Diogenes, the eccentric Greek philosopher (*c.* 400–325 BC) describes him as being 'so crabbed he ought to have lived in a barrel like a dog' which led to the misconception, claiming Seneca as authority, that Diogenes did in fact live in a tub.

**CRACKED UP TO BE:** *Reputed to be.*

As in 'wisecrack', the word 'crack' has, since the late seventeenth/early eighteenth century, meant the kind of amusing repartée that can enliven the early hours of a drinking session. The Irish still ask: 'Where's the crack?' meaning 'Where's the fun?' At such gatherings, the exploits of absent friends are embellished with each succeeding drink and their reputations swell, although, in fact, they are 'not all they are cracked up to be'.

**CRACKERBARREL PHILOSOPHY:** *Homely philosophy.*

The name of this Will Rogers type philosophy owes its existence to the large barrel of biscuits, or crackers, which was to be found in most nineteenth-century rural American stores, and around which the small-town intellectuals gathered to chat and put the world to rights.

**CRAP:** *Excrement or verbal rubbish.*

Ultimately based on the Dutch '*krappen*', to pluck off, cast off or separate, which emerged in Middle English as '*crappe*', rejected matter, residue, or dregs. The OED notes its use as such as early as the fifteenth century, which, alas, confounds any claim on behalf of that much cited, but nebulous, nineteenth-century sanitary engineer, Thomas Crapper.

**CRAZY AS A COOT:** *Completely mad.*

The bird's cry is reminiscent of a maniacal cackle.

**CRAZY LIKE A FOX:** *Extremely astute.*

A perverse, reverse statement based on the fact that foxes are extremely intelligent.

**CREAM OFF:** *To defraud by persistent theft.*

The allusion is to dairy work which entails repeated removal of the creamy richness from the top of milk stored in vats.

**CREOLE:** *A person born in the West Indies.*

The word is from the Old Spanish '*criollo*', the diminutive of '*criado*', foster child, a term linked with 'create'. In modern Spanish, '*criadero*' means a nursery or breeding place, and '*criado*' a servant. The application of 'creole' is highly confused and corrupted. Originally, it denoted the offspring of a slave or a native West Indian woman and a Spaniard. Spanish slavers fathered many such children as a matter of economics! By the eighteenth century, it had come to designate a person of European descent who was raised in the West Indies, as opposed to European immigrants to the islands. Napoleon's wife, Josephine, was therefore a Creole though she had no black blood in her. In eighteenth century America, slaves adopted the word for children born there, whether of pure Negro blood or mixed, to distinguish them from blacks shipped in. Currently, in Louisiana it denotes a French-speaking white, in Mexico whites of Spanish blood, in Brazil a black, and in Alaska a person of mixed Russian and Amerindian blood.

**CRETIN:** *One affected by a specific condition of mental deficiency caused by the malfunction of the thyroid gland.*

Etymologically the word is linked to 'Christ' and 'Christian' both of which words stem from the Greek

'*Christos*' – anointed. Cretinism is endemic in Central Switzerland and the Pyrenees, and the inhabitants of these areas called a simple-minded person a 'cretin', this being a corruption of '*chrétien*' – Christian – since they believed imbeciles to be touched by the hand of God. The notion that fools are divinely blessed in their innocence existed in this country too as evinced by the expression 'a bit touched'.

**CROCK:** *A decrepit person or thing.*

The source is the Low German '*krakke*' – broken down person or animal, a term allied to 'crack' but its spelling was undoubtedly influenced by the other 'crock' which was based on the Old English '*krog*', pitcher, since this crock could also mean *broken* household items.

**CROCODILE TEARS:** *A display of assumed grief.*

This is based on the old notion that the crocodile cries and moans while eating its victim. Naturally, this is not true, but there is, as with some old wives' tales, a kernel of truth in it. The animal does emit a melancholy-sounding noise while eating and there is a gland in the top of its mouth which, activated during feeding, promotes a flow of water from the tear ducts. Also, after feeding, crocodiles lie facing up wind with their mouth open to cool it and to allow plovers time to give them a 'denticure'. This too promotes tears as yawning does in humans.

**CRONY:** *An intimate companion.*

A piece of seventeenth-century Oxford and Cambridge slang that is based on the Greek '*chronos*', time. It used to apply only to friends who were 'up' at university at the same time.

**CROSS THE RUBICON:** *To take an irrevocable step.*

The Rubicon was a rather insignificant stream that separated Julius Caesar's province of Cisalpine Gaul from Ancient Italy. As he marched towards Rome in 49 BC, his ambassadors were conducting hurried negotiations, but his crossing of the Rubicon at the head of his army was a virtual declaration of war against Pompey and Rome.

**CROSSPATCH:** *An bad-tempered person.*

'Cross' in this word obviously means 'peevish', but 'patch', a fool, a jester, comes from Cardinal Wolsey's personal jester who was known throughout society as 'Patch', his real name being Sexton. Whether he took his name from his patched costume or from the Italian '*pazzo*', fool, which also produced PATSY, is not clear.

**CRUSHERS:** *Policemen.*

Possibly arising because policemen tend to be large powerful men with big feet, this was first noted in the early part of the nineteenth century. As far as the civil police are concerned, it has long since given way to less complimentary nicknames but it is still alive and well in the British Navy where it is slang for a ship's policemen, not only because of their big feet, but also because of the charming notion that, when patrolling the decks at night, their presence is announced by the popping noise of the cockroaches they tread on and crush.

**CRY WOLF, TO:** *To persistently cause false alarms.*

Ancient indeed is the fable common to most cultures telling of a shepherd boy who thought it great fun one day when bored to set the whole village on its ear in panic by screaming out that a wolf was attacking the flock. Needless to say, after a few such false alarms the villagers ignored his cries so when the wolf really did come calling and kill the lad and a few sheep, no one paid any attention to his screams.

**CUDDLY TOY, CUDDLY TOY:** *A saying that indicates the need for time to think.*

In the long-running British TV series *Generation Game* prizewinners watched goods passing a conveyor belt, after which they got each prize they could remember and name. There was always a cuddly toy and temporarily bemused contestants repeated that over and over again.

**CUMSHAW:** *A tip or a gift.*

Based on the Chinese '*kan*', to be grateful and '*hsich*', thanks. It was shouted out by Chinese beggars in ports at which the nineteenth-century European merchantmen called.

**CUNT:** *The female genitalia; vulgarly, a term of abuse.*

It is not possible to point to one particular source for this word, but one can look to a groundswell of cognate terms that existed in the Mediterranean area throughout time. The most influential was probably the Latin '*cunnus*', which gave rise to such term as '*cunabula*', a place where something is nurtured, but similar words abounded, ranging through the Hittite '*kun*', tail, the Egyptian '*qefen-t*', vagina or vulva, the Persian '*kun*', posterior, the Italian '*conno*', and the French '*con*'. There were also Germanic terms such as '*kunta*' and '*kunte*', which were reflected in Dutch, Old Frisian and Old Norse. The word today is in some disrepute, having been pushed into the shadows by imports from other languages regarded as more refined. Its decline may have been helped by the fact that it is an ugly, curt word, and does sound crudely blunt; the same has not happened to the French '*con*' which is quite acceptable and doubles in normal conversation for 'idiot'. 'Cunt' was not always BEYOND THE PALE, and in times gone by it was so widely accepted that it was even used of an empty receptacle. Here are some examples of its erstwhile usage: The street directory of thirteenth-century London included 'Gropecuntlane', obviously popular with lovers. It must be remembered that folk were not so prissy of speech in such times and those surnames not built on the person's trade reflected personal traits or peculiarities. Early records mention such female names as Gunoka Cuntles (1219), Bele Wydecunthe (1328) and presumably promiscuous males sporting such names as Godwin Clawecunte (1066), John Fillecunt (1246) and Robert Clevecunt (1302).. The standard method of stacking barrels in a pyramid was called 'cunt-line and bilge free', the cunt-line being the concave, delta-shaped apertures between adjacent barrels. ('Bilge free' meant that the bottom line was raised off the ground on rails for ventilation purposes.) In the sea-faring world, 'cut-splicing', joining two ropes to form an elliptical eye, was once called 'cunt-splicing', and the spiral groove in a rope was properly 'cunt-line', until sailors, with uncharacteristic coyness, changed the word to 'contline'. Shakespeare puns on it in *Twelfth Night* when Malvolio says: 'By my life this is my lady's hand/These are her very C's, her U's and ['n] her T's and/Thus she makes her great P's.' John Wilmot, 2nd Earl of Rochester (1647–80), referring to Nell Gwyn in his poem 'The Royal Angler' says: 'However weak and slender be the string/Bait it with cunt, and it will hold a king.' In 1743, Horace Walpole advocated in his *Little Peggy* that 'distended cunts with alum shall be braced' and even in 1800, Robert Burns, praising a woman's beauty in his *Merrie Muses of Caledonia*, says: 'For ilka hair upon her cunt/Was worth a king's ransom.'

**CUPBOARD LOVE:** *A show of love with a material end in view.*

Children can often cajole grown-ups into opening up a store of sweets by being excessively loving.

**CURATE'S EGG:** *Something that is good in parts.*

An expression born of a 1895 issue of *Punch* (vol. C ix), which on page 222 carried a cartoon of a young, nervous curate having breakfast with his bishop. The unfortunate man is forcing down a bad egg, too frightened of his superior to reject it. In the caption, the bishop remarks: 'I'm afraid you've got a bad egg, Mr. Jones.' The curate's reply: 'Oh, no, My Lord, I assure you! Parts of it are excellent.'

**CURIOSITY KILLED THE CAT:** *A cautionary saying.*

Cats are incurably inquisitive creatures and, despite their reputation for having nine lives, this frequently leads them into danger from which there is no escape. Modern householders have allegedly opened up their washing machine to find one very clean, but very dead, domestic pet.

**CURMUDGEON:** *An ill-natured miser.*

The origin is obscure, but suggestions are not lacking. It could be a variant of the sixteenth-century 'cornmudgin', 'mudgin' meaning a thief or a hoarder, and the whole word referring to one who hoards local corn to force the price up, or of 'curmudgin', a base fellow who steals dogs. It could perhaps be of Scottish extraction from '*curmullyit*', a dark, unpopular man or from '*curmurring*', a low, threatening growling, '*cur*' being based on the Old Norse '*kurra*', to grumble. Last but not least, there is the French '*coeur mechant*', evil heart, this being the source of one of the most notorious mistakes in the field of word origins. In his *Dictionary* (1755), Samuel Johnson discussed the word and, without any assertions, put forward '*coeur méchant*', followed by: 'credited French, an unknown correspondent' because an unknown correspondent had suggested this French origin to him. Twenty years later, one John Ash, having 'researched' most of his work in Johnson's publication, brought out a dictionary; it included the word 'curmudgeon' which he stated to be derived from the French 'coeur' (unknown) and 'méchant' (a correspondent).

**CURRY FAVOUR, TO:** *To try to ingratiate oneself.*

This has its source in a fourteenth-century satirical play entitled *Roman de Favel*, in which Favel, a chestnut horse, represented the baser side of human nature, e.g. duplicity and cunning. Other characters wishing to enlist his aid in their schemes would curry, or stroke, Favel to gain his favour. The similarity of the name to 'favour' ensured the shift from 'curry Favel' to 'curry favour'.

**CURTAIN LECTURE:** *A wife's reproof to her husband.*

When the curtains around the four-poster bed were closed, the couple were alone and the wife could indulge in criticism without fear of being overheard.

**CUSHY / CUSHIE:** *Easy and undemanding.*

The ultimate source seems to be '*kush-kush*', an African dialect word for a food which took its name from the Hindustani '*khush*', pleasure, and which is better known to Europeans as 'couscous'. 'Cushie' first made its appearance in America in the mid-1700s during the massive influx of slaves, who at first used the word to describe a kind of soft, sweet, fried oatmeal cake, and then extended it to describe a job that was also soft and sweet, and hence a 'cushie number'.

**CUSTOM MORE HONOURED IN THE BREACH THAN IN THE OBSERVANCE.**

In Act I Scene iv, when Horatio is puzzled by an uproar from within, Hamlet tells him that the existing custom of accompanying the king's carousals with the beating of drums and the blowing of trumpets is one that has brought contumely upon the Danes as drunken revellers, and uses the above meaning the custom would be *better* breached than observed. The tag is widely used of a custom regrettably falling into disuse, though this is the very antithesis of what Hamlet was implying, and in 1987, even Kenneth Baker regrettably used the expression wrongly when, as Education Secretary for the Thatcher Government, he was talking on Radio 4 about the falling standards in education.

**CUT ABOVE:** *Better.*

This is an old butchery term; as a general rule, the finer cuts of meat are to be found higher up in the carcase.

**CUT AND DRIED:** *Settled in advance or finished completely.*

This refers to crops, such as silage for winter feed, that have been cut, baled, stored and dried out, or possibly to herbs similarly treated. It has been alternatively suggested that the allusion could also be to timber which has been sawn and allowed to cure.

**CUT AND RUN:** *To make off quickly, perhaps just ahead of trouble.*

The crews of sailing ships anchored in open road-stream sometimes furled the sails and tied them off in such a way that cutting a few strategic strings allowed all canvas to fall into immediate use, and this preparation was seen as indicating a suspicious need for a speedy get-away. Some prefer to believe that the anchor cable was cut in an emergency, but this is hardly likely; by the nature of things, ships cannot take off like startled deer and there was always time to haul up the anchor – something that in any case a ship would be ill-advised to leave behind.

**CUT AND SHUT:** *Workmanship so sloppy as to be dangerous.*

From the shady end of the British car trade, this describes a process whereby two similar cars, which have sustained damage to front and rear ends respectively, have the damaged parts cut off. The two good ends are then 'shut' together, welded up and dumped on the market.

**CUT AND THRUST:** *Aggressive behaviour.*

This is an allusion to serious sword-fighting, the objective of which was to wound or kill.

**CUT BLOCKS WITH A RAZOR:** *To achieve the impossible with next to no resources.*

When Tarquin the Elder wished to enlarge his army by increasing the number of centuries prescribed by Romulus, Accius Naevius, himself an augur, warned him not to do so without consulting the augurs first. Seeking to belittle Naevius and his powers, Tarquin asked: 'Is the thought in my mind at this moment possible?' The augur replied that it was, whereupon Tarquin held out a whetstone and challenged Naevius to cut it in two with the sacrificial razor he was holding at the time. The priest gave the block a sharp tap and it obediently fell in two, leaving Tarquin speechless.

**CUT NO ICE:** *Make no impression.*

This figure-skating idiom implies that one who uses skates too dull to cut the ice will similarly fail to make an impression on the judges.

**CUT OF YOUR JIB:** *Your appearance.*

The jib is one of the triangular sails set from the foremast, which, in the old days, tended to vary in profile from nation to nation, and so served to identify the nationality of a vessel, even if her flag was not visible.

**CUT OFF WITH/WITHOUT A SHILLING:** *Disinherited.*

Under Scottish Law, a son cannot be disinherited by default; he must either be specifically disinherited in the will, or left *something*. Wayward sons were virtually disinherited by a bequest of only a shilling.

**CUT OUT:** *To leave; excluded.*

Both these derive from card games, such as bridge, in which only a specified number can participate. If there are more players than places at the tables, everybody cuts the pack (deck) and those cutting the lowest cards sit out the next deal.

**CUT OUT FOR:** *Ideally suited.*

This is from the skill of the tailor's cutter who cuts his cloth to just the right shape.

**CUT THE GORDIAN KNOT:** *To solve a problem by direct, forceful action.*

Legend tells that, when the people of the ancient city of Phrygia asked the oracle of Zeus for advice in selecting a king, they were told to choose the first man who turned up at the temple in a cart. This transpired to be Gordius, a peasant, who gave his name to the city and became an excellent ruler. Once king, he dedicated his cart to Zeus, tying it to a beam outside the temple with a rope made of cornel bark twisted into an ingenious knot and the oracle stated that whoever could untie the knot would rule all Asia. Many tried and failed, but Alexander the Great boldly severed the rope with his sword and fulfilled the prophecy.

**CUT THE MUSTARD:** *To do a job well.*

'Cut' here is used in its meaning of to perform or achieve. Mustard is hot and sharp, both of which adjectives have come to mean 'able and clever'.

**CUT TO THE QUICK:** *Really offended.*

Originally, this meant literally wounded by a sword thrust that cut through armour to the living flesh. This phrase, and 'the quick and the dead', are just about the only remaining examples of the word 'quick' used in its true and original sense, which derived from the Old English '*cwicu*', alive or living.

**CUT UP ROUGH:** *To turn disagreeable.*

This is an allusion to the sea becoming choppy.

**CUT YOUR STICK:** *To leave.*

Before embarking on any significant journey, people used to cut a stout walking stick, which also served for self-defence.

# D

**D, TAKE A:** *To commit suicide.*

It is popularly held in America that the last of the huge letters atop Mount Lee, proclaiming H O L L Y W O O D to the world, marks a leaping-off spot much favoured by aspirants to movie fame who commit suicide because they have failed to achieve their ambition.

**DAB HAND:** *An expert.*

'Dab', skilled, emerged as early as the late seventeenth century and was a slurred contraction of '*adept*', from the Latin '*adeptus*', especially in the phrase '*adeptus artem*', having attained an art. In the Middle Ages, alchemists assumed the title *Vere Adeptus* (One who has *really* attained the secret or skill), indicating their claim to have fathomed all the mysteries of science and learned how to convert base metal into gold.

**DAFT AS A BRUSH:** *Stupid, or soft and sentimental.*

This North of England expression was originally '*soft* as a brush' and meant gentle, if a little naive. Because of other sayings like 'soft in the head', non-Northerners interpreted it as 'stupid', hence 'daft as a brush'.

**DAG:** *An unpleasant person.*

Possibly enjoying some relationship with 'tag', a 'dag', from the Middle Ages onward, was understood to mean a part or portion hanging down, and a 'daggle-tail' meant a bedraggled slut, or even a low whore. In Australia, where 'dag' is popularly used, its meaning drifted towards the unpleasant because any muck-caked fleece hanging on a sheep, especially from its rear end, was referred to as a 'dag'. The currency of the expression is growing in Britain through the influence of Australian entertainers and soap operas.

**DAG UP:** *To smarten up.*

This Australianism has its source in the cleaning up of a sheep by removing any DAGS.

**DAGO:** *Properly a Spaniard, but generally any Iberian or Latin.*

Known since the turn of the eighteenth century, this racial insult is seemingly built on 'Diego', a typical Spanish Christian name which is the equivalent of James. Any name which is over-used seems to acquire slighting overtones, viz CHARLIE, DICK.

**DAMN THE TORPEDOES, FULL SPEED AHEAD:** *To proceed irrespective of danger.*

This is one of the few influences directly exerted on English by the American Civil War. On 5 August 1869, Admiral David Glasgow Farragut entered Mobile Harbour to do battle with the Confederate Fleet. At the opening of the engagement, he lost his lead ship, *Tecumesh*, to a mine. Despite the fact that several more of the devices (known at that time as torpedoes) were spotted, the Admiral gave his famous command.

**DAMON AND PYTHIAS (MORE PROPERLY PHINTIAS):** *Faithful friends.*

During the fourth century BC, Pythias was condemned to death by Dionysius of Syracuse, but was granted a stay of execution so that he could first return home and put his affairs in order. This was made possible by his friend, Damon, who remained in Syracuse as a hostage, to be executed if Pythias defaulted. Pythias, however, *did* return to meet his fate, and the tyrant was so impressed with this proof of loyal friendship that he promptly released them both.

**DAN TO BEERSHEEBA:** *From one end to the other, literally or metaphorically.*

These two cities were respectively the most northern and the most southern in the ancient Holy Lands, and this Middle Eastern version of 'John O'Groats to Land's End' is used as metaphor ten times in the Bible.

**DANCE ATTENDANCE:** *To wait on hand and foot.*

Inconsiderate superiors tend to keep their subordinates pacing up and down in outer offices or scurrying around in anxious circles to satisfy every instruction to the letter, rather as if they were involved in some complicated dance routine. It has also been suggested that the expression is a development of 'to dance the attendance' which described the tradition that a bride had to dance with all comers from the guests (attendance) at the wedding celebration, which tended to leave the poor girl giddy and exhausted.

**DANDY:** *One overly concerned with his appearance and clothes.*

Both this eighteenth-century development and its seventeenth century predecessor, 'Jack-a-dandy', could well derive from 'dandiprat', a coin of insignificant value first issued by Henry VII (1457–1509) towards the end of his reign. The transfer could have been occasioned by two influences. (1) the meaning of dandiprat spread to encompass a worthless, petty fellow, especially of the jumped-up variety. (2) From as early as the year 1000, the second half of the name, 'PRAT', had been associated with foolishness. Indeed, 'prat' might have been incorporated in the name of the coin to indicate its insignificant nature. In any case, in the edition of the *Northampton Mercury* dated 17 April 1819, one Bishop Fleetwood discussed the origin of 'dandy' and linked it to the name of the coin, which, he averred, had spread to servants and other 'worthless and contemptible fellows'. There are other suggestions: (3) The French '*dandin*', ninny, could be connected, or the French '*dindon*', which is pronounced in much the same way and can also mean a dupe or a simpleton, but which literally means a turkey cock, a creature noted for its stupidity and its vain strutting. (4) The old Scottish pet form of Andrew was 'Dandy' and it was applied in much the same way as 'Jack-the-lad' to young blades who thought they knew it all. (5) The Scottish and North Country 'dander', to saunter, might have implied the 'casual', but deliberately eye-catching, sauntering of the poseur.

**DANIEL COME TO JUDGMENT:** *An infallibly wise judge.*

In *Merchant of Venice* Act IV Scene I, Shylock, sensing that he is actually going to be awarded his pound of flesh, praises the judge, who is Portia in disguise, as: 'A Daniel come to judgment! yea, a Daniel!' The Daniel to whom he refers is, of course, the biblical character who, while still young in years, displayed great wisdom. A Bible story from the Apocrypha tells that Susanna was condemned to death for adultery, but Daniel established her innocence. Her accusers, two elders whose advances she had rejected, each attested that they had seen her lying under a tree with a young man. Daniel insisted on asking each accuser separately to describe the tree under which the adultery took place. Each man described a different tree.

**DANIEL IN THE LION'S DEN:** *Someone who shows fortitude in great danger.*

The source of this is, of course, the Bible. Daniel 6 recounts how Darius, King of Persia, had Daniel thrown into the lions' den on the strength of false accusations. Daniel was resigned, but the Angel of the Lord intervened and the lions did not attack him. His innocence was thus proved and his traducers were put to death instead.

**DARBY AND JOAN:** *A devoted, elderly couple.*

This came about through the publication in *The Gentleman's Magazine* of a ballad entitled 'The Joys of Love Never Forgot', the third stanza of which includes the lines: 'Old Darby, with Joan by his side/You've often regarded with wonder/He's dropsical, she's sore-eyed/Yet they're never happy asunder.' Credit for the authorship is laid at the door of Henry Woodfall Snr whose son, Henry Sampson Woodfall, (1739–1805) was an English printer and journalist who started his apprenticeship in the printing works of John and Joan Darby, the model couple who inspired the poem.

**DARK HORSE:** *A person whose abilities are undisclosed.*

Taken from the race-track, this previously described a horse with no track record, whose chances of winning were impossible to assess. 'Dark' is used in the sense of unknown.

**DAVID AND GOLIATH:** *A small opponent pitted against massive odds.*

I Samuel tells that when the champion of the Philistines, Goliath the giant, challenged any one of the Israelites to single combat, only the boy David came forward. An unlikely victor, David nevertheless killed his opponent with a single shot from his sling and won the day. Since real life confrontations rarely end this way, the metaphor is sometimes used to indicate the impossibility of fighting a 'Goliath'.

**DAVID AND JONATHAN:** *Inseparable friends.*

The Biblical David dearly loved his friend Jonathan, the son of Saul. In II Samuel 1:26, David laments his passing, proclaiming: 'I am distessed for thee, my brother Jonathan/Very pleasant hast thou been unto me:/ Thy love to me was wonderful,/ Passing the love of women.'

**DAVY JONES' LOCKER:** *A sailor's nickname for the sea, or its malignant spirit.*

The origin can only be conjectured, but it does seem highly likely that part of the name at least is linked to Jonah of whale fame, who was also referred to as Jonas; this could have been corrupted to Jones and preceded by the archetypal Welsh Christian name. On the other hand, some see 'Davy' as being derived from 'Duffy', a West Indian sea-devil, and claim that 'Jones' is a corruption of 'Shonee', a Celtic sea-god. There are also countless stories concerning alleged characters named Davy Jones. Some cite unscrupulous inkeepers who sold their sleeping clients to the press gangs; others recount the gory escapades of Davy Jones, a pirate with an apparently clinical obsession for making his victims walk the plank. Maritime history neglects to mention this pirate, nor is there any record of 'walking the plank', which, like the Jolly Roger, is a gruesome invention. If a pirate wanted someone off his ship, he threw him over the side.

**DAYS ARE NUMBERED:** *The end is known and in sight.*

Daniel 5: 25–29 tells of the WRITING ON THE WALL which prophesied the collapse of Belshazzar's kingdom. He is told that 'God has numbered thy kingdom, and finished it', meaning that his allotted time was over.

**DEAD-AND-ALIVE:** *Dull and inactive.*

In the sixteenth century, this appeared as 'dead-alive' (as much dead as alive); the transition to 'dead-and-alive' had already begun by the nineteenth century and was completed by the 1850s.

**DEAD AS A DODO:** *Finished, right out of fashion.*

The name of the dodo, a large, flightless bird indigenous to the Mauritius Islands, is rooted in the Portuguese '*duodo*', fool. It was an incredibly stupid bird, and the fact that it became extinct in the 1680s is hardly surprising since the female, having laid its annual egg, usually wandered off and forgot where the nest was, a trait unlikely to ensure the survival of the species. The story that their meat was so tasty that they were eaten into extinction by the early explorers is groundless; the Dutch actually called them '*walgvogels*', nauseous birds, since no method or amount of cooking could render them palatable.

**DEAD AS A DOORNAIL:** *Having no life or usefulness.*

The origin lies in carpentry in which there is a process known as 'dead-nailing'. When constructing a particularly stout door, carpenters fastened the panels to the batons using extra long nails which, driven into the outside, protruded on the inside of the door and were hammered flat, so that they could not be removed. The nails were then said to be dead. Some sources maintain that the saying derives from the heavy stud nails found adorning the outside of many old doors, particularly the one directly beneath the knocker; this has been hit on the head so often that it must be dead!

**DEAD CAT BOUNCE:** *A misleading portent.*

Originally a Wall Street expression to describe a deceptive and temporary recovery in share prices when the market itself is generally low. The allusion is to a dead cat which, if dropped from a sufficently great height, will still bounce off the ground.

**DEAD CAT ON THE LINE:** *An indication that something is wrong.*

This was born in the Southern states of America and refers to a method there of catching catfish. In the morning a fisherman lays stretch lines baited with several hooks along the river; at night he returns to see what he was caught. If someone pulls up another's line and finds on it a dead fish, he knows the owner has left it untouched for some time. Why? What's happened to him?

**DEAD LETTER:** *A project or law currently unenforced and ignored.*

'Letter' in this case means a writ or statute and the expression was born of two biblical sources. Firstly Romans 7:6: 'But now we are delivered from the law, that being dead wherein we were held, that we should serve in newness of spirit and not live in the oldness of the letter.' Secondly, II Corinthians 3:6 which advises that people heed the spirit, not the letter, 'for the letter killeth, but the spirit giveth life'.

**DEAD MAN'S SHOES:** *Slow promotion.*

Shoes were once extremely expensive, and when a member of a family died, his shoes were passed down.

**DEAD RECKONING:** *The estimation of a ship's position simply by the log book.*

The calculation starts off with the last known position of the vessel, then, taking into account travelling speed, bearing, drift and currents, arrives at a hypothetical fix as to where the ship would have been at a specific time had she been dead or absolutely stationary in the water. Naturally, the figure can be a projected one, or retarded. The usual origin attributed to this expression is that 'dead' is a corruption of 'ded', an abbreviation of 'deduced'. This seems logical, but it is wrong.

**DEAD RINGER:** *One with an identical appearance.*

'Dead' is here used in its sense of 'absolute' or 'unerring'. The expression originated in the United States, and could have derived from the world of horse racing. Before the advent of stringent controls on the race-courses and the mass media, it was not unknown for a top-class runner to be entered in a race under the name of a lesser performer which it resembled, or had been made to resemble, a ploy which ensured long odds, but which required the connivance of all parties concerned, owners, trainers, jockeys etc. and was therefore known as a ring-deal. Alternative theories point to 'ringer', a forged coin, which makes a tinny, ringing noise when dropped on a hard surface and does not RING TRUE.

**DEAD SEA FRUIT:** *Transient pleasure or items of apparent value soon lost.*

Behind this expression lies the legend of a fruit which grew beside the Dead Sea near the cities of Sodom and Gomorrah and was said to appear rich, ripe and juicy, but to turn to ashes in the mouth. Deuteronomy 32 states: 'For their vine is of the vine of Sodom, and the fields of Gomorrah: their grapes are grapes of gall, their clusters are bitter.' The legend most probably referred to the madar, a member of the asclepiadaceae family of shrubs and woody vines which is not only common in that area but has fleshy pods particularly vulnerable to insect attack that leaves the fruit a mess of galls. The use of 'apple' in the synonymous 'apples of Sodom' is a modern perversion of the original legend which also took place in the tale of Adam and Eve wherein again the apple was used by later Western scholars to symbolise greed or lust.

**DEAD SET:** *A determined, single-minded onslaught.*

On the battlefield, a field piece which was locked in the required elevation was said to be 'dead set'. In the workshop, too, a piece of equipment was lined up correctly and then locked 'dead', exactly, in position.

**DEADBEAT:** *A lazy, idle bum.*

An expression of American origin relying on the use of 'dead', absolute, and 'beat', scrounger, a meaning applied in the States since the eighteenth century, and arising from their application of the word to mean 'avoid', i.e. a deadbeat avoids paying his way, just as a criminal 'beats the rap' when he evades conviction for a crime he actually committed. The suggestion that the term was born of 'beatnik' is thus defeated by chronology, and the OED includes a quotation from 1877: 'A system of local government controlled by 30,000 bummers, loafers and deadbeats'. There could however have been some reinforcement from the eighteenth-century watchmakers' use of 'dead-beat' to describe a beat which, for no apparent reason, did not swing the latches far enough to engage on the teeth of the main wheel, thus causing the whole mechanism to come to a sudden halt until shaken or jarred.

**DEADLEG:** *A useless idler.*

This is a metaphorical use of a term

which describes the physical result of having your leg struck hard on the outside of the thigh by, for example, an assailant's knee. When this happens, the limb loses all sensation, cannot support you for some time and must be dragged around as so much dead weight.

**DEADLINE:** *A fixed, unchangeable date for the completion of a task.*

Adopted by the American public after reading press reports on the war crimes trial of Captain Henry Wirz. Wirz was the Confderate Commandant of Andersonville POW camp, one of the great scandals of the American Civil War. Crammed into the sixteen and a half acre camp, situated some fifty miles south of Macon in Georgia, were more than 30,000 Union prisoners of whom over 13,000 died in thirteen months. A line was drawn outside and parallel to the stockade wall, and any man in the corridor was considered to be attempting to escape and shot out of hand. Wirz was hanged in 1865.

**DEADPAN:** *An expressionless, inscrutable, face.*

A simple blend of 'dead', without animation, and 'pan', a utensil whose round shape is suggestive of the face, the handle perhaps representing the body.

**DEAL FROM THE BOTTOM OF THE DECK:** *To cheat or deceive.*

A card sharp surreptitiously deals from the bottom of the pack or deck where certain cards have previously been placed.

**DEAR JOHN:** *A letter to a man ending a romantic relationship with him.*

This was born in WW2 to describe the sort of letter received by servicemen separated from partners who were then writing to terminate the relationship. Recent popularity of the term has been assured by the American and British sit-com of the same title centring on a hapless husband returning to find such a letter awaiting his return and his problems thereafter.

**DEAR ME:** *Exclamation of exasperation or surprise.*

This could be a corruption of the Latin '*Dio me salvi*', God save me.

**DECK IS STACKED AGAINST YOU:** *All the odds are against your success – especially if this has been deliberately contrived.*

A stacked deck of cards has been deliberately arranged by a card sharp to disadvantage the other players.

**DEEP SIX:** *Death, or a metaphorically sticky end.*

The Admiralty dictates that a burial at sea must take place in a minimum of six fathoms of water and this is a far more likely origin than any reference to a land grave, popularly assumed to be six feet deep. This has not been the case for many a long year.

**DEKE, TO:** *To cheat or defraud.*

Seemingly of early twentieth-century Canadian origin this is likely a spin-off from 'decoy' in that the term was initially restricted to diversionary or trap-setting tactics in a sporting situation. In turn, 'decoy' is derived from the Dutch '*de kooi*', the cage, and arrived in English as a hunters' term for the caged but live bird forced to make distress calls to lure other birds down and under the guns.

**DEKKO:** *A quick, possibly surreptitious glance.*

In the nineteenth century, British soldiers serving in India adopted and adapted the Hindustani '*dekho*', which is the imperative of '*dekhna*', to look.

**DELPHINIAN:** *Oracular, especially if ambiguous or gratuitously convoluted.*

Allusive to the activities of the female visionaries of the ancient temple of Delphi in Phocis, Greece, supposedly situated over the womb of the Great Earth Mother, hence the place name as based on the Greek '*delphos*', a womb. Direct sister-words are the names of the dolphin whose body resembles the shape of that organ in relaxed mode and the delphinium with a similarly shaped nectary. To act as the mouthpieces of Gea, the Great Mother, the priestesses put themselves into a drug induced hysteria by chewing the sacred cherry-laurel leaves, hence the convoluted or downright incomprehensible nature of the answers given to those who came for wisdom. In the Greek culture the wresting of control from the hands of women was symbolised by Apollo slaying the temple guardian, a massive, unnamed and female serpent which he decreed should not be buried but lie there and rot like some grotesque tribute to his victory. From the Greek '*pytho*', to rot, comes the term 'python' and the Greeks celebrated Apollo's victory with the commencement of the Pythian Games; it was here that the victorious athletes were awarded laurel wreaths – victors at the Olympic Games received wreaths of wild olive.

**DEMI-MONDE:** *The somewhat decadent fringe of society.*

Dumas the Younger created this expression and used it as the title of a play staged in 1855. *Demi-monde* (Half World) concentrated on the activities of the more colourful sectors of society, of which he and his father, known as Dumas Père, were so inordinately fond. His best-known work, *La Dame aux Camelias* for example, was inspired by his long affair with a tubercular prostitute called Marie Duplessis, who had a passion for the flowers and was eventually buried in a coffin full of them. Despite his lifestyle, Dumas adopted a highly moral tone in his work.

**DEMI-REP:** *A person, especially a woman, of dubious morals.*

A contraction of demi-reputable, this was an eighteenth-century invention to describe ladies who inspired so much gossip that it was felt they must have indulged in sexual impropriety, even though nothing definite was known.

**DEMI-VIERGE:** *A sexually enthusiastic female who can claim to be a virgin only in the strictest sense.*

The French for 'half-virgin', this was coined by the novelist Marcel Prèvost (1862–1941) who caused a sensation in 1894 with his *Les Demi-Vierges* which examined the effect of Parisian society and education on young girls. The title was perhaps inspired by the play DEMI-MONDE by Dumas Fils.

**DEMMICK:** *Unwell, run down or wholly defunct.*

A corrupt contraction of 'epidemic'.

**DERBY DOG:** *The inevitable minor upset preceding a major event.*

An allusion to the stray dog which so often wanders onto the course at Epsom, after it has been cleared for the big race of the day.

**DERRING-DO:** *Daring action.*

According to the OED, this is a pseudo-archaism 'misconstrued as a substantive phrase, and taken to mean daring acts or feats'. It would appear that all the trouble started with a misinterpretation by Spenser of a passage in Chaucer in which Troilus is referred to as being second to none 'in dorryng don that longeth to a knyght'. This line properly meant 'in daring to do what is rightly a knight's task', but Spenser mistook the verb for a noun and thought the line meant 'in bold achievement, which is a knightly duty'. The error was compounded by a misprint in a work by John Lydgate and this gave us the current spelling of the phrase, which is essentially a nonsense.

**DEUS EX MACHINA:** *An auspicious arrival which magically resolves an impasse.*

Taken directly from the Latin, this literally means 'a god from out of the machine', and was anciently used in Roman theatre for the figure of a particular god which was winched onto stage to extricate a character in the play from a sticky end.

**DEVIL AMONG THE TAILORS:** *A heated slanging match or a violent free-for-all.*

The origin is uncertain but the most likely theory cites the children's game which involves releasing a spinning top amidst a set of nine wooden men. The top was called the devil, which was and still is to some extent a common name for a tool or machine that performed a destructive function; the wooden men were called tailors, probably from the old saying: 'It takes nine tailors to make a man', an unflattering comment on their weak physical condition brought about by the sedentary nature of their work. Another origin has been suggested; it is said that, in 1830, a large body of London tailors rioted outside the Haymarket Theatre during a benefit performance in aid of the actor William Dowton, protesting that the play, a burlesque piece entitled *The Tailors: A Tragedy for Warm Weathers*, was a vile slander on their profession.

**DEVIL AND HIS DAM:** *Tremendous trouble, followed by something worse.*

The implication here is that the mischief caused by the supernatural Devil is increased two-fold when he is accompanied by his wife. In some traditions, such as the Rabbinical, Satan's wife is Lilith, Adam's first wife who found Eden too tame, and the Devil more to her liking.

Isaiah 34:14, discussing the coming together of various abominations, is referring to Lilith when it states: 'The screech owl also shall rest there, and find for herself a place of rest.'

**DEVIL TAKE THE HINDMOST:** *Every man for himself.*

Medieval folklore held that the Devil ran a black magic school at Toledo, Spain. On graduation day in this subterranean 'University of Evil', successful students had to race through a lengthy passage back into the world, to cause havoc in their master's name. The last man to reach the door at the end was trapped by Satan and had to remain as his imp until released by the slowest graduate the following year.

**DEVIL TO PAY, THE:** *We are in a highly dangerous situation.*

As is the case with BETWEEN THE DEVIL AND THE DEEP BLUE SEA, the reference here is not to Satan, but to a ship's seam, which, being between the garboard-strake and the keel, was the most difficult to get at and keep clear of water when the ship was being careened. Nevertheless it had to be cleaned out and caulked with the greatest of care because, being next to the keel, it was the most dangerous place for a leak to occur, and was almost impossible to reach from the inside. The original, full expression was: 'There is the devil to pay and no hot pitch', and 'pay' is actually a corruption of the Old French '*peier*', to daub or fill with pitch. Thus, despite its increasing misuse, the saying does *not* indicate that great wrong has been committed and that the Devil will be seeking restitution. Scholars have suggested that this seam was called the devil because it was 'a devil of a job to get at', but, if this were the case, given the colourful turn of phrase for which sea-faring types have long been famed, one feels that a shorter, much blunter name would have emerged. It seems far more likely that it acquired its name because it was an ever-present danger below everyone on board, for if the devil leaked, the ship was doomed.

**DEVIL'S ADVOCATE:** *Someone who opposes a motion, not from conviction, but to test its validity.*

The final step in canonisation is a favourable judgment from the Papal Court and, although a refusal is unlikely at this stage, and the hearing little more than a formality, tradition dictates that the hearing is conducted on adversarial lines so that all possible objections can be ventilated and overcome. The Advocatus Dei supports the canonisation, but the duty of the Advocatus Diaboli is to propose objections to it, even though he is really in favour of it.

**DICK:** *An idiot.*

As happened with 'CHARLIE', this, as a by-form of Richard, fell to such use through the popularity of Charles or Richard as boys' names generated by the string of monarchs bearing these names. As soon as a name is over-used, connotations of stupidity automatically creep in – much the same is happening today with Wayne and Craig.

**DICKER:** *To haggle; to prevaricate.*
This is based on the Latin '*decuria*', a lot of ten, especially a bundle of ten animal pelts, once a standard unit of barter. The German descendant '*decher*' emerged in America with its original trading application, and, because of the argy-bargy and mind-changing which takes place during the striking of a deal, with its more modern application.

**DICKEY (also DICKY):** *Sick or somehow infirm or malfunctioning.*
This is probably from some sort of rhyming slang such as 'rickey-dick' = sick, although an influence from Tumbledown Dick, the inept Richard Cromwell (1626–1712) has been conjectured.

**DIDDLE:** *To cheat.*
This was certainly popularised by the character Jeremy Diddler, a foxy swindler in James Kenney's farce *Raising the Wind* (1803) although it is unlikely that Kenney created the name out of whole cloth. There are several examples of 'diddle' in use since the seventeenth century ranging in meaning from 'to walk unsteadily' to 'to sing in a frivolous and indistinct manner'. There could thus be some connection with 'doodle'. It is not beyond the realms of possibility also that some debt is payable to the Old English '*didrian*', to cheat or delude.

**DIE IN HARNESS:** *To go down fighting or striving for success.*
'Harness' appears here in its now obsolete sense of 'armour' and does not signify the tackle of a draught animal. The expression properly means to die in battle or, in the modern vernacular, with one's boots on.

**DIE IS CAST:** *An irrevocable step has been taken.*
This 'die' is the singular of the gaming 'dice'; there is no connection with the system of metal-moulding called die-casting for this expression was in existence long before such methods were known, viz the parallel Latin saying, '*jacta alea est*' allegedly Caesar's words at the crossing of the Rubicon. However, at the end of the day, both senses of 'die' are linked, since the die used for casting metal objects, being often a perforated metal cube, derives its name from the gaming die which it resembles.

**DIG YOUR HEELS IN:** *To become obdurate.*
When a tug-of-war team is in danger of being dragged across the line, its members quite literally dig their heels in, lean back and lock off, until the opposition, hopefully weakened by the strain, provides them with the opportunity to regain ground.

**DIGGER:** *An Australian.*
This epithet has been in vogue since the Australian Gold Rush of the 1850s when everyone down-under seemed to be digging for gold. The usage lapsed a mite until WW1, when the Anzacs involved in the fiasco at Gallipoli were said to have shovelled half of Turkey into sandbags when digging in.

**DIGS:** *Lodgings.*

In the American gold rushes of the early–mid nineteenth century a miner who had found gold prudently took up residence in his diggings lest an intruder 'worked a night-shift' whilst the true owner was tucked up in bed in town.

**DIKE/DYKE:** *A lesbian of mannish appearance who assumes the dominant role in a relationship.*

This arose some time in the nineteenth century but its origin is wholly obscure. It could perhaps be a crude comparison between Lesbian penetration practices and the tradition of the Dutch boy stemming a flood by sticking his finger in the hole in the dike, or perhaps some play on the fact that a dike is a dam. There is also the possibility that it is connected to the American rural 'morphodyke', this being a play on 'hermaphrodite', the last syllable of this term itself having been postulated as the progenitor.

**DILDO:** *An artificial substitute for an erect penis; a complete idiot.*

The origin, which is uncertain, perhaps lies in the Italian '*diletto*', delight, a word by which the sexual device was known in early Italy. This would seem to be supported by the fact that dildoes were first put on open sale in England in the early seventeenth century in a shop in St James' Street which imported all its stock from Italy. In English the word once meant a foolish youngster; this is perhaps the basis for its second meaning, although this could have been a natural development. It also served to describe any cylindrical object such as a sausage or test tube; it was once even used in a senseless refrain in songs but, obviously, no more. Perhaps the earliest reference to such a device is to be found in Ezekiel 16-17: 'Thou has also taken thy fair jewels of my gold and silver, which I had given thee and made to thyself images of men and didst commit whoredom with them.'

**DIM AS A TOC H LAMP:** *Stupid.*

In July 1915 Lieutenant Gilbert W.L. Talbot was killed at Hooge – the first engagement involving the use of flame-throwers by the Germans. Talbot was the son of the Bishop of Winchester who resolved to perpetuate his son's memory by creating a leisure club for soldiers in the Flemish town of Poperinghe, which lay in the Ypres salient. This was to be but the first of many Talbot Houses, all of which kept a dim, low lamp lit to remind everyone who used them of those lost in action. 'Toc H' is signals parlance for 'T.H.' as in Talbot House, and the above expression developed in Army slang as a tag for those unencumbered with too much intelligence.

**DINE WITH THE CROSS-LEGGED KNIGHTS:** *To go hungry.*

The allusion here is to the stone figures of Temple Church, London, formerly a famous meeting-place for lawyers and clients. This attracted vagabonds and undesirables of all sorts who hoped to be hired as 'witnesses' but who, if they failed to sell their perjury, spent the night there and 'dined' with the cross-legged knights.

**DINGBATS:** *Insane.*

It is unclear whether this arose in America or Australia, but if the latter, it could be a blend of 'dingo' and 'bat', since an early application of the term most certainly related to the hallucinations of delirium tremens, in which nightmarish compounds of various animals are conjured up.

**DINKUM / FAIR DINKUM:** *Honest, genuine.*

The origin of this Australian slang, sometimes rendered as 'dinky', probably lies in the English rural dialect 'dincum' (work, especially hard, physical work). In the late nineteenth century, *The English Dialect Dictionary* records 'dinkum' as holding in Lincolnshire a meaning of 'an equitable share of work in hand'.

**DIOMEDEAN EXCHANGE:** *An agreement whereby one side reaps all, or nearly all, the benefit.*

During the Trojan Wars, Diomed, commander of the Lycian forces, came face to face with his old and dear friend, Glaucus, who was unfortunately leading a body of opposing Trojans. To show their respective forces that they did not intend to engage in combat, the two commanders met in the no man's land between them and exchanged armour. Glaucus's was finely wrought and decorated with gold and silver, while that of Diomed was plain bronze. Such a one-sided deal is also sometimes called a 'Glaucus swap'.

**DIP OUT:** *To miss out on something good.*

In birdwatchers' slang, this means to miss seeing a rare bird spotted by other 'twitchers' in the locality, and probably originated with the idea of a spotter settling, or dipping, back down in his hide at just the wrong moment. To spot a rarity, in the same jargon, is to 'dip in'.

**DIPPY:** *Insane or eccentric.*

Perhaps a distorted application of 'dip', to go up and down, although some connection with 'dipso', dipsomaniac, cannot be ruled out. Nor, some think, can the Romany '*divio*', mad.

**DIRTY WORK AT THE CROSSROADS:** *Foul play.*

It is doubtful that any single influence produced this but rather a number of unpleasant activities which once took place at crossroads, if only because so many people passed that way. For example, the bodies of hanged criminals were left to rot in metal cages at crossroads, a grisly deterrent indeed, though not to the highwaymen who found crossroads highly lucrative catchment areas. Again, suicides were buried at crossroads – with a stake through the heart to prevent them rising as vampires to stalk the night – since none of the bordering parishes would accept their being interred within their boundaries.

**DISCUSSING UGANDA/ UGANDAN AFFAIRS:** *Engaged in sexual intercourse, especially if casual or extra-marital.*

This is one of several entertaining euphemisms coined by the British satirical magazine *Private Eye.* In Issue 293, March 1973, the tongue-in-cheek 'gossip' columnist 'Grovel' reported that, at a party hosted by Neal and Corinna Ascherson, he was encouraged by his hostess to go upstairs to listen to a former Cabinet Minister of the recently deposed Milton Obote regime 'talking about Uganda'. Anxious to '. . . learn the latest from the Dark Continent', he rushed upstairs but, finding the alleged Ugandan statesman heavily engaged with a lady features editor, he withdrew to allow the two to continue 'discussing Uganda'. However, it would appear that, in this case, *Private Eye* was not entirely original. In April 1928, the suitably named British economist, Sir Leo Chiozza Money, a one-time junior minister in Lloyd George's government, was caught in a similar situation on a park bench in Hyde Park with one Miss Irene Savidge. When both were charged with indecent behaviour, Money insisted he had simply been advising Miss Savidge on her career, and that they had sat down for a short while to 'discuss matters of industrial economics'. Both were acquitted, but the jury was not so ready to believe Money's story on a subsequent occasion.

**DISHED:** *Thoroughly beaten or frustrated.*

Several sources, most notably the OED, suggest that this in some way refers to the fact that, when food is 'done', it is then 'dished' out. The more likely progenitor is the verb 'to dish', meaning to beat out into a concave, dished shape.

**DISH THE DIRT:** *Engage in slanderous gossip.*

This is taken from gold-mining jargon in which it signifies the swirling about of the dirt in the prospector's pan to separate out the particles of gold – or juicy scandal, in the case of the modern application.

**DIVE:** *A low club or bar.*

Originated because so many of these establishments were set up in basements and cellars – and indeed still are.

**DIXIELAND:** *The southern states of America, or a style of music played there.*

The origin actually lies in the French '*dix*', ten. During the 1830s, America was inundated by counterfeit banknotes and the public, quite justifiably, became suspicious of anything other than gold or silver coin. The Citizen's Bank and Trust Company of New Orleans consequently produced a series of highly complex notes printed in a mixture of French and English on distinctive, long-staple paper brought in from Europe. Not only did these notes defeat the forgers, they were also solidly backed and quickly won public confidence. The first denomination to be issued was the ten dollar bill which was popular in trading circles; this had 'DIX' printed on the back and almost overnight New Orleans became 'Dixietown' and the South in general 'Dixie'. The fact that most of the area lies south of the Mason–Dixon Line is sheer coincidence.

**DO A BRODIE:** *To commit, or attempt to commit, suicide by jumping; to perpetrate a hoax; to fail.*

One night in 1886, a man called

Steve Brodie claimed to have jumped off New York's Brooklyn Bridge for a $200 bet. He made enough money out of the stunt to open a bar in the Bowery and became a noted character, later portrayed by George Raft in a feature film of the era. The meaning of the term transferred to 'failure' because Brodie, unaccountably, performed his stunt without witnesses. The men who fished him out of the East River did not see him jump, so the 'daring exploit' always remained in doubt.

**DO A BUNK:** *To decamp.*

This originated in the late 1800s and, though the origin is obscure, it might well have arisen in either the British Forces or Public Schools in the sense of 'do up a bunk' i.e. to make one's bed appear occupied while one made good one's escape.

**DO BIRD:** *Imprisonment.*

The inspiration was the Cockney rhyming slang 'birdlime' = time reinforced by the fact that the said birdlime was a sticky substance used to entrap birds for caging.

**DO SOMETHING BY NUMBERS, TO:** *In an easy if not infantile manner.*

In the 1950s there was a short-lived craze for 'painting by numbers' which provided the artist manqué with a landscape, seascape, or whatever, this being divided into numbered squares, each number denoting a paint colour also supplied in the kit.

**DO SOMETHING ON A SHOESTRING, TO:** *On a limited budget.*

A simple reference to the one such item.

**DO THE DECENT THING:** *To obviate an embarrassing situation by removing oneself.*

This has its roots in the 'stiff-upper-lip' morality of the previous century when a gentleman who had been caught out contravening the accepted standards of his class was expected to go quietly away and shoot himself, thus saving everyone from potentially embarrassing consequences.

**DOBBER:** *Anything excellent.*

This is army slang from the latter part of WW1. British troops on the expedition into Northern Russia adapted the Russian '*dobra*', good.

**DOCTOR LIVINGSTONE, I PRESUME.** *A quotation that is now a humorous greeting, especially on a first meeting.*

This first appeared in the colourful account by Stanley, later Sir Henry Morton (1841–1904) of his incredible 236 day trek to find David Livingstone (1813–71), the Scottish missionary and explorer, whose disappearance while on an expedition into central Africa to discover the source of the Nile had caused enormous public concern. When Stanley, a newspaper correspondent at the time dispatched to trace him, eventually found him in Ujiji, it must have been the most exciting meeting of the century. Nevertheless, he reported that he greeted Livingstone with the now famous laconic words which, typifying the Englishman's ability to preserve his traditional sang-froid even in the outlandish and dangerous milieu of darkest Africa, became a catchphrase overnight. It is interesting to note that, shortly before he was sent on his mission by GORDON BENNETT, Stanley had attended a performance of Sheridan's *School for Scandal* which, in Act V, Scene 1 when two characters encounter each other, includes the line 'Mr Stanley, I presume'.

**DODGING THE COLUMN:** *Evading work.*

This British Army slang referred to the practice of being counted as present by obeying the order to muster for a task but sloping off when unobserved as the column moves from the parade ground to the place of work.

**DOG DAYS:** *Hot summery days, properly the period from 2 July to 11 August.*

It is pure coincidence that Sirius, the bright Dogstar, begins its heliacal rising at the same time as the height of summer, but the Romans, when they noted this, wrongly attributed the increased heat to the visibility of the star during the days they therefore called 'Caniculares Dies'.

**DOG IN THE MANGER:** *One who hangs on to something that is useful only to others.*

This refers to the old parable of the dog, asleep in a manger of hay. When it is awoken by various farm animals wanting their fodder, it barks and snarls and keeps them at bay, although it cannot eat the hay itself.

**DOG WATCH:** *Properly, either of the two-hour ship's watches between 4p.m. and 8p.m., but in general speech any late-hours tour of duty.*

There has been much conjecture about the origin of this term which may have arisen through the watches being short and 'dog' being a corrupt shortening of 'docked'. It has also been suggested that this is straightforward use of 'dog' due to the watches being shortened and thus perceived as inferior. This would draw a parallel with terms such as 'dog Latin'. The suggestion that the term is a play on the watches being shortened – or 'cur-tailed' – is at least amusing. Although often referred to by landlubbers as First Dog and Second Dog, these watches are properly called First Dog and Last Dog and the reason for their short duration is to ensure an uneven number of watches within the twenty-four hour period to ensure that no man on the watch rota works the same watch day after day.

**DOGIE:** *Young calf.*

This is most probably a development from 'dough-nut' applied in America to a calf orphaned before it has been completely weaned. Such animals are not sufficiently mature to digest grass properly, and their stomachs distend under the effort of attempting to do so. There is also a suggestion that the Afro-Creole '*dogi*', short or small, could have had some influence; there were a considerable number of black cowboys.

**DOG'S AGE:** *An exceptionally long time.*

Since dogs do not enjoy any great

particular longevity one can only presume this to be founded on the mistaken notion that a dog's age equated to that of humans in multiples of seven. Since a dog has reached full maturity within two years the true rule of thumb is to count the animal's first year as fifteen, the second as ten and every one thereafter as equivalent to five human years.

**DOGSBODY:** *A lowly subordinate undertaking menial tasks.*

In the nineteenth century, this was British Merchant Navy slang describing a meal made up of ships' biscuits and left-overs from the passengers' and officers' tables that was served to the crew, who likened it to eating dog. Even when conditions improved, this dish was still served, but only to the lowest of the low, who, in the end, inherited its nickname.

**DOLDRUMS:** *State of depression; an area of becalmed sea.*

Probably based on the now obsolete 'dold', a spin-off from 'dull' meaning an idiot or a lethargic person, 'doldrums', in the late eighteenth century, described sluggards or those who slept over-long. By the middle of the nineteenth century, this had transferred to those areas of sea so calm that ships languished there for days. The usage 'in the doldrums' is seemingly born of the misconception that there is only one such location. This is not so, although the best-known maritime doldrum is that near the Equator where the north and south trade winds meet and neutralize each other.

**DONKEY'S YEARS:** *An inordinately long time.*

A corruption of 'donkey's ears'; the creature may be noted for several qualities but longevity is not one of them; its ears however are renowned for their length.

**DOOLALLY/DOOLALLY TAP:** *Insane or irrational.*

Deolali is a town to the north-west of Bombay in the Indian province of Marashtra, and '*tap*' is Hindustani for 'fever'. Until the beginning of the twentieth century, Deolali served as a staging post for all time-expired British troops on their way home. The troop-transporting season, however, only ran from October through to March, and some men, finding themselves in Deolali for a frustratingly long time, took to drunkenness, brawling, and generally outrageous behavior, whereupon they were said to have caught 'Deolali tap'.

**DOOZIE:** *A person or thing considered to be exceptional.*

This arose from Deusenberg, the name of a very expensive and opulent motor car produced in America during the 1920s and 30s.

**DOPE:** *Narcotics; an idiot; inside information.*

The Dutch '*doopen*', to dip, gave rise to 'doop', a thick, viscous sauce into which food could be dipped, and inspired all the applications above which are closely linked to each other and to the quality of viscidity thus: there is a thick residue left after the addict has heated his opium. Anyone high on narcotics is going to act like an idiot and in the world of horse-racing, inside information often meant knowing which horses had been doped.

**DOT THE I's AND CROSS THE T's:** *To check a completed task and polish up the details.*

Children were once made to go over a piece of work, especially a sample of handwriting, to make sure all the letters were complete.

**DOTTY:** *Feeble minded or simply eccentric.*

Related to terms such as 'dotage' and likely a modern variant of 'dote', which has denoted a fool since the fifteenth century.

**DOUBLE CROSS:** *Intricate swindle, ultimate betrayal.*

First used in the horse-racing fraternity of the early nineteenth century to denote a double-deal set up to rook all parties involved, they each thinking they would be robbing each other. The classic double cross was set up by a jockey who let it be known he was prepared to cross his own boss by losing the race. When approached with sufficient funds the same jockey either did his best to win or used the money to bribe the other jockeys in the race and then bet heavily on himself to win – that being the second cross.

**DOUGHBOYS:** *American infantrymen.*

This first saw the light of day during the American Civil War, but came into prominence in WW1. Its origin is obscure but one theory put forward in the writing of Elizabeth Bacon Custer (widow of Lt Col. Custer – he did not hold the rank of General at the time of his death), holds that American sailors so nicknamed the infantry whose large, brass tunic buttons reminded them of the cornmeal biscuits known as doughboys. Another theory suggests the white clay dough once used by soldiers to keep their belts and webbing whitened, while yet another sees 'adobe' as the source because so many barracks in the American Southwest were constructed of it.

**DOWN AND OUT:** *Thoroughly beaten, at the end of one's resources.*

A boxer who is not only knocked down on the canvas but unconscious is finished.

**DOWN AT HEEL:** *In reduced circumstances.*

Shoes were once very expensive and have long been taken as an indication of the wearer's financial health, so if a man's heels are worn down, his bank balance probably is too.

**DOWN IN THE DUMPS:** *Depressed.*

Several terms have produced this; the Middle Dutch '*domp*', mental haze; the Low German '*dump*', mentally depressed, and also the German '*dump*' which emerged in Elizabethan times meaning a funeral song or dirge, and was based on the other meaning of the Low German '*dump*'- dull or hollow of sound.

**DOWN THE TUBES:** *Ruined or lost forever.*

A reference to domestic plumbing, the 'tubes' being those connecting the lavatory to the main sewer.

**DOWN TO CASES:** *Down to basics.*

In the eighteenth and nineteenth centuries, the heavy-duty boots worn by soldiers were called 'cases'.

**DOWN-BEAT:** *Gloomy and pessimistic, or extremely relaxed.*

This is the downward stroke of the conductor's baton which indicates the first, or most heavily accented, note of a measure. The antonym 'up-beat' is also frequently heard.

**DRACONIAN RULE:** *An extremely harsh regime.*

Draco, an Athenian legislator of the seventh century BC, drew up in 621 BC the first comprehensive code of law under which almost every crime in the book called for the death penalty.

**DRAG:** (1) *A tedious person or situation.* Although this could certainly be a simple extension of 'drag', to haul along a weighty object, the term was in use in America in the mid nineteenth century, which is long before such 'hip' language became fashionable. It is possible, therefore, that this usage has its roots in the jargon of cowboys, for whom the most tedious job on the trail was 'riding drag' i.e. riding behind the herd, eating dust for mile after mile. (2) *Female attire worn by a man.* The most likely explanation is that this was born in nineteenth-century theatre slang describing a part that required a man to dress up as a woman and 'drag' his skirts and petticoats around the stage. Having said this, it would be unwise wholly to dismiss the French '*dragee*', a sugar-coated pill, the association being fairly obvious.

**DRAG YOUR HEELS:** *To hang back and procrastinate.*

If a reluctant prisoner, for example, or a sit-down protestor goes limp and has to be forceably moved, this is often done in such a way that his heels drag on the ground behind him.

**DRAW:** *An even contest.*

A contraction of 'withdraw' since, in a way, both contestants withdraw from the contest leaving the matter unresolved.

**DRAW A BEAD:** *To line up on target.*

This alludes to the small globular foresight that was once fitted to the muzzle of the nineteenth and early twentieth-century firearms.

**DRAW A BLANK:** *To come up empty-handed.*

This refers to the sort of lottery in which all the tickets, save the winning ones, are blank.

**DRAW STUMPS:** *To conclude a matter.*

In the game of cricket, the end of play for the day is indicated by the three wooden stumps at either end of the pitch being pulled out.

**DRAW YOUR HORNS IN:** *To step down or cease belligerence.*

Reference to the snail which, at the slightest touch to its sensory 'horns' will retract them and proceed no further in the direction of the obstruction.

**DREADED LURGY:** *A viral infection going around.*

Wholly fictitious disease invented by the BBC Radio series *The Goon Show* which, in the 1950s, gave regular bulletins reporting its supposed rampage through the countryside.

**DRESSED TO THE NINES:** *Dressed in your best clothes and other finery.*

'To the nines' is generally accepted to be a corruption of the Old English '*to then eyne*', to the eyes, the whole expression suggesting well turned out from head to toe.

**DRESSED TO KILL:** *Attired in gorgeous, eye-catching clothes.*

Primitive warriors painted and adorned themselves before battle. Possibly consequential are such expressions as 'knock 'em dead', 'knock-out' etc.

**DRESSING DOWN:** *A severe reprimand.*

Either butchers' jargon, signifying the initial cutting into a carcass hanging from the beam, or from the building trade wherein it describes the scouring of a brick's front face to make it appear bright and new.

**DROP A BRICK:** *To disconcert by making a blunder.*

This certainly seems to have originated in Cambridge University slang, and was allegedly prompted by the ineptitude of the Trinity College Company of University Volunteers. While marching them through the town during the May term of 1905, their Sergeant Major had suddenly to bark out the order to halt since the street ahead, Trumpington Road, was blocked by building works. The order reduced the column to such chaos that some of the builders dropped their bricks in surprise. When relating the incident to his friends, the S.M. averred that, thereafter, he feared his orders would result metaphorically in the sound of cascading bricks.

**DROP A CLANGER:** *To make a singularly ill-timed gaffe.*

'Clanger' is British Service slang for a testicle, that which clangs or claps about, so this is a euphemistic version of 'drop a bollock' or 'make a balls/bollocks of things'.

**DROP OFF:** *To fall asleep unintentionally.*

It has been suggested that this was born in the coaching era; when the poorer passengers, who had to suffer long periods on the roof of the coach, became weary and drifted into sleep they quite literally dropped off.

**DRUM:** *Dwelling place; home patch.*

Although this came into English through the Romany '*drom*', street or section thereof, it is ultimately rooted in the Greek '*dromos*', a course or a run, and is therefore allied to 'aerodrome' and 'dromedary'.

**DRUM OUT:** *To dismiss for unacceptable behaviour.*

In most armies, when an officer is cashiered the reasons for his dismissal are read out before the entire regiment while his uniform is stripped of insignia, after which, he must walk off the parade ground alone to the distinctive drum beat known as the rogue's march.

**DRUM UP:** *To muster support or business.*

Army drum-squads once played through towns and villages to call all able-bodied men to the standard.

**DRUMHEAD COURT MARTIAL:** *An impromptu or hurried, but not illegal, trial.*

In previous centuries, it was military custom to maintain discipline by holding courts in the field so that punishment could be meted out on the spot. The hearings were traditionally held outside the commanding officer's tent around the regimental bass drum.

**DRUNK AS A FIDDLER/FIDDLER'S BITCH:** *Completely intoxicated.*

At wakes and village parties, the fiddler was usually unpaid, but could eat and drink his fill – a rather short-sighted economy which often had disastrous results. His female companion was afforded the same privilege and did not even have to waste good drinking time playing the fiddle!

**DRUNK AS A LORD:** *Completely intoxicated.*

When cheap imports of Portuguese wines were organised by the Methuen Treaty of 1703, the eighteenth-century British aristocracy, a drunken lot at the best of times, went absolutely overboard on port.

**DRUNK AS CHLOE:** *Completely intoxicated.*

The lady in question, wife of a cobbler of Linden Grove, had a long-standing affair with the English poet Matthew Prior (1664–1721). Her alcoholic excesses made her a legend in her own lunchtime.

**DRY GULCH:** *To ambush or defeat by foul means.*

An unpleasant trick once common during the American range-wars was to round up a man's cattle and drive them off a cliff into a dried-up river, thus bringing about his financial ruin.

**DRY RUN:** *Experimental trials.*

This is most likely adopted from America but it is unclear whether the inspiration was the bootleggers' driving of a route to check it out before bringing the trucks through, or from the teenagers' use of the term for simulated sex 'without penetration or divestiture', this previously being known as a 'dry fuck'.

**DUD:** *False, inoperable, worthless.*

This has probably developed from the English dialect 'dud', a sham, a paper tiger, a contraction of 'dudman' – scarecrow – which in turn was inspired by 'DUDS' – clothing. It is also highly likely that there has been some influence from such terms as the Dutch '*dood*', dead.

**DUDE:** *A foppish man, especially an American one.*

Coined in 1883 in New York, the precise inspiration for this is unclear. Since the dude is obsessed with his appearance, it would seem logical to ally the word with 'DUDS' as used to mean clothes. However, considering the significant Teutonic influence in America, it would be unwise to ignore the German dialect '*dude*', fool. Moreover, the word could be an over-fastidious or mocking pronunciation of DUD – false, which most dudes certainly are.

**DUDS:** *Clothing.*

This is a hand-me-down from the Middle English '*dudde*', covering of cloth, which also produced 'dudsman' which first described a pedlar hawking materials and haberdashery and later came to mean a scarecrow.

**DUFFER:** *An inefficient or useless person; an old fogey.*

This was built on 'duff' and first denoted a man trading in sub-standard merchandise. The Scottish word '*duffar*' has probably given 'duffer' a helping hand to its current meaning.

**DUKES:** *Hands or fists.*

Possibly from the rhyming slang 'Duke of Yorks' = forks, long used for 'hands', as in 'fork out', to pay. It may, on the other hand, be an allusion to the Marquis (Duke) believed to be responsible for the QUEENSBERRY RULES, or it may have arisen from the Romany '*dook*', which referred to the hand when being 'read'.

**DUMMY RUN:** *A rehearsal, a try-out.*

When the British Navy holds trial runs of torpedoes, these are fitted with false, or dummy, warheads to maintain trim.

**DUN:** *To importune for the repayment of a debt.*

The origin is in some doubt, but probably either a variant of 'din', terrible noise, or a play on the now obsolete 'dun', to make threatening noises, based on the Old Norse '*duna*', thunder, the allusion being, in both cases, to the noise created by the bailiff's pounding on the debtor's door. There is also an intriguing suggestion that there may be a link with 'Dunkirk', which was used of old for a pirate or chivvying raider since many privateers in the opening years of the seventeenth century sailed from that port to relieve English merchantmen of their cargoes. In addition, many believe the term to be an eponymous one inspired by Joseph Dun of Lincoln (and several other towns and cities), who thrived during the reign of Henry VII (1457–1509) and was allegedly a bailiff and debt-collector of such verve that he earned national acclaim; however, there are no written contemporary references to him, nor did the term appear until the opening of the seventeenth century. In fact, the OED gives one of the earliest quotes (1656) which declares the word to be 'lately taken up by fancy' and deems it necessary to explain its meaning. The only eponymous origin that makes sense is the possibility that 'John Dun' might have appeared on writs of debt in the same way that JOHN DOE once did on early legal documents when the miscreant's real name was unknown or his identity needed to be kept secret.

**DUNCE:** *A blockhead, the dullest pupil in class.*

It is ironic, but this was taken from the name of John Duns Scotus (*c.*1265–1308), one of the most respected scholars and theologians of his time. Born at Duns, near Roxburgh, Scotland, he was known throughout Europe and most universities regarded his writings as standard reference works, until the sixteenth century when they came under fierce attack from Humanitarians and Reformers who dismissed his philosophies as nebulous sophistry and his élitist followers as outmoded thinkers blindly resistant to new ideals. The obstinacy of these disciples, who were called Scotists, Duns men, or Duncers, inspired the use of 'dunce' in academic circles. As for the shape of the dunce's cap this was a sneer at the previously respected apex as worn by many pagan priests and wizards. Most education was imparted by a not entirely impartial Church and for them the shape of hat signifying ignorance was an obvious one.

**DUNDERHEAD:** *A stupid person.*

Certainly of Scottish origin, the actual source of this is unclear. It is perhaps linked with the Scottish '*donner*' – to stun with a severe blow or a loud noise – from the Old Norse '*duna*', to thunder. Alternatively there could be a connection with the Scottish '*redunder*', to overflow, which produced the colloquial '*dunder*', scum rising up and over the side of a vat during the fermentation of liquor. When this was drunk by the less fastidious distillery workers of the seventeenth century, it gave rise to decidedly irrational behaviour and a convincing parallel exists in the origin of BARMY.

**DUNSTABLE:** *Plain, direct speech.*

This is an ellipsis of 'as plain as the road to Dunstable', the British town in Bedfordshire. Lying some thirty miles to the north-west of London, it is connected to the capital by part of the old Watling Road which, being a Roman road running straight and true from one conurbation to the other, is easy for the traveller to follow.

**DUTCH:** *Inferior or unacceptable.*

Centuries of animosity between England and The Netherlands caused by their rivalry for maritime supremacy resulted in the birth of a number of expressions using 'Dutch' in this way. For example, the 'Dutch disease' was a sexually transmitted disease, taking 'Dutch leave' meant leaving without paying one's host the normal courtesies, 'doing the Dutch' was committing suicide, and so forth. Similar expressions still in use speak for themselves: Dutch uncle, Dutch courage, Dutch treat, Dutch auction, Dutch bargain, Dutch comfort, Dutch gold. England's interminable squabbling with France, too, created parallel expressions using 'French' in the same way.

**DYED IN THE WOOL:** *Stubbornly fixed in attitude.*

The formative woollen trade was plagued by the impermanence of the dyes to which garments were subjected. They then discovered that, if the wool was dyed before being made up, the colouring had a far better chance of remaining fixed and stable.

# E

**EAR-MARKED:** *Set aside for a purpose.*

A monogrammed metal clip is fixed into the ears of cattle or sheep to show who owns them.

**EARS ARE BURNING:** *You are being discussed in absence.*

From the old belief that angels hold blazing torches to the ears of the one under discussion; if the left ear burns, the talk is uncomplimentary and the subject should bite his little finger whereupon the slanderer will bite his tongue and be unable to continue.

**EAT CROW:** *To endure enforced humiliation.*

The expression is said to come from an undoubtedly apocryphal incident of the Anglo–American War of 1812 when, during a cease-fire, a bored American soldier, who went hunting, strayed behind the British lines and shot a crow. A British officer, alerted by the shot, approached; for reasons known only to the inventor of the tale, he was unarmed, but managed to get hold of the American's gun by dint of flattering his markmanship and fine weapon, which was then given him to inspect. He promptly turned it upon its owner, forcing him to take a bite of the crow to punish him for infringing British territory, after which – and this strains credulity even further – he allegedly returned the gun to the American who, not to be outdone, forced *him* to eat the rest of the bird.

**EAT DOG FOR ANOTHER:** *To do another's dirty work in return for payment.*

Mainly American usage and stems from pow-wows between early settlers and Red Indians. Dog, or more usually, puppy, was considered a delicacy by the Amerindians, but a white settler, presented with such food at a meeting, could not bring himself to eat it, and, to avoid a refusal offensive to his hosts, adopted a custom of placing a dollar in the dish and passing it on to the Indian next to him, who would pocket the dollar and eat the dog. It is probably safe to assume that the Indians themselves came up with this doubly beneficial idea.

**EAT HUMBLE PIE:** *To abase oneself.*

Originally 'eat umble pie', 'umble' was rooted in the Latin '*lumbulus*', the diminutive of '*lumbus*', a loin, and properly signified offal, particularly of deer. After a hunt, the lord and his guests dined off venison while lesser mortals were served umble pie, which, in a way, demeaned them, hence the shift from 'umble' to 'humble'.

**EAVESDROP:** *To listen secretly to the private conversation of others.*

Originally 'eavesdrip' which described the area around a medieval dwelling overshadowed by the extended eaves, an ideal place for clandestine listeners to lurk.

**ECONOMICAL WITH THE TRUTH:** *Deceitful.*

Edmund Burke in his *Letters on a Regicide Peace* (1796) wrote: 'Falsehood and delusion are allowed in no case whatsoever. But . . . there is an *economy* of truth . . . a sort of temperance, by which a man speaks the truth with reason that he may continue to speak it longer.' In 1942, a Foreign Office memo written by Sir William Strang referred to the Czechoslovak president-in-exile, Edvard Benes, as being 'economical with the truth', so the expression was by no means new when the Press pounced upon it as if it were on 17 November 1986 when it was used by the British Cabinet Secretary, Sir Robert Armstrong, during the *Spycatcher* trial in Australia. In the Supreme Court of New South Wales, the British Government was trying to prevent the publication in Australia of the book by the disaffected former British Intelligence Officer, Peter Wright. Under cross-examination by defence counsel Malcolm Turnbull, Sir Robert, accused of making misleading statements in writing, defended himself by stating that he had, perhaps, been 'economical with the truth'. Sir Robert had in fact prefaced his comment in a rather wry tone with, 'As someone once said', adding when the ripples of laughter had faded: 'It's not very original, I'm afraid.' And, how right he was. Nevertheless, all these examples rest on a misunderstanding, or a ridiculing, of the theological application in which 'economy' was considered synonymous with 'dispensation' describing an administration of events by God. For example, St. John Chrysostom, or St John the Golden-mouthed (345–407) discusses in his writings the deception practised by Jacob on his aged, near-blind father to supplant Esau, referring to it not as a fraud, but as an economy orchestrated by God. Later European writers, however, notably Voltaire (1694–1778), ridiculed such usage as sophistic juggling and brought the expression into disrepute.

**EGG ON:** *To incite.*

A corruption of the Old Norse '*eggja*', an edge, and so means to edge someone further on into action.

**EGG ON YOUR FACE:** *The embarrassment caused by the revelation of an error.*

A person is often unaware of the tell-tale signs on his face of a recently eaten egg – until someone puts him wise.

**EGGS ARE EGGS, AS SURE AS:** *With no doubt whatsoever.*

This is based on the old mathematics maxim 'as sure as x is x'.

**EIGHTY-SIX:** *To remove, kill or render insensible.*

American catering staff in the 1920s used a number code to convey messages quickly and, sometimes, secretly. 'Eighty-six' initially meant 'we have run out of that', but in barman's jargon it came to signify a drunken customer who was not to be served with more. The choice of the number could well have been dictated by the fact that it rhymes with 'nix', nothing.

**ELEVENTH HOUR:** *The very last minute.*

In Matthew 20, an owner hired men progressively later and later in the day to work on his land, some at the break of day, some at the third, then the sixth, the ninth and finally the eleventh hour. When all were paid the same amount, those who had toiled longest complained about those who had started eleven hours later.

**EMBER DAYS:** *Erroneously, the last years of life or a dynasty.*

Properly the title of a group of four Christian festivals fixed by the Council of Placentia (1095) to occur on the Wednesday, Friday and Saturday following the first Sunday of Lent; Whitsun; Holy Cross Day (14 September) and St Lucia's Day (13 December) The festivals take their collective name from the Old English 'ymbrene', a circuit, since together they run the course of the year. The associations with the ashes of penitence, most notably at Lent, became mixed in the popular mind with the image of dying coals and this led to the misapplication of the expression.

**EMINENCE GRISE:** *A shadowy figure exercising power in the background.*

The French for Grey Eminence, this was the nickname given to Cardinal Richelieu's confidant and counsellor, the rather Machiavellian Francois Leclerc du Tremblay (1577–1638); also known as Père Joseph, he was a Capuchin monk who wore grey robes. The head of Richelieu's highly efficient spy networks, Tremblay wielded considerable influence over the decisions of the Cardinal who, as Louis XIII's Chief Minister, completely dominated the government of France from 1624 until his death in 1642.

**END IS A-WAGGING:** *The end of the job is in sight.*

Sailors in the British Navy spent much of their time hauling in lines etc. The job of dragging in a heavy cable was almost complete when the loose end rose out of the water and waggled about.

**ENTER THE LISTS:** *To become involved in active participation.*

'List' was anciently used for a strip of land used for a jousting competition, and any knight who rode onto that area indicated his intention to fight.

**ESPRIT D'ESCALIER:** *Thinking of the perfect conversational riposte when the opportunity for using it is past.*

Adopted from the French in

which the proper form is '*l'esprit d'escalier*', this translates as 'the wit of the staircase'. All society salons of eighteenth/nineteenth century Paris were located on upper levels; the ground floors mainly taken up by concierge accommodation and laundry facilities etc. Thus, anyone flouncing out of a salon in high dudgeon would likely be on the stairs on his way back to the street before thinking of the ideal riposte to the jibe that occasioned their leaving in the first place.

**ET TU, BRUTE?:** *Classic riposte to treachery.*

Allegedly the last words of Julius Caesar, this is instead the invention of playwrights. Suetonius, the Roman historian who flourished in the first half of the second century, recorded the details of the killing only a few years after the event. He wrote: 'Caesar did not utter a sound after Casca's blow had drawn a groan from him' and Casca struck first. Another allied myth, fostered by Shakespeare to mention but one, was that the assassination happened in the Capitol, whereas Caesar was stabbed, rather ironically, at the foot of a statue of Pompey in a room sometimes used as a meeting place by the Senate.

**EUREKA, more properly, HEUREKA:** *An exclamation announcing a discovery.*

'*Heureka!*' is Greek for 'I have found it!'- and the usage has its origins in the following story. When King Hiero II of Syracuse received a crown he had commissioned to be made out of gold provided by the court, he suspected that the goldsmith had substituted silver for some of the gold, and asked Archimedes to prove whether this was the case or not. To ponder the problem of establishing the bulk of irregularly-shaped objects, the mathematician went to relax in a bath, where the displacement factor of his own body allegedly sparked off and formed the basis of Archimedes' principle. The story goes that, staggered by the simplicity of the idea, he ran through the streets shouting 'Heureka!' He used his theory to prove that the goldsmith had indeed cheated, so he too lost his head over the principle, but in a far more literal fashion.

**EVEN BREAK:** *An equal chance.*

From the world of live hare-coursing, referring to the fact that the dogs are not handicapped, but are released (allowed to break) at the same time. The expression 'to break even' is also connected, in that one who breaks even neither gains nor loses but is back to where he started.

**EVEN STEVENS/STEPHENS:** *Quits, on a par, especially financially.*

Apart from the fact that it trips nicely off the tongue, the name would appear to have been chosen for its similarity to '*stuiver*', a small Dutch coin known in English as a 'stiver', and, in sixteenth-century English, 'stiver' came to mean any trifling amount of exchange. From this, 'Stephen' was chosen as slang for money in general.

**EX PEDE HERCULEM:** *To deduce the whole from one insignificant piece of information.*

The Latin for 'Hercules from his foot', this was born of the tale that Pythagoras calculated the height of the hero from the known size of his foot.

**EXCEPTION PROVES THE RULE:** *The unusual tests the accepted.*

From the Latin '*exceptio probat legem*', the word 'prove' is here used in its all but redundant sense of 'test the validity, or the quality, of'. Another example of this is 'the proof of the pudding is in the eating'.

**EYE-OPENER:** *A revelation that shocks.*

Originally, this was slang for the first drink of the day intended to shock the system into action.

**EYE-WASH:** *Humbug, deliberate deception.*

This was used in mid nineteenth-century British military slang to describe a cosmetic cover-up; for example, a first-class parade could, as it were, wash over the eyes of a senior officer and blind him to any existing practical problems.

# F

**FABIAN TACTICS:** *Cautious, delaying tactics.*

The Roman, Quintus Fabius Maximus, headed the army sent to deal with the Carthaginian invasion led by Hannibal. He eschewed formal combat, engaging instead in what would now be known as guerrilla tactics, constantly manoeuvring Hannibal into hilly terrain where his cavalry was useless. These were by no means standard Roman military tactics, and he was strongly criticised by the Senate whose members dubbed him 'Cunctator', delayer. His policy, however, proved sound; Hannibal's army disintegrated, he was defeated, and Fabius Maximus retained as a title of honour the nickname originally intended as a slur.

**FACE THE MUSIC:** *To accept the worst consequences of one's actions.*

Deriving from the ceremony in which an officer being cashiered was required to stand facing the drum squad whilst the reasons for his disgrace were read out to the regiment, his uniform defaced and his sword broken. *See also:* DRUM OUT.

**FACE VALUE:** *Apparent, or stated value.*

The self-evident meaning was probably reinforced by the fact that certain currencies and negotiable instruments have a value shown on them, but can command a different price on the open market at times.

**FAG:** (1) *A cigarette.* There is most probably a connection with 'fag' (remnant, or flap hanging loose), as a cigarette does from the mouth of an uncultivated smoker; certainly, when cigarettes were introduced in the 1850s, they were despised as lower-class by the cigar-smoking gentry. Again, there could be a link with 'fag end' (short piece cut from a rope) or 'FAGGOT' (substitute for a cigar). It has also been suggested that there is a connection with the English dialect '*vag*' (turf or peat for burning). (2) *Anything exhausting or boring.* This is probably a product of 'fag' in its earlier meaning of 'to droop', as does the exhausted person. (3) *A junior schoolboy whom the British public school system compels to undertake menial tasks for older pupils.* Although this is generally accepted to be simply an allusion to the boy's getting fagged out (See 2), or droopy with exhaustion, one cannot ignore the possible influence of (4) and the not wholly unjustified suspicion that certain young fags were used as such. The purely military application of 'FAGGOT' could also be involved since the fag is a substitute and undertakes tasks the senior would otherwise have to perform himself. (4) *An effeminate male homosexual.* See FAGGOT.

**FAGGOT** (1) *Effeminate male homosexual.* The origin of this word, which is often abbreviated to '*fag*', is obscure, but perhaps the most convincing theory, since the expression almost certainly grew up in America, is that it derived from the Yiddish '*faygele*' (literally a little bird, but understood to mean 'homosexual'). Nevertheless, in the seventeenth century, 'faggot' held, as one of its many meanings, a man who took another's place in the muster of a regiment and became his substitute for the purpose of military service. Not only could this have influenced the public schoolboy '*fag*' who worked on behalf of another, but it could have transferred to the homosexual partner who became a substitute woman. (2) *A bundle of sticks or twigs.* This could have a connection with (1) in its military sense, since this faggot was the poor man's substitute for the logs he could not afford. (3) *A concoction of cheap meat.* Again a sort of substitute, this time for pork, being a mix of a pig's internal organs all minced up and compressed.

**FAIL-SAFE:** *Self-operating safety device intended to create an acccident-proof system.*

This was coined just after WW2 during the tension that then prevailed between Russia and America. The American Strategic Air Command used it to describe the system they employed to prevent their bombers' accidentally triggering a third world war; their aircraft took off for a real target with a payload of bombs but with orders to abort and return if Command did not confirm their mission before they reached their destination.

**FAIR CRACK OF THE WHIP:** *An equal share.*

In nineteenth-century naval slang 'whip' denoted money collected from every member of the mess in order to buy extra drink for a special occasion. The usage arose either from the speed with which the collecter completed his task or to the methods employed to extract the necessary funds. Naturally each man who had contributed felt it only right that he received a fair share of the drink purchased. Should a member of the mess be retiring or transferred, the money for a farewell round of drinks would be extracted by a whip, hence the modern whip-round to buy the farewell gift for a colleague.

**FAIR GAME:** *A legitimate target.*

In hunting terminology, this is game that is of age and is targeted during the open season.

**FAIRY:** *Effeminate male homosexual.*

One of the many terms of insult to shift from women to homosexuals, this was sarcastically applied in the nineteenth century to ugly old women who insisted on exaggerating the insult paid them by nature by highlighting their facial short-comings with much rouge and powder. It is possible that this particular word was chosen in allusion to the atrocious parodies of women appearing on the pantomime stage and the like, whereon most fairy godmother characters were undertaken by men in DRAG and grotesque make-up. This would have re-inforced the first shift in application which was to androgynes, especially if getting on in years and starting to look a mite pathetic.

**FALL FOUL OF:** *To clash with.*

One ship is said to fall foul of another if the preceding vessel is slower and there is no room to pass it, in for example narrow straits. The anchor too is 'fouled' if it becomes entangled in its own cable. Incidentally, a fouled anchor for some unfathomable reason was for a long time the device of the Lord High Admiral of Britain and, since the Queen assumed that office in 1964, now serves as the emblem on her personal flag.

**FALL BY THE WAYSIDE:** *To lose the capacity to finish and drop out.*

In the parable of the sower, Luke 8:5–8, some of the seed fell by the wayside and was eaten up by birds.

**FALL GUY:** *A dupe or scapegoat.*

From America where criminals 'take a fall' when sentenced, so the above properly alludes to one who is framed.

**FALL IN WITH:** *To join company with.*

This follows the meaning of the military command 'Fall in': take your place and line up in the ranks.

**FALL ON STONY GROUND:** *To fail through lack of appreciation.*

From the same parable as FALL BY THE WAYSIDE. Some of the seed died through lack of nourishment in the soil.

**FALL OUT:** *To quarrel.*

After the military command 'Fall out', the orderly ranks break up and each man goes his own way.

**FAN:** *A devotee or enthusiastic admirer.*

This term almost certainly started life as a contraction of 'fanatic'. It was first noted in English in 1682, some time after which it disappeared, only to be re-imported in the late nineteenth century from America where it had remained in continuous use thanks to English settlers. There is, however, an alternative theory which sees the origin in 'fancy': 'The Fancy', mainly used today to describe pigeon-fanciers, was applied in the nineteenth century to the adherents of any sport. The earlier appearance of 'fan', however, defeats this; examples of 'The Fancy' as late as 1873, quoted in the OED, were still being put in inverted commas, and one as late as 1889 felt the need to explain its meaning. One of the 1682 examples of 'fan' is spelt 'phann', and from this some argue that it must indeed come from 'fancy' which in earlier times was spelt 'phansey' or 'phansie', being a contraction of 'fantasy' or 'phantasy' from the Greek '*phantazein*' – to make visible. In one of its earliest appearances in 1533, 'fanatic' was spelt 'phanatik'.

**FANDANGLE:** *Elaborate nonsense or foolery.*

This is probably based on '*fandango*', the Spanish name for one of their elaborate dances which, in the eyes of some British at any rate, may appear to be foolishly extravagant. The spelling could well have been influenced by 'new-fangled'.

**FANNY:** *Vagina or buttocks.*

Possibly the origin lies in the Naval 'fantail' which describes the fanned out overhang of a ship's stern, which would fit with both the American usage for buttocks and the English for female genitalia. After all, the two are close together and such terms as 'arse' and 'tail' are widely used for 'CUNT' and, indeed, for the act of sexual union itself. The origin, though, is disputed; some relate it to John Cleland's *Memoirs of a Woman of Pleasure* (1748–49), popularly referred to as *Fanny Hill*, which recounts some pretty torrid sessions, and some see a connection with SWEET FANNY ADAMS.

**FARM OUT:** *To delegate to others something for which one is responsible.*

The word 'farm' has changed so much that this expression is the only widely used example of its original meaning. The first 'farmers' bought the tax-collecting concessions for various areas from the Crown and then set about collecting more in taxes than they had paid for the concession. 'Farm' is derived from the Latin '*firma*', fixed payment, and only in the sixteenth century did the word start on its march to its current application through its use to describe a tract of land leased out at a fixed rent.

**FAZE:** *To perturb or discompose.*

Based on the Old English '*fysian*', to drive away, this term in the various forms of 'feeze', 'pheeze', 'feise' and 'veese' was in common use in England from as early as the ninth century. Although by the eighteenth century it had largely become redundant in England save for limited rural use, it travelled to America with early settlers, and survived there. Though regarded by many as a modern Americanism, its reappearance in England is a fine example of a term's surviving only in its adoptive country to be reimported much later.

**FEEL AS IF SOMEONE HAS JUST WALKED OVER YOUR GRAVE:** *Uttered after an involuntary shudder.*

An ancient superstition holds that the site of one's death and/or burial is pre-ordained and that if another person walks across that plot wherever it may be then the fated occupant will momentarily experience the shiver of death.

**FEEL THE PINCH, TO:** *To suffer financial stricture.*

This suggests being unable to afford to replace shoes that have become uncomfortable.

**FEEL YOUR OATS, TO:** *To get frisky.*

Such a diet given a horse can produce a rather ebullient demeanour.

**FEET OF CLAY:** *Unsuspected weaknesses in an admired character.*

In the Book of Daniel 2:31–41; Nebuchadrezzar dreamt of a mighty figure which had a head of gold, torso and arms of silver, belly and thighs of brass, legs of iron and feet made partly of iron, partly of clay. A stone struck the feet and the whole figure collapsed.

**FEISTY:** *Small but spirited.*

The now redundant 'fist' or 'fyest' – to break wind – was based on the Middle High German '*visten*' meaning the same and, in turn, inspired by the Latin '*fistula*' – a pipe. Most animals, man included, get flatulent when agitated, and a horse in an animated frame of mind is a fine example. In Southern American dialect, '*fice*' developed for a small but aggressive lap-dog on which the owner could put the blame for his farts.

**FELL SWOOP:** *One decisive, possibly ruthless, action.*

Properly applies to the sudden, savage attack of a bird of prey when it goes into its stoop. The Middle English '*fell*' meant cruel and vicious, and is from the Late Latin '*fello*', traitor, whence also 'felon' and the use of 'felo de se', a kind of Anglo-Latin for a cruel, criminal act against oneself – suicide.

**FELLOW-TRAVELLER:** *Someone in sympathy with the greater part of a political ideology, especially Communism.*

This is really a translation of the Russian '*popuchik*' which was used by Trotsky to describe one who, whilst not entirely in tune with a point of view, was sufficiently sympathetic to the cause to go most of the way down the road. In America, the Macarthyite witch-hunt of the 1950s made much use of the term when describing those suspected of being 'in the closet' Communists, but it was a later development of the word which really took off in the form of 'sputnik' which means 'one who travels the same path'.

**FENCE:** *Dealer in stolen goods.*

The origin lies in the ordinary use of 'fence' for a defensive boundary and is a play on the fact that the dealer forms such between the police and the end-purchaser who remains ignorant of the identity of the thief.

**FIASCO:** *A complete failure, an atrocious performance.*

Although it is known that the term is taken directly from the Italian '*fiasco*', a flask or bottle, the reason for this application both in English and Italian is obscure. It has been suggested that it is an ellipsis of '*far fiasco*', to make a bottle, since, in the Italian/Venetian glass-blowing industry, abortive attempts at fine items were set aside to cool and sold off as wine flasks in the local taverns. Be this or no, the word surfaced in eighteenth-century Italian theatrical jargon to describe a poor stage performance, at which the jeering crowd chanted 'Olà, Olà fiasco', and it was with theatrical connections that it first appeared in early-mid nineteenth-century English.

**FINE/PRETTY KETTLE OF FISH:** *An awkward, messy state of affairs.*

An ironic reference to the old Scottish border term for a picnic centred on newly caught salmon cooked on the spot in a large cauldron known as a 'kettle'. The orchestral timpano is popularly called a kettle-drum because its shape resembles that of the cauldron. Such affairs were invariably rowdy and accompanied by much drunken revelry.

**FIT AS A FIDDLE:** *In extremely good shape or state of health.*

In the seventeenth century when the expression and the instrument itself rose to popularity the term 'fit' more usually meant suitable or pleasing but the issue is further clouded by the fact that 'fiddle' could also then denote the player who was perhaps perceived as extremely hale and hearty for all the general leaping about and cavorting in time to the music issued.

**FIDDLE:** *To swindle.*

This emerged in the middle of the nineteenth century and could well have been inspired by 'fiddle' as used by the Stock Exchange to describe a specially low commission paid by a jobber to a broker to handle a transaction carrying no risk. The 'tic-tac' enacted on the Floor for this was the sawing of one extended index finger against the other. In turn, the inspiration for this might have been the older expression 'fiddler's money' – small change.

**FIDDLE WHILE ROME BURNS, TO:** *To indulge whims whilst serious issues are afoot.*

This is born of the myth recounting how Nero played such an instrument with a nonchalant air as the city blazed away for over a week. The yarn is palpably untrue if only for the fiddle being an instrument of sixteenth-century development. At virtually every road intersection of the city there was a noble family's tomb or memorial. As these would have to be flattened for road-widening schemes Nero's plans for the wholesale redevelopment of Rome were thwarted. To the criminally insane the solutions to complex issues are always blissfully simple, so Nero torched his own capital but made sure he was away from the city at the time. It does seem fairly certain that he mounted his own private stage and entertained his guests with lyre music and songs about the destruction of Troy whilst the city burnt on the horizon. Whatever the truth, Rome got her new streets; while the Christians got the blame for the inferno and the lions got a good feed.

**FIDDLESTICKS:** *Nonsense.*

Whilst this could refer simply to the cheapness and simplicity of the bow as opposed to the instrument, it is not beyond the realms of possibility that the slang usage of the same term as a synonym for penis gave rise to the modern usage.

**FIELD DAY:** *A day of unusual activity and success.*

This alludes to the open days of military parades and splendid manoeuvres designed to impress visiting dignitaries.

**FIFTH COLUMN:** *Spies and saboteurs operating inside enemy territory.*

General Emilo Mola coined this phrase in 1936 during the Spanish Civil War when, just before advancing on Madrid, he was asked if he felt his army was up to the task. He replied that it was, for in addition to the four columns in his army, he had a fifth column already secretly working inside the city.

**FIFTH MAN:** *An as yet unidentified, highly placed traitor.*

An expression created during the never-ending aftermath surrounding the Burgess–Maclean espionage scandal of the early-mid 1950s, in which Kim Philby and Anthony Blunt were also deeply involved. The term, now used for any 'mole', came into being because of the continuing speculation that there was yet another highly placed British traitor. The expression no doubt owes much to the earlier 'fifth column' and much also to the numbering of batsmen in cricket, as does the famous fictional Third Man.

**FIFTH WHEEL:** *An unwelcome person or thing.*

This harks back to the nuisance of having to carry a spare wheel for a coach. Being both large and cumbersome, the wheel took up a great deal of room, had to be strapped at the rear, and unlashed and re-lashed whenever anything was required from the storage area behind it.

**FIG UP, TO:** *To make an article for sale more attractive.*

This 'fig' is an old horse-traders corruption of 'fake', itself originally a term of the same trade and based on the German '*fegen*', to sweep or clean up. In bygone days faking a horse involved tricks such as filing its teeth into a more youthful profile and making most improper use of the spice ginger as explained in GINGER UP.

**FIGHT SHY OF:** *To avoid.*

In the world of boxing, a boxer fights shy if he keeps his distance from his opponent.

**FIGUREHEAD:** *Any nominal leader.*

Obvious reference to the carved figure – almost invariably of the female form – set at the prow of a ship and intended to represent some power of speed of fortune, but which is nothing but a craven image. The reason for the favouring of the female form is as ancient as it is repugnant. Whilst sailors regarded the presence of women on board as unlucky they also believe that the sight of the naked female body would calm rough seas. Countless unfortunate women were kidnapped and held below decks, subjected to repeated rape and only saw the light of day when stripped naked and lashed to the prow during a storm. Mercifully, carvings gradually became accepted as being equally effective as the real thing.

**FILCH:** *To steal, especially in a petty way.*

The etymology is obscure but there may be a clue in the fact that, in the early seventeenth century, a 'filch' was a kind of bent stick which beggars and vagabonds used for hooking things out of hedgerows – and houses.

**FILIBUSTER:** *To obstruct legislation by making excessively long, irrelevant speeches and by insisting on the observance of formality and procedure to the last detail.*

The Dutch '*vrijbuiter*' – freebooter, i.e. one who roams freely looking for booty – first made its appearance in sixteenth-century English as 'flibutor', later changing to 'filibuster' through the re-importation of the French '*flibustier*' and, in the mid-nineteenth century, the Spanish '*filibustero*'. In America the political application came into being in the latter half of the nineteenth century, apparently due to 'filibusters' being used to describe either the American mercenaries who followed Narcisco Lopex (1798–1851) on his private invasion of Cuba in 1850, or those who went with William Walker (1824–60) on his abortive attempt to capture Nicaragua in 1856, probably because of the harassing guerilla tactics employed by these forces.

**FILL SOMEONE IN:** *To beat someone up.*

This was originally a low, macho vulgarism meaning to make a woman pregnant; because it smacked of prowess the expression drifted towards its present sense and, its original crudity forgotten, gained a level of respectability.

**FILTHY LUCRE:** *Perjoratively, riches, money.*

The source for this expression, which many assume to be modern slang, is biblical; the text of Timothy 3:2–3 discusses the qualitites required of a bishop saying, *inter alia*, that he 'must not be given to wine, nor striker [brawler], nore greedy of filthy lucre' – that obtained by bribes. This association with 'filthy' had condemned 'lucre' to the DEMI-MONDE of English, while its brother 'lucrative' enjoys the sunshine of respectability.

**FIN DE SIECLE:** *Decadent.*

The French for 'the end of the century', this was used of the closing years of the nineteenth century which were marked by what was seen by the Conservative Establishment as a decline in morals and attitudes.

**FINAL SOLUTION:** *The attempted genocide of the Jews by Nazi Germany.*

This was the chilling phrase, almost certainly dreamed up by Hitler, that enabled the paperwork setting up the plan to flow without giving away the enormity of the horror. On 31 July 1941, Goering wrote the following memo to Heydrich: 'I herewith commission you to carry out all preparations with regard to . . . the total solution of the Jewish question . . . I further commission you to submit to me as soon as possible a draft showing the administrative, material and financial measures already taken for the execution of the intended final solution of the Jewish question.' The expression has been applied in other theatres of war in which such wholesale slaughter has occurred, but it was gortesquely ironic that, in a 1988 televised discussion between Israelis and Palestinians, one minor politician talked of the need to move towards a 'final solution' to the Palestinian question.

**FINE FETTLE:** *Excellent condition.*

From the Old English '*fetel*', girdle, the allusion is to a warrior all girded up and ready for battle.

**FINE ITALIAN HAND:** *An indication of* SKULDUGGERY.

This first described the highly distinctive writing style of the Vatican scribes. At one time, the Vatican's reputation as a hot-bed of vice, murder and intrigue was justly deserved.

**FINGER IN EVERY PIE:** *Many diverse business interests.*

This could simply refer to a bakery supervisor's having a little to do with every item of production, but, since the expression usually implies interference, it could stem from a more literal criticism of one who sticks his finger into everyone else's pie to see what it tastes like.

**FINGERS AND THUMBS, ALL:** *Awkward and clumsy.*

A corruption of the original 'all my fingers are thumbs', which makes more sense, all of us having fingers and thumbs anyway.

**FINK:** *An unpleasant, treacherous person.*

At the close of the nineteenth century in America this appeared in Trades Union jargon for a 'blackleg', and is probably an amalgam of 'fucking' and 'Pink' arising out of the Homestead Steel Strike of 1892 during which the management hired large numbers of Pinkertons to protect the non-union strike-breakers they had shipped in. This theory does not go unchallenged; some point to the German '*fink*', finch – old German university slang for an egg-head who stayed out of the macho drinking and duelling set – but the first explanation must remain the most likely unless a viable link can be established between Prussian students and American labour disputes.

**FIRE AND BRIMSTONE:** *Hell and damnation.*

From the Old English '*bryne*', burning, brimstone was the old name for sulphur, now essentially obsolete save in certain entomological designations, and in the above which is still heard in relation to pulpit rantings of the worst kind.

**FIRST BLUSH:** *On the first impression.*

Derived from the Middle English '*blusche*', glance or glimpse, but there has been a perhaps inevitable confusion with 'blush', grow red, which has led to a similar expression 'at first flush'.

**FIRST CHOP:** *The finest quality.*

In China and India a 'chop' is a seal, from the Hindi '*chhap*' – an official seal or product brand. British troops returning from India brought the expression with them.

**FIRST DIBS:** *First turn or choice.*

This is based on 'dibstones', a dialect term for a game, not unlike jacks, once played by children in rural Britain. 'Dib' is most probably a variant of 'dip' in that players had to dip down and snatch up as many dibstones as they could before catching a ball they had previously tossed in the air.

**FIRST MAGNITUDE:** *Of the highest calibre.*

In the world of science, the brightness of stars and the force of earthquakes can be measured on a scale of magnitudes. This adaptation is, for some reason, generally used in a derogatory way, e.g. a traitor of the first magnitude.

**FIRST ORDER:** *Of the best available.*

An elliptic of FIRST (ORDER OF) MAGNITUDE.

**FIRST RATE:** *The very best.*

In the days of the wooden men-of-war the various ships of the Navy were rated by their cannon-power – ships of the First Rate carried over a hundred; Second Rate, between ninety and a hundred; Third Rate, seventy to ninety; Fourth Rate, fifty to seventy; Fifth rate thirty-two to sixty, and Sixth rate less than thirty-two.

**FIRST STRING:** *Leading or important.*

This is an allusion to the favourite or strongest string possessed by an English longbow-man who always carried several back-ups, hence 'second string' and 'extra strings to your bow'.

**FIRST WATER:** *Highest calibre.*

The classification of diamonds refers to the colour or lustre of one of these gems as its 'water'. Like FIRST MAGNITUDE, this too can be tacked on to an unworthy subject e.g. 'a cad of the first water'.

**FISHWIFE:** *Any foul-mouthed woman.*

The cataract of obscenities pouring forth from the mouths of the women of nineteenth-century Billingsgate fish market made these ladies a legend in their own lifetime.

**FIT AS A FIDDLE:** *In the best condition.*

Something of a puzzle, this is perhaps an example of 'fit' meaning pleasing and suitable for its purpose, as a fiddle certainly was.

**FIT THE BILL:** *To be suitable for the purpose.*

This was originally theatrical slang based on the fact that the size of the lettering used for an actor's name on advertising posters was dictated by his status. If a gap was created by the non-availability of one performer, then the name of another of equal calibre would fit neatly into it.

**FIT-UP:** *Fabricated evidence to secure criminal conviction.*

Theatrical jargon, this expression originally described a venue other than a theatre proper at which the company erected collapsible scenery brought with them to create the desired illusion.

**FIZZER:** *A charge, or the punishment resulting from it.*

Of military origin, the actual inspiration for this is unclear though it could simply be that 'on the double' punishments were considered mighty lively. There could, though, be a link to a 'facer', anything daunting, through 'phiz/phizog', a contraction of physiognomy, the slang for a face. Two other expressions would then seem relevant: 'put through your facings' and 'face the music'.

**FLAG DAY:** *A day of organised street collection by a charity.*

In days not so long distant, those who made a donation had a miniature flag pinned on their clothing and, although this has now been replaced by the safer use of stickers, the name remains.

**FLAK:** *Harsh criticism.*

This acronym, built on the German '*Fliegerabwehrkanone*', anti-aircraft gun, and used in military slang for the missiles fired from it, came into general usage in 1940 though it had been known in military and armament circles for at least two years before that.

**FLAKE, A:** *An eccentric or pleasantly insane individual.*

A transfer from turn-of-the-century parlance in which 'flake' was cocaine – an elliptic of 'snow-flake' in allusion to the whiteness of the powder. Those who made over enthusiastic use of the drug were 'flaked-out', hence the modern meaning of 'to collapse with exhaustion'.

**FLANNEL:** *Flattery intended to blind or persuade.*

The old printing trade used 'flannel' to describe the colouring on, for example, a letter-head, which was broken up into a textured finish as if it had been dabbed with an ink-soaked flannel. Prententious shopkeepers of the mid-nineteenth century put such headings on their letters and invoices, accompanied by scroll-work, bogus coats of arms etc., in an effort to impress their carriage trade who actually considered it gross. Partridge quotes from the 1858 *Ask Mama* by Robert Surtees (1805–64); in this, such an invoice is discussed and dismissed as having 'all the crowns, arms, orders, flourish and flannel peculiar to an aristocratic tradesman'. In addition, of course, the texture of the material itself must have contributed to securing the use of its name in this way.

**FLAP:** *A panic, a fluster.*

Born in early twentieth century British Forces slang, this certainly refers to flags but whether it is a straightforward allusion to their agitation in blustery conditions or to their use in signals before impending action is unclear.

**FLAPPER:** *A young, flighty girl.*

Adopted from the hunting jargon for a young bird, because of its exuberant wing movements, this usage can be compared with 'quail' for a desirable young woman, and the German '*Backfisch*' – flapper. Its application to the 1920s bright young things was aided by their hair bobbed, so that, wing-like, it flapped up and down at the sides and their habit of leaving their galoshes unfastened to flap about. It was said that they took their fashions from the Parisian prostitutes and their mental attitudes from the shallow women featured by Scott Fitzgerald (1896–1940) in his novels.

**FLASH IN THE PAN:** *Initial enthusiasm that comes to nothing.*

The flintlock weapons of yesteryear were notoriously unreliable. When the gun was loaded, a little powder was placed in the priming pan, located to the side of the weapon under the side-hammer. On firing, the hammer fell, the flint sparked, the priming charge ignited the main charge and the gun went off – unless, of course, the process failed, in which case all one got was a useless flash in the priming pan.

**FLAT OUT:** *At top speed.*

This is a hand-me-down for the older 'flat to the boards'; at top speed, an accelerator pedal was pushed down to the car floor which used to be made of wooden boards.

**FLAT SPIN:** *An excited panic.*

An expression from the early days of flying which referred to a pilot's terrible predicament if his aircraft went into a spin of tight circles while remaining on an almost horizontal plane.

**FLAVOUR OF THE MONTH:** *Enjoying transitory popularity.*

Of American origin, this derives from a sales gimmick employed by early twentieth-century ice-cream manufacturers who, every month, dreamed up a new, or one-off, flavour that was pushed hard by the sales force.

**FLEA IN THE EAR:** *A severe rebuke.*

This was first applied to people shaking their head in disbelief after being given distressing news, as if trying to dislodge it – as a dog does with a real flea in its ear. The meaning altered since a severe reprimand also causes distress.

**FLEA MARKET:** *A street market selling second-hand goods.*

This is a translation of the French 'Marche aux Puces', a large nineteenth-century outdoor market in Paris which specialised in second-hand clothes. The poor found it useful but the better off gave it this nickname for obvious reasons.

**FLESHPOTS:** *High living, sensual luxury.*

Exodus 16:3 relates: 'And the Children of Israel said unto them [Moses and Aaron] Would to God we had died by the hand of the Lord in the land of Egypt, when we sat by the fleshpots [pots for cooking meat], and when we did eat bread to the full; for ye have brought us forth into this wilderness, to kill the whole assembly with hunger.' From this, 'the fleshpots of Egypt' became synonymous with easy living; by the eighteenth century, 'of Egypt' had been dropped and the expression had also acquired overtones of sensuality, probably because 'flesh' was thought to mean the pleasures of the flesh. The original problem afflicting the Children of Israel was remedied by 'manna from heaven'.

**FLIBBERTIGIBBET:** *A flighty person.*

A fanciful invention of the sixteenth century which was apparently built on the notion of a flapping tongue spouting gibberish and first applied to empty-headed chatterboxes. In 1549, Hugh Latimer (*c.* 1492–1555), the English preacher and reformer, used the word for a malicious gossip, and in 1603, Samuel Harsnet(t) (d. 1631), in his *Declaration of Egregious Popish Impostures* talked of four demons: 'Fraterretto, Fliberdigibbet, Hoberdidance, Tocobatto'. Shakespeare too used the name for one of the five fiends in *King Lear*.

**FLIM-FLAM:** *To con or deceive.*

An onomatopoeic duplication suggestive of fast talking that is perhaps based on a variety of Scandinavian terms such as '*flamflew*', trinket or bauble, or the Old Norse '*flim*', lampoon, or '*flimta*', to flout.

**FLIP-FLOP:** *A sudden reveral of policy.*

This American usage, which is the equivalent of the English 'U turn', is based on the British meaning of a backwards somersault. It is sometimes used in the States for 'the return trip' e.g. 'catch you on the flip-flop' – see you on the way back.

**FLIP-SIDE:** *Literally or metaphorically, the reverse, especially if second-rate.*

1950s disc jockeys so referred to the 'B' side of a 45 r.p.m. which they played by flipping over the record on the turntable.

**FLOGGING A DEAD HORSE:** *Wasting effort.*

Although the allusion is obvious, it is worth mentioning that the expression took on a specific meaning in the British Navy to describe having a crew that had been paid in advance to sign up and had blued their wages in port before leaving. Both the crew and the period they would have to work without pay were called 'the dead horse'; the men knew that no matter how hard they worked there would be no more money and the officers knew that no matter how they pushed, the men would only work at a barely acceptable pace.

**FLOTSAM AND JETSAM:** *An assortment of odds and ends.*

These words are taken from Maritime Law in which they have far more precise meanings; the former applies to goods found floating at sea after a shipwreck, and the latter to goods washed up on shore after being deliberately thrown overboard to lighten a ship in danger. 'Flotsam' is derived from the Old French '*floter*', to float and 'jetsam' shares its source with 'jettison', coming from the Latin '*iactare*', to throw.

**FLUNKEY:** *An obsequious servant.*

A demeaning varient of 'flankie', which, based on 'flanker' denoted a servant who stood around the side walls of, for example, a banqueting hall, in case his services were required.

**FLY A KITE:** *To raise money by questionable means.*

Specifically, this describes the passing of a cheque with no funds to meet it and issuing another dud cheque to cover the first. The increasing spiral of dishonesty is likened to the dizzying ascent of a kite.

**FLY BLIND:** *To feel your way.*

This was originally used of a pilot navigating his way through fog relying only on his instruments.

**FLY BY THE SEAT OF YOUR PANTS:** *To judge by gut instinct and experience.*

Before the days of sophisticated instrumentation, an experienced pilot gauged the degree of bank and the steepness of climb by the way the centrifugal and gravitational forces slid him about in his seat.

**FLY IN THE FACE OF DANGER:** *To ignore obvious risks.*

Originally said of birds, usually crows, which frequently turn on and mob a bird of prey in an attempt to make it drop its catch.

**FLY IN THE OINTMENT:** *A small but significant flaw.*

Ecclesiastes 10:1 states: 'Dead flies cause the ointment of the apothecary to send forth a stinking flavour: so doth a little folly him that is in reputation for wisdom and honour.'

**FLY OFF THE HANDLE:** *To go suddenly into a violent rage.*

If an axe-head flies off its handle in mid swing, it presents a very real danger to everybody in the immediate vicinity.

**FLY TOO CLOSE TO THE SUN:** *To tempt fate by ignoring a known danger.*

For certain treacherous acts, Daedalus and his son Icarus were imprisoned in the Labyrinth that Daedalus himself had built for Minos. To engineer their escape, Daedalus designed and constructed for each of them a pair of wings made of feathers stuck together with wax. Despite repeated warnings, Icarus insisted on flying too high; the warmth of the sun melted his wax and he fell into the sea and drowned.

**FLYERS:** *Small hand-bills or posters.*

This is an ellipsis of 'flying sheets' which we adopted from the French '*feuilles volantes*' – flying leaves. In the days immediately before the French Revolution of 1789, this was used of the political lampoons and cartoons that circulated under threat of dire penalty, the name arising either from the rapidity with which they were passed or because the distributors, to reduce the risk of arrest, often flung handfuls of them from top floor windows whence they fell to the street like autumn leaves.

**FLY-BLOWN:** *Tainted with flies' eggs.*

At one time, naturalists thought that the group of flies that include the blue and green bottle actually blew their larvae onto meat or carrion, hence also the term 'blowfly'. In the not too distant past, blowflies were used in hospitals to clean infected wounds since the larvae will eat only rotten flesh, shunning healthy tissue.

**FOB OFF:** *Disingenuously to free oneself of an unwanted person or thing.*

Most probably derived from the German '*foppen*', to jeer or dupe, the meaning altering because fobbing off is usually accompanied by a thinly disguised excuse.

**FOGEY, OLD/YOUNG:** *An old dodderer/a twenty-year old already in their fifties.*

As reflected in the American usage of 'foggy bottoms' for a misty, marshy area, 'foggy' on its own meant a marsh or boggy reach in sixteenth and seventeenth century English. Next, and up to the early nineteenth century, the term came to mean bloated or puffed up through eating too much and exercising too little which caused the variant 'fogey' to be adopted by late nineteenth-century military slang to denote an elderly or invalided soldier relegated to garrison or outpost duties to while away what was left of their lives. Relatively recent is the development of 'young fogey', first spotted in the 1980s.

**FOLLOW SUIT:** *To do as others do.*

In bridge, whist and a host of other card games, the rules require that, where possible, each player must play a card in the same suit that led.

**FOOL'S PARADISE:** *A state of illusory happiness.*

The early Church decided that there were areas on the borders of Hell set aside for those who were unfit for Heaven through no fault of their own and who therefore did not deserve to suffer in Hell. Lunatics and simpletons went to this Limbus of Fools, otherwise known as the Paradise for Fools.

**FOOTLING:** *Trifling, of no value.*

This could have come about from the French '*foutre*', originally a vulgarism equivalent to FUCK but still used in expressions like '*se foutre de*' – not to care a damn for.

**FOOTLOOSE AND FANCY FREE:** *Unhampered.*

A sail on which all the restraining ropes at the base (foot) have been slackened off (loosened) flaps about capriciously.

**FOR PETE'S SAKE:** *Cry of exasperation.*

A corruption of 'for pity's sake'.

**FORCE ANOTHER'S HAND:** *To push another into an action he would rather not take.*

In the game of bridge, one player can, through cunning play, force an opponent to lay a card he would rather retain until a more advantageous time.

**FORLORN HOPE:** *An aspiration with no chance of realisation.*

The Old Dutch '*verloren hoop*' literally meant lost troops, and described the first wave of attack usually sent in to test the enemy fire-power; the French equivalent was '*enfants perdus*', lost children. The expression entered sixteenth-century English in the military sense, but the last word changed to 'hope' since the chance of survival for such shock troops was small. In the Navy, the term was further corrupted to 'flowing hope', the allusion being to something floating past out of reach.

**FORTY WINKS:** *A short nap.*

'Winks' is in all probability a play on the Middle English '*winkis*', sleep. The reason for 'forty' can only be guessed at, but it may have something to do with the frequent use of that number in the Bible, e.g. forty days and forty nights, which in turn may have come from Old Mosaic Law, and indeed Greek Law, wherein time limits for the fulfilment of certain obligations, payment of fines, and even terms of imprisonment were set at forty days. Further, under Mosaic Law Jews were forbidden to inflict more than forty lashes on a criminal, so, to avoid any accidental infringement of this, they always stopped at thirty-nine – as was the case in the scourging of Jesus. English law and superstition has inherited this obsession with forty, viz the forty days of quarantine, and the forty days of rain associated with St Swithin.

**FOSSICK ABOUT:** *To rummage or search about for any kind of profit.*

The English dialect 'fossick' meant a troublesome, interfering person and probably owed something to 'fuss'. The Australian mining industry adopted the word and, in that context, it means to work over another's gold mine or waste heap in the hope of picking up the odd nugget.

**FOUR CORNERS OF THE EARTH:** *The furthest flung parts of the planet.*

This may hark back to the old notion that the earth was flat and, no doubt, square. Strangely enough, in science the expression does have a quite specific meaning; they are four areas of the planet which are significantly above the geodetic mean and where the gravitational pull is measureably greater, namely Ireland, an area to the south-east of the Cape of Good Hope, an area between New Guinea and Japan and part of the Peruvian coast.

**FOUR-FLUSHER:** *A cheat or conman.*

In the game of poker, five cards of the same suit constitute a 'flush' and, in certain types of play, four of them may be turned face up. Only a good bluffer can convince the others that his fifth card completes the flush – even if it does not.

**FOUR HUNDRED, THE:** *The upper echelons of society in any American city, but especially in New York.*

Mrs William Astor was giving her annual ball in New York in 1892 and her guest list was restricted by the size of the ballroom to 400. To help her draw it up, she enlisted the aid of Ward McAllister, a social parasite who justified his existence by performing such tasks. He reputedly snorted that there would be no difficulty since there were only 400 people in New York who could possibly consider themselves 'society'.

**FOURTH ESTATE:** *The Press.*

A realm is considered to be made up of three estates: the Lords Spritual, the Lords Temporal and the House of Commons, and, originally, this expression was used to denote any significant power or force outside these; for example, in 1752, Henry Fielding (1707–54), the English novelist and dramatist used it in *The Covent-garden Journal* to decribe the mob. It is, however, impossible to pin-point its application to the Press; it is generally ascribed to Edmund Burke (1729–97), the English man of letters and politician, but there is no supportive evidence for this claim.

**FOURPENNY ONE:** *A swingeing blow.*

The origin is the rhyming slang 'fourpenny bit' = hit. The silver fourpenny bit, coined since 1662 only as Maundy Money, is better known as a groat which, though now proverbially a trifling sum, was in its day moderately valuable. The silver fourpenny-piece coined from 1836–56 was not officially called a groat. It has also been suggested that the expression derives from the payment of four pennies paid in days gone by to the beadle for every beggar he whipped beyond the parish boundary.

**FOXED:** *Puzzled or bewildered.*

Although perceived as alluding to those in such a state being perplexed by the creature's legendary cunning this is not the case as the first noted usage in 1611 was in reference to drunkeness. In the same era are found references to men 'foxing their noses' with drink in allusion to the reddening effect on the organ of over-indulgence, but it is also fair to state that the fox was the symbol of Bacchus, Roman god of wine, and that the presence of his familiars in a vineyard could either guarantee a fine crop or its total failure. This belief is reflected in the Song of Solomon 2:15, a verse which blames the presence of 'little foxes' for the withering of the grapes on the vine. At the end of the day it is but a short step from the seventeenth-century usage to the modern application.

**FRAGGING:** *A very severe reprimand.*

This meaning is a watered down version of the original. During the closing years of the American involvement in the Vietnam war, the word was used to describe the killing by his own men of an American officer unpopular perhaps because he was inefficient or because he was too keen on action. If the former, a *fragmentation* grenade was usually rolled into his tent; if the latter, it was lobbed at him during some action which could then be broken off. The choice of device rendered ballistic tests impossible.

**FRED KARNO'S ARM/CIRCUS:** *A laughably disorganised operation.*

At the opening of the twentieth century, Fred Karno, whose real name was Frederick John Westcott (d. 1941), achieved fame through his vaudeville shows and slapstick comedies. This epithet was originally applied to the 'New Army' of raw recruits, hurriedly raised in Britain for WW1.

**FREELANCE:** *An independent operator.*

Sir Walter Scott (1771–1832), the Scottish novelist, coined this in 1820 to describe a knight with no allegiance to any cause who simply sold his services to the highest bidder.

**FREELOADER:** *A scrounger.*

A sponger does not pay his way, and in the world of transport, freight carried free of charge is called 'freeload'.

**FREEWHEELING:** *Acting or living without constraint.*

The term first appeared in 1899

with the advent of the free-wheel for bicycles which, unlike the previous fixed wheel, allowed the rider to stop pedalling without impeding progress. In the 1930s in America, a similar device was fitted to motor cars making it possible for the driver to 'coast' simply by taking his foot off the accelerator.

**FRENCH LEAVE:** *Depart without notice or permission.*

The use of 'French' as a perjorative originated in the days when the English and the French were traditional enemies and tended to trade insults; the French equivalent of the above is '*filer à l'anglaise*' – take English leave. Other examples of this are the use of 'French disease' for syphilis and 'French letter' for condom, known in France as a '*capote anglaise*'. English hostilities with the Dutch have also affected the language.

**FRESH:** *Cheeky.*

The language of America has been much influenced by the people who emigrated there; this is from the German '*frech*' – insolent.

**FRIG ABOUT:** *Popularly, to mess about.*

Basically a euphemism for 'fuck', and ultimately rooted in the Latin '*fricare*', to rub, 'frig', in the sixteenth century, meant to move in a violent or nervous manner, and because of this, it became, early in that century, synonymous with 'fuck' and 'wank'. It has been suggested, though none too convincingly, that the name of the Norse goddess of love, Frigg, could have helped the term survive.

**FROG IN THE THROAT:** *Sudden attack of hoarseness.*

In the Middle Ages when frogs and toads were feared because of their occult connections, our ancestors lived in dread of there being frog spawn in the water they drank from streams etc., believing that the frogs would then mature within them; they quite seriously thought that this otherwise inexplicable hoarseness with attendant coughing and gagging was due to one such creature coming back out of the stomach and up the throat to escape.

**FROG-MARCH:** *To hustle forward, pinning the arms from behind.*

This properly describes the carrying off of a miscreant, face down, by four people each of whom restrains a limb, thereby giving the offender all the appearance of a captive frog. Today, it is more often applied to what the Americans call the 'bum's rush' i.e. being removed in a running half-nelson.

**FROGS:** *The French.*

Popularly believed to derive from the French prediliction for the consumption of the nether regions of frogs, this does in fact date back to the ancient Frankish Kingdom under the rule of Clovis (466–511). His heraldic device – later assumed by the city of Paris – displayed three golden toads salient, or springing upwards. Tradition has it that Clovis had a heavenly dream in which he saw his toads transmute to lillies of the valley and, whether this be true or no, France acquired the fleur-de-lys. Through their adoption of the toad device, Parisians were nicknamed 'toads' by non-Parisian French, not foreigners. After the French Court had established itself at Versailles the nobility, perhaps harking back to the grandeur of the Frankish kingdom, hijacked the title of 'toad' for themselves and thenceforth slightingly referred to the Parisians as frogs, they being the smaller of the two species – '*Qu'en disent les Grenouilles?*', What do the frogs say?, was the typical way of inquiring after the mood of the city in pre-revolution days. Jean Crapaud, Johnny Toad, long remained a popular nickname for any Frenchman, the influx of whom to New Orleans introduced a new dice game which the locals aptly named Crap's dice, now simply known as craps.

**FROM THE SUBLIME TO THE RIDICULOUS:** *Wild swings in mood or reason.*

Although this is the usual mode of employ the expression actually indicates something far more subtle. The first usage appears in Tom Paine's *Age of Reason* (1794) in the following context: 'The sublime and the ridiculous are often so nearly related that it is difficult to class them separately. One step above the sublime makes the ridiculous, and one step above the ridiculous makes the sublime again.' Thus it is evident that the usage is far more akin to sentiments such as the dividing line between genius and insanity being disturbingly fine rather than results diametrically opposed to each other.

**FROM THE WRONG SIDE OF THE TRACKS, TO BE:** *To come from a humble background.*

In the typical layout of a nineteenth-century American Western town the railroad also formed a social boundary with the stockyards and less desirable areas to one side and the middle-class section on the other. Invariably this was the more western side since in the northern hemisphere the winds are predominantly westerlies and thus the smell of cattle and slaughter was kept where it belonged.

**FRONT AND CENTRE:** *A call to those about to be punished.*

In most armies, a sergeant uses this phrase to order a miscreant out of the ranks to a position centre front of the assembly to receive his reprimand.

**FRONT FOR SOMEONE:** *To act for one who wishes to remain unidentified.*

In nineteenth-century criminal slang, this described the action of a pickpocket's accomplice who stood in front of him, almost obscuring him from the view of the victim.

**FRUIT:** *Male homosexual.*

In the 1930s this applied to a promiscuous young woman regarded as 'easy pickings'. The notorious promiscuity of young male homosexuals in pre-AIDS days caused the shift within the GAY community itself. By the 1950s/'60s it was being directed from without as a blanket term for any ostentatious homosexual.

**FUCK:** *To copulate.*

The origin is obscure and perhaps there is no one single source, rather a blend of influences. The German '*ficken*', to strike or penetrate, will have been of significant influence (in current German it means 'fuck'), although 'fuck' cannot have derived unaided therefrom. There is some conjecture that there was a blending with the French '*foutre*', to fuck, which, it is postulated, produced the assumed mid-point of 'fucken' but no trace of this word has been found. However, there is no proof of this, and there could well have been a union between 'ficken' and the no-doubt related Old Norse '*fikja*', to move about relentlessly through violent emotional stimulation. The related '*fikjask*', to desire passionately, ultimately produced 'fidget' in English. These Norse terms also inspired the Middle English '*fike*' which, as well as retaining all its applications of agitated movement, could also mean 'to fawn or deceive'; 'deceiving a woman' frequently has sexual connotations. Possibly involved is yet another 'fike', totally unrelated in that it derives from the Latin '*ficus*', fig, which was used in fourteenth-century England for the fruit and for many centuries throughout Europe 'fig' has been synonymous with both fuck and CUNT. Perhaps 'fuck' was produced by a blending of both 'fikes' and the French '*foutre*'. The Old Norse word '*fukja*', to drive, could be another source. The kestrel was known in the seventeenth century as the 'windfucker' or 'fuckwind' and in Scotland the foresail was called the 'fucksail'. There is at any rate no substance to the idea that the term was generated as an acronym of the criminal charge relating to 'Full Unlawful Carnal Knowledge'.

**FULL BORE:** *At top speed.*

This is a reference to the chamber of a carburettor when the butterfly is pulled open by the accelerator cable, allowing the full bore of the inlet tube to become operational.

**FULL MONTE:** *Absolutely everything.*

Based on the Spanish '*monte*', mountain, which applied to the stack of cards remaining after a deal in a Spanish–American gambling card-game of this name.

**FULL OF BEANS:** *To be in vigorous form.*

Whilst sexually aroused horses are said to be FEELING THEIR OATS, the above was originally said of humans for much the same reasons. The bean has since the most ancient times been considered by the gullible to be an aphrodisiac; in both Greece and Rome the bean was a yonic symbol and still in modern Italian '*fava*' is understood to mean both 'bean' and 'vagina' and in Sanskrit '*mundra*' meant both 'kidney bean' and 'woman'. The Pythagoreans shunned the bean for this reason and advised others to do likewise with the 'love bean' and Aristotle held 'bean' synonymous with rampant lust and advised those who wished to remain chaste of spirit and celibate of body to 'abstain from beans'. In more recent English balladry a work entitled 'The Love Bean' puts is quite directly: 'My love hung limp beneath the leaf/Oh bitter, bitter shame/My heavy heart was full of grief/Until my lady came./ She brought a tasty dish to me/Oh swollen pod and springy seed/My love sprang out right eagerly/To serve me in my need.' Most, if not all, fairy tales are a mite bawdy in their original form – Sleeping Beauty was not woken with a kiss but by more protracted and intimate attention from a knight who tarried not to remove his armour! Early forms of Jack and the Beanstalk left little to the imagination either.

**FULL-BLOWN:** *Complete.*

This is an application of 'blow' meaning 'to flower or blossom forth'.

**FULL FIG:** *Dressed up in your finest clothes.*

This 'fig' is a variant of the German '*fegen*', to clean up, this also giving rise to the English 'feague', the tarting up of a horse for sale, which ultimately produced 'fake'.

**FULL TILT:** *Top speed.*

During jousting tournaments, two knights galloped towards each other for quite a distance over rough terrain before they met. Carrying their long, heavy lances horizontally the while would have imposed a considerable strain, so they held them upright until they were almost on each other, whereupon they lowered, or tilted, them downwards. This was gauged to coincide with the point at which their horses were up to full gallop.

**FUNK:** *A state of terror.*

This has its origins in three influences, the most important of which is the Flemish '*in de fonke siin*', the metaphorical meaning of which is 'to be in a state of abject fear'. Its literal meaning, however, is 'to be in the smoke' which connects it to the other two influences, the Middle Dutch '*vonke*' and the Middle High German '*vunke*', both of which mean 'spark' (spark, fire, smoke). From the fourteenth to the seventeenth century, 'funk' was used for tinder, or for a spark, or for a miasma, especially that created by smoke. The connection with smoke could not only have caused the transfer in meaning to 'fear' in the early eighteenth century, since the blowing of smoke in another's face was then a challenge or a gross insult which only the cowardly would ignore, it could also go some way towards explaining the strange expression 'in a blue funk'. On the other hand, a much less pleasant, but equally possible theory is that the 'funk' could be that miasma surrounding one whose bowels have been loosened by fear.

**FUNKY:** *Descriptive of music, especially black disco music, with a driving beat.*

From 'funk', this adjectival form meaning malodorous, foul, or excessively smoky, largely died out in England but remained in American dialect and most early American examples apply it to the smell which, according to prejudiced whites, emanated from blacks. It is therefore possible that the term transferred to describe the sort of music played mainly by blacks in smoky dives.

**FURPHY:** *Falacious information, nonsense.*

It is generally accepted that this, arising in WWI Forces slang in Australia, was based on the name of the Furphy Company of Shepperton, Victoria which as it were dealt in garbage; not only did it make the garbage trucks which ostentatiously sported its name, it also had the contract for removing rubbish from Melbourne and from military camps – to which it also supplied latrine buckets. Less convincingly, the term has been connected to Joseph Furphy (1843–1912), a famous Australian author who, under the pen name Tom Collins, wrote highly colourful tales; the title of his most famous novel, *Such is Life* (1903) which described frontier life in the 1880s was apparently the last sentence spoken by the infamous Ned Kelly (1855–80) just before he was hanged in Melbourne jail. In any case, James Furphy came of the Shepperton family and joined his brothers at the foundry to the north east of Melbourne in 1884.

**FUZZ, THE:** *The Police.*

This certainly started life in America in the early part of the twentieth century and it has been suggested that it was a development from the black slang 'fuzzy-balls', a white man, particularly one in authority, a term based on the fact that blacks have little body hair. Alternatively, it may be a contraction of 'fuzzietail', a stern disciplinarian or a hard-to-please superior, an allusion to the way an angry or agitated animal bushes out its tail. The last, and least likely, suggestion is that 'fuzz' is a slurred version of 'Feds', officers of the Federal Bureau of Investigation.

# G

**G.I.:** *American Army serviceman.*

Initially the designation for the galvanised iron rubbish bin which was standard issue in military camps, this came by the mid 1930s to stand for the soldier himself because every piece of equipment he drew from stores had a General Issue number stencilled on it.

**G-STRING:** *Crotch or loin string.*

If not simply 'G' for 'groin' which is a distant possibility this could well refer to the lowest-toned, thickest string on a violin. The turn-of-the-century striptease acts, more sedate affairs than their modern counterparts, were usually performed at private functions to the strains of a string quartet.

**GAFF:** *A house or other premises, especially if disreputable.*

Most probably based on 'gaff', hook, this first applied to a fair or other place of entertainment where the punters were hooked like fish. In the twentieth century the word came to mean a brothel or low dive, whence its present use.

**GAFFE:** *A social blunder.*

This is from the French '*gaffe*', unwise.

**GAFFER:** *Boss or foreman.*

This is a corruption of 'granfer', itself a contraction of 'grandfather'.

**GAG:** *Joke or hoax.*

Early nineteenth-century theatre jargon used this to describe anything unscripted said or done by an actor; it was an extension of the meaning of 'gag', to bind the mouth since it usually stunned the other performers into temporary silence. Because it often served to cover up a late arrival on stage, for example, or the falling down of some scenery, or the steadfast refusal of a prop to function – all such contretemps inevitably eliciting laughter from the audience – it gradually acquired its current meaning.

**GAGA:** *Senile.*

This piece of nineteenth-century French theatre slang is a deliberately moronic corruption of yet another slang term, '*gateux*' – incontinent old fool – based on the verb '*gater*' – to spoil or damage.

**GALL AND WORMWOOD:** *Bitter torment.*

The Bible does make much of gall and wormwood, e.g. Jeremiah 9:15 talks of God's giving people wormwood to eat and water of gall to drink, and Revelations, which some believe foretells the end of the world, talks of a great star called Wormwood that falls to earth contaminating the water and resulting in countless deaths. Prophets of doom were beside themselves in May 1986 after the Chernobyl disaster which contaminated the water table; '*chernobyl*' is Ukranian for wormwood and its ultimate native etymology is even more revealing in that it breaks down to mean 'black or dark truth or reality'.

**GALLIVANT:** *To gad about, usually engaging in flirtation.*

Of obscure origin, this could be a blend of 'gallant', (which was used in the seventeenth century as a verb meaning to cut a dash or to flirt) and the even older 'galliard', once a popular court dance whose name is the French for lively.

**GALOOT:** *A clumsy idiot.*

Although its origin is unclear, this certainly started life as a nautical expression denoting anyone unused to the sea, especially a newly recruited marine. Some say that the earlier variant 'geloot' could indicate a Dutch origin, perhaps '*gelbut*', eunuch, or '*genoot*', companion. Others favour the Spanish '*galeoto*' or the Italian '*galeotto*', both of which mean galley-slave.

**GAME IS NOT WORTH THE CANDLE:** *The venture is not worth further investment of labour, money or time.*

In the days when candlelight was the norm, a boardgame such as chess, which had reached stalemate, did not warrant lengthy consideration whilst the expensive candle burned away.

**GAME PLAN:** *Plan of action.*

This American intensification of 'plan' was born on the American Football field and used in the 1960s for the overall strategy worked cut by the coach. Richard Nixon (b. 1913), a devoted fan of the Washington Redskins, put the expression into the general swim when he used it repeatedly in broadcasts in the late 1960s.

**GAMESMANSHIP:** *The art of winning by putting your opponent off.*

Stephen Potter launched this term in 1947 publication *The Theory and Practice of Gamesmanship* or *The Art of Winning Games without Actually Cheating*. In an amusing manner, and none too seriously, he gave advice on how best to disadvantage your opponent.

**GAMMON:** *Humbug or disingenuous talk.*

Something of a mystery, this could possibly be based on the Middle English '*gamen*' – game; the same descendant cropping up in 'backgammon', a game in which pieces are sometimes taken up and obliged to go *back* into play. The term can be intensified by the addition of 'and spinach' to mean absolute rubbish, and this is the most likely inspiration for 'spinach' used as such.

**GAS, A:** *Anything considered hilarious.*

The allusion is to nitrous oxide, or laughing gas, which has been used in anaesthetics since the late eighteenth century.

**GASCONADE:** *An outrageous vaunt.*

In seventeenth-century France, the district of Gascony was notoriously poverty- stricken but its inordinately proud inhabitants were allegedly much given, when travelling, to covering this up with outrageous claims of wealth. There were countless Parisian jokes about this, the most often cited being that of the Gascon who, after seeing Versailles for the first time, remarked that it reminded him very much of his father's stable block back home.

**GASH:** *Free for the taking, extra or spare.*

This piece of nautical slang came from the French '*gaché*', bungled, spoiled, wasted – hence unwanted.

**GAY:** *Homosexual.*

This is simply an extension of 'gay', happy and lively, an application now seldom used through fear of misunderstanding, and the currently accepted meaning of the word looks as if it is here to stay. Long before it designated a homosexual male, in fact since the seventeenth century, it was attached to a woman of loose morals, she being said to be 'gay in the tail', and, by the eighteenth century it had most certainly come to mean a female prostitute. It could then also mean a toy or item of ornament or pleasure, this meaning only serving to reinforce the notion of frivolous dissipation. Although homosexuals had doubtless used the word among themselves before, one of its earliest significant appearances in this context arose in 1889 with the Cleveland Street scandal which centred on a vice ring of Post Office boys operating a homosexual brothel. In police statements and in the subsequent court proceedings, John Saul, one of the leading male prostitutes, repeatedly referred to both male and female whores as 'gay'.

**GAZUMP:** *To go back on an agreement, especially in real estate deals, and raise the price.*

This term was already used in the American motor trade before it arrived in Britain in the 1920s so it quite possibly arose from the Yiddish '*gezumph*', swindle. Modern developments include 'gazwelsh', a simple extension of WELSH, renege, and 'gazunder', to drop an accepted bid, this last no doubt influenced by the pun on 'goes under'.

**GEECHEE:** *An American black, especially one from the rural South.*

In post Civil War America, many freed blacks settled along the banks of the Ogeechee River in Northern Georgia and maintained their peculiar patois developed on the plantations. Another suggestion is that, if not itself the origin, there has been at least a strong influence from the Geejee dialect of the Gullah language spoken in the Kissy region of Liberia.

**GEEZER:** *A man, especially if peculiar.*

There are several possible origins

though none is certain. Conservative opinion generally favours a dialect corruption of 'guiser' – mummer, or one in disguise – the appearance of mummers often being strange indeed. On the other hand, troops with the Duke of Wellington when he finally drove the French out of Spain in 1813 could have picked up the Basque '*giza*', man, or British personnel on Malta could have built the term on the local 'gisem', body or person.

**GEHENNA:** *Hell or any place of torment.*

According to Jeremiah 19:4–6, the Israelites sacrificed their children by fire to the god Baal in the valley known as Ge ben Hennom, or the Valley of the son of Hinnom.

**GEN:** *Information.*

This was born in British Forces slang during WW2. It could be a contraction of 'intelliGENCE', 'GENuine', or 'GENeral', the latter because posted bulletins were always headed 'for the general information of all ranks'.

**GEORGE:** *An automatic pilot.*

Partridge is tempted to see this as little more that the generic name for an aircraftsman who undertakes tasks for others – the Air Force equivalent of the British Army 'Tommy' – but perhaps there is more to it than that. The first auto-pilots emerged in 1913 in America, a country where the Pullman rail-car company had long symbolised the ultimate in travel comfort. Possibly because the founder's name was George Pullman (1831–97), everybody addressed all the servicing personnel as 'George', and much of the company advertising was slanted towards the idea that the traveller could sit back and let 'George' take care of everything. There may also have been some reinforcement from LET GEORGE DO IT.

**GERMAN MEASLES:** *Rubella.*

Compared to measles proper, German Measles, previously known as false or French measles, is mild indeed and 'German' is here used as FRENCH or DUTCH can be to indicate inferiority. In the surge of anti-German feeling during the lead-up to WW1, even this use of 'German' was dropped; in America, German Mealses became Liberty Measles, German Shepherds became Alsatians, and in Britain, the Battenburg family changed its name to Mountbatten and George V changed his family name from Wetlin to Windsor.

**GERONIMO:** *A war-cry.*

The main training camp of the famous American 82nd Airborne was, in 1938, near Lafayetteville, Indiana, and in the summer of that year, some recruits, given the traditional day off before their first, full-drill jump from a plane, drifted into town to see the new Western *Geronimo*. The film featured what was supposedly a true incident in the Indian's life when, to avoid army pursuers, he rode off a near-vertical cliff at Medicine Bluffs, Oklahoma, shouting 'Geronimo' as he plummeted into the river below. The recruits jumping the next day could not resist the temptation to emulate the cry, and when everybody followed suit, the Division adopted the call as its official battle-cry. On the subject of the Indian himself, whose real name was 'Goyathlay' (roughly, he who yawns), he was called Geronimo by the Mexicans, though why is not altogether clear. There is, however, a Spanish expression 'sin Jeronimo duda', their equivalent of our 'without a shadow of a doubt' and perhaps this arose because, in reprisal for the murder of his family, Geronimo made numerous raids on Mexico after which he seemed to melt away like a shadow.

**GERRYMANDER:** *To re-arrange electoral boundaries to ensure the continuance of the existing government.*

This was coined in America to describe a practice that was far from new but was not named until 1812 when one Elbridge Gerry (1744–1814), then governor of Massachusetts, later Vice President 1813–14, engaged in such political SKULDUGGERY to ensure his party's success in the coming elections – a ploy which engendered a deal of discontent in some quarters. Gilbert Stuart, the resident cartoonist of *The Boston Sentinel*, produced a drawing of the new boundary of Essex County which so reminded him of a salamander that he drew it as such. His editor, Benjamin Russell, made further suggestions, and the salamander, renamed a gerrymander, appeared with a face which was a caricature of Gerry's. Incidentally, the governor's name was pronounced with a hard 'g', so perhaps 'gerrymander' should be too.

**GET/GIT:** *An idiot.*

This was taken from 'beget' but with definite intimations of low breeding and bastardy since that word was, after the eighteenth century, more properly used of animals, especially horses. 'Git' is an ill-educated slovening which is steadily increasing in currency at the expense of the term that begot it.

**GET AWAY SCOT-FREE, TO:** *To escape without penalty.*

Whether the Scots deserve their reputation for parsimony is a matter for debate, but this is no racial slur merely an example of the Old Norse meaning a contribution or a tax.

**GET COLD FEET:** *To become fearful and withdraw from a venture.*

When the body is in a state of shock or fright, the blood withdraws from the surface and the extremities, and the feet do literally become cold.

**GET DOWN TO BRASS TACKS:** *To start talking about solid facts and figures.*

This originated in the cloth retailing trade which used long counters marked by brass-headed tacks at measured intervals of yardage. It has been suggested that 'brass tacks' could be rhyming slang for 'facts', but no such usage has been traced. Furthermore, the American equivalent, 'get down to brass nails' backs up the other origin.

**GET DOWN TO THE NITTY-GRITTY:** *Eliminate frills and concentrate on the hard, unvarnished truth.*

A relatively recent addition to phraseology from the black GHETTOES of American cities wherein the inhabitants frequently had to delouse each other's heads – an unpleasant but necessary task. The bugs themselves are, of course, the nitty-gritty so called for the headlouse's tough casing. The nature of afro hair produced the 'get down' element in that the de-louser would have to quite literally dig down to find the nits.

**GET IT IN THE NECK, TO:** *To receive heavy punishment.*

Allusive to the nineteenth-century Americanism 'to get it where the chicken got the axe'.

**GET KNOTTED:** *Crude dismissal.*

The vaginal muscles in bitches, especially vixens, sometimes knot during copulation, which results in the male's penis becoming jammed by them for anything up to an hour.

**GET OFF ON THE RIGHT FOOT:** *To strike an auspicious commencement.*

Yet further legacy from the prejudice against anything connected with the left side, this is a hand-me-down from the superstition concerning the beginning of any important journey with the right foot. If started with the left step, the journey was doomed to disaster or failure hence 'get off on the wrong foot'.

**GET ON SOMEONE'S WICK, TO:** *To annoy them intensely.*

Rhyming slang citing the London district of Hampton Wick = dick.

**GET ON THE RIGHT SIDE OF A PERSON, TO:** *To engender someone's trust and liking.*

Dating from the Royal Courts of old this is a reference to the custom placing the more elevated or trusted officials on the right-hand side of the monarch.

**GET ON YOUR HIGH HORSE, TO:** *To stand on your dignity.*

The gentry rode tall, thoroughbred animals.

**GET OUT ON THE WRONG SIDE OF BED:** *To start the day disgruntled.*

One of the oldest superstitions is that God and the Devil sit at the head of each bed disputing for control of the occupant's life throughout the next day. Getting out on the Devil's side spells bad luck.

**GET SOMEONE'S GOAT:** *To annoy them intensely.*

Highly strung horses have always been stabled with their own 'comforter' which is usually a goat. There seems to be something about the smell of such creatures which exerts a calming influence on horses. It is said that the above arose from the old trick of sneaking into a racehorse's stable the night before a big race and leading away its pet goat to ensure the horse has a restless night and is not on form in the morning.

**GET THE BULLET:** *To be discharged from a post, or unceremoniously dumped by a friend or lover.*

In the days when a gentleman was expected always to DO THE DECENT THING, an officer who had disgraced himself or his regiment was handed a single round for a service pistol with which to shoot himself.

**GET THE DROP:** *To gain the advantage, especially unfairly.*

In nineteenth-century America, this signified having the opportunity to fire first at someone who had not yet drawn his weapon. The murderous overtones of the expression do make it likely that it was born of taking a POT SHOT from ambush, 'drop' signifying the lowering of the gun's muzzle to bring it on target.

**GET THE SHORT END, TO:** *To be placed in an invidious position.*

When it is required that one of a group undertake an unpleasant or dangerous task to the collective benefit, the time honoured method of selecting the 'volunteer' is the drawing of straws from a clenched fist. All – bar one – are of uniform length.

**GET THE WIND UP, TO:** *To become frightened.*

It is common for horses to become agitated when caught up the rear by a sudden gust of wind.

**GET THE WRONG END OF THE STICK, TO:** *To wholly misunderstand the situation.*

They who fail to grasp the situation correctly are likened to those who foolishly grasp the wrong end of the stick used to prod something nasty from the shoe.

**GET YOUR DANDER UP, TO:** *To get in a temper.*

This may have derived from the Dutch '*donder*', thunder, or from the Victorian 'dander', dandruff (implying that one was so irate that the very dandruff was flying from his hair), or possibly from the Scottish '*dunder*', to be stirred by anger or emotion. The expression is rapidly fading from modern usage, having been largely replaced by more colourful alternatives.

**GHETTO:** *Segregated and deprived sector of a city.*

In Venice in 1516, an islet was turned into a Jewish quarter complete with curfews and Christian watchmen. It took its name from the presence there of a foundry, or 'getto', a word built on such as the Old French '*geter*', to throw or cast. The 'h' was added as the term spread across Europe. Attempts to link 'ghetto' to the Italian '*borgo*', borough, through its diminutive 'borgetto', are unconvincing.

**GHOST WALKS, THE:** *Payment is imminent.*

A truly bizarre expression of theatrical origin, this has been actors' slang for many a year and derives from *Hamlet* in which Horatio asks the ghost if it walks because 'Thou hast uphoarded in thy life/Extorted treasure in the womb of earth.' If a show is going so badly that the actors are likely to remain unpaid, they conversely bemoan this fact with: 'The ghost won't walk.'

**GIBBERISH:** *Meaningless gabble.*

Geber or Jebir, more fully Abu Musa Jabir ibn Hayyan, was the most celebrated alchemist of medieval times; his writings and his incantations were highly cryptic and his mumblings, unintelligible to the uninitiated, soon became known as 'gibberish'. Some prefer to see the word as a ricochet from 'jabber' but have as yet failed to establish this connection.

**GIG:** (1) *Dance or a band engagement.*

This term, which also described any event of great merriment or hilarity, is probably based on the use of 'gig', anything that whirls like a top and appears in 'whirligig', though there could be a connection with the Middle French '*gigue*', fiddle, violin. (2) *The vagina or anus.* Along with 'giggy', this was used until the nineteenth century to mean a flighty girl of loose morals, a 'piece of tail' who no doubt took part in many a merry gig, in which case a correlation with the first meaning emerges. It is, too, remotely possible that there is a link to an old fertility statue known as 'Sheela' or 'Sheila-na-gig', an anglicised version of the Irish '*Sile na gcioch*', Julia of the breasts. Such statues were full-frontal, highly erotic female forms with hands positioned so as to direct the gaze to greatly exaggerated vulvae. These could also perhaps explain the Australian use of SHEILA.

**GIGOLO:** *A man paid by an older woman to be her escort or lover.*

Ultimately rooted in the Middle French '*gigue*', violin or fiddle, which produced the diminutive '*gigolette*' – a female prostitute who made her contacts on the dance floor – 'gigolo' first applied to a man living off immoral earnings, later softening a shade to indicate a professional male dancing partner whose services often went beyond that.

**GILD THE LILY:** *To embellish unnecessarily.*

A misquotation from Shakespeare's *King John:* 'Therefore, to be possess'd with double pomp/To guard a title that was rich before/*ITo gild refined gold, to paint the lily*/To throw a perfume on the violet/To smooth the ice or add another hue/Unto the rainbow, or with taper-light/To seek the beauteous eye of heaven to garnish/Is wasteful and ridiculous excess.'

**GINGER:** *Highly sexed or promiscuous.*

If this is not a straight reference to the spice's hot flavour and its effervescent effect when added to soft drinks there could be some connection with the use by prostitutes of 'gingering', robbing a client, this word perhaps implying that the extra money added spice to the night. Whores indulging in this practice were called 'ginger-girls'. Ginger is also used to describe a male homosexual; it is rhyming slang: ginger beer = queer.

**GINGER UP:** *To inspire with enthusiasm or activity.*

Unscrupulous horse-traders in the previous century used to insert a pinch of ginger up a horse's rectum before parading it in front of prospective buyers. The hapless animal then pranced around in a highly animated manner, appearing more spirited than it really was.

**GINGERLY:** *With extreme delicacy, cautiously.*

The origin is the Old French '*gensour*', dainty, delicate, and all the attempts to link this to the spice are spurious.

**GINGHAM:** *Cotton fabric.*
This is from the Malay '*ginggang*', striped cloth.

**GINK:** *A boring man.*
Of obscure origin, this is possibly associated with the dialect 'gink', a term related to 'jink', both of them meaning a trick or a dodge. A woman of loose morals was once known as a 'ginkie' and it is possible that this simply shifted its ground and became an insult to a man – not the first to make this sort of transition. Alternatively, this step could have been taken through 'gink's baby', a child born of casual or bought sex, in which case it would be paralleled by the American 'trick baby'.

**GIOTTO'S CIRCLE:** *Any simple statement of perfection.*
An apocryphal story tells how the Vatican demanded a test piece of the Florentine master, Giotto di Bondone (1266–1337) before offering him a formal commission. After a few moments' thought, the painter drew a perfect circle free-hand – and got the commission.

**GIP:** *To cheat, defraud.*
This is an allusion to the unfortunate reputation for dishonesty that gypsies have acquired.

**GIPPY TUMMY:** *Upset stomach, mild food poisoning.*
The adjective derives from Egypt – British troops stationed there in the nineteenth century regarded it as a highly insanitary place. It was no doubt helped into being by the expression 'give someone gip'.

**GIRD UP YOUR LOINS:** *To prepare for strenuous effort.*
The Bible makes much use of this expression; Jews wore long, flowing garments which were tucked up out of the way and folded over a belt or girdle when activity was called for.

**GISMO:** *Any little contrivance or piece of equipment.*
The origin of this is obscure, but it has been suggested that, since it originated in WW2 among American forces as slang for something whose name was unknown or forgotten, its source could be the Arabic '*shu ismo*' – thingummybob – picked up through Arab–American contact in North Africa.

**GIVE AIM:** *To stand aloof or to act only to help others to achieve an objective.*
On an archery range, one person stands well down toward the target and signals to the archer after each arrow is shot so that he can adjust his aim if necessary.

**GIVE A WIDE BERTH:** *To keep your distance.*
Vessels entering port have to be steered well clear of ships already berthed since allowance has to be made for the fact that these can swing out on their anchors.

**GIVE IT SOME STICK, TO:** *To inflict dire punishment or impart maximum effort.*
In WW2 RAF bomber-pilots jargon, a load of bombs designed to hit the ground in a line was called a stick and to give the target plenty of stick meant to bomb it to smithereens.

**GIVE SOMEONE A BIT OF LEEWAY, TO:** *To make allowances.*

At sea, 'leeway' is that distance between the set course of a ship and the line to which she is driven by prevailing winds and currents.

**GIVE SOMEONE SHORT SHRIFT, TO:** *To deal with or dismiss someone in a summary manner.*

Derived from the Anglo– Saxon '*scrifan*', to receive confession, 'shrift' was the time given a condemned man to make his peace with his maker and confess any outstanding sins to wipe clean the celestial slate. Those strung up out of hand were those given short shrift.

**GIVE SOMEONE THE BIRD:** *To express disapproval.*

Frequently done by booing and hissing, this expression was originally 'to give someone the big bird' and referred to the goose which hisses loudly when annoyed.

**GIVE YOUR EYETEETH, TO (BE WILLING TO):** *Willing to pay any price.*

It was once believing that the upper canines extended all the way up to the eyesockets and that blindness would be a natural ramification of their being pulled out.

**GLORY HOLE:** *A repositary of assorted junk or memorabilia.*

The Scottish '*glaury*', filthy and muddy, inspired the construction industry's 'glaury hole' to describe the water-tight enclosure created by the building of a coffer-dam. As the hollow, double-skinned dam is being constructed, the river-bed with all its slime is exposed and any unwanted materials are dumped into it – hence the modern usage. The word 'glaury' was also presented as 'gloary', so perhaps the transition to 'glory' was inevitable.

**GLOSS OVER A SUBJECT, TO:** *To hide or explain away.*

No reference to the gloss paint but derived instead from the Middle English '*glossen*', to explain, as is 'glossary'. As a verb the term took on connotations of speciousness and 'to gloss the truth' meant to pervert it with spurious arguments. Associations with the paint may well have helped the expression survive but anyone who has ever used gloss paint will know only too well that its application to an ill-prepared surface will only accentuate any faults and not hide them.

**GLOVE MONEY:** *A bribe.*

Gloves are significant in several ancient customs. In legal circles, a client often presented a pair of gloves to the advocate who accepted his case, and it was not unknown for a little sweetener to be placed inside them. One of the most famous examples of this occurred when Mrs Croaker, trying to enlist the aid of Sir Thomas More (1478–1535), presented him with gloves containing £40. More, a man of the utmost integrity, retained the gloves indicating that he was willing to accept her case, but returned the bribe. Incidentally, as a spin-off from the custom of glove money, sitting judges are forbidden to wear gloves, a prohibition that underlines their complete impartiality.

**GNOMES OF ZURICH:** *Swiss financiers.*

The gnomes of mythology hoarded and guarded the treasures of the earth, as do Swiss bankers in their underground vaults. Although the expression was no doubt current in the financial world before then, it made its first significant impact when Harold Wilson, speaking in the House of Commons on 12 November 1956 of the financial ramifications of the Suez affair, referred to 'all the little gnomes of Zurich and other financial centres'.

**GO BY THE BOARDS:** *To go to ruin.*

The boards in this expression are those which make up the side of ship's hull; all the rubbish from the vessel is thrown past these.

**GO FOR A SONG, TO:** *To be sold well below the market price.*

The glut of minstrels and poets in Elizabethan times brought into play the law of supply and demand and it was common to see musicians and writers outside London trying to sell their works for a pittance.

**GO FOR BROKE:** *To go all out to succeed no matter what the risk.*

The most likely source is surfers' slang in which the 'broke' is the foaming edge of the wave at its breaking point. Riding this edge is spectacular and exciting; it is also difficult and hazardous, there being absolutely no recovery from error on the broke. It has been suggested that the expression is a gambling one referring to a player's staking his all on one big bet, but 'going for broke' would be an unlikely objective for a gambler.

**GO FOR SOMETHING BALD-HEADED:** *To launch an all-out attack.*

In the days when gentlemen wore wigs, it was advisable to cast them aside before indulging in sword-play; the risk of their slipping forward over the eyes at a potentially fatal moment was only too real (*See also*: PULL THE WOOL OVER THE EYES). The suggestion that the expression arose from the Dutch '*bald dadig*', audacious, seems far-fetched as does the story of the Marquis of Granby (1721–70) who successfully led a daring charge in the Battle of Warburg in 1760, during which, it is said, his wig flew off. It hardly seems likely that he would have worn his wig when accoutred for battle.

**GO LIKE THE CLAPPERS:** *To move fast.*

From Forces slang in which 'clapper' is synonymous with 'clanger', testicle, and is probably a ribald allusion to the way the testicles move in copulation. The origin is sometimes presumed to concern the clappers in bells, but these seem an unlikely source for Forces slang, and, in any case, move quite slowly.

**GO NINETEEN TO THE DOZEN, TO:** *To work at maximum effort.*

If not simple reference to the disparity of the numbers, it has been suggested that this was born of the rated output of the Watt's shaft pump used to control the universal problem of flooding in mines. When operating at peak efficiency it could raise 19,000 gallons of water per dozen bushels of coal burnt in the boiler.

**GO OFF HALF-COCK:** *To act precipitately.*

The allusion is to hauling back the cock hammer of a firearm which, if the firer is not careful, can slip from under his thumb and discharge the weapon prematurely before aim has been taken.

**GO PHUT, TO:** *To break down or fail.*

Surprisingly this is not simply onomatopoeic but comes from the Hindustani '*phatna*', to burst or explode, and was brought into general usage by troops on service in India.

**GO THE WHOLE HOG:** *To go all out.*

In the days when a shilling was a considerable sum of money the nickname of this coin was 'hog' and to spend all indicated lack of restraint.

**GO THE WHOLE NINE YARDS, TO:** *No half measures; full and focused effort.*

A twentieth-century Americanism completely unknown in Britain before the Gulf War when it was used several times by American military spokesmen – General Schwarzkopf included – when giving televised updates. The phrase is taken from the construction industry and 1930s ready-mix cement lorries which carried nine cubic yards maximum, thus it first meant a full load, no half deliveries.

**GO THROUGH FIRE AND WATER:** *Suffer a great ordeal.*

In bygone trials by ordeal, the defendant was subjected to burning, branding and near drowning.

**GO TO POT, TO:** *To go to ruin.*

It is unclear whether the pot is that in the jeweller's workshop where damaged items are re-melted or the cooking pot of old where meat and vegatables past their best were made into a rather unpleasant stew eaten by those who could not afford to waste anything.

**GO TO THE DOGS:** *To come to ruin.*

Probably from decomposing meat thrown to the dogs. On the other hand, there is an interesting notion that the saying could be a corruption of the Old Dutch business maxim '*Toe goe, toe de doges*', which translates loosely as 'Money gone, credit gone'.

**GO TO THE WALL, TO:** *To face ruin.*

With the finger of heresy and witchcraft pointed all too easily in earlier times, the churches were better attended than they are today but not so well furnished. The common herd had to stand and in summer the press could prove too much for the old and frail who were given first choice of positions round the walls where it was cooler and they found some support – sometimes even stone seats let into the masonry.

**GO TO TOWN, TO:** *To go full out.*

In nineteenth-century America those settlers in the more remote regions rarely ventured the long journey into the nearest town for not only could the trip itself be perilous but the homestead would be left largely unprotected. The most was made of each sortie, complete with getting dressed up for a good time.

**GOD BLESS THE DUKE OF ARGYLE:** *A Scottish expression accompanying vigorous scratching.*

Some time around the opening of the nineteenth century, the Duke of Argyle compensated for the dearth of trees on his land by erecting numerous posts which his sheep could scratch against to clean their fleeces of pests. Since most of his shepherds and labourers had cause to use the posts for similar reasons, they humorously blessed the Duke while doing so.

**GOD BLESS YOU:** *Rejoinder to a sneeze.*

The Plague first afflicted Europe in the fourteenth century and re-emerged periodically thereafter, the last serious outbreak in London being in 1665–66, and one of its early symptoms was violent sneezing which, in those days, naturally elicited this pious hope. It is thought that the Great Plague also inspired the nursery rhyme *Ring a ring of roses/A pocketful of posies/Atishoo, atishoo/We all fall down*. The roses allude to the appearance of the red pustules and 'atishoo' to the sneezing. Posies were traditionally carried to ward off the infection.

**GOLDBRICK:** *A sham, a poser; to do less than your share.*

Both usages derive from the word 'goldbrick', a forerunner of 'ingot' which soon fell from grace and described only phoney ingots dummied up to look like the real article. In WW1, American regulars adopted the word for a lieutenant appointed direct from Civvy Street with no formal training or experience. The expression 'to sell someone a goldbrick' gave rise to the verb 'to goldbrick'.

**GONE FOR A BURTON:** *Died, or become unserviceable.*

This euphemism originated in Royal Airforce Slang in WW2. It has been suggested that the expression arose because the RAF took over the premises of Burton's men's outfitters in Blackpool and used it eventually as a centre for keeping records of their casualties. It could also refer directly to the tailors through a wry allusion that someone had gone to get a (wooden) suit. Another possible origin quotes a Burton Ales advertising campaign, which many people 'remember', consisting of posters depicting a group of people (e.g. an orchestra) with one person very obviously missing, the never-changing caption being: 'He's gone for a Burton.' This would dovetail with the fact that many pilots were shot down over the sea, which the RAF referred to as 'the drink' or 'the big drink'. Unfortunately no firm proof of this campaign has yet been found and, significantly, Eric Partridge makes no mention of 'a burton' being used as slang for 'a beer'.

**GOOD FIELD, NO HIT:** *An expert in one area but not in another.*

A baseball expression meaning 'a

good fielder but a poor batsman', this was the burden of a telegram that Miguel Gonzales, a St Louis Cardinals coach, sent to Mike Kelly when asked to assess Moe Berg with a view to purchasing him for the team. It is thought to be ironic that this laconic, even ungrammatical, assessment was applied to the extremely well-educated Berg who spoke seven languages. During WW2 Berg was America's top spy in the field of atomics, monitoring the labours of German scientists in the race to produce the atomic bomb.

**GOOD NIGHT, VIENNA:** *An expression denoting an abrupt ending or quick dismissal.*

This was the title of an extremely popular song from a romantic operetta of the same name written in 1932 by Eric Maschwitz and George Posford especially for Richard Tauber (1892–1948). The song was heard everywhere and its title was taken up as a common expression.

**GOOD RUN FOR YOUR MONEY, A:** *Enjoy the proceedings even if there be no profit.*

A horse-betters' expression to describe a race in which the horse backed made an exciting run leaving everyone guessing the outcome, but then failed to take the tape.

**GOOD WINE NEEDS NO BUSH:** *Quality speaks for itself.*

In the days before pubs had individual signs, a drinking haunt specialising in wine announced its wares to travellers by hanging out an ivy bush, that plant being sacred to Bacchus. Ale houses tended to display forked or angled sticks, hence the popular pub name 'The Crooked Billet'.

**GOODY TWO-SHOES:** *An unrealistically virtuous person.*

In a story most probably written by Oliver Goldsmith (1731–74) for Sir John Newbury (1713–67), one of the first publishers of children's books, the central character was an unbelievably sugary little girl called Goody. She was so poor that she had only one shoe; when she was given a pair, she she was overjoyed and proudly drew everybody's attention to her 'two shoes'.

**GOOK:** *Insultingly, an Asian, especially a Japanese or Korean soldier.*

The ultimate origin would appear to be the Vicol '*gugurang*', spirit or demon, from which came the Philippino '*Gugu*', the name adopted by the Filippino guerrillas in the 1899 Insurrection which occasioned the arrival of American servicemen. It is possible that the Forces slang 'Gook' was additionally influenced by GOON and by the Korean '*kuk*', pronounced 'kook' or 'gook', which basically means 'country', Korea being 'Han-gook' and America 'Mei-gook'.

**GOON:** *A stupid person; a professional thug.*

If not inspired, as seems likely, by the incredibly stupid gooney bird, then this could be a blend of 'gorilla' and 'baboon'; the Hindi '*goonda*' – hired killer – seems an unlikely source. At any rate the term, which originated in the early 1920s as a piece of Forces slang, was launched into general use by E.C Segar (1894–1938) when he introduced a large, clumsy stupid creature named Alice the Goon into his successful strip cartoon *Popeye* .

**GOOSE:** *To prod in the backside to annoy or surprise.*

The rear end of a human being is, conveniently for a snapping goose, at beak height. Goose as a synonym for 'to fuck' came about from the eighteenth-century use of the word to denote a prostitute or a venereal disease. It was an ellipsis of Winchester Goose, so called because the seventeenth-century brothels of Southwark came under the jurisdiction of the Bishop of Winchester.

**GOOSE HANGS HIGH, THE:** *All augurs well for the future.*

The origin is obscure but this could allude to the fact that the clearer the weather, the higher returning geese fly or hang in the sky. There is no evidence for the assertion that 'hangs' is a corruption of 'honks'. The term could, on the other hand, hark back to the once popular pastime of 'goose pulling' in which a live goose with its neck greased was hung by its feet from a tree or a pole and participants rode past trying to break its neck or pull its head off, the implication being that the higher the goose was hung, the better the sport.

**GOOSEBERRY BUSH:** *Euphemistic explanation of childbirth.*

The gooseberry bush was most probably selected because of its association with lovers, e.g. PLAY GOOSEBERRY, and perhaps this expression was originally used to explain the advent of the 'six-month baby' after a hurried wedding occasioned by a conception incurred while the chaperone was off 'picking gooseberries'.

**GOOSE PIMPLES:** *Constriction of the skin producing a mass of pimples.*

The popular term for horripulation alludes to the appearance of a plucked goose. A reaction to fear or surprise, this is a hangover from the days when humans, more hairy than they are now, could present a frightening appearance when the subcutaneous muscles contracted, crushed the follicles and made the body hair stand out. Much the same happens with the hackles of cats and dogs.

**GORDON BENNETT:** *Exclamation of surprise.*

Son of one of the most famous men in newspaper history, James Gordon Bennett Jnr followed his father at the helm of the *New York Herald*. He pulled off the greatest scoop ever by dispatching Stanley to find Doctor Livingstone, whom most people believed to be already dead, and his name lives on as a monument to the amazement of a stunned world when Stanley actually succeeded in his mission. Some maintain that even rival newspapers published cartoons of an excited Stanley telephoning his editor from Africa with captions such as 'Gordon Bennett, I've found him!' The fact that the name makes a convenient euphemism for 'Gawd!' will, no doubt, have reinforced the usage.

**GOTHIC:** *A genre characterised by horror, violence and the supernatural.*

The archetype of this form is set in medieval times against a backdrop of the Gothic architecture prevalent at the time – e.g. in dark, haunted castles. The prototype was *The Castle of Otranto* published in 1764 by Horace Walpole, who also spear-headed the revival of the architectural style.

**GOWK:** *An idiot.*

This could have arisen because '*gowk*' was an Old English dialect name for the cuckoo, which have a repetitive, rather foolish call.

**GRAFT:** *Hard physical work; corruption in public life.*

The term 'grafter', once common in the North of England, Northern Ireland and certain parts of Scotland, designated the kind of flat, rectangular spade ideal for trenching and grave-digging, both of which demand such physical effort – hence 'graft' itself, incidentally, a variant of 'grave'. The same tool was really useful for squaring away a trench or grave and skimming off the bottom until it was flat; illicit profits are usually made by a process of 'skimming' off. 'Graft' in this sense of corruption was originally an American expression, and no doubt it was the Irish immigrants who took the tool and its name with them. At any rate, the usage does seem to have arisen in New York during the Prohibition era when, significantly, almost the entire police force was manned by the Irish.

**GRAND GUIGNOL:** *Grotesque drama.*

Inspired either by the French '*guigner*', to cast an envious eye, to cheat by looking at another's playing cards, or '*guigne*', bad luck, or by the name of a local 'character' of Lyons. Guignol was the name given to the eighteenth-century French equivalent of the puppet known elsewhere as 'Punch'. The puppet shows in which he appeared were characterised by much violence and gross behaviour and the term spread to live drama featuring such elements. One of the theatres in Paris specialising in short plays of horror was actually called the Grand Guignol.

**GRAND PANJANDRUM/ PANJANDARUM:** *A pretentious, self-important official.*

The word was invented by the English dramatist Samuel Foote (1720–77). He overheard the self-opinionated, hot-tempered Irish actor/playwright Charles Macklin (real name, McLaughlin, *c.* 1697–1797) boasting that he could commit anything to memory after reading it once. Foote challenged this and penned the following as a test: 'So she went into the garden to cut a cabbage leaf to make an apple pie and at the same time a great she-bear came running up the street and popped its head into the shop. 'What, no soap?' So he died, and she, very imprudently, married the barber. And there were present the Picinnies, Jobillies, the Garyulies, and the Grand Panjandrum himself, with the little red button a-top, and they all fell to playing the game of catch-as-catch-can till the gunpowder ran out at the heels of their boots.' Only a truly photographic memory, which

Macklin did not possess, could recall such ramblings and he withdrew from the challenge, imperiously pronouncing Foote's writing to be beneath an actor of his calibre.

**GRANDFATHER CLOCK:** *A clock in a tall wooden cabinet.*

Properly termed a long-case clock, this pet name developed from the song 'My Grandfather's Clock' (1878) written by the American Henry Clay Work (1832–84) who also penned *Marching Through Georgia* (1865). The actual clock that inspired the song ended up in Britain and currently stands in the George Hotel, Piercebridge, County Durham.

**GRANDFATHER'S AXE:** *Something that has been completely renewed, bit by bit.*

This is from the tale of the young man, hefting his trusty axe and proudly announcing it to have been his grandfather's. It had, however, had three new heads and six new handles.

**GRAPEVINE, THE:** *Rumoured abroad.*

The vine spreads everywhere, as do the chains of communication along which run gossip and rumour. The early American telegraph was certainly nicknamed the Grapevine for the way the wires draped from pole to pole. News and information have never travelled so fast and this Americanism most certainly appeared in the form of 'the grapevine telegraph'. By WW2 'telegraph' had been abandonned.

**GRASP THE NETTLE FIRMLY:** *Act boldly to succeed.*

Folklore has it that a nettle grasped boldly and firmly has no time to sting before it is crushed.

**GRASS:** *Police informant.*

The old Cockney rhyming slang for a policeman was 'grasshopper' = copper, but this specifically referred to one who went about in plain clothes 'hopping' from one criminal haunt to another with the intent of assimilating intelligence. In time it transferred to those who fed information to the police. There is also a slightly more fanciful theory that links the term with the song 'Whispering Grass', first made popular by the Inkspots in 1940, but 'grass' appeared in print in this context several years before that date.

**GRASS WIDOW:** *A wife temporarily living without her husband.*

In the sixteenth century this denoted a woman seduced in a field or stable and then deserted, and there are equivalents in other languages like the German '*Strohwite*' , straw widow. The term later applied to a deserted mistress – which is getting closer to the modern meaning – and, in the nineteenth century it was rendered more respectable by its use among the colonial British in India where, in high summer, the wives and children were sent away from the intolerable heat into the hills where the grass still grew because it was cooler. There have been several attempts to clean up the history of this word by hailing it as a corruption of '*veuve de grace*', widow by dispensation of the Church, a divorcée, but the other European parallels point straight back to the stable.

**GRAVEYARD SHIFT:** *A tour of duty spanning the midnight hours.*

The graveyards of the wealthy used to be patrolled after dark by watchmen hired to deter grave robbers.

**GREAT SCOTT!:** *Exclamation of surprise.*

Already a hero of the 1812 war against the British, General Winfield Scott captured the American imagination with his exploits in the Mexican War of 1846–48. 'Great Scott' started life as a soldier's expression, but its later use by the man himself in his abortive run for the presidency brought it into general usage.

**GREEKS HAD A WORD FOR IT:** *It is unmentionable.*

This arose from a play of the same title, written by Zo Atkins and produced on Broadway in 1929; it concentrated on the antics of the Hetairai, girls of Ancient Greece trained to be sexually proficient.

**GREEN-EYED MONSTER:** *The epitome of jealousy.*

In *Othello*, Iago says: 'O, beware, my lord, of jealousy; it is the green-ey'd monster which does mock the food it feeds on.' The allusion is to cats, which often have green eyes and habitually play with their prey before eating it. Jealous love, too, consumes or destroys the object of its desire.

**GREEN ROOM:** *A rest room for actors.*

The walls of the original restrooms used by actors when not required on stage were painted green to rest their eyes from the glare of the lights.

**GREENHORN:** *A raw, inexperienced youth.*

Analogy based on the fact that the horns of young deer and the like are protected by a green, velvety covering.

**GREMLIN:** *Any imaginary, mischievous agency.*

This was first an RAF slang term; it seems to have appeared in the early 1920s and could perhaps have been simply an 'in' form of 'goblin', possibly with 'grinning goblin' in mind. At any rate it designated an imp-like creature at whose door any vexatious mystery was laid, although later on the gremlin's forte became inexplicable mechanical failure. The uncertainty of the origin of the word has prompted a stream of conjectures; there is the Irish '*grauimin*', an irascible little creature, the Old English '*greme*', to vex, and the long redundant Danish '*gram*', devil, to mention but a few. There has also been a suggestion that the gremlin was an evil creature of drunken imagination born from the beer bottles of Fremlin, a Kentish brewery lost in corporate mergers of the mid 1950s. The trouble with all of these, proposed long after the time of origin, is that they attribute a somewhat evil character to the gremlin whereas pilots regarded him with wry affection as a merely mischievous being.

**GREY MATTER:** *The brain, intelligence.*

This is based on something of an anatomical misunderstanding since only the nerve tissue of the brain is grey. This is the surface layer, the brain itself being essentially white, although, to be fair, there are certain grey masses embedded within it.

**GRIN LIKE A CHESHIRE CAT:** *Smile broadly.*

Popularized by Lewis Carroll's *Alice in Wonderland*, this extremely odd expression is of obscure origin. The most widely accepted is that, at old produce fairs, Cheshire cheese was moulded in the form of grinning cats, and this is possible but slightly suspect in view of the very crumbly texture of this cheese. Partridge put forward the notion that 'Cheshire' was a corruption of 'cheeser', in which case the expression would refer to a contented cat fed on cheese to which it is much addicted, but then cats have never been proverbially associated with cheese. Etymologists may have been seeking a too respectable origin. Cheshire is a county nationally famed for its hospitable inns and, if one thinks of 'cat' in its age-old meaning of 'whore', then some sort of logic emerges; the expression could then allude to a girl in a well-patronized Cheshire inn smiling invitingly, or contentedly after a good night's trade.

**GRINGO:** *A Mexican word used slightingly of someone whose language is not Spanish, especially an American.*

The word is based on the Spanish '*Griego*', Greek (after the style of 'All Greek to me'); Funk and Wagnall's dictionary points out that the word appeared in a Madrid newspaper as early as 1787 when it meant 'any person with a peculiar accent that prevents him from achieving the pure, Castilian accent.' Apparently the Irish were the first to be labelled gringos, however, it first acquired widespread attention during the Mexican War of 1846–48 and this gave rise to many spurious derivations based on the misconception that conflict spawned the word. For example, it has been proposed that the origin is the Mexican version of the first two words heard when the American troops were singing either 'Green Grow the Lilacs' or 'Green Grow the Rushes O'. Also cited is Major Samuel Ringgold whose surname spoken by a Mexican would resemble 'gringo' and who, before being mortally wounded at the Battle of Palo Alto in 1846, mounted several punitive raids against the Mexicans.

**GRIST TO THE MILL:** *Something of value.*

'Grist', a variant of 'grind', originally denoted the average quantity of corn a mill could grind at one time – i.e. its source of profit.

**GROG:** *Alcoholic drink in general, rum in particular.*

The rum ration in the British Navy used to be one full pint of thick traditional rum per man per day which, needless to say, resulted in a great deal of drunkenness. In 1740 Admiral Edward Vernon (1684–1757), nicknamed by his men Old Grog because he sported a highly distinctive grogram boat cape, decided to stamp this out by ordering that the ration be diluted with water and issued in two parts, one at noon and one at 6p.m. The new diluted ration was promptly named 'grog' and one who was partly intoxicated was said to be 'groggy', a word that has now expanded to mean weakened by illness or exhaustion.

**GROOVY:** *Pleasing, sexually exciting, fashionable.*

This is an extension of the 1940s American jazz musicians' jargon 'in the groove', playing to perfection, which probably arose by analogy with the perfect reproduction obtained by the accurate positioning of a stylus in the groove of a record. The expression became *démodé* after the 1960s but enjoyed a revival in the '80s.

**GROTTY:** *Inferior or socially unacceptable.*

A Liverpudlian truncation of 'grotesque' much popularised by The Beatles in the early 1960s. Grotesque came to hold such meaning due to the excessively ornate and bizarre nature of the decor found in the Roman grottoes by early archeologists.

**GROUND SWELL:** *A movement of opinion or feeling whose existence is evident though its source is not.*

Properly, this denotes a condition of the sea characterized by low, powerful undulations which are caused by a distant storm or seismic disturbance and which do not deepen like ordinary waves until they near the shore. The experienced sailor is nevertheless aware of the condition and able to sense it through the movement of his craft. It would appear that Samuel Coleridge (1772–1834), whose Devonian childhood would have rendered him familiar with seafaring terms, was the first to use the expression metaphorically; in *Zapolya, A Christmas Tale* (1817), he talks of the ground swell of teeming instinct.

**GROUSE:** *To grumble.*

The Northern French dialect '*groucer*' – to grumble and complain without cause – is the source.

**GRUB STREET:** *The lower end of the literati.*

In mid seventeenth-century London, Grub Street, which took its name from a medieval property dealer called Grubb, was the haunt of pamphleteers and writers purveying material of much volume but little merit. The name was changed in 1820 to Milton Street after the owner of the lease.

**GRUB-STAKE:** *Money required to fund the start of a venture.*

The term developed in the American Gold Rush of the mid–late 1800s when investors funded experienced mine prospectors in return for a share of the proceeds. Whether this is built on the fact that the investor provided food and supplies for the trip or on the fact that the prospector was off to the hills to grub about in search of gold is irrelevant since both these two senses of 'grub' are directly linked in their common derivation from the Middle English '*grubben*', to dig or poke about, as a person does in his food.

**GUBBINS:** *Assorted rubbish.*

This is the Devonian variant of 'gobbons', small pieces or portions, used in that country for the waste matter of a fish catch, i.e. heads, guts and parings. The word ceased to be regional in the early seventeenth century after it had shifted to describe the highly uncivilised people infesting Brent Tor at the edge of Dartmoor in Devon, a group with such a long-standing reputation for savagery that even the Romans are recorded as making a point of leaving them strictly alone.

**GUNG-HO:** *Given to bravura heroics.*

This is built on the Chinese '*kung-ho*', more fiery, fierce and awesome, a term which was somewhat misunderstood by the American Marine Officer Evans F. Carlson (1896–1947) when serving as an observer with the Chinese 8th Route Army from 1937–39. He thought it meant 'to work together' and, when in command of the 2nd Marine Raider Division (Carlson's Raiders) in WW2, he adopted it as the divisional motto. Effectively a little army on their own, paying scant attention to standard authority, his men fought with the ruthless guerilla tactics that Carlson had learnt in China. They were undoubtedly brave, but outsiders thought them unnecessarily reckless.

**GUSSIED UP:** *Dressed in finery.*

This harks back to earlier times when the more ornate the style of court gowns and suits, the greater the number of gussets and inserts required for them.

**GUY:** *A man.*

This is almost certainly born of the Hebrew '*goy*', Gentile, especially since it developed in American English in which there is a pronounced influence from Hebrew and Yiddish. Another suggestion is that the origin is the seventeenth-century application of 'guy' to one of grotesque and ragged appearance based on the effigies of Guy Fawkes; if this is the case there is a long, unexplained gap since the word did not start to serve as a synonym for 'man' until the nineteenth century. When used to mean 'to poke fun at' guy is probably taken from the Dutch '*de guig aansteken*' – to make fun.

# h

**HACKNEYED:** *Dulled by over-use.*

The Old French 'haquenée' was an ambling horse which, unlike the draught or war horse, had no specific role to play. Such plodding nags tended to become hire horses which are traditionally over-worked and of poor quality – hence the modern 'hackneyed', trite, 'hack', horse for hire, and 'hack', a literary drudge. The element of hire is further reflected in 'hackney cab', originally horse-drawn. The belief that the cab is etymologically linked with the Borough of Hackney in London is therefore wrong. Oddly enough, though, the very first fatality caused on the public highway by a motor vehicle occurred on Stockmar Road, Hackney and the vehicle involved was an early motorized taxi, which retained the old name. The furore caused by this incident could explain the mistaken association with the borough.

**HAG-RIDDEN:** *Obsessed by troubles.*

This derives from the old belief that those who rose in the morning looking worn out had spent the night being tormented and ridden about by witches. Horses and ponies were also believed to be similarly used, which is why the knots in their manes are called 'hag-knots'.

**HAIL FELLOW WELL MET, TO BE:** *To be on extremely or overly friendly terms with another.*

Recorded since the sixteenth century one must assume there to have been some element of punctuation in the original form; perhaps 'Hail, fellow, well met.' On the other hand there are plenty of examples of 'hail-fellow' meaning a thoroughly good chap, so perhaps the expression alluded to a fortuitous meeting with a boon companion.

**HAIR OF THE DOG:** *The first alcoholic drink taken 'the morning after' to cure a hangover.*

A strong medieval belief held that the only guaranteed cure for a dog-bite, and one which would ward off any infection to boot, was a mixture of bread and milk containing some of the offending animal's hair, which had to be either eaten or applied as a poultice. This 'cure' was no doubt as effective as the modern hair of the dog treatment is.

**HALCYON DAYS:** *A time of peace and happiness.*

In Greek mythology, Alcyon, the daughter of Aeolus, became the wife of Ceyx; she and her husband were turned into kingfishers as a punishment for calling themselves Hera and Zeus. There is a legend that the kingfisher uses its magical powers to calm the seas at a particular time so that it can build its nest on the waters and breed. The Ancient Greeks actually logged these days on their calendars as the seven days before and the seven days following the winter solstice, when the weather patterns and the seas do tend to be calm. Because of this tale, the spelling altered to include the 'h' through the erroneous notion that the origin was the Greek '*hals*', sea, and '*kyon*', conceiving.

**HALF MAST:** *Not properly positioned.*

This really denotes the required position of flags lowered in respect for the dead or as a distress signal. It is a misleading expression, the ruling being that the flag should be lowered only by its own depth. A large flag on a short pole might be flown literally half-way down, but this would be simply coincidental.

**HALF SEAS OVER:** *More than a little drunk.*

Possibly a corruption of 'half sea's over' – i.e. the journey is half completed – and the jubilation this would induce in the crew, but others maintain this alludes to a ship floundering drunkenly in a heavy storm, heeled hard over, with the prevailing sea breaking half-way across the upper deck. There could also have been a pronounced influence from the eighteenth-century Dutch '*op-zee zober*', over-sea beer, their extra-strength, export beer that was extremely intoxicating.

**HAM ACTOR/HAM IT UP:** *Anyone given to theatrical excess.*

Of late nineteenth-century American origin, this is a contraction of 'hamfat' actor, a slang name for one of the flamboyant, blacked-up minstrels who were so popular at that time and whose heavy make-up had to be removed with hamfat. There was a song entitled 'The Hamfat Man', which told the tragedy of one such, and there were countless turn of the century references to worn out, old actors as 'Hamfats'. There have been attempts to link the term instead to Shakespeare's Hamlet who, in the opening of Act III, Scene 2, cautions the players against indulging in exaggerated acting, excessive gesticulation and strutting and bellowing with too much passion, but the time and place of origin still point to the 'hamfat' theory.

**HANDICAP:** *A disadvantage.*

An abbreviation of 'hand-in-cap'. In medieval times two parties wishing to barter had to avail themselves of the services of an umpire. Each of the three placed a token sum of money in a cap and the umpire then decided which of the two articles for barter held the least value and how much money should be added to make a fair exchange. The deal went ahead only if both barterers indicated their satisfaction by putting another token into the cap, otherwise no exchange took place. In either case, the umpire kept what was in the cap. In the seventeenth century, a similar method was used to decide which horses should carry extra weight to make for a fair race.

**HANDSOME IS AS HANDSOME DOES:** *It is one's actions that count.*

An example of 'handsome' in one of its very early meanings – chivalrous and well-mannered. Built on 'hand', it originally applied to someone who was not recalcitrant but easy to 'handle'. The second 'handsome' is properly an adverb.

**HANG A LEFT/RIGHT:** *Make a left/right turn in a car.*

This comes from the world of surf-riding; a board is manoeuvred in either direction by shifting the position of the feet so that the toes hang over the edge.

**HANG BY A THREAD:** *To depend on precarious conditions.*

This is an allusion to the suspension of the SWORD OF DAMOCLES.

**HANG FIRE:** *To hesitate or delay.*

In the days of the old, muzzle-loading cannon, if the gun had not been properly loaded and primed, or if the powder was damp, there could be a considerable time-lag between the ignition of the powder in the touch-hole and the discharging of the gun – which was then said to be hanging fire.

**HANG ON IN THERE, TO:** *To persevere despite adversity and exhaustion.*

Turn-of-the-century American sporting jargon, this could well have developed specifically in the boxing fraternity as a shout of encouragement to a fighter near dead on his feet, near the end of a round, and simply hanging onto his opponent in a hug for support and waiting for the bell.

**HANG OUT:** *To reside.*

A shortening of 'hang out one's shingle', this alludes to the old practice, now used only by barbers and pawnbrokers, of hanging out a sign to indicate the trade or practice being carried on in that place. It is one of the many expressions that went out to America on the Mayflower and survived there long after its abandonment here, only to be re-imported much later.

**HANGED, DRAWN AND QUARTERED:** *Severely punished.*

This was a particularly revolting death sentence first used in 1284 on David, the Welsh Prince. A typical reading of the sentence went as follows: 'You are to be taken to the place of execution where you are to be hanged but not till you are dead; for, while still living, your body is to be taken down, your bowels torn out and burnt before your face; your head is then cut off and your body divided in four quarters.' This terrible sentence is not lost in the mists of time; it was last passed in a British court in 1867 though, mercifully, it was never carried out. There was another sentence, 'Drawn, hanged and quartered', under which the victim was drawn on a hurdle to the place of execution.

**HAPPY AS A CLAM AT HIGH TIDE:** *Feeling pleased and secure, and even a little smug.*

When the tide is in, people cannot go down to the beach and dig clams out of their hidey-holes in the sand.

**HAPPY AS A SANDBOY:** *Carefree.*

In the nineteenth century, sand was used to scour stone floors etc. and the street urchins of London hawked it in buckets from door to door. Their life was doubtless short and miserable but it was perceived by their customers to be devoid of any pressure or responsibility.

**HAPPY AS LARRY:** *Extremely happy.*

The origin, although obscure, is most probably the British dialect 'larry', confusion and excitement which, in turn, is built on 'larrikin', a dialect corruption of 'larking'. Various persons forenamed or surnamed 'Larry' have been put forward, but all are groundless.

**HARD AND FAST:** *Fixed and rigid.*

A ship run aground on a sandbar was so described until the tide lifted her free of obstruction.

**HARD-BITTEN:** *Tough and uncompromising.*

A horse that has a hard, leathery mouth is unresponsive to the pull of the bit.

**HARD-NOSED:** *Tough, uncompromising and stubborn with it.*

Originally said of a hunting dog that consistently picked up the wrong scent and would not leave it, however many times it was lead away to the correct trail.

**HARD UP:** *Short of money.*

The nautical command to push the tiller full windward to bring the ship's head right away from the wind, a maneouvre usually undertaken when the vessel could not cope with the heavy weather and had to ride out the storm as best she could – as one in financial difficulties has to.

**HARK BACK:** *To revert to.*

'Hark' actually means to hear or to listen, but this usage arose from the command 'Hark back!' (Listen! Go back!) given to a pack of hounds when it had over-run the scent or trail. Similar commands like 'Hark away!' or 'Hark forward!' exist but have had no similar outcome.

**HARP ON, TO:** *To dwell mercilessly on the same topic.*

The original and fuller expression of the sixteenth century was 'to harp on the same string' and it is not unlikely that some influence was exerted by the ultimate meaning of 'harp' as explained under HARPY. This would produce allusion to someone picking away at the same sore.

**HARPY:** *A shrewish or rapacious woman.*

The original female Harpies were Minoan funeral priestesses who stood in attendance naked to the waist and shrouded in feathered cloaks. Thus they were intended to represent the vulture which was in turn regarded as the transporter of souls to the heavens through their habit of devouring the dead and winging their way skyward. Their title was based on the Greek '*harpazein*', to seize or pluck, but it is unclear whether this was applied for their resembling the bird that plucked at the corpses or for their plucking at the harps they played at the service. Perhaps it was nothing more than associations with death that ensured the gradual degradation of the Harpies until they were portrayed in Greek culture as foul and winged demons sent to plague men but, curiously enough, never women. The Harpies emerged in Early Christian iconography as winged creatures of angelic aspect escorting souls to heaven, playing their harps the while.

**HARUM-SCARUM:** *Wild, giddy, confused.*

Derived from the long redundant verb 'hare' – to harass or harry – and 'scare', it would appear that this initially described a hit-and-run military tactic executed in the dead of night to cause maximum disruption and fear.

**HARVEY SMITH:** *An offensive, two-fingered gesture.*

At the Hickstead show-jumping finals of August 1971, it was alleged that, upon completing his last and winning round, Harvey Smith made the gesture at Mr Douglas Bunn, one of the judges. He was threatened with the loss of all prize money but staunchly maintained that he had merely made a victory sign to his numerous fans because he felt he had done so well. He was later exonerated and the matter was dropped.

**HAS THE PENNY DROPPED?:** *Do you understand yet?*

Reference to the old penny coin operated locks on the public conveniences which made an instinctive 'clunk' as the heavy copper coin activated the mechanism and laid clear the objective.

**HASSLE:** *Trouble and vexation.*

In the Southern states of America, the term is applied to the quick, agitated panting of hounds after a fight or a long run on the hunt. Etymologically, 'hassle' could be a blend of 'haggle' and 'tussle', an old North of England word meaning to hack at with a blunt knife, or the German '*hassen*', to hate.

**HAT TRICK:** *A set of three achievements or victories.*

In the game of cricket, in earlier days, a player was awarded a special cap if he took three wickets with three successive balls.

**HAULED OVER THE COALS:** *Severely reprimanded.*

One of the old methods of torture was to drag the victim slowly over hot embers.

**HAVE A CHIP ON THE SHOULDER, TO:** *To be defiant and ready to take offence.*

In America truculent boys, sometimes even men, carried around a wood-chip which they would put on their shoulder as a challenge to others to knock it off and start a fight.

**HAVE A COB ON:** *Be in a bad temper.*

'Cob' means anything hard and round and is slang for the head, this saying implying a bad head, and therefore a bad mood.

**HAVE A CRUSH ON:** *To be infatuated.*

The verbs 'to crush' and 'to mash' mean much the same thing, and this saying probably arose by analogy with 'masher', an aggressively romantic male, a gypsy word for 'fascinator'. In the 1880s, youngsters professed to be 'mashed' on someone.

**HAVE A DERRY ON, TO:** *To be in a foul mood, or to have a 'downer' on something.*

The most likely source would appear to be the old nonsensical refrain 'Hey, derry, derry, down', although there has possibly been a helping hand from the old dialect 'deray', uproar, based on the Old French '*derroi*', confusion and destruction. Perhaps 'derelict' has also had some influence?

**HAVE A LOT OF FRONT:** *Ostentatious.*

It is said that this arose in America where some stores in the Mid-West had frontages grossly disproportionate to their internal size, making them look grander than they were.

**HAVE A LOT OF NECK, TO:** *To be audacious.*

Allusive to the way most animals lower and extend the head forwards when adopting a fighting stance. Similarly, the admonition 'wind your neck in' means calm down.

**HAVE A YEN FOR SOMETHING, TO:** *To have a strong hankering.*

A term arising in mid nineteenth-century America as a result of the influx of Chinese coolie labour to whom '*yen*' was the smoke from an opium pipe.

**HAVE NO TRUCK WITH SOMEONE, TO:** *To avoid them at all costs.*

Likely derived from the French '*troquer*', to barter or exchange, 'truck' has held such meaning here since the Middle Ages. There is no connection with the vehicle.

**HAVE OVER A BARREL, TO:** *To have someone at your mercy.*

At one time, an offender in the British Army or Navy was subjected to Field Punishment Number One during which he was tied helpless across the barrel of a gun and flogged. If the seriousness of the crime warranted it, further punishment was inflicted by the gun's being discharged, thus also ensuring several cracked ribs. The death of the offender during the execution of this brutal sentence was not uncommon.

**HAVE THE BIT BETWEEN YOUR TEETH:** *To be set determinedly on a course of action.*

A horse which has managed to shift the bit forward and clamp it between its teeth is no longer subject to any control.

**HAVE THE INSIDE TRACK:** *Have an advantage.*

In athletics or horse-racing, the competitor on the inside track has the advantage of having less distance to cover.

**HAVE THE MAKINGS OF, TO:** *To have obvious potential.*

Another piece of nineteenth-century American cowboy jargon, this refers to the kit of tobacco, cigarette papers and matches known as the makings. This word came to describe a person as yet immature or unskilled who nevertheless had all the right ingredients for success.

**HAVE THE PIP, TO:** *To take umbrage; be in a temper.*

Use of 'pip' as denoting a disease afflicting fowl and hawks which causes the birds to lose appetite and pine away.

**HAVE TOO MANY IRONS IN THE FIRE:** *Attempting too many jobs at the same time.*

If a laundry-maid put too many of the old flat irons on the fire at once and the rotation was therefore too slow, the irons overheated and she singed the clothes. Attempts to link this with the blacksmith's forge are unconvincing since the best place for his irons is in the fire.

**HAVE YOUR CAKE AND EAT IT, TO:** *To have two irreconcilable benefits.*

Seemingly incongruous since one must first have a cake before one can eat it, this is the modern distortion of the more logical sentiment expressed in John Heywood's *Proverbs*, published 1546: 'Would you both eat your cake and have it?'

**HAVE YOUR CARD MARKED, TO:** *To be cautioned.*

Developed in the 1970s from British football; the referee can mark a player's card each time he infringes the rules and send him off the pitch if he repeatedly offends.

**HAVE YOUR CARD STAMPED, TO:** *To be allowed out for pleasure.*

The reference here is to the military pass which allows a soldier out of camp and which must be stamped by the Duty Officer or Sergeant.

**HAVING KITTENS, TO BE:** *To be in a state of extreme agitation.*

The modern hand-me-down from the medieval belief that pregnant women experiencing pain had 'cats in the bellie' as a result of having offending a witch who placed them there for revenge.

**HAY, HELL AND BOOLIGAL:** *The least desirable of places or situations.*

Hay and Booligal are towns of unpopular reputation in New South Wales, Australia and the expression was made famous by Andrew Barton Paterson (1864–1941), a lawyer, poet and journalist from NSW, perhaps best remembered for the song 'Waltzing Matilda'. In his 'Rio Grande's Last Race' (1902): 'Oh, send us to our just reward/In Hay or Hell, but Gracious Lord /Deliver us from Booligal.' Paterson was in all likelihood inspired by the much older English expression used by beggars and thieves in their pleas namely: 'From Hell, Hull and Halifax'.

**HAYMAKER:** *A wild swing, particularly an uppercut.*

The allusion is to a farmer pitching a forkful of hay onto a cart already piled up high.

**HAYWIRE:** *Out of control, all wrong.*

The wire used to bale hay is held in a coil by restraints; it is thin and whippy, and, if the restraints break, it uncoils itself like lighting and at random, presenting a very real danger to everyone in the vicinity.

**HEAD HONCHO:** *Supreme leader.*

An Americanism based on the Japanese '*hancho*', a squad leader.

**HEAD START:** *A significant advantage.*

In horse racing, one animal can be given an advantage over the others by starting in front of them by a distance equal to the length of its own head.

**HEADS, THE:** *Urinals.*

A Naval expression, this is a contraction of 'bulkheads', since urinals on board ship are located against these.

**HEAP COALS OF FIRE ON ANOTHER'S HEAD:** *To encourage repentance by returning good for evil.*

Proverbs 21-22 reads: 'If thine enemy be hungry, give him bread to eat; and if he be thirsty, give him water to drink: For thou shalt heap coals of fire upon his head and the Lord shall reward thee.' The apparent incongruity of heaping coals of fire is explained by the ancient symbolism of the purifying power of hot coals – especially those taken from an altar. Isaiah 6:6–7 reads: 'Then flew one of the seraphims unto me, having a live coal in his hand which he had taken with the tongs from off the altar: "And he laid it upon my mouth and said, Lo, this hath touched thy lips: and thine iniquity is taken away, and the sin is purged." '

**HEAR, HEAR!:** *Indication of complete agreement.*

In the House of Commons in the seventeenth century, those in opposition to a speaker indicated their disapproval by setting up a monotonous humming noise; those who agreed with him counteracted with shouts of 'Hear him! Hear him!', which, by the early nineteenth century, reduced to 'Hear, Hear!'

**HEATH ROBINSON:** *Unnecessarily complicated, slung together with weird components.*

The British cartoonist Heath Robinson (1872–1944) produced for *Punch* and other such publications numerous cartoons depicting weird and wonderfully complicated machines that performed simple, even unnecessary, functions. Drawings emulating his style, still widely available on greetings cards, keep the expression alive.

**HECTOR:** *To bully or intimidate.*

Surprisingly, this is ultimately from the noble, Trojan warrior in Homer's *Iliad*; in seventeenth-century London his name was adopted by a street gang who saw themselves as jolly brave fellows but were regarded by everybody else as cowards who ganged up on the defenceless and the out-numbered.

**HEDGE:** *To prevaricate.*

This spin-off from HEDGE YOUR BETS alludes to the fact that a gambler who does this is not following any firm conviction.

**HEDGE YOUR BETS:** *To make contingency plans, to protect oneself from loss.*

A farmer protects his land from the ravages of the wind by planting hedging all around it. The gambler too protects his interests when he makes compensatory transactions by, for example, wagering on both sides, placing an each-way bet, or backing more than one horse in a race.

**HEELTAP:** *To drink more slowly than your companions.*

Originally a 'heeltap' was one of the layers of leather that went to make up the heel of a shoe but it came to be applied to the small amount of liquor left in a glass that had not been completely drained in one draught, these dregs being thought to resemble the leather heeltap in shape. This 'tap' appears to be allied to 'taper' and could be applied to any diminishing shape or tail end. Heeltap is also used to mean 'to scrounge drinks'; this development from the first meaning is understandable since one who has never actually finished his drink is never 'ready' to buy the next round.

**HELD/LOCKED IN CHANCERY:** *Trapped in an invidious position at the mercy of another.*

Chancery is the court of the Lord Chancellor so, properly, the term should be 'chancellery', but that great modifier, lazy speech, has worked its magic. This application has arisen because the court of chancery functions mainly in the field of bankruptcy and equity, and deals with issues so complex that cases before it incur a great deal of legal wrangling and tend to remain unresolved for a very long time. By association, in wrestling, a 'side chancery' is a hold which involves locking an opponent's head under one arm and abusing it until the unfortunate victim can extricate himself.

**HELL FOR LEATHER:** *Breakneck speed.*

Originally used in the nineteenth century in relation to someone riding a horse at such a speed, this could be a simple reference to the damnation of the rider if he fell from the leather of the saddle. It has, on the other hand, been suggested that the expression is a corruption of the German '*zum Heil verlaufen*' run for your life or salvation.

**HELL ON WHEELS:** *A state of supreme misery or degradation.*

Originating in America, this was initially the moralists' metaphor for the travelling brothels, gambling dens and saloons that trailed along behind railway-track layers and the like to provide entertainment at night.

**HELLO, SAILOR:** *Camp greeting.*

Born of sailors' reputation for homosexuality induced by long periods at sea, this has been in wide use since the 1950s and has been promoted by several British radio and TV programmes, most notably *The Goon Show* and *The Dick Emery Show.* It is, unfortunately, untrue that the family motto of the French Admiral Le Compte de Villeneuve (1763–1806) who was trounced by Nelson at Trafalgar was '*A l'eau, c'est l'heure*'.

**HENPECKED:** *A man dominated by women, especially the members of his own family.*

The younger and immature cockrels in the chicken yard are bullied mercilessly by the hens.

**HERE WE GO GATHERING NUTS IN MAY:** *Folly is afoot.*

This is a corruption of 'here we go gathering knots of may (blossom)' as previously chanted by children sent out by the villagers to collect floral decoration for the May Day celebrations. As with children today, or any era, the allotted task was accomplished amidst much horseplay.

**HERE'S MUD IN YOUR EYE:** *Popular drinking toast.*

Originally this was something of a vaunting challenge over a stirrup cup before a steeplechase. The proposer of the toast was insinuating that the other riders would spend the race clearing from their face the mud dashed up by the lead mount of the proposer.

**HEX:** *A jinx.*

Since a hex is normally 'put on' someone as a spell that brings about disaster, this is from the German '*Hexe',* witch, which entered English by way of the so-called Pennsylvania Dutch who painted the sides of their barns with hex-signs to ward off evil spirits.

**HEYDAY:** *Period of greatest success, prosperity or gaiety.*

This is a simple combination of 'hey' – exclamation of pleasure or enthusiasm – and 'day' – time of existence.

**HIDE YOUR LIGHT UNDER A BUSHEL:** *To conceal your talents modestly.*

Matthew 5:15 reads: 'Neither do men light a candle and put it under a bushel, but on a candlestick; and it giveth light unto all that are in the house.' A bushel was a measuring container for corn which took its name from the Gaelic '*bas*', palm of the hand.

**HIDEBOUND:** *Rigidly narrow-minded.*

Originally the term applied either to cattle whose hide, through malnutrition, was clapped so tight about the body that it could not be raised with the fingers, or to a tree whose bark was gripped so tight about the trunk as to impede growth. The intimations of rigidity and restriction caused the shift in meaning, this being also reflected in STRAIT-LACED.

**HIGH AND DRY:** *Left helpless with no further resources.*

The allusion is to a beached ship stranded so high up the beach that no tide can refloat her.

**HIGH BALL IT:** *To travel at top speed.*

In the American railroad system of the late nineteenth century, the track signal consisting of a large ball raised to the upright position indicated a clear track ahead; in these conditions the driver piled on the speed. In the twentieth century, the term 'highball' transferred to a cocktail based on whiskey. The American railroad is also responsible for the terminology 'club soda' as the Pullman club cars of the early twentieth century were selected as the market test ground for the option of individually bottled soda water which eventually brought about the downfall of the more traditional syphon.

**HIGH DAYS AND HOLIDAYS:** *Rare or special occasions.*

The word 'high' here denotes great formality or pomp as in 'high tea' or 'High Church', so these days, embracing solemn rites and religious pomp were infrequent, notable festivals, as were holidays (holy days) – especially to the hard-working common multitude.

**HIGH DUDGEON:** *Offended, indignant and resentful.*

Although the origin is unclear, this could be based on the sixteenth-century 'dudgeon' – a kind of boxwood used in the making of dagger handles; if so, the allusion could be to a person so angered that he lifted his dagger high to strike back. Alternatively, the Welsh '*dygen*' – dark and evil feeling – is no mean contender.

**HIGH FALUTIN':** *Absurdly affected or unrealistic.*

This is most probably a whimsical corruption of 'high fluting' in allusion to a high ethereal ramble of notes drifting this way and that. Alternatively, it may be from the Dutch '*verlooten*' – lottery, high gambling game.

**HIGH HANDED:** *Overbearing, autocratic.*

The reference here is to a haughty rider holding the reins high up towards his chest.

**HIGH MUCK-A-MUCK:** *A person of great importance or, perjoratively, a person who sees themself as such.*

This is from the Chinook '*hui muckamuck*' – plenty of food. In the Alaskan wastes inhabited by the Chinook, food was all that really mattered so a man with plenty of it was an extremely important person.

**HIGH PROFILE:** *Significant, prominent.*

In the US Navy, this originally described certain kinds of large shipping as seen against the horizon.

**HIGH ROLLER:** *A person who operates on a financially impressive scale.*

This expression originated in the gambling world where vast sums of money ride on the roll of the dice.

**HIGH SIGN:** *To indicate that all is well; to give the go ahead.*

Originating in con men's jargon, this was a surreptitious sign given to tell a partner that it was time to implement the main gambit or 'sting'. Usually, the sign was an arching of the brows or the placing of the hands on the head or some other pre-arranged upward gesture.

**HIGHBROW:** *Intellectual, sometimes loftily so.*

Allegedly coined by the American journalist and humorist Will Irvin (1873–1948) and included in his *The Hamadryads*, this was a direct reference to the old notion that those of high intellect have high foreheads to accommodate their supposedly larger brain. If Irwin did coin the word, the idea was hardly original, being reflected in countless much older epithets like 'longhead'.

**HIGHJACK:** *To steal in transit, to usurp command of an aircraft etc.*

The term was born in America in the late 1800s and first applied specifically to the activities of criminals in dry states who robbed BOOTLEGGERS, relieving them of the bottles hidden inside their *high jackboots*, so this seems a plausible origin. With the advent of Prohibition in the 1920s, the meaning shifted to convey one gang's stealing another's shipment of booze, which moved the word closer to its current usage.

**HIGH JINKS:** *Ludicrous revels or devious trickery.*

'Jink' once meant sudden or erratic and jerky movement intended to delude or evade. 'High jinks' is first noted in 1700 when it was a dice game in which the loser had to drink in one draught a massive bowl of booze or pay a forfeit.

**HIGH JUMP, FOR THE:** *In trouble.*

This was coined by British troops to describe the punishment of having to go over the assault course at the double in full kit. The course was known as the high jump because of all the obstacles that had to be surmounted. Reinforcing this is the fact that a really high jump in athletics or steeplechasing presents the greatest danger.

**HIGH TAIL IT:** *To run away at high speed.*

A horse at full gallop holds its tail high.

**HIP:** *Aware, in tune with surroundings, street-wise.*

A straightforward development from 'hep', the spelling could well have been influenced by the Wolof '*hipicat*', person who is aware, the 'hipi' element meaning 'to open the eyes'. This could have also brought about the use of 'cat' to designate a 'hip' person.

**HIP! HIP! HURRAH!:** *Cry of exaltation.*

This is, in all likelihood, nothing more than a cry echoic of joy and pleasure, but this has not prevented some wild conjectures, the most inventive of which holds 'hip' to be a notarikon representing '*Hierosolyma est perdita*'. The meaning is to be taken as either 'Jerusalem is destroyed', as shouted in joy by German knights on a Jew-bashing jaunt, or 'Jerusalem is lost [i.e. taken from the infidel]', a chant raised by the Crusaders. This latter theory further postualates that 'hurrah' is derived from the Slavonic '*hu-raj*', paradise, thus giving the overall cry a meaning of 'Jerusalem is lost to the Infidel and we are on our way to heaven or paradise.'

**HIS NIBS:** *A person of importance, or one who considers himself as such.*

Aping such expressions as 'His Excellency', the 'nibs' element is probably a corruption of 'nobs', a contraction of 'nobility' or 'nabs', a contraction of 'nabob'.

**HIT THE PANIC BUTTON:** *To instigate pandemonium.*

Located next to the pilot of each WW2 American bomber was a button used to alert the crew to bale-out status. Generally referred to as the Panic Button, English civilians acquired such usage from the airmen stationed here during the conflict.

**HITCH-HIKE:** *To go on foot but beg rides from passing motorists.*

It has been asserted that this was originally 'hitch and hike' and was applied to two men travelling with one horse. To avoid over-tiring any one of the three, one would ride ahead, tether the animal to a tree to await the arrival of the other who would then ride ahead by the same distance and again tether the horse, the process being repeated until the journey was completed. This procedure was also known as a 'ride and tie' and, in America, could take the form of a race. As recently as 1971, Levi – the jeans company – organised a ride and tie in California.

**HIVE OFF, TO:** *To move assets to safety.*

At times the beekeeper moves some of the combs and part of the population of one hive to a fresh one to start off a new colony with its own queen.

**HOBBLEDEHOY:** *An awkward, clumsy youth.*

'Hob', a by-form of Robert or Robin, denoted in the fourteenth to nineteenth centuries a rustic dolt or clown. The second element is perhaps rooted in the French '*de haie*', of the hedgerow.

**HOBBY-HORSE:** *Personal obsession or pet subject of lecture.*

Probably akin to 'hobble' in allusion to clumsy or ungainly movement, the term 'hobby' in earlier times was descriptive of a small falcon or ambling horse for everyday use. During the day a gentleman-farmer would do the rounds of his tenants and workers on his hobby-horse whilst keeping the thoroughbred mounts for hunting and pleasure. Typically this resulted in the hobby-horse treading a well worn path and covering the same ground day after day. To examine the falcon for a moment, it is interesting that when Peter Adolph devised a new table-football game in 1947 he tried to register it under the name Hobby but found this disallowed as the word was considered public domain. Aware of the etymological history of 'hobby' he resorted to Subbuteo from the Latin name for the bird in question – *Falco subbuteo subbuteo.*

**HOBNOB:** *To associate with familiarly.*

From the Anglo-Saxon '*hab*', give, and '*nab*', take, the expression appeared in Chaucer's times as '*habnab*', to have and have not, and referred to the give and take of close companionship.

**HOBO:** *A tramp or itinerant worker.*

Apparently from the expression 'hoe boy', which, in the nineteenth century, was applied to an itinerant farm labourer who trekked from job to job with his tools on his back. Although 'hobo' now denotes any old tramp or bum, it properly describes a man who works on the move and is not in search of handouts. There is, however, another suggestion that the word derives from 'Ho beau!', known to be a form of greeting between eighteenth/nineteenth-entury tramps.

**HOBSON'S CHOICE:** *No choice at all.*

The most widely accepted and published theory lands the eponymous honour squarely on the shoulders of one Thomas (or Tobias) Hobson (1544-1631), a Cambridge-based carrier and haulage contractor who hired out his horses on what was alleged to be an inflexible system of rotation which afforded no choice to the hirer. The horse closest to the stable door was the next one to be hired out and the customer took that one or none at all. That this nationally known carrier did exist is beyond dispute for reference is made to him in Samuel Fisher's *The Rustick's Alarm to the Rabbies* (1660), and in *The History of the Worthies of England* (1662 post.) by the Cambridge born and educated Thomas Fuller (1608–61); the poet John Milton (1608–74) mentions him twice and a reference to him appears in Issue No 509 of *The Spectator* dated 14 October 1712. However, Hobson's fame seems to have been largely posthumous and, though it may seem positively iconoclastic to impugn his involvement, one must be fair. During his lifetime, in 1617, this appeared in print: 'We are put to *Hodgson's* choice to take such privileges as they will give us, or else go without.' A case can be argued for an origin in 'Hodge' which, a variant of Roger, was a generic name from the fourteenth to the nineteenth century for any rustic, and the life of medieval rustics was decidedly lacking in freedom of choice. 'Hodgson's choice' could have developed into 'Hobson's choice' to indicate the Devil's alternative since 'Hob' was once used as a name for the Devil, but it could also have been influenced by the fame of the Cambridge carrier.

**HOBSON-JOBSON:** *Disparagingly, a native ceremony, or the process of adopting a foreign phrase and anglicising it.*

In the nineteenth century, British soldiers serving in India thus slightingly mimicked the Muslims in the Muharram procession who repeatedly cried out: 'Ya Hassan! Ya Hosain! O Hassan! O Hosain!'. In Muharran, the first month of the Muslim year, there is a fast commemorating the grandsons of Mohammed, Hassan and Hosain.

**HOCUS-POCUS:** *Deception, mumbo jumbo.*

It is unclear whether this originates in the dog-Latin title of an actual conjurer of old, or in the corruption of a phrase much used in the consecration of the Mass 'Hoc est Corpus [filii]' (This is the body [of the Son of God]), or in a combination of both. Thomas Ady in *A Candle in the Dark* (1656) mentions a magician who styled himself: 'The Kings Majesties most excellent Hocus Pocus, and so was called because that at the playing of every trick, he used to say, "Hocus Pocus tontus talontus, vade celeriter jubio", a dark composure of words, to binde the eyes of the beholders, to master his trickpass the more currently without discovery.' It is nevertheless highly probable that the 'magic' words Hocus Pocus were based on the Latin phrase from the Mass; all magicians and showmen used parodies of Latin to impress the audience whose 'knowledge' of that language was mostly restricted to what they heard in Church services. The theory that the term was originally a direct steal from the Mass is supported by the Scandinavian '*hocuspocusfileokus*' and the still current chant of American children 'hocus-pocus-dominocus'. There is, in any case, nothing to recommend the alternative suggestions that the word derives from variously named mythological wizards, such as Ochus Bochus, of whom no record can be found. There have been two modern spin-offs from 'hocus-pocus': 'hokum' and 'hoax'.

**HOGWASH:** *Verbal insincerity or nonsense.*

This is from the medieval use of 'wash', slops or swill, and the term originally described what today is called 'pigs' swill'.

**HOI POLLOI:** *The common herd.*

This is Greek for 'the many', which is why purists point out that '*the* hoi polloi' is tautological. The phrase is increasingly misused to designate the upper classes, perhaps because of some imagined connection with 'HOITY-TOITY'.

**HOIST WITH YOUR OWN PETARD:** *Caught out by your own machinations.*

A petard was a medieval military mine used to breach walls or gates. It was notoriously unreliable, often capriciously detonating as soon as a flame came anywhere near it, thus many a hapless sapper was blown up by, or hoist by, his own device. One may hazard a guess at the sort of noise a petard made; it takes its name from the French '*peter*', to fart.

**HOITY-TOITY:** *Supercilious.*

The origin is obscure but it seems likely that there is some play on 'high' or 'haughty' or both, and, indeed there was an eighteenth-century version 'highty-tighty'. Although there are problems associated with a possible origin in blend of 'hoit', to move about in a boisterous manner and the dialect 'toit', to stagger, it must be said that the term's earliest application was to a wild and frivolous demeanour. There is no foundation to the suggestion that the origin lies in the French '*haut toit*', high roof, alluding to the fact that the dwelling places of the nobility had high, vaulted roofs.

**HOKEY-POKEY:** *Trickery and decei;. cheap ice-cream.*

Both senses are derived from HOCUS-POCUS. The second was most probably occasioned by the poor quality of the product which was nothing more than ice fragments flavoured with syrup, hence sham ice-cream. There is, however, a wholly fictitious claim that it came about because nineteenth-century American ice-cream vendors of Italian extraction allegedly called out '*O, che poco*' (Oh, how little) – a cry that was hardly likely to engender a high turnover.

**HOLD AT BAY:** *To fend off.*

The 'bay' in question is actually the sound made by an excited hound but here the clarity ends. The expression was first used of the denouement of a stag hunt when the quarry was cornered by the hounds until the huntsmen arrived. It is, however, now unclear as to whether the phrase applied to the stag as it warded off the baying pack with its antlers, or to the hounds themselves which held captive the stag whilst baying to summon the hunters.

**HOLD OUT THE OLIVE BRANCH, TO:** *To offer peace.*

As attested by the name of Athens, the goddess Athene was a major deity to the Greeks and her main attribute was the olive, this followed closely by the dove. Olive branches were much easier to handle in ritual ceremony and so became a symbol of peace.

**HOLD THE FORT, TO:** *To manage despite difficulties.*

Popularly believed to be part of the signal sent by General William 'War is Hell' Sherman to fellow Union General Corse whom he had required to hold Allatoona Pass in the October of 1864 during the Atlanta Campaign. What Sherman actually signalled from his HQ on Kenesaw Mountain was 'Hold out, relief is coming'. As is so often the case the words were altered by the Press and in this particular case the distortion is even more remarkable in that there was no fort there to be held. Undeterred by this irksome detail an American hymn writer, Phillip Paul Bliss (1838–1876) put the words into the mouth of Jesus in the form of a beseechment to the faithful to 'Hold the fort, for I am coming' and this atrocious hymn was a great favourite at evangelical meetings in England in the early 1870s which secured the expression a place in the language. As for General Corse, he survived the war and went on to more dark and bloody deeds as a tax collector in Chicago.

**HOME AND DRY:** *Indisputably the winner.*

The allusion is to a horse-race home when one rider has not only reached the stables first but with such a lead that he can rub down and retire his mount before the others arrive.

**HOMER SOMETIMES NODS:** *Even the best of us is not perfect.*

The Latin poet Horace (65–68 BC) wrote: 'I think it shame when the worthy Homer nods but, in so long a work, it is allowable if drowsiness comes on.' Homer (*c.*850 BC) was the great poet of Greece attributed with the authorship of the *Iliad* and the *Odyssey*, although this has been disbuted. In fact there is an on-going debate, as there is over Aesop, as to whether such a character ever really existed or whether he was a 'blanket' author invented to cover a collection of several tales; Homer's name does mean 'one who puts things together'.

**HOMERIC LAUGHTER:** *Strong, lusty laughter.*

The allusion is to the '*asbestos gelos*', inextinguishable laughter, paralleled to that of the gods of Olympus in the *Iliad*, allegedly written by Homer.

**HONI SOIT QUI MAL Y PENSE:** *The sin is only in the eyes of the beholder.*

Popularly rendered as 'Evil be to him who evil thinks', this is the well-known motto of The Most Noble Order of the Garter as instituted by Edward III *c.* 1348. Tradition has it that the king was dancing at court with the Countess of Salisbury when a garter slipped from her leg to the floor causing a hush in the assembly. Edward then caused further stir by putting the garter on his own leg and uttering the above. Again it is the tradition that in this act of 'gallantry' he saved the lady any further blushes arising from an item of her under-attire falling to public gaze. The story is unsatisfactory for many reasons. Firstly, stockings had not yet been invented so no garter would be needed to hold up such an item and why should anyone think evil of a woman suffering such an accident of dress? Secondly, ladies of the time were not so easily embarrassed; they were made of bawdier stuff – none wore underpants and lifting their skirts to show their bare behind at others in derision was pretty standard behaviour. What the king was actually doing was saving the Countess's life for the garter was a leg emblem which symbolised the ring of the coven. Many bored ladies of station were into witchcraft for the sex and drugs – naturally occurring narcotics and hallucinogenics were available even then. Basically the king was cutting dead any speculation regarding the Countess's involvement in such antics by himself donning the garter and asking the assembly if anyone present fancied accusing him of witchcraft as well. The first word of the motto actually means 'dishonour' and dishonour then meant death, so Edward was effectively placing himself between Salisbury and any potential accuser who would face death for levelling any similar charge against the Crown.

**HONKIE/HONKY:** *Pejorative term applied by a black to a white man.*

Derived from 'Hunky' or 'Bohunk', first used by nineteenth-century American whites to designate an immigrant labourer from a middle-eastern European country, most notably Hungary. Because it was an insulting term denoting low status, the blacks adopted it for any white and, in their slightly back-of-the-throat manner of speech, 'Hunky' became 'Honky'.

**HOOCH:** *Alcohol, especially of poor quality.*

The Hutsnuwu Indians of Adriraly Island, Alaska, distilled a rough spirit. Their name, meaning 'grizzly bear fort', and rendered as 'Hoochinoo' by whites, transferred to the drink.

**HOOD/HOODLUM:** *Thug; member of a criminal organization.*

The origin is obscure but the most acceptable theory so far is that it derives from the Bavarian '*Hodalum*', rowdy, street-thug, this being a variant of '*Huddellump*', raggedy beggar or scoundrel. The term emerged in Chicago *c.* 1870 and first denoted a street yob who specialized in roughing up immigrant Chinese, this being well in keeping with the original Bavarian meaning.

**HOODWINK:** *To fool or dupe.*

In use since the sixteenth century, this could well refer to a custom of muggers of the time; they pulled their victim's hood over his eyes to disorientate him and to prevent his identifying his attackers.

**HOOK, LINE AND SINKER:** *Completely.*

The reference here is to a fish that not only takes the bait, but greedily swallows the hook, the fishing line and the lead weight that sinks the bait.

**HOOKER:** *A prostitute.*

Although tempting to see this as a simple allusion to a whore's hooking a client like a fish, it would appear instead that two very definite influences were at work here, one toponymal and the other eponymous. Chronologically speaking, the first is the preponderence of whores operating in the early nineteenth century in Corlears's Hook, an infamous New York brothel area much frequented by seamen. There are therefore examples in print of the usage before the American Civil War, whence came the later, but more significant influence – General Joseph 'Fightin' Joe' Hooker (1814–79). He was certainly one of the Union Army's more flamboyant characters; Charles Francis Adams once said: 'General Joseph Hooker is a man of blemished character whose headquarters is a place that no self-respecting man liked to go and no decent woman could go, for it can only be described as a combination of bar-room and brothel.' Hooker's reputation for hedonism, no doubt greatly embellished, spread throughout the Army and, when the red-light district of Washington swelled to cope with the demands of the massive military presence, it was called 'Hooker's Camp' or 'Hooker's Division'. The constant movement of personnel in and out of the city carried the term 'hooker' with it and dispersed it across the States.

**HOOLIGAN:** *A street thug.*

There has been much conjecture about the origin of this term, the most widely held view being that it derived from the name of Patrick Hoolihan (or Hooligan) who, in the late 1800s, made of the *Lamb and Flag* pub in London's Southwark a base from which he ran a petty crime empire. The word certainly first appeared in print in Police commentaries in daily newspapers in the summer of 1898, although it had already enjoyed a certain vogue due to a series of songs and ripping yarns in the early 1980s regarding the adventures of a rowdy Irish family named Hooligan. Indeed, there was also an 1824 farce by T. G. Rodwell

*More Blunders than One* in which there was a drunken, disreputable character called Larry Hoolagan. Some think there is a possibility that there was a street gang run by someone by the name of Hooley, hence 'Hooley's gang' and 'hooligan'. There seems to be no end to the speculation and, perhaps, after all the word is simply a development from the Irish '*hooley*', noisy, drunken party. Although a digression, it is interesting to note that, when the Russian and British royal courts enjoyed a close relationship in the 1890s, visiting Russians picked up the word, which is still alive and well in Russia in the form of '*gooligan*'. (The Russians have no 'h' in their alphabet.)

**HOOSEGOW:** *Prison.*

This approximates to the pronunciation of the Spanish word from which it is derived, '*juzgado*', a tribunal or court, which could send one to prison.

**HOP THE TWIG:** *To decamp just before capture.*

This is from hunting jargon and refers to birds that take to the air just before, or just as, the hunter fires at them.

**HORATIO ALGER STORY/ CHARACTER:** *A tale of one proceeding from rags to riches.*

The American author Horatio Alger (1834–99) wrote a series of moral tales for youngsters extolling honesty and hard work. Despite the current usage, not one of Alger's characters became even remotely rich; they rose from nowhere to achieve lower middle-class respectability, no more. Alger was also a Unitarian minister and very much one of the New England moralists but had to resign from the Church in 1866, quitting his native Massachusetts for New York, due to persistent rumours about him and the little boys to whom he loved to preach.

**HORN OF PLENTY:** *A source of teeming abundance.*

Alternatively known as the cornucopia, this refers to a character in Greek mythology called Amalthea. The legend is that Zeus was reared in secret to prevent his father Cronus eating him along with his brothers. Although one version has Amalthea as a nymph in his attendance, the main one says that she was a magic she-goat, used to suckle the infant god. At some point, Zeus removed one of the goat's horns, presenting it to his nurses and assuring them that it would provide whatever they wanted in endless supply. He later, somewhat ungratefully, killed the goat and used its skin as his shield covering.

**HORNS OF A DILEMMA:** *Having to choose between two courses, neither of which is desirable.*

'Dilemma', from the Greek '*di*', twice, double, and '*lemma*', assumption, is therefore a double assumption. The inclusion of 'horns', apart from the obvious intimation of discomfort, allludes to the philosophers' designation '*argumentum corutum*', basically a horned argument which, like a bull, is going to toss you, whichever horn (or lemma) you grab.

**HORNSWOGGLE:** *To prevaricate or deceive.*

Originating in the nineteenth century American West, this then denoted the evasive tactics of a longhorn which knew how to dodge the lasso. Not only did it twist and turn as it ran, but it also waggled, or woggled, its horns to make roping difficult or impossible.

**HORSE LATITUDES:** *Areas of becalmed sea abutting the North East trade winds.*

Although the origin is obscure, there are three possibilities. (1) The inspiration may have been the self-explanatory saying FLOGGING A DEAD HORSE which was already in existence and may have been further popularised by 'horse latitudes'; in the days when sailing ships often left Britain manned by a crew which had been paid in advance for anything up to a month's work, the ship would have reached these latitudes when the 'dead' wages were paid off. (2) This relies on the effect of the calm waters found in the area. Ships bound for the New World and the West Indies with cargoes of horses were sometimes when becalmed there, forced to jettison some or all of the animals to ensure there was enough fresh water for the men. (3) This explanation relates to the fact that these seas are sometimes positively unruly. The Spanish, moving from the pleasant, predictable seas governed by the trade winds which they called 'El Golfo de las Damas' (Sea of Ladies, Ladylike Seas) called the horse latitudes 'El Golfo de las Yeguas' (The Mares' Sea) since, in colloquial Spanish and throughout South and Central America '*yegua*' can also mean a slut or anything coarse and crude – as these seas can be at times in contrast to those governed by the trade winds.

**HORSE-SENSE:** *Common sense.*

A nineteenth-century Americanism which cannot possibly allude, as claimed by horse-lovers, to the animal's innate intelligence since this is not a quality for which the species is noted or famed. The reference is made instead to the cunning and savvy of the horse-trader, a calling long noted for comprising dealers who know all too well on which side their bread is buttered.

**HORSES FOR COURSES:** *The most suitable is the best.*

On the race track it is well established that some animals run better on wet turf while others are more suited to dry.

**HOT BED:** *Breeding ground, especially of evil.*

As early as the seventeenth century, growers were building hot beds by using fermenting manure as a source of heat, covering the beds with glass to produce a forcing house. Why an innocent horticultural term should acquire connotations of evil is obscure, unless the smell was responsible.

**HOT LINE:** *Any channel of priority communication.*

First used in 1952, this was the nickname for a multiple direct line linking all USAF bases to alert them for mass, co-ordinated action. It was not until 30 August 1963 that the Washington–Moscow link was established and so named, though it is not the 'red telephone' of films and popular imagination; it is a teletype machine which has not yet been used for anything more dramatic than New Year greetings and hourly test messages.

**HOT PURSUIT:** *Determined chase.*
Figuratively, of course, 'hot' can mean 'passionate' or 'eager', but this expression had a quite specific meaning in the early English Navy when 'hot pursuit' described a Naval chase in which the quarry was actually in sight and not over the horizon heading for a known destination, which was known as 'cold pursuit'. Hot pursuit would generally be carried on into territorial waters, but cold pursuit would be broken off if it became apparent that the quarry would make safe harbour before it could be overtaken.

**HOT SEAT:** *A difficult uncomfortable situation from which there is no escape.*
This originated in America, and alludes to the most undesirable seat of them all – the electric chair.

**HOTCHPOTCH:** *A random mixture.*
From the Middle French '*hocher*', to shake, and '*pot*', pot, this originally meant a stew made with anything to hand thrown into a pot and stirred up. In law, the term has acquired a quite specific meaning relating to property inheritance. In the event of there being a group of beneficiaries to an estate, one of whom has received some funds in advance of the formal division, the stipulation of a 'hotchpotch' in the will demands that these funds be returned to the 'pot' before the estate can be divided in total.

**HUE AND CRY:** *A great outcry against, a clamour.*
From the Norman '*hu e cri*', ('*hu*' meaning a hunting or war cry), this was originally the term for the general turnout of a community in full pursuit of a felon.

**HUGGERMUGGER:** *In secrecy or disorder.*
This is seemingly an Anglo–Irish construction resting on the Irish '*cogair*', whisper, and the Middle English '*mokeren*', conceal.

**HUMBUG:** *Spurious talk or trickery.*
The origin is clouded but the most convincing theory is that this is a compound of 'hum', to cajole or coax, and 'bug', ghost or bugbear, giving the concept of a sham bugbear. There is however another suggestion worthy of consideration which is the Irish '*uim bog*', soft or base copper, this being the term for the spurious coinage circulating in Ireland during the reign of James II. There seems little to recommend the theory that points to the Italian '*uomo brigiard*', a lying man.

**HUNKY-DORY:** *In an ideal situation.*
First appearing in print in 1856, this is based on the Old Fresian '*honcke*', place of refuge, through the Dutch '*honk*', a goal, which was adopted by New York children as 'hunk' to denote a goal or home base

in a game of tag. Thus 'hunk' and 'hunky' became established as meaning fine and dandy. The addition of 'dory' could well have come from Japan, unlikely though that may seem. After Commodore Perry had gained permission for American ships to have access to Yokohama in 1854, American sailors discovered the delights of the bars and brothels on Huncho-dori, a street leading away from the docks, whereupon 'hunky-dory' could have emerged as an expression of their appreciation.

# I

**I SHOULD COCO!** *Expression of agreement, or, ironically, disagreement.*

An ellipsis of the Cockney rhyming slang 'I should coffee and cocoa' = 'I should say so'.

**I WANT TO BE ALONE**

Always copied with a heavy Slavonic accent, this is popularly believed to have been said by Greta Garbo (1905–90) when she retired at the age of thirty-six from the glitzy world of Hollywood and became a recluse in New York City. She turned down all requests for interviews and a certain sector of the Press, who were greatly intrigued, simply made up 'quotes' including the above. What she actually said when exasperated by the intrusiveness of the press was: 'I just want to be let alone' but, by sheer coincidence, 'I want to be alone' had been one of her lines in 1932 film *Grand Hotel* .

**IF THE MOUNTAIN WON'T COME TO MOHAMMED . . . :** *Assertive action must replace passive attendance.*

Completed by 'then Mohammed must go to the mountain', this relates to a traditional account of how Mohammed, when preaching to a sceptical crowd, was asked to perform a miracle to prove his powers – as Jesus was in similar circumstances. Obediently, he ordered Mount Safa to move towards him, but it did not, whereupon he told the people to offer thanks since, if the mountain had moved it might have toppled over and crushed them.

**I'M FROM MISSOURI, (YOU'LL HAVE TO SHOW ME):** *I'm a cynic; I need hard evidence.*

This expression has long been associated with that American state which is otherwise known as the Show-Me State; natives therefrom taking pride in their self-bestowed reputation for shrewdness. As with many axioms and expressions, this has no specific origin yet one can pinpoint the incident which launched the phrase into general usage. In 1899, Willard Duncan Vandiver, Congressman for Missouri, was attending a Naval banquet in Philadelphia and at some point in his speech he said: 'I come from a state that raises corn, cotton, cockleburs [a coarse weed] and Democrats. Frothy eloquence neither convinces nor satisfies me. I am from Missouri. You will have to show me.' His speech was well reported and the term came into general use.

**IN A CLEFT STICK:** *In a dilemma.*

The reference here is to forked sticks which can be used to pin down snakes or other small creatures.

**IN CAHOOTS:** *In collusion for shady dealings.*

Originating in America, this was born of the French '*cahute*' (hut or shanty) which was the traditional hide-away of bandits.

**IN CLOVER:** *In luxury.*

Cows prefer and thrive on pasture that contains a high concentration of clover. The saying has nothing to do with the four-leafed variety.

**IN FULL CRY:** *Aggressively on the trail.*

The allusion is to the excited baying of hunting hounds when the pack is in hot pursuit of its quarry on open ground.

**IN HOCK:** *In debt or in pawn.*

It would appear that the phrase originally meant 'in prison' and derived from the Dutch '*hok*', hutch, hovel or prison; the strictures applied by debt caused the transfer in general usage. The extension to 'in pawn' is a straightforward analogy to an item's being held prisoner by the pawnbroker.

**IN STIR, TO BE:** *To be in prison.*

'Stir' has been applied to prisons since the mid 1800s; there are three possible origins of the word. First, the Romany '*stirpen*', a prison; secondly the English dialect '*styr*', a penalty, and lastly the 'porridge' theory which maintains that the prisoners' staple diet generated the term since porridge has long been nicknamed 'stirabout'.

**IN THE AIR:** *Present in an indefinite form.*

Possible reference to the 'smell' of rain in the air when a change in the weather is imminent, or to the scent of the quarry carried on the wind to the nose of the predator. The same construction also appears meaning 'everything is up for grabs' but this is from the American football pitch and allusive to the ball having been punted high in the air and therefore the trophy of the first man to catch it when it falls.

**IN THE ALTOGETHER:** *Completely naked.*

In the early 1800s drunkards, wasters and rakes were known collectively as 'The Altogethery' and anyone who was so drunk that he collapsed was said to have 'joined the altogethery' or to be 'in the altogethery'. The transfer to nudity came about because nearly all the turn-of-the-century paintings of nudes that were displayed in public places showed women reclining so languidly on *chaises-longues* that they looked just as if they had over-indulged.

**IN THE BAG:** *Absolutely certain.*
This is an allusion to game shot or captured and already in the hunter's bag.

**IN THE BUFF:** *Stark naked.*
An analogy between the colour of the human skin and that of cured ox-hide.

**IN THE CAN:** *Ready for its purpose.*
This originated in the motion picture business. Reels of film which were ready for release used to be stored in round tins.

**IN THE CART:** *In severe trouble.*
The reference here is to a condemned criminal's last journey – in a tumbril.

**IN THE CATBIRD SEAT:** *Sitting pretty.*
The catbird is an American songbird whose alarm cry resembles the mewing of a cat and the expression probably arose in the Southern States where it was a popular cage bird and therefore pampered. Red Barber, the sports announcer for The Brooklyn Dodgers, launched the phrase when he described how he lost to a poker opponent who later thanked him for continually raising the ante saying that he (the opponent) had been in the catbird seat all along because of an ACE IN THE HOLE. Barber liked the saying, and, having paid so dearly for it, decided to adopt it. The expression gained further status when James Thurber (1984–1961) used it as the title of one of his most popular stories in *The Thurber Carnival*, first published in 1945.

**IN THE DOGHOUSE:** *In disgrace.*
This is, of course, a direct reference to a dog's being banished from the house for misbehaviour and relegated to its cold kennel. The expression was greatly aided by J.M.Barrie's *Peter Pan* (1904) in which Mr Darling was punished by his wife by being relegated to living in the dog-kennel until the children returned safely from their adventures. He had unjustly chained Nana, the family dog and children's nanny, in the back garden with the result that Peter Pan was able to slip into the house and spirit the children away.

**IN THE LAP OF THE GODS:** *At the mercy of fate.*
The gods, when eating their wondrous food, drop crumbs in their lap, just like mortals. When they stand up, these miraculous crumbs of fortune fall to earth completely at random.

**IN THE NICK OF TIME:** *Success in the last second.*
This dates from the days when game scores were kept on a stick called a tally into which were cut, or 'scored', marks to indicate points. The duration of play was marked off by wider notches incised each time the sandglass drained – perhaps four such sections to a game. Play would have to cease as the last such notch, or nick, was to be cut.

**IN THE OFFING:** *In the near future.*
Properly, the offing is that expanse of sea between a ship and the shore. Landlubbers distorted this meaning to that part of the sea to the horizon,

so any incoming vessel within view would soon be in harbour.

**IN THE PINK:** *At the peak of health.*

Although now only used in the above context one could previously have been in the pink of anything – fashion, business or social acclaim. But one such example is found in *Romeo and Juliet*, Act 2, Scene iv; 'Nay, I am in the very pink of courtesy.' This line is uttered by Mercutio and draws from Romeo the response 'Pink for flower?' for in Shakespearean times the admittedly exquisite flower was a metaphor for excellence. Now almost redundant is the verbal 'pink' as meaning to cut or make a sharp puncture – we still talk of pinking shears and the flower, the pink, is so named for the sharp indentations in the petals for the blooms are not always pink in colour. Thus, to be in the pink of something was to be at the exact point where one wished to be.

**IN THE SWIM, TO BE:** *To mix with the right people.*

A rather obscure use of 'swim' as denoting the thickest part of a shoal of fish into which the clever fisherman casts his net or line.

**IN YOUR ELEMENT:** *Literally or metaphorically in your natural or most agreeable environment.*

This is a reference to the ancient concept that earth, air, water and fire were the four basic elements which formed the foundation of everything. Mammals are most at home on the earth, birds in the air, and fish in water – presumably the fire was the final refuge of the heretic.

**INDEPENDENT AS A HOG ON ICE:** *Arrogantly indifferent to advice; independent to the point of self-detriment.*

The origin of this puzzling expression is obscure, but it has been conjectured that it lies in the North of England and Scottish '*hog*' – a curling stone thrown with insufficient force to make it travel far enough across the ice to be considered 'in play' – a usage perhaps occasioned by the notion that such a stone is 'pig-lazy'. Various other theories depend on the creature itself but none is even remotely convincing since the animal becomes completely helpless on smooth surfaces; its legs splay out as it collapses and, after a few attempts to rise, it simply lies where it is until it is rescued or it dies. It is, of course, possible that the phrase is now used in almost the reverse of its original application and that it once denoted the helpless and pathetic; there are examples of an earlier expression likening someone of awkward demeanour to a hog on ice.

**INDIAN CLUBS:** *Heavy wooden clubs thrown or swung to exercise the upper body.*

It was said that American Indians used similarly shaped wooden clubs in exercise. In addition, there could have been an influence from the use in the gym of the term 'medicine ball', a contrivance also allegedly used by these Indians, a people to whom 'medicine' conveyed the idea of a powerful influence, mentally or physically.

**INDIAN FILE:** *Single file.*

A party of American Indians on a hunting trip or a raid into enemy territory walked one behind the other, the last man shuffling along backwards brushing out the footprints.

**INDIAN GIVER:** *One who gives and takes back, or gives only to receive.*

This was a slur aimed by white settlers at American Indians, whom they largely held in contempt. An exchange of gifts on meeting was an essential part of the Indian culture, and the settlers interpreted this as giving in the hope of receiving, especially as, whenever whites were involved, the Indians always seemed to end up with something better than what they had given away.

**INDIAN SUMMER:** *Dry warm weather in late autumn.*

Such weather was common on the western plains of America where once the native Red Indian roamed.

**ISH KABIBBLE:** *Exclamation indicating total lack of concern.*

This corruption of the Yiddish '*ich gebliebe*', '*nisht gefildt*' or, possibly, '*es is mein diege*' – all of which mean 'it's my problem' or 'I should worry' – was made extremely popular by the American Fanny Brice (neé Borach, 1891–1951) whose life story was told in the hit musical and film *Funny Girl*.

**IVORY TOWER:** *A place of retreat from the realities of life.*

Although the expression was already common in literary circles, no doubt inspired by the reputation for purity held by ivory and its colour, it was the quite specific use by the French man of letters, Charles Augustin Saint-Beuve (1804-69), that launched it to its current prominence. In 1837 he wrote *Pensées d'Aot, à M. Villemain* in which he mildly pilloried contemporary writer Compte Alfred Victor de Vigny (1797–1863), drawing a distinction between him and Victor Hugo (1802–85), (with whose wife he, Saint-Beuve, was conducting an affair), using in the text these words: 'Hugo, a strong partisan . . . fought in armour and held high the banner in the midst of the tumult; he still holds it; and Vigny, more discreet, as if in his tower of ivory, retired before noon.' Vigny, whose work is characterized by bleak bitterness, had retired from all public and social life to live as a recluse.

**IVY LEAGUE, THE:** *A select group of Eastern American Universities.*

The relevant universities – Harvard, Yale, Columbia, Princeton, Dartmouth, Cornell, Brown and the University of Pennsylvania – are the long-established colleges built in the old style with walls covered in ivy. The designation started in sports journalism in the mid-1930s when, it is said, sports writer Caswell Adams of the *New York Herald Tribune,* discussing the relative merits of various college teams, referred to both Princeton and Columbia as 'ivy league' and his editor was so taken by the epithet that he started using it in editorials. Adams later commented that he had intended to be disparaging when he said it, but only in a mild and humorous way.

# J

**J. ARTHUR:** *Wank or wanker.*

This is Cockney rhyming slang based on the name of Lord Joseph Arthur Rank (1888–1972), the British industrialist and film magnate whose film productions, known to millions, were always signed off after the credits by 'J. Arthur Rank'.

**JACKANAPES:** *An impudent fellow.*

This is most probably a blend of 'Jack' and 'ape': 'Jack', a generic term for the male of a species, e.g. jackass, was in medieval England also a generic term for an ape, especially a trained one, so such a combination would be similar in usage to 'tomcat'. In fact, the word could even be a collision of 'Jack, an ape'. In addition it has been suggested that the word is a blend of 'Jack-à-Napes', meaning a monkey brought in from Naples and sold as a trained foil to dandies out to impress the ladies but chronology disputes this since the word predates the influx of such Italian-trained monkeys. Its use as an insult seems to have begun with its application to the extremely unpopular William de la Pole, Duke of Suffolk, (1396–1450), whose device was that of an ape shackled by a ball and chain. He was exiled by Henry VI in 1450, but murdered almost as soon as the ship was out of sight of land, most probably on the orders of the then Duke of York.

**JAM SESSION:** *Gathering of jazz musicians playing together ad lib.*

Almost certainly of African origin, this emerged in the jargon of black American musicians in the 1920s and '30s. Possible sources are the Wolof '*djam*', a sort of divine inspiration, or the Swahili '*jaame*', anything good, a special friend. It could be a blend of the two, a group of friends sitting round making good music together, extemporizing in an inspired way.

**JACKPOT:** *The main prize.*

In a game of poker, the kitty is known as the jackpot since, to enter the play for it, a player has to have a pair of jacks or better.

**JAMBOREE:** *A wildly festive occasion.*

In the card game of euchre, a call of 'jamboree' announces the holding of all five top-point-scoring cards, which accrues to the holder sixteen points and negates the need to play that round at all since it sweeps the board. The origin of the call itself is obscure but is conjectured to be a combination of 'jam', impact together, and the French '*bourrée*', stuffed or packed tightly together, underlining the fact that all the important cards are jammed into one player's hand.

**JAMMY:** *Exceptionally lucky.*

This is a modern reduction of the 1930s British Navy slang 'jam-strangling' applied to a man who could extract the very best from any situation and somehow convert it to his own advantage. This was based on the use of 'strangle', to extract by unfair or illegal means.

**JANISSARY:** *A bodyguard.*

This is derived from the Turkish '*yeni ceri*', new troops. In 1330, the Ottoman Empire drafted initially 1,000 Christian youths to form the nucleus of a new army and, shortly afterwards, increased the draft to one out of every five Christian youths throughout the empire. The fact that the Janissaries were drawn exclusively from Christian stock gave rise to the notion that the word is based on the Turkish for 'pale-faced', but this is not so. The corps enjoyed great status for many years but when their position was threatened in 1826 by reform they rebelled and were disbanded through slaughter.

**JANKERS:** *Punishment.*

This is most probably a variant of 'janglers' since it started life as early twentieth-century British Army slang in which it described not only the punishment but also the camp cell block where the jangle of keys sounded.

**JAYWALKING:** *Crossing the road as a pedestrian without due care.*

The Americans regard the jay as a rural bird and have therefore used this expression to represent the way a rustic, unused to a city's busy traffic, would simply wander out into the street as if he were at home.

**JEEP:** *An all-terrain vehicle.*

Two influences produced this, the designatory initials G.P. (General Purpose) and Eugene the Jeep, a character introduced into the Popeye cartoons on 16 March 1936 by E.C. Segar. Eugene, a small, rugged, dog-like creature, lived on orchids, could go anywhere, do anything and become invisible at will. The only sound he could make however was 'Jeep, Jeep'.

**JERKWATER TOWN:** *An excessively rural place.*

In early-mid nineteenth-century American railroad jargon, a jerkwater stop was a place where the fireman had to go down to a stream, jerk water out in buckets and carry it back to the engine; it later denoted a small town built around the water tower from which the fireman had to jerk the pipe across to the engine. The system was modernized in 1870 so that pans inside the tracks jerked water up into the tender as it passed over.

**JEROBOAM:** *Large bowl or wine bottle.*

The reason for the attribution of

this biblical character's name is usually put down to the Bible describing him as a 'mighty man of valour', presumably capable of downing capacious quantities of wine, but this is wholly unsatisfactory if for no other reason than the Bible's marked reluctance to associate courage and valour with drunkenness. Far more likely an explanation is to be found in 1 Kings, 11:29–40 which recounts that Jeroboam was leaving the city of Jerusalem when accosted by Ahijah, the Prophet of Shiloh, who removed his new robe and tore it into twelve strips. These were intended to represent the twelve tribes of Israel; only ten of them were handed to Jeroboam, Ahijah explaining that he would have control of ten of the tribes but the entire kingdom of Solomon would not pass to him, two tribes would be withheld. This explanation would also account for the divided opinion as to whether a Jeroboam contains ten or twelve normal bottles (one for each piece of cloth from the robe). Once the biblical pattern was set in the early 1800s, other names such as Rehoboam and Methuselah were applied on a random basis with no numerical significance whatsoever.

**JERRY:** *A chamber pot.*

This is a diminutive of JEROBOAM which is large bowl or bottle. 'Jerry' as applied to a German was probably occasioned by the first meaning in that the German helmet resembled a chamber pot.

**JERRY-BUILT:** *Cheaply and hurriedly constructed.*

Likely from the maritime 'jury built' which was applied to an emergency, running repair to a ship damaged by storms etc. As for the 'jury' element, there are two possibilities, both from French; one is '*jour*', day, since the temporary repair was not intended to be long-lasting, the other the Old French '*adjurie*', relief. It has also been suggested that this 'jury' is but a contraction of 'injury' since its first recorded usage refers to a sailor's peg leg. Of the folk etymology that abounds concerning this expression, the most frequently postulated claims it refers to the walls of Jericho which came tumbling down at a mere trumpet blast from Joshua; there are in addition a few digs at the Germans and a putative connection with a non-existent firm in Liverpool infamous for throwing up shoddy dwellings.

**JEW'S HARP:** *Musical instrument.*

This is in all likelihood a slur based on the Jews' reputation for parsimony with which, deservedly or no, they are now saddled; the implication is that a Jew would make do with this cheap thing because the proper harp is so expensive. In an attempt to remove the slur, some etymologists have nudged forward the improperly constructed French; '*jeu trompe*', play horn or trumpet, which is baseless, as are suggestions of 'jaw's harp'.

**JIGGERED:** *Extremely tired; confounded.*

The origin is obscure but there are some possibilities. It may be from 'jig' i.e. exhausted from dancing too much, or from 'jigger', a measure of spirits, i.e. intoxicated or, as has been conjectured, it may be a blend of 'Jesus' and 'buggered'. It is also possible that 'jigger', a variant of 'chigoe' is responsible; the chigoe (possibly named from the Spanish '*chico*', small) is a parasite that bores into the hands and feet.

**JIGGERY-POKERY:** *Underhanded trickery.*

Originating in Scotland, this is from 'joukery-paukery', a ricochet based on the Scottish '*jouk*', dodge, and '*pauk*', shrewd, cunning.

**JILT:** *To abandon (a lover).*

From 'Jillet' (a pet form of Jill) this originally applied only to the dumping of a man by a woman. In essence, it is very similar to the use of 'Jack' in expressions like 'he jacked her in' and 'jilt' could have been chosen as the female equivalent due to the nursery rhyme association of Jack and Jill.

**JINGOISM:** *Chauvinism of the right-wing British variety.*

This dates from the tremendous success with armchair generals of a popular music hall song of 1877 in a time of mounting tension between Britain and Russia. Written by G. W. Hunt and first performed by the Great MacDermott, the song contained the lines: 'We don't want to fight/But, by Jingo, if we do/We've got the ships, we've got the men/ We've got the money too.' As for the origin of 'Jingo' itself, this is not quite so clear. It is first noted in the seventeenth century as conjurers' jargon, 'Hey Jingo' being used to make things appear (as opposed to 'Hey Presto' which was originally used exclusively to make things disappear). A suggestion that the word derives from the Basque '*Jinko*' (God) is given some backing in that the 1694 translation of Rabelais by Motteux substitutes 'by Jingo' for the original French '*par Dieu*'.

**JINX:** *A bringer of bad luck.*

Ultimately from the Greek '*iyinx*', the wryneck woodpecker, which produced 'jynx' and finally 'jinx'. The bird, which spends much of its time in Africa, was much used there, and throughout Europe where it summers, in witchcraft and the casting of spells; in medieval times the bird itself was presumed to have supernatural powers, its selection for such a role no doubt due to its many strange habits and characteristics. When disturbed in her nest, the female distorts her neck grotesquely and hisses like a snake, and she can be induced, through daily removal, to continue to produce anything up to fifty of her translucent eggs. There is some difficulty with this origin in that the OED and other authorities do not record its appearance in print until 1911: on the other hand, this could be attributable to its lying 'underground' in black American slang, based on the original African influence, which no one bothered to record.

**JOB'S COMFORTER:** *Someone who gives no comfort at all.*

Job was a prosperous, God-fearing man who was afflicted by successive disasters. He retained his faith in God, who had wagered on this with Satan, but when he sought comfort from his friends they could give him none and even suggested that he, the blameless Job, must have kindled God's wrath in some way.

**JOE MILLER:** *A hackneyed joke; a joke book.*

This is a reference to Joseph Miller (1684–1738), a famed Drury Lane comedy actor, but there may not be any real connection since it rests on a publication entitled *Joe Miller's Jest Book or The Wit's Vade Mecum* published in 1739 by one John Mottley who used the recently deceased comic's name simply as a hook for sales; there were none of his jokes or witticisms therein, only three stories told about Miller.

**JOHN:** *The lavatory.*

Although now seen as decidedly American, the origins of this term lie in early sixteenth-century England and the misconception that Jack is the pet form of John. The earliest noted use in 1553 makes reference to Jacques, this spawning several variant spellings, including the obvious anglicization of 'Jackes'. It was doubtless with a pun on this spelling that Sir John Harington, courtier to Elizabeth I, published a pamphlet in 1596 entitled *The Metamorphosis of Ajax* – this last word then being pronounced 'a-jakes' and the publication being a publicity puff for his invention of the first primitive yet practicable inside flushing toilet. Certainly by the early 1600s, the term 'john' was in use – perhaps this was perceived as a more English nomenclature than Jack but, as already stated, Jack is the diminutive of James as clearly demonstrated by the supporters of James II being termed the Jacobites.

**JOHN AUDLEY IT:** *To cut things short.*

Originating in theatrical slang, this was a call traditionally used in companies of strolling players. When the next audience was massed outside and becoming restive, an attendant would enter the tent or barn calling out: 'Is there a John Audley here?' – as if there were a message for him – which indicated to the players that they should hurry the current performance along before the people outside became bored and moved off.

**JOHN DOE:** *Any unidentified male, especially if dead.*

Until abolished by the Common Law Procedure Act of 1852, John Doe warrants and eviction notices were an accepted legal convenience. The papers were effectively open in that John Doe was a generic term for the common man so the holder of the warrant could then arrest whosoever he chose. Other names used were Tom Styles, John Noakes and, for women, Jane Doe.

**JOHN HANCOCK:** *One's signature.*

The name of the American statesman (1737–93) whose signature is the most prominent on the Declaration of Independence, which led to the tradition that he was the first to sign it though, in fact, nobody knows who this was. 4 July 1776 was the day on which the final draft was voted upon, but no signatures were added on that day; the main signing process went on until August and indeed, some signatures were added years later.

**JOHNNY APPLESEED:** *A rustic, especially if itinerant.*

This was the nickname of the mildly eccentric American, John Chapman (1774–1847), who was famous for scattering apple seeds from cider mills all over the country, even passing out bags of dried apple seed to travellers on waggon trains heading west. He personally established a great many orchards though the number is not known and has been grossly exaggerated by legend.

**JOINT:** *A place of low repute.*

This is most probably due to the fact that a deal of disreputable activity once took place in annexes *joined* to a main building. In the nineteenth century, for example, a girl picked up in a bar would be taken to some hovel attached to it; most back rooms in such places were merely huts built on at the rear. The word 'joint' applied to a marijuana cigarette alludes to its tapering shape resembling a leg-joint of meat.

**JUMBO:** *Excessively large.*

Jumbo was an extremely large African elephant exhibited at London Zoo from 1865 to 1882. He was possibly named from the Swahili 'jumbe', a chief, from the Gullah '*jamba*', elephant, or from MUMBO-JUMBO.

**JUMP ON THE BANDWAGGON:** *To join a successful enterprise.*

A bandwaggon, which was ornately decorated and had a high deck for accommodating a band, was used in nineteenth-century America to parade a politician through the streets of a town in which he was campaigning. To indicate their support, and possibly to curry favour, leading citizens climbed onto the waggon of their chosen candidate and this gave a lead to lesser mortals who followed suit.

**JUMP THE GUN:** *To act prematurely.*

An athlete who is too quick off the mark begins his sprint before the starting pistol has been fired.

**JUNKET:** *A dessert; a feast; merrymaking.*

The Latin '*juncus*', a reed or rush, gave rise to the French '*jonquette*', a kind of sweet custard which, once made, was stored inside rush baskets to keep away the flies. The term spread to encompass any large, wicker basket, such as a picnic basket, and thence to the sort of occasion on which it might be used.

# K

**KANGAROO COURT:** *An improperly constructed tribunal before which a fair hearing is impossible.*

The origin is clouded by the fact that, whilst it is almost beyond doubt that there is a direct influence from Australia, the expression arose in nineteenth-century America and there is no record of its being in circulation in Australia before then. The term was first applied in America to courts set up in prisons by inmates either to judge one of their own or to decide what payment to extract from new prisoners wishing to avoid painful initiation ceremonies. Possibly those undergoing 'trial' saw parallels with earlier British courts which, in order to supply much needed settlers and labour for the new colony of Australia, found guilty and transported almost everybody who came before them, often on the flimsiest evidence: or, possibly, since 'kangaroo' (=SCREW) or 'kange' was prison rhyming slang for a prison officer, it reflected their view that the 'judge' and 'jury' were acting like warders. It is just possible too that the notion of being 'jumped up' or of leaping about had some influence.

**KEELHAULED:** *Severely punished.*

Keelhauling, which was common to most early navies, involved attaching a miscreant to a line which was passed under the keel of the moving ship to the other side; the hapless victim was then hauled up to one yardarm, dropped sharply into the sea and dragged slowly under the ship and up to the other yardarm, the process being repeated as often as thought necessary to fit the crime. Severe injury was inflicted on the offender by barnacles on the underside of the craft and a cannon was also discharged as he was hauled past it to the other yardarm to startle and disorientate him before he was dropped back for the return trip. Keelhauling was abandoned by most navies in the opening years of the eighteenth century and replaced by the notorious cat o'nine tails.

**KEEN AS MUSTARD, AS:** *Very adept or dilligent.*

Basically this rests on the application of 'keen' in its original sense of sharp – 'arms akimbo' being a corruption of 'in keen bow', as in bent sharply at the elbows. The second impetus came from Keen's mustard as a brand leader at the turn of the century when posters announced grinning families to be 'Keen on Keen's Mustard' or that 'Nothing is as keen as Keen's Mustard'.

**KEEP IT UNDER YOUR HAT:** *To maintain confidentiality.*

This probably alludes to the Victorian messenger boys of London who were mainly urchins and riff-raff of the cloth cap brigade. Entrusted with a letter or message, they tended to keep it under their cap since most of them wore tattered clothes whose pockets had long since been torn off.

**KEEP MUM, TO:** *To hold absolute silence.*

Simple allusion to the only sound a person can make with sealed lips.

**KEEP ON TRUCKING:** *To persevere.*

Whilst it is true that in 1930s America there was a dance craze called truckin'- the style involving a fair amount of undignified cavorting with one index finger held high and wiggling above the head – there does not seem to be any established link between the name of the dance and the above phrase which emerged quite some time later in the 1960s, more likely as a result of the dance marathon craze as in *They Shoot Horses Don't They?* The contestants who had to keep going through the night were perceived as haulage truckers pressing on to their destination and the above served as a shout of enthusiasm to those on the dance-floor.

**KEEP SOMEONE POSTED, TO:** *To supply them with up-to-date information.*

Since the opening of the eighteenth century 'to post' in accountancy terminology has meant to transfer the most recently available figures from informal day or note books to the formal accounts record books. In nineteenth-century America the term shifted in business circles from the specific to the more general meaning of keeping a superior supplied with developments pertaining to a particular set of circumstances.

**KEEP THE WOLF FROM THE DOOR, TO:** *To just get by.*

An oddity at first glance in that the wolf of folklore would be more likely to come a-calling if he thought there was something to be had. In this instance the wolf is a metaphor for hunger, the creature all too frequently portrayed as a ravenous predator. The human perception of the wolf is indeed a dichotomy with the salivating devil-dog on the one hand and on the other the kindly wolf taking abandoned children in and caring for them. It is worth mentioning that there has never been a single authenticated wolf-attack on man.

**KEEPING UP WITH THE JONESES:** *Emulating your neighbours.*

The title of a cartoon, penned by Arthur Momand, which began in 1913 in New York's *The Globe* and ran for nearly thirty years. It was originally to be named *Keeping up with the Smiths* but, it is said, since Momand's neighbours were actually called Smith and the strip was inspired by his ritualistic manoeuvres with them, he decided to change the name in the interests of domestic harmony. It is possible that the expression received a boost in Britain after the marriage of Princess Margaret to Antony Armstrong-Jones.

**KEEP YOUR EAR TO THE GROUND:** *To keep oneself informed and abreast of events.*

Perhaps a reference to the Red Indian scout all too often seen in Westerns pressing one ear to the ground before announcing the distant presence of a specified number of riders, or to the misconception that a worm-hunting bird with its head cocked sideways is listening, whereas this attitude is necessitated by its monocular vision. On the other hand, this could be an intensifier of the older 'incline one's ear', meaning to listen intently to important information.

**KEEP YOUR NOSE CLEAN, TO:** *To stay out of trouble.*

When first heard in British military circles at the opening of this century the expression meant to stay off the drink – an allusion to the beer froth that can sometimes end up on the nose of the over-enthusiastic drinker. Since most of the trouble caused amongst the ranks was drink-associated 'keeping your nose clean' came to mean stay sober and thus out of trouble.

**KEEP YOUR NOSE TO THE GRINDSTONE, TO:** *Work without pause.*

The exhortation initially cautioned the careless to pay more attention to what they were doing, for anyone sharpening a scythe with a hand-held stone whilst looking the other way and chatting ran the risk of losing the odd finger or two. Over the years the phrase has moved slightly to mean keep on with the task in hand.

**KEEP YOUR POWDER DRY:** *To proceed with caution.*

The reference is to gunpowder and the original usage said to be that of Cromwell addressing his troops during the Irish Campaigns prior to their crossing a river to do battle when he allegedly shouted 'Put your trust in God, but keep your powder dry.'

**KEEP YOUR SHIRT ON:** *Caution to remain calm.*

A allusion to the readiness of the aggressive to strip down for a fight.

**KEEP YOUR WEATHER EYE OPEN, TO:** *To remain wholly vigilant.*

At sea there is a temptation for those on watch in bad weather to keep the eye closest to the prevailing wind closed and thus be blind to dangers on that side.

**KENTUCKY WINDAGE:** *Adjustment made by intuition based on experience.*

The skill of nineteenth-century Kentucky riflemen with their long muskets, though admittedly exaggerated, was legendary; they laid off their aim to allow for the influence of the prevailing wind on the musket ball.

**KIBOSH:** *The kiss of death.*

All the indications are that this is derived from the Yiddish '*kye bosh*', eighteen pence, an arbitrary sum picked to represent a physical or metaphorical blow, and thus very similar to the British FOURPENNY ONE. There are two factors corroborating this: the first is the use of 'kibosh' among criminals for an eighteen-month sentence, the second is that the term is first recorded in print in 1836 as 'kye-bosh' – by Boz (Charles Dickens) describing a fight between two street-girls in the East End of London back streets during which a spectator shouts: 'Hooroar, put the kye-bosh on her, Mary.' There are other suggestions, including the Irish Gaelic '*cie bais*', cap of death, the Yiddish '*kabas*', suppression, the German '*Keibe*', carrion, and '*caboshe*', the action of beheading a fallen deer.

**KICK INTO TOUCH:** *To abandon.*

In the game of football, a player in possession of the ball with no clear idea of what to do with it can deliberately kick it over the touchline, which will immediately bring play to a halt until a throw-in starts it up again.

**KICK OVER THE TRACES:** *To throw off all restraint.*

The reference here is to draught animals that rear and prance to such an extent that they get their legs over the trace reins that run up the side of the team.

**KICK THE BUCKET:** *To die.*

The early French '*buquet*' denoted a beam from which something was hung; a pig for slaughter was bled to death suspended upside down from such a beam and, not unnaturally, kicked hard against the beam with its hind legs. The idea that the expression comes from someone hanging himself by fixing the noose while standing on a bucket then kicking it away is wrong, if only because this would not provide the suicide with an adequate drop.

**KICKSHAWS:** *Small cheap trinkets.*

This is a corruption of the French '*quelquechose*' – something. The word was once used of small delicacies (somethings) to whet the appetite.

**KID:** *To joke or dupe.*

If this is not a simple implication that the butt of the joke is being treated like a kid – child – there is a possibility of some influence from the wholly separate 'kid' – FAGGOT, or the binding together of loose soil by driving in faggots. 'Kidder' arose from this 'kid' to become fairground jargon for a person 'planted' in the crowd whose function was to hold the audience together and encourage them to start spending, thus 'kidding' them into buying rubbishy goods or entertainment.

**KIKE:** *Insultingly, a Jew.*

Probably from the Yiddish '*kikel*', circle, as first aimed at illiterate Jews entering the US in the 1880s by literate Jews who, already established in that country, looked disparagingly upon their poor fellows from Eastern Europe. Illiterate immigrants were asked to sign their documentation with a cross, a symbol with too strongly Christian associations for many Jews who opted for a circle instead.

**KILL THE GOLDEN GOOSE:** *Foolishly to destroy a source of benefit.*

An old fable tells how a poor couple who acquired a magic goose that laid golden eggs killed it and opened it up thinking they could then take out all the eggs at once.

**KILROY WAS HERE:** *Ubiquitous graffito.*

Immediately before the Japanese attack on Pearl Harbor (1941), one James J. Kilroy took up employment at the shipyard of the Bethlehem Steel Company of Quincy, Massachusetts. As an inspector, he was given to chalking the above on jobs examined to let the crews know they had been checked. The men of the yard adopted it as a slogan, daubing it all over the place and from there it moved into Forces' tradition. After the war a campaign was mounted to find the Kilroy in question; it verified the aforementioned's claim to be the originator. He died in Boston in 1962.

**KITH AND KIN:** *All of one's acquaintance.*

In the Middle Ages 'kith' meant one's native land and, by extension, friends, neighbours and fellow countrymen in general. 'Kin', on the other hand, applies only to one's blood relatives, as reflected in the German '*Kinder*'. Over the years this collective usage seems to have confused the terms which now stand as almost synonymous in general speech.

**KITTY:** *A communual fund; a stake in a gambling game.*

Whilst the origin is obscure, this could be rooted in the early nineteenth-century North of England 'kitty', a prison, based in turn on 'kidcote', a secure bed for a child.

**KNACKERED:** *Extremely tired.*

Based on the idea of a horse so worn out that it is fit only for the attentions of the knacker, or horse slaughterer. The origin of 'knacker' most probably lies in 'knack', onomatopeia for a rapping sound, since the knacker's cart, which had heavily cleated wheels, made a highly distinctive rapping sound on the old cobbled streets.

**KNACKERS:** *Testicles.*

This harks back to 'knack', a term echoic of things rapping together – in this case the testicles of a man running or copulating.

**KNOCK FOR SIX:** *To strike mightily; to stun.*

In the game of cricket, a score of six runs is made when the ball is struck so hard that it leaves the play area without touching the ground.

**KNOCK FROM PILLAR TO POST:** *To knock hither and thither.*

The forerunner of tennis was played by the nobility in their own courtyards where the pillars and posts formed natural obstacles from which the ball ricocheted unpredictably. The notion that the expression is based on the concept of a miscreant's being whipped *en route* from the pillory to the stocks has no foundation.

**KNOCK INTO A COCKED HAT:** *To beat decisively.*

The significance of 'cocked hat' in this expression has been much debated; the following suggestions are the most plausible, but it must be said that none of them has more supportive evidence than any of the others. (1) In sailing navigation, a 'cocked hat' occurs on a chart when poor calculations have been made to determine the ship's position. After plotting the three bearings, the lines should intersect at one point but, if the calculations have been inaccurate, the lines fail to do this and a triangle, nicknamed 'the cocked hat', appears. The greater the errors made, the bigger is the cocked hat. (2) The cocked hat could be the Navy or Army hat of the eighteenth/nineteenth centuries which could be knocked flat to be carried under the arm. (3) Again with hats, when the fashion for triangular hats arrived in the late seventeenth century, those who could not afford to buy one simply soaked and bent up the brim of their old pilgrim style hat. This was thought to be the ruination of a perfectly good hat by those who shunned the new trend. (4) In America, where the expression does seem to have originated, the setting up of three bowling pins in a triangle is known as a cocked hat, and, in a normal game of ninepins, if the inner six pins have been removed by a fluke shot, then the somewhat ruined game was said to have been 'knocked into a cocked hat'.

**KNOCK SPOTS OFF:** *To defeat convincingly.*

The spots on dominoes and the symbols on playing cards seem the most likely source for this; in certain games, the losing side has the value of their remaining dominoes or cards knocked off their score and added to that of the opposition. It has also been suggested that the expression comes from displays in which sharpshooters tried to shoot the spots out of playing cards, but this is not convincing since one is generally said to knock spots off some other person.

**KNOW YOUR ONIONS, TO:** *To be knowledgeable in your own field.*

There have been flattering attempts to tie this into the name of Mr C. T. Onions, a previous editor of the Shorter OED, but it is more likely rhyming slang – onion rings = things.

**KNUCKLE DOWN:** *To apply oneself seriously.*

In a game of marbles, a player's hand is in this position when he sets himself to aim and play. An alternative assertion is that, since in early times the word 'knuckle' could describe any joint, including those in the spine, the allusion is to someone bending his back in effort, but the expression originated in the nineteenth century, and 'knuckle' (of a human) was no longer used of anything other than a hand joint by the end of the seventeenth century.

**KNUCKLE UNDER:** *To submit.*

In a game of dominoes or cards, the traditional way of indicating that one cannot play is by knocking with one's knuckles on the underside of the table. In alehouses and the like, this was also a sign that one had conceded an argument. As with KNUCKLE DOWN, chronology disputes any connection with bowing in submission since this expression arose in the early eighteenth century.

**KNUCKLEDUSTER:** *Metal fist guard.*

The original knuckleduster was an early pepperbox pistol which dusted the firer's knuckles with powder burns; the gun also had a heavy brass trigger guard which was large enough to accommodate the whole hand and looped for the knuckles so that, after all the shots had been fired, one could still use it as a weapon.

**KOWTOW:** *To abase oneself in homage.*

The Mandarin '*k'o-t'ou*', to knock the head, alluded to the ceremony of abasement in which a subordinate prostrated himself before a superior, banging his head on the floor in a gesture of respect.

**KRISTALLNACHT:** *A night of great violence and civil disturbance.*

A German word meaning 'crystal night'- implying 'night of the broken glass' – which was applied to the night of 9 November 1938, when Nazi agitators went on a rampage that was proclaimed to be in retaliation for the alleged murder of a German diplomat in Paris by a Jew. Nearly 8,000 Jewish-owned shops were destroyed and looted, and countless synagogues set on fire. In Nuremberg, the arson was actually perpetrated by the Fire Brigade.

# L

**LACKEY:** *A menial servant or a servile follower.*

The Arabic '*al kaid*', leader or chief, originally applied to the élite of the Moorish army. When the Spanish reclaimed their land from the Moors, who dominated it from the eighth to the fifteenth century, they enslaved many of them and, in mockery of their vaunting title, created the Spanish corruption '*lacayo*', meaning the lowest of lowly slaves.

**LAG:** *A convict, especially a recidivist.*

This could be related to 'lag', a variant of 'lug', to cart away or transport as once were convicts to Australia. It has also been rather unconvincingly argued that the source is the maritime 'lagan', goods dumped at sea with a marker attached to facilitate later reclamation, likening the convict to one temporarily abandoned in a penal colony.

**LALLAPALOOZA:** *Any thing or person that is large and remarkable.*

The author's guess, and it is pure conjecture, is that this could be a combination of some dialect term for a large lumbering person, or possibly a corruption of 'lulu' – thing or person that is remarkable – and the Italian '*peloso/a*', hairy. In his opinion, the only postulated derivation sounds decidedly contrived; it is said that, when the French landed in Ireland in 1798, they engaged themselves in trying to organise an armed uprising against the British. In the mouths of the Irish, the French '*Allez fusil!*' – Forward the muskets! – became corrupted to 'lallapalooza'.

**LAME DUCK:** *One who cannot cope.*

Originally a quite specific Stock Exchange term for a defaulter, this alludes to the way ducks fly in a chevron formation, their bodies held absolutely horizontal for maximum speed; a lame duck's useless leg hangs down and acts as an airbrake, so it must eventually break formation and be left behind.

**LAND OF COCKAIGNE:** FOOL'S PARADISE *comparable to* CLOUD CUCKOO LAND.

This is a very old term indeed, being originally the title of a poem satirizing monastery life, translated from the French by Ellis in the thirteenth century. Cockaigne was an imaginary land where the rivers flowed with wine, fatted fowl wandered around beseeching people to eat them, and so forth. Etymologically, 'Cockaigne' is based on the Middle Low German '*Kokenje*', small cake, and is therefore allied to 'cookie'. Both London and Paris have in their time been ironically dubbed The Land of Cockaigne.

**LASH UP:** *Total confusion; a badly done job.*

In seamen's jargon, this originally meant anything botched up such as a load of old rubbish lashed together to form a make-shift raft.

**LASHINGS:** *An amplitude.*

Originally a nineteenth-century Navy expression denoting a large amount of drink as extracted by money collected on the whip, as explained under FAIR CRACK OF THE WHIP.

**LAST DITCH EFFORT:** *A final and desperate attempt.*

In warfare, an army in retreat is forced farther and farther back from one defensive ditch to the next; at the last one they must stand and fight or die.

**LAST KNOCKINGS:** *The end of anything.*

In British public houses, this was another term for last orders at closing time when anxious customers are knocking on the bar to attract attention.

**LAST STRAW:** *Whatever finally breaks the limits of one's endurance.*

In the old fable, a camel is constantly overloaded until, one day, just one extra straw added to its burden breaks its back.

**LAUGH ON THE OTHER SIDE OF HIS FACE:** *To take revenge on a derider.*

This oddity is of doubtful origin. It might be that, since mocking laughter usually issues from one side of a twisted mouth, the expression implies a threat to twist the mouth to the other side by administering a blow. It might also be an allusion to the two masks representing Comedy and Tragedy, one the obverse of the other.

**LAUGH UP YOUR SLEEVE:** *Laugh inwardly or surreptitiously.*

In bygone eras, sleeves were so wide and full that a mocker could hide his face in one.

**LAUGHING STOCK:** *A butt of general ridicule.*

This is a sixteenth-century development from the now obsolete 'laughing post'; both 'stock' and 'post' here mean an object to which things are attached.

**LAW OF THE MEDES AND THE PERSIANS:** *Immutable law.*

Taken from Daniel 6:8 'Now, O king, establish the decree, and sign the writing, that it be not changed, according to the law of the Medes and the Persians, which altereth not.'

**LAY AN EGG, TO:** *To blunder, or fail miserably.*

From the world of cricket, this was originally 'lay a duck's egg', being out for a duck, zero. In tennis, 'LOVE' is a corruption of the French '*l'oeuf*' – the egg.

**LAY IT ON THICK:** *To do anything to excess, e.g. flatter, make excuses, charge.*

The expression refers to spreading bread with an unnecessarily thick coating of honey or butter, so this is comparable to 'buttering someone up'.

**LAY SOMETHING AT ANOTHER'S DOOR, TO:** *To hold them responsible.*

Illegitimate children were often left abandoned on the doorstep of the 'gentleman' who had taken advantage of some servant girl and then thrown her out.

**LE MOT CAMBRONNE:** *Euphemism for 'shit'.*

It is alleged that, at the Battle of Waterloo in 1815 when the English called upon Pierre Jacques Etienne, Baron de Cambronne (1770–1842), to surrender, he made this gallant response: 'The Guard dies but never surrenders.' If he did say this, events did not bear him out for he himself was captured and the Guard did surrender. However, Cambronne denied uttering the fine words, continuing to protest during the remainder of his life that what he actually said was '*Merde!*' (Shit!). He was nevertheless saddled with the vaunt which was engraved at the foot of a statue raised to him by his name town, Nantes. *See also:* OLD GUARD.

**LEAD A MERRY DANCE, TO:** *To deceive or to involve another in complex situations.*

A direct reference to the old ring dance or to procession-like, follow-my-leader dances enacted in the streets. *See also*: RINGLEADER.

**LEAD UP THE GARDEN PATH:** *To mislead or seduce.*

This probably harks back to the house parties of the nineteenth century when propriety was maintained by the matrons of society. A man with designs on a young woman could stroll in the garden with her in full view of the chaperones until he led her up a path screened by bushes.

**LEAD WITH YOUR CHIN:** *To invite defeat.*

In boxing, a fighter is said to lead with one fist, which he holds ready to deliver a punch, and guard with the other. If he leads with his chin, he obviously renders himself highly vulnerable.

**LEADING LIGHT:** *The prominent figure in a group.*

Properly called a 'leading mark', this is a light, either shore-mounted or fixed in the shallows, which, when lined up with another, leads a ship safely past some local danger. The importance of such a navigational aid caused the shift in meaning.

**LEARN THE ROPES:** *To become acquainted with the details of some procedure.*

It was necessary for a sailor to become familiar with the ropes and rigging of a sailing ship. The suggestion that the source is bell-ringing is unconvincing; managing a maze of rigging is much more complicated.

**LEFT FOOTER:** *Roman Catholic.*

Originally a piece of twentieth-century Northern Irish slang, this developed from a spate of jokes aimed at the people of Eire who were deemed to be so stupid that labourers there pushed a spade in with their left foot when generally the right and stronger leg is used.

**LEFT HOLDING THE BABY:** *Saddled with an unwelcome responsibility.*

In centuries gone by, the mother of an unwanted baby would sometimes offload it by dint of asking some affluent and kindly looking person to hold it for a moment or two while she attended to some minor matter and then just disappearing, hoping that the victim of the ruse would have enough compassion to give the baby a home.

**LEFT HOLDING THE BAG:** *Left in a ridiculous, invidious position.* A country practical joke played on green townies was known as 'hunting the snipe' or 'hunting the gowk'. The dupe was led off into the wilds and left crouched over a trail or footpath along which, he was told, the quarry would be driven by the others. He was also told that the birds were so silly that they would not deviate from the path and would therefore walk straight into the bag he was instructed to hold across the trail. The jokers then left him to it!

**LEFT IN THE LURCH:** *Abandoned in a difficult situation.*

Probably based on the Middle Dutch '*lurz*', left-handed or unlucky, the French coined '*lourche*' for a player in a game who is either last or is so far behind that he has no chance of catching up. The term was further refined in the game of cribbage and applied to one who had failed to score thirty-one or move his score peg up one side of the board before the other side had finished play. *See also*: PEG OUT.

**LEMON, A:** *Any disappointment or failure.*

More than simple reference to the tartness of the fruit, the early one-armed bandits generated such use. The first machine was produced in 1889 in America by German immigrant Charles Fey of San Francisco. With perhaps misguided fervour for his adoptive country, Fey used images of the Liberty Bell for the jackpot line and fruit symbols for the lesser prizes – so was born the Bell-Fruit machine. Fey's equivalent of the zero on a roulette wheel was the lemon; even a complete line of lemons netted the player nothing at all.

**LESBIAN:** *Female homosexual.*

The Greek island of Lesbos was the home of the great poetess Sappho, who is quite erronіously said to have been inclined to lesbianism.

**LESBIAN RULE:** *A regulation that is flexible and open to interpretation.*

The original was an actual, pliable, lead rule used by Lesbian masons (i.e. masons on the Island of Lesbos) to measure mouldings and arches. There is no connection with lesbianism.

**LET FLY:** *Suddenly to attack either verbally or physically.*

When archers were soldiers, they attacked by letting their arrows fly. This was also a seafaring expression in the days of sail when it meant to let go of the ropes holding the mainsail in position, but, since this manoeuvre deprived the vessel of forward thrust, it seems an improbable source.

**LET GEORGE DO IT:** *Let someone – anyone – take the responsibility.*

Coined at the French court as a derisory remark aimed at Louis XII who was given to passing the buck to Cardinal George, George d'Amboise (1460–1510). The original French '*Laissez faire à George*' became popular throughout France and eventually crossed the channel, reaching peak popularity at the beginning of this century, boosted by the advent of the automatic pilot which was nicknamed GEORGE.

**LET THE CAT OUT OF THE BAG:** *To let slip a secret and give the game away.*

At fairgrounds in times gone by, a prime piglet would be displayed, then tied up in a sack and offered for sale. While the haggling took place, the sack was unobtrusively replaced by one containing either a muted cat with its claws drawn, or a muted puppy. If this sack was opened before the sale was concluded, then the cat was out of the bag like a rocket and the game was up. This same piece of sharp practice also produced the expressions 'being sold a pup' and 'buying a pig in a poke', 'poke', being allied to 'pocket', meant a sack.

**LET THE DEAD BURY THEIR DEAD:** *Let each see to their own.*

Matthew 8:18-20, tells how a scribe, wishing to follow Jesus, asked to delay his departure in order to bury his father, whereupon Jesus answered: 'Follow me; and let the dead bury their dead.' Theologians explain that 'to bury' the father here meant to wait until he was dead, for the man was not actually dead, but terminally ill. Jesus, aware that his own days were numbered, and that he had still much to do, needed immediate commitment from his disciples. Hence, let the dead (i.e. those older members of the family who were themselves approaching death) attend to the dying.

**LET THEM EAT CAKE:** *Used to indicate total lack of concern.*

Marie Antoinette allegedly said this during the Paris Bread Riots of 5 and 6 October 1789, but Rousseau, in his *Confessions* (1766), referring to the Grenoble Bread Riots of 1739 which took place sixteen years before she was born, states: 'A great Princess callously remarked: "Let them eat cake".' The truth of the matter is that the Revolutionaries circulated this rumour against Marie Antoinette in order to discredit her further with the people – not a difficult task. It does seem to be a matter of record that the Duchesse de Polignac, a close friend of the Queen, did say *to* her: 'How is it that these silly people are so clamorous for bread when they can buy such nice brioches for a few sous?' (A brioche is a sort of sponge cake.) Similar heartless inanities have been attributed to members of other royal families; in Britain at the time of the French Revolution, Princess Charlotte allegedly proclaimed that she would rather eat beef than starve, and asked of the assembled company if anybody could explain why the French population so stupidly and persistently demanded bread when everybody knew it was so scarce.

**LET US RETURN TO OUR MUTTONS/SHEEP:** *Let us return to the matter in hand.*

The fourteenth-century French play *La Farce de Maître Pathelin* centred on a court case in which a woollen-draper, accusing a shepherd of ill-treating his flock, and giving what is for the most part perjured evidence, constantly digresses to hurl all sorts of peripheral and unassociated accusations. The judge repeatedly drags him back to the charge at issue with the original French, which is also used, '*Revenons à nos moutons*' (Let us return to our sheep).

**LET YOUR HAIR DOWN, TO:** *To abandon formalities.*

In previous and perhaps more elegant eras women habitually wore their hair up in dressed styles and only unclipped this when relaxing in the privacy of their boudoir or bedroom.

**LEVEL BEST, YOUR:** *Your utmost.*

In the days of steam locomotives, this indicated the best turn of speed that could be achieved by an engine on a level track unaided by a downhill slope.

**LEVEL PEGGING:** *A state of equality in competition.*

When the pegs in a cribbage score board are level, both players hold the same number of points.

**LICK INTO SHAPE:** *To discipline and organize.*

Ancient folklore had it that bear cubs were born shapeless balls of fur which the mother bear moulded into form by licking.

**LICKSPITTLE:** *A toady.*

Subservient dogs in a pack lick clean the muzzles of the dominant ones after feeding etc.

**LIFE OF RILEY:** *A life of ease and pleasure.*

Although this may simply have evolved from the fact that the Irish seem to have a capacity for enjoying life to the full, the following specific origins have been put forward: (1) The American poet James Whitcomb Riley (1844–1916), much of whose writings dealt with carefree summer jaunts. (2) A song written by Lawber and Blake entitled 'The Best in the House is None Too Good for Riley'. (3) A song by Pat Rooney, widely performed in the music halls of the 1880s and entitled 'Are You The O'Riley?' which became a sort of dissolutes' anthem for it told how, when O'Riley struck it rich, he was going to pay for everything for everybody.

**LIGHT OUT:** *To decamp at speed.*

Originally a Naval term for slipping a ship's cable from the bollard and leaving port, this was the opposite of 'light to', to secure a ship to the quayside, a use of 'light' in the sense of 'alight' as in 'arrive'. 'Light out', a later development, was no doubt helped to its present meaning because ships sometimes made a clandestine departure at night without navigation lights.

**LIKE A BAT OUT OF HELL:** *Very quickly.*

This implies that bats, though traditionally regarded as nightmarish creatures, would find the light and heat of Hell so abhorrent that they would flee from it with all speed.

**LIKE CAESAR'S WIFE:** *Absolutely above suspicion.*

In 62 BC, the Roman ladies' ceremony of paying homage to Bona Dea (The Good Goddess) was celebrated in the house of Julius Caesar and his second wife, Pompeia. During the rites, a male infiltrator was discovered (almost literally) and a scandal ensued, exacerbated by the fact that the man was Publius Clodius, whose name had been linked to Pompeia's in court gossip. There was no evidence of adultery, and Caesar himself asserted that there was none, but, having said that, he announced their divorce on the grounds that he could not afford to be associated with a woman whose name had been tainted by scandalous speculation.

**LIKE IT OR LUMP IT:** *There is no choice but to accept with good grace or ill.*

'Lump' once meant 'to scowl or complain'. When writing about Ireland in 1577, Richard Stanyhurst said: 'They stand lumping and lowering . . . for they imagine that their evill lucke proceedeth from him.'

**LILY-LIVERED:** *Cowardly.*

Associated with the archaic meaning of humour, this assumes that a liver would be white if lacking bile, a fluid once thought to generate ill-humour and aggressiveness. *See also*: YELLOW.

**LIMBER UP:** *To tone up the body in preparation for physical effort.*

There are three possible origins. The first comes from the world of eighteenth-century gunnery in which the limbers were the detachable forepart of a gun carriage consisting of two wheels, the axle, the shaft for the horses and two ammunition chests. Naturally this would need to be hooked up before the gun crew could move out so perhaps the military command of 'Limber Up!' prefaced the strenuous business of moving an artillery battery from one location to another on the double. This 'limber' is derived from the French '*limon*', shaft, which in turn is derived from or strongly influenced by the Old Norse '*lim*', branch of a tree. Next, there is the limber which means to make pliable or supple, as are the muscles in preparatory exercises; there is a double connection here since this is derived from the first 'limber' in that the front shafts of a light carriage need to be whippy and supple to act as shock absorbers for the benefit of both passengers and draught animals. Lastly, and admittedly least likely, comes the 'limber' that is derived from the French '*lumière*' meaning a light or a hole cut to allow its passage. On a sailing ship, a limber was one of a series of holes cut through the timbers about the side of the keel to allow free passage of bilge-water down to the pumpwell. Through these holes were threaded ropes of chain which, when pulled to and fro, cleared any blockage that might create a stink or a breeding ground for disease, getting everything running nicely free and loose again.

**LIMBO:** *A state of suspension or oblivion.*

Based on the Latin '*limbus*', a fringe, hem or border, Limbo was a place invented by the early Church to tidy away those souls who, whilst not actually deserving to burn in Hell, nevertheless could not be allowed into Heaven; these included persons who had died before the coming of Christ and stillborn babies or those who had died in infancy before being baptised. This nowhere land was imagined to be on the borders of Hell and all those languishing there had to await the Day of Judgement. The idea is not unique – see FOOL'S PARADISE.

**LIMEHOUSE:** *Political invective.*

Lloyd George (1863–1945) made a famous and bitter speech in the London district of Limehouse on 10 June 1909 when he vehemently attacked all the aristocracy, private landlords, banks and financial institutions.

**LIMELIGHT, IN THE:** *The centre of attention.*

An actor with a spotlight playing on him is literally 'in the limelight'. In 1826, Thomas Drummond invented this type of light which was operated by burning a mixture of oxygen and hydrogen on a surface of lime; because it threw a very powerful beam but generated comparatively little heat, it was ideal for stage use. Drummond also envisaged it as a lighthouse beam, but trials for this were not successful.

**LIMERICK:** *A five-line jingle.*

The origin of this is obscure and it may be nothing more than a suggested analogy between the absurdity of the poem and the proverbial illogicality of the Irish, Limerick being a well-known Irish county. Of the more specific theories that have been put forward, it must be said that none is convincing or even tenable. The suggestion that 'limerick' is a corruption of 'Learic' (of Edward Lear, (1812–1888) is quite without foundation; Lear's rhymes did not even conform to the strict rules of limerick construction, those in his *Book of Nonsense* (1846) boasting a last line which is merely 'choric repetition, employing one of the previous rhymes, and adding little or nothing to the sense' (Encyclopaedia Britannica). To quote further from the Encyclopaedia Britannica, 1953 edition, 'Langford Reed, the only collector of limericks who has toiled valiantly with their history, suggests that this peculiar form of verse was brought direct to Limerick by the returned veterans of the Irish Brigade who were attached to the French Army for a period of nearly 100 years from 1691. The Brigade was organised in Limerick and, when disbanded, was no doubt responsible for giving currency to many rude barrack-room songs. Evidence of a French origin for the five-lined metrical scheme of the limerick rests on very feeble foundations. Langford Reed quotes from Boswell's *Life of Johnson* (properly titled *The Life of Samuel Johnson, LL.D.* and published 16 May 1791): *'On s'étonne ici que Caliste/Ait pris l'habit de Moliniste;/ Puisque cette jeune beauté /Ote à chacun sa liberté/N'est-ce pas un Janseniste?* – an epigram in *The Menagiana* (1716) on a young lady who apppeared at a masquerade dressed as Jesuit during the fierce contentions of the followers of Molinos and Jansenius. Finally, there is a suggestion that 'Will you come up to Limerick?' was widely used as a chorus line in ad-libbed dirty ditties, being repeated several times whilst players thought up their rhymes; this is unlikely since there is no evidence of this chorus anywhere in print.

**LIMEY:** *An Englishman.*

All ships in the British Navy were once required to carry a supply of fresh limes for the crew. They sucked the juice which was rich in vitamin C and protected them from scurvy.

**LIMOUSINE:** *Plush/chauffeur-driven car.*

In the district of Limousin in Central France, the inhabitants wear a distinctive type of hooded cloak, and the French gave this name to an early type of chauffeur-driven car in which the owners sat under a hood while the chauffeur braved the elements.

**LINE ONE'S POCKETS:** *To amass money from dubious sources.*

This may simply allude to the fact that the lining of a pocket does not show, but the expression is commonly linked to a story about Beau Brummel although the sources are careful not to state categorically that it is the origin. It is said that an unnamed tailor, wishing to advertize his workmanship in high society by winning the patronage of the Beau, delivered to him a dress coat which was not only free but had its pockets lined with banknotes. Brummel supposedly wrote the tailor saying he liked the coat, especially the lining. In actual fact though, tailors had a hard time trying to get money *out* of Brummel who was somewhat cavalier about his debts. In any case, he thoroughly disapproved of pockets since they spoiled the line of his clothes, and, according to him, a gentleman did not need them for he carried nothing about with him save his wit.

**LINGO:** *Any language or jargon, especially if not understood.*

This is based on such terms as the Italian '*lingua*', language.

**LINGUA FRANCA:** *Any pastiche of languages.*

This is named from the original Mediterranean mixture which was based on Italian expressed without inflexion and adulterated with other languages, predominantly French. '*Lingua franca*' is Italian for 'Frankish language'.

**LINKS:** *Golf course.*

Ultimately linked to 'lean', incline, this term properly described undulating, sandy land near the sea. Because so many early golf courses, especially Scottish ones, were located near the sea, the term gradually transferred.

**LION HUNTER:** *One who seeks out celebrities.*

Since the lion is king of the jungle, the allusion is obvious. Its survival was doubtless ensured when Dickens included in his *Pickwick Papers* (1836/37) one Mrs Leo Hunter who obsessively sought to give her gatherings prestige by inviting any prominent person to them.

**LIP MOVER:** *An idiot or dullard.*

The doltish move their lips when struggling to read.

**LIQUIDATE:** *To kill off.*

This comes from the Bolshevik use of the Russian '*likvidirovat*' (to clear up, wind up) to describe their murderous purges of the 1920s.

**LITTLE AUDREY LAUGHED AND LAUGHED AND LAUGHED:** *Quotation from a series of jokes.*

The prototype of these jokes, in general circulation and on radio throughout the 1930s, told how little Audrey went into the bathroom where her uncle was lying in the bath listening to the radio. Staring at a certain part of his anatomy, she asked what it was and her unwitting uncle replied that it was his Bush (then a popular make of radio). At this, little Audrey laughed and laughed and laughed because she knew it was Ferranti (another make of radio).

**LITTLE BIRD TOLD ME, A:** *I will not reveal my source.*

There has been much speculation on the origin of this which must remain obscure. It could derive from Cockney rhyming slang 'little bird' = quiet word, which would be substantiated by an allied expression 'I haven't heard a dicky bird.' It might on the other hand be rooted in fairy tales in which birds are frequently the speaking spies of princes and wizards. A typical example of such supernatural usage occurs at Ecclesiastes 10:20. 'Curse not the king, no not in thy thought; and curse not the rich in thy bedchamber; for a bird of the air shall carry the voice, and that which hath wings shall tell the matter.' Worthy of mention too is the Dutch '*Er lij t'el baerd?*', I should betray another? but whilst interesting this is nevertheless untenable.

**LITTLE GROUP (or BAND) OF WILFUL MEN:** *A deliberately destructive group.*

The American President Woodrow Wilson (1856–1924) speaking in 1917 said of a group of eleven senators led by Robert La Follette and George Norris: 'A little group of wilful men, representing no opinion but their own, have rendered the great government of the United States helpless and contemptible.' He was referring to their FILIBUSTER against a bill authorising the arming of American merchantmen just before America's entry into WW1. It is often stated that Wilson was denoting another group who opposed American involvement in the League of Nations, but this is not the case.

**LITTLE LORD FAUNTLEROY:** *A 'precious' boy or man.*

*Little Lord Fauntleroy* was an extremely sweet story by Frances Hodgson Burnett (1849–1924) published in 1886. Its hero, a boy named Cedric Errol who would have inherited the Fauntleroy title had his father not gone off and married an American woman of whom his family disapproved, is, on his father's death, summoned to England and comes to visit the family there, leaving his 'Dearest Mother', at her own behest, in the slums of New York. His angelic appearance and sweet disposition win over the Fauntleroy family who then invite his mother and a tearful reconciliation takes place. The tremendous success of the tale and its subsequent stage versions condemned hordes of little boys to be dressed in velvet suits with lace collar and cuffs as was Little Lord Fauntleroy.

**LIVE HIGH ON THE HOG, TO:** *To live extremely well.*

The better cuts of pork are to be found higher up the carcass and at banquet these would be presented to the head of the table.

**LIVERY:** *Stabling facilities; distinguishing colours or clothes of household servants.*

Both meanings are derived from a reduced form of 'delivery'; the owner of a horse delivered the animal to be tended and the master of the servants provided them with their clothes which were normally in the household colours.

**LIVING DAYLIGHTS OUT OF SOMEONE, TO BEAT, FRIGHTEN OR SCARE THE:** *To soundly trounce them.*

Some confusion here for since the eighteenth century in Britain 'daylights' has signified the eyes whilst in America the term has signified the intestines. So, if not a direct parallel of 'I'll punch your eyes out!' and an expression of pure British origin, there could be some influence from the American source which in turn might be a usage of 'daylights' born of confusion with 'lights' as descriptive of intestines. This has long been slaughtermen's/butchers' terminology for the offal which is lighter than any meat. Perhaps 'living daylights' is an intensifier arising as a corruption of 'liver and lights', itself a composite designating the guts in their entirety.

**LLAMA:** *South American pack animal.*

This Spanish word derived from Quechua is worthy of inclusion if only to put to rest a ridiculous tale. It is said that a Spanish explorer, seeing the animal, asked the native South Americans: *'Como se llama?'* (What is it called?) whereupon they, not understanding, simply repeated his last word, which the Spaniard incredibly took to be the name of the beast. Exactly the same sort of story is told about the boomerang, the kangaroo and countless other animals and placenames.

**LLOYD:** *A housebreaker.*

This is a corruption of 'loid', an abbreviation of celluloid – a piece of which is often used to slip locks.

**LOADED FOR BEAR:** *Ready for anything.*

An American hunting term, this describes a hunter out in the woods carrying a gun loaded with the most powerful ammunition available for the calibre just in case he encounters a bear, against which an ordinary round would be ineffective.

**LOADSAMONEY:** *The unacceptable face of capitalism.*

This was the name of a character created by British Comedian Harry Enfield who ridiculed through him what he saw as the most evil and divisive 'benefits' of Thatcherism. A crass Londoner, flush with Thatcherite wealth, he never missed an opportunity to brandish a massive wad of notes shouting 'Loadsamoney!'.

**LOADSTONE/LODESTONE:** *Magnetic ore.*

The Old English '*lad*' (journey or way) produced the Middle East '*lode*', a term akin to 'lead' (guide); early lodestone compasses guided sailors around the seas. An old name for the guiding Pole Star was Lodestar.

**LOAFER:** *An idler.*

The origin is either the German '*Landlaufer*' (tramp) or the Dutch '*loof*' (weary).

**LOBSTER SAUCE, TO DIE FOR THE WANT OF:** *To come to grief over a trifling matter.*

The story goes that M. Vatel, a leading chef during the reign of Louis XIV (1638–1715), was so dedicated to his art that, having prepared a special banquet for the King at Chantilly, he ran himself through with a sword when he was informed that the lobsters required for a new sauce he had devised as the PIÈCE DE RÉSISTANCE would not be arriving in time.

**LOBSTER SHIFT:** *An early morning stint of work.*

The precise origin is unclear but it is known that the expression came to light in New England and was apparently first applied to the shift of newsmen who started work at 4a.m.; this was about the time that the lobster smacks set out to sea, and indeed, many of the early twentieth-century newspaper offices in New York overlooked the docks from which they departed. An alternative suggestion is that pressmen, being notoriously heavy drinkers, turned up for work sporting a boozer's flush. Yet a third theory points to the well-established use in America of 'lobster' for an idiot or easy dupe, this probably going all the way back to colonial America when the occupying British Redcoats were nicknamed Lobsters. The allusion would then be that only an idiot would be drafted in to work at that time of the morning.

**LOCK HORNS:** *To argue or fight.*

Male moose and deer in the rutting season engage in fights over females and sometimes their antlers do become locked together.

**LOCK, STOCK AND BARREL:** *Everything.*

This refers to the three main sections of an early flintlock firearm: the firing lock, the wooden shoulder stock and the barrel which together make up the whole gun. Suggestions of a link with the sale of a farm right down to the key to the door*lock*, the *live*stock and the water*barrel* are quite groundless.

**LOCO:** *Mad.*

The Spanish '*loco*', insane, transferred to English in the American West in the early 1800s when it was blended with 'weed' to denote certain plants which maddened any livestock that ate them. Horses especially would rear and career wildly if fed locoweed.

**LOG:** *Ship's record book.*

Although now used to record all information pertinent to the voyage, navigation and crew, the original purpose of the log was to note details of the ship's speed, which was once calculated by counting the number of knots in a line attached to a log of wood and pulled out by the passage of the ship through the water.

**LOGGERHEADS, AT:** *In violent dispute.*

This certainly has a Naval origin, although which particular loggerhead is responsible is not clear. Based on the old, well-established 'logger' (any thing or person that was stupid, clumsy, heavy or awkward), a 'loggerhead' on board could denote either a long pole topped by a heavy ball which was heated to melt pitch for deck maintenance, or a barshot with a cannon-ball at each end. Since the former made a formidable weapon with which sailors were prone to sort out their differences, and the latter was fired in close-quarters battles, whirling about like a lethal weight-lifting bar to sweep clear the enemy's decks, either one could have inspired the saying.

**LOGROLLING:** *Political concession-making.*

This American coinage refers to the way early settlers used to help each other to clear land of timber and haul it away.

**LOLITA, A:** *A schoolgirl seductress.*

The novel *Lolita* by Vladimir Nabokov (1899-1977), published in France in 1955 and in America in 1958, caused something of a storm. In it, Professor Humbert Humbert, a man afflicted with an obsessive desire for pubescent girls, marries the mother of twelve-year-old Dolores Haze in order to be close to the daughter. When the mother dies shortly afterwards, Lolita (Humbert's pet name for Dolores) takes the initiative and seduces *him*.

**LOLLIPOP:** *A sweet on a stick.*

This is most likely a blend of the British northern dialect 'lolly' (tongue) and 'pop' (put) as in 'pop it in your mouth'.

**LOLLY:** *Money.*

This is almost certainly a contraction of LOLLIPOP; it could have its source in a simple analogy between the pleasure of sucking the sweet and that of having money to spend, or in the rhyming slang 'lollipop' = drop – a drop being a tip or a *sub rosa* payment.

**LOLLYGAGGING:** *Lazing about.*

Although this is its present meaning, this originally meant heavy kissing, especially if in public, thus the origin could lie in the dialect 'lolly', tongue, and 'gagging', choking, i.e. heavy, French kissing.

**LONG AND THE SHORT OF IT:** *The sum of the matter.*

It is possible that the source of this is the drawing of straws, one of which was shorter than the others, a form of lottery used to settle disputes or allocate a task to one of a group. The matter was clearly resolved when the short straw was drawn, no further discussion being required.

**LONG IN THE TOOTH:** *Old.*

As horses, and indeed humans, get older, their gums recede; as the teeth become more and more exposed, they look as if they are becoming longer.

**LONG TIME NO SEE:** *Form of greeting.*

This is Chinese pidgin based on the literal translation of the Chinese construction '*hao jiu mei jian*'.

**LONG HOT SUMMER:** *A time of violent civil unrest.*

This has been current in the United States since 1928, being a favourite expression of William Faulkner (1897-1962) who used it as the title of one of his numerous short stories about the poor and dispossessed in the Southern states of America; a film of the same title followed in 1958. The phrase became attached to the riots that erupted amongst the underprivileged blacks in eighteen cities across America in the summer of 1967 when the heat made life in the rubbish-filled tenement blocks intolerable.

**LONG STOP:** *An additional precaution.*

The long stop in a game of cricket is the one who stands behind the wicket-keeper ready to catch any ball that gets past him.

**LOO:** *Lavatory.*

The obscurity of the origin of this term has not inhibited conjecture; there are many theories, the more plausible pointing to a French origin. (1) There could have been an influence from '*l'eau*' for the lavatory was once referred to as 'the water'; this could have intensified after Wellington trounced the French at Waterloo, a name which gave a double, Franglais description. (2) A now outmoded name for the lavatory in French was '*lieu d'aisance*', place of easement. (3) Still with French, the term could be a contraction of '*bordalou*', a kind of portable chamber-pot which ladies carried in their muff when travelling or attending lengthy functions. The bordalou was made of silver and embellished so that, in later times, examples of them were apparently mistaken for sauce-boats and sold as such. It was supposedly named after Louis Bourdaloue (1632–1704), a high-profile Jesuit preacher in the reign of Louis XIV, who was prolix in the extreme, the lengths of his dissertations being as famed as they were tedious. The term prolix is derived from the Latin '*pro*', forward, and '*liqui*', to flow! He was, if you like, constantly pouring forth – or maybe those forced to listen were in constant need of the aforementioned item. (4) The Breton for urinating is '*louein*' so this too has a valid claim to be considered as the forerunner of the word. If the French is not responsible, the term could be simply a prissy piece of baby-talk based on 'lav' or 'lavatory' or a dialect variant of 'lee' as in 'leeward', the side of the boat selected by those wishing to relieve themselves without 'getting their own back'. It is possible that 'loo' arose from a composite influence from countless terms associated with washing and gushing water i.e. the 'loo' sound in terms such as 'dilute' and 'ablute'. It has also been mooted that the Old Flemish '*loo*', a bog, could be responsible or the old cry of '*Gardez l'eau*!' or 'Watch out belooooow!' allegedly shouted by those about to empty a chamber-pot out of the window. Lastly there is a possibility that the term was born in British India where a particularly hot, booming wind was called the loo, this being the Hindi name based on the Sanskrit '*ulka*', flame. This would then allude to the booming wind sometimes emitted in the lavatory and make the word a parallel term to the 'thunder box'.

**LOON:** *(1) An idiot.*

This is a corrupt shortening of LUNATIC. (2) A man or a boy. Derived either from the Middle Dutch '*loen*', stupid fellow or from the Old Norse '*luenn*' beaten, bemused or exhausted, this was in Medieval times highly pejorative, denoting a thoroughly unpleasant, villainous person. In time 'loon' retreated to the north-east of England and to Scotland where it lost all its ugly connotations and is now used in a much more friendly manner. (3) A type of bird. A seventeenth-century alteration of the earlier and more proper 'loom', this is derived from the Old Norse '*lomr*', an echoic word which refers to the bird's cry and which is ultimately rooted in the Latin '*latrare*', to bark.

**LOOPHOLE:** *A metaphorical chink in the armour of e.g. a contract or law.*

Originally the term denoted those ball-thermometer shaped slits in the walls of ancient castles through the rounded end of which archers fired their arrows and boiling oil was poured. The slit took its name from either the Middle Dutch '*lupen*', to look slyly, perhaps like a wolf, or to lie in wait with malicious intent, or from the Dutch '*loopgat*', a runway or escape route. If this last be the sole or co-progenitor, 'loophole' would be a sister word of 'gauntlet' as in RUN THE GAUNTLE.

**LOOSE END, AT A:** *Having nothing to do or no specific aim in mind.*

This certainly has a maritime origin harking back to the ropes on a working ship, but it is not clear whether it alludes to an unemployed rope dangling loose or to a frayed rope with a loose end that needed whipping. If the latter, then the expression would indicate that sailors with nothing better to do filled in time by mending ropes.

**LOOSE, ON THE:** *Indulging in unrestrained behaviour.*

A tethered animal that has broken loose trails its line behind it, and is free to wander at will and eat forbidden fruits.

**LOOT:** *Plunder; money.*

From the Hindustani '*lut*', plunder, this has also been influenced by 'lootie', hill bandit, a term more frequently heard by the British in India who used it somewhat disparagingly of any Indian irregular soldier; to be fair, many of these soldiers were little better than hill bandits and some were part-time bandits in actuality.

**LOSE FACE:** *To be humiliated.*

Largely an Eastern concept, this is the literal translation of the Chinese '*tiu lien*', the covering of the face with a fan in the event of disgrace or humiliation. This hiding, or losing, of one's face was also expected in the presence of some great superior, suggesting that his presence was so awesome that no mere mortal could look at him.

**LOSE YOUR CHERRY:** *Lose one's virginity.*

Apart from the fruit's imagined similarity in shape to the unbroken hymen, the cherry has been a symbol of the Virgin Mary since medieval times. An ancient ballad entitled 'The Cherry Tree Carol' recounts how when Joseph and Mary were strolling through a cherry orchard Joseph refused to climb up and pick her some fruit. The unborn child in her womb promptly caused the tree to bow down and render up its fruit to her.

**LOSE YOUR MARBLES:** *To become irrational, even clinically insane.*

This is possibly an allusion to the tantrums enacted by petulant little boys when they have lost their treasured playing marbles. Alternatively, it could hark back to the mid nineteenth-century when the working classes mocked the upper classes for using the French '*meubles*', furniture. In this case a parallel would be found with such expressions as 'he hasn't got all his chairs at home'.

**LOSE YOUR RAG:** *To get into a temper.*

This may be a development from the Naval 'lose the cloth'. If a ship's captain was having a power struggle with his officers, or with the crew in general in a small ship, and was so dissatisfied that he intended to turn them off the ship at the next opportunity, then 'the Custom of the Sea' decreed that he indicated this by removing the tablecloth from the dining table three times; since there was only one cooked meal a day, this was equivalent to three days' warning. It would be a short step from 'the captain's losing his cloth' to 'the captain's losing his rag'.

**LOSE YOUR SHIRT:** (1) *To venture and lose all.*

This is a straightforward reference to a gambler's staking all he has down to the shirt on his back. (2) *To become extremely angry.* The allusion is to a man who is so incensed that, far from simply throwing an impulsive punch, he strips to the waist in preparation for a full-scale fight.

**LOST GENERATION:** *A generation without aim or direction.*

Although sometimes applied to a generation largely wiped out by war, the expression was coined in relation to the living. Although both Ernest Hemingway (1899–1961) and Gertrude Stein (1874–1946) have been accredited with it, it really came from France. Stein and her secretary, Alice B. Toklas, driving through France encountered mechanical problems in Belley, where they put up at Hotel Pernollet. During a conversation the owner, M. Pernollet, talking of the plight of the generation who had gone off to WW1 and returned with an inability to settle to normal life, used the expression '*une génération perdue*', a lost generation, perhaps as a play on '*enfants perdus*' to describe these young men who, he said, were epitomised by the mechanic working on Stein's car with whom she was becoming increasingly impatient. She picked up the phrase, and used its English translation so much that Hemingway himself thought she had coined it, going so far as to say so in print on the dust jacket of *The Sun Also Rises* (1926).

**LOTUS POSITION:** *Cross-legged yoga position.*

The position is named after the leaf of the lotus tree which, whilst it rests on the water, remains dry and is thus taken to represent detachment.

**LOTUS-EATER:** *One given over to idleness and pleasure.*

Odysseus, on his homeward journey, lived for a while among the legendary Lotus-eaters, a people whose staple food was the fruit of a plant the Greeks called '*lotos*' which induced in them a delicious languor; when Odysseus and his men also ate of this fruit, they too succumbed to idle pleasure and forgot all about the homeland to which they were trying to return. There are several plants bearing the name lotus, and some were anciently used as a food source by the poor who made from it a bread-like substance and, from its berries, a fermented wine which was unusually stupefying.

**LOUNGE:** *To loll; a sitting room.*

The origin is essentially clouded; 'lounge' certainly suggests a recumbent (long) attitude and the actual word 'long' has almost certainly had some indirect influence, but it cannot be the sole, direct source. The most likely origin is the Middle French '*longis*' meaning 'a tall and dull slangam, that hath no making to his height, nor wit to his making'. (Even today, a person, irrespective of his actual height, is often slighted as 'a long streak of misery' or 'a long, tall nothing'.) To enter an even more shady area, there is quite a lot of support for the notion that, at the root of '*longis*' lies the invented name 'Longius' or 'Longinus' applied to the Roman centurion who allegedly pierced with a spear the side of Christ on the cross; an abbreviation of the name of the perpetrator of such an abomination could well have served thenceforth for a brutish dullard. It seems a fair assumption that the name was built on the Latin '*longus*', a long-armed thrust.

**LOVE:** *A zero score in tennis.*

This is a corruption of the French '*l'oeuf*', the egg, the shape of which is taken to indicate zero. The allusion is reflected in a player's being said to be 'out for a duck' and in the American expression LAY AN EGG.

**LOVE APPLE:** *The tomato.*

When the Spanish, who inherited the tomato from North Africa, called it '*pomo dei Moro*', apple of the Moors, the French misnamed it '*pomme d'amour*', apple of love, thus inadvertently bestowing on the humble tomato the reputation for being an aphrodisiac and it was with this accolade that the plant entered England in the very early 1600s. The Puritans, alienated by such a claim to fame, put about rumours that the tomato was highly toxic so that people largely eschewed it until its reputation was restored in the early-mid 1800s.

**LOW-DOWN:** *Inside information.*

This has developed from expressions like 'low-down trick' or 'do the low-down on someone' since the holder of such information which is usually confidential or even incriminating can use it to damage someone.

**LOWER THE BOOM ON:** *To borrow money from.*

At sea, lowering the boom on another would inflict severe injury on him, so it seems likely that this originally maritime description of soliciting a loan from a fellow crew member is parallel to such landlubberly expressions as, 'Can I hit (on) you for a few quid?'

**LUCIFER:** *The Devil.*

The word is derived from the Latin '*lucifer*' (bringer of light) but the Bible does not associate it with Satan, for the name appears only once in the whole book and then as an epithet for Nebuchadrezzar (note the spelling which is the correct form), the fallen king of Babylon. The relevant passages occur in Isaiah 14:12–15: 'How art thou fallen from heaven, O Lucifer, son of the morning . . . For thou hast said in thy heart, I will ascend into heaven, I will exalt my throne above the stars of God . . . Yet thou shalt be brought down to hell' when Isaiah was crowing over the fall of the pagan king. The overall description of the fall of Nebuchadrezzar does sound very like the popular but erroneous idea about the fall of Satan who was not cast down to Hell for the sin of false pride, but because he lost a power struggle with Michael, which is hardly the same thing. The confusion over the name must be of relatively recent development since there was a famous Bishop Lucifer in the fourth century, who is still regarded as a saint in Sardinia. So strong is the mistaken association however that the Church would be unlikely to permit the christening of a boy child with that name, though the stigma does not seem to attach to all the female equivalents like Lucy, Lucinda or Lucille, all of which also derive from '*lux*', light.

**LUCKY BREAK:** *To have fortune on your side.*

Based on the game of snooker where each player's turn is called a 'break', because each turn breaks the game up into stages.

**LUCULLAN:** *Lavish.*

Lucius Licinius Lucullus (*c.* 115–57 BC), having made his fortune from a successful military and administrative career, enjoyed upon retirement a life of luxury that became the talk of Rome. His banquets, renowned for their opulence, also gave rise to the expression 'Lucullus sups with Lucullus' – said of one settling down by himself to a lavish meal. This latter rests on the tale that someone who saw the preparation of a banquet to end all banquets asked Lucullus which important guests he expected that night; Lucullus replied that he would be dining alone.

**LUCUS A NON LUCENDO:** *An absurd explanation, especially an etymological one.*

Literally meaning 'a grove [named] from its not shining', this was coined by the Roman grammarian Honoratus who flourished towards the end of the fourth century AD. He was ridiculing the habit of inventing false etymons by attempting to derive one word from another of similar appearance but opposite meaning; in this case the Latin for grove, which is shaded and dull, is falsely derived from the Latin for shining.

**LULU:** *Anyone or anything considered remarkable.*

This origin is totally obscure, but it has been said that it derived from the nineteenth-century cowboy term 'loo loo', built on the French card game '*loo*' which was built in turn on the French card game '*lanterlu*'. (This incidentally started out life as a wholly meaningless chant used in the refrains of rounds, as was the English 'folderol'). In any case, to a passing-through-town cowboy, a 'loo loo' was a non-standard poker hand which he strongly suspected to be invented for the occasion though all the locals stuck together assuring him that the rules and the hands were those genuinely accepted in that particular locality. The meaning would have been reinforced by the use of 'loo' deriving from the French '*lieu*', place or locality. So, the card-playing loo loo was remarkable in that it was not only surprising, it was also unbeatable. It has also been suggested that 'lulu' stems from the Christian name 'Louise' although no explanation as to why that particular name was chosen.

**LUMP, THE:** *Illegal labour, especially in the building trade.*

Originally, this seems to have denoted gangs of men who moved from job to job, tendering for a lump sum of money as opposed to specific wages per week. However, it is not impossible that the expression is but an intensifier of what is still known as 'piece' work. The shady overtones were caused by men who worked on the lump and, at the same time, claimed social security money or did not declare their earnings to the tax man.

**LUNATIC:** *Madman.*

Deriving from the Latin '*luna*', moon, this illustrates the ancient belief that the insane were in some way controlled by the moon or subject to its influence. As with many ancient beliefs, there does seem to be some basis to this one. Whether by coicidence or not, certain mental conditions do seem to wax and wane in parallel with the lunar cycle.

**LUNATIC FRINGE:** *Extremists attached to a group or creed.*

If not coined by him, this was at least given currency by Theodore Roosevelt who used it of factions of his own Republican Progressive Party in 1913. In a letter to Henry Cabot Lodge, Roosevelt, musing on the recent defeat of the Bull Moose Party, so-called after he himself had joined it as presidential candidate and pronounced himself as 'fit as a bull moose' for the forthcoming fight, and pondering the possibility that some of his more fanatical partisans might have cost him votes, declared that various groups of supporters had 'always developed amongst their numbers a large lunatic fringe'. Later in the same year he said of the same people: 'There is apt to be a lunatic fringe in the votaries of any forward movement', by which, if he was not exactly justifying them, he was perhaps trying to minimize the damage they were doing by suggesting that they were a political reality for which no one could be blamed.

**LUSH:** *A drunk or dipsomaniac.*

This is possibly akin to the 'lush' that is applied to luxuriant plant growth in that both the drunk and the vegetation are full of watery juice, the term being akin to 'laxative' which also carries a meaning of loose and watery. There is, too, the gypsy '*lush*', to eat and drink, which could have had some influence. There is in addition a much mooted explanation which, whilst it smacks of invention, cannot be dismissed out of hand. The first appearance of 'lush' in this context was in 1790 and, claiming to have existed since 1740, there was an actors' club called *The City of Lushington* which met until 1895 in the *Harp Tavern* in London's Russell Street where their drinking bouts were said to be marathon and prodigious. The club's name has been variously ascribed to sundry persons surnamed Lushington but none has any foundation, as has not, to introduce a note of scepticism, the club's claim to have been founded in 1740; it could well be that its name was in fact a pun on the previously established use of 'lush' for liquor or a drunk.

**LUTESTRING:** *A fine, lustrous silk.*

Whilst it is broadly held that this is a curious, unexplained corruption of 'lustring' (ie that which has lustre), it must be said, as the OED takes the trouble to point out, that reference to the material as 'lutestring' first appears in 1661 whereas 'lustring' does not make its appearance until 1697! It is surely not beyond the bounds of possibility that the cloth's lustre was likened to the sheen on the strings of a lute.

**LYCEUM:** *A literary institute or one in which lectures are given.*

This is the Latin translation of the Greek '*Lukeion*', (a gymnasium wherein Aristotle gave talks and lectures) which took its name from a neighbouring temple erected to Apollo Lukeois. This epithet is variously derived; it may be from '*lux*' light (i.e. the solar god) or it may straightforwardly indicate his Lycean origins since he was the Hellenic counterpart of the Arab god Hobol, the God of Lycia. On the other hand, the Greek '*lukos*', wolf, could be the source since Apollo was also the protector of flocks, being therefore regarded as the wolf-killing god or perhaps even the wolf-god.

**LYNCH:** *To judge and put to death, especially by hanging, without reference to the due processes of law.*

A number of eponyms have been put forward, probably because, in some early appearances, the word began with a capital letter and there were references to 'Lynch's Law', but none can be verified to any satisfactory degree. Instead, one can look to the well-established 'linch', 'lynge' or 'linge', to punish by beating or flogging, which long predated any of the eponymous characters, especially as early references are to floggings, beatings or tarring and featherings, not hangings. Although not certain, the likely origin of this term lies in the Norman '*lincher*', to whip. As far back as 1600, there are references to men being 'lindged', the spelling change was perhaps influenced by the seafarers' use of the linchpin as a weapon. It is, of course, possible that the word 'Lynch came about by way of a fictional personification in the same way as did shadowy characters such as Jack Straw or Captain Lud who allegedly led the LUDDITES, or Captain Swing of the Swing Riots, all of these titles being ascribed to *anyone* involved in the associated activities. As for the eponymous claims, they are as follows: James Lynch Fitz-Stephen who, as a sixteenth century Warden of Galway, Ireland, sentenced his own son to death for murder (an extremely unpopular verdict since his son was beloved by one and all) and, to circumvent rescue by the mob, personally strung him up. It is, however, unlikely that anyone would sit in judgment on his own kin, and, in addition, identical yarns exist in countless other cultures, so this 'source' is extremely suspect. The two best backed claims, in opinion rather than hard fact, come from America's State of Virginia, one citing a Charles Lynch (1736–96), the other a Captain William Lynch (1742–20); both men did exist and both set up rough justice systems to combat lawlessness, but their surnames could have been coincidental.

# M

**McGUFFIN, A:** *A hopelessly convoluted red herring.*

A term invented by film director Alfred Hitchcock to describe any elusive item or person pursued relentlessly by the main characters but which has absolutely no relevance or bearing on the outcome of the plot. Hitchcock claimed that his choice of McGuffin came from an old shaggy dog story in which two old gentlemen are travelling on a train bound for Scotland. One gentleman enquires as to the contents of the other's large and mysterious parcel and is told it contains a McGuffin used for trapping lions in the highlands. When the questioner points out that there are no lions in the highlands he receives the riposte: 'Well then, there's no such thing as a McGuffin.'

**MAD AS A MARCH HARE:** *Excessively deranged.*

A corruption of the original 'mad as a marsh hare', a form noted in the early sixteenth-century writings of Erasmus (1466–1536). In his 'Aphorisms' (1527) Erasmus discusses the nature of the phrase and explains that 'hares are wilder in the marshes from the absence of hedge and cover.' This absence ensures that when a hare does break cover it moves across the open reaches of the marsh in an erratic series of dog-legs and sudden changes of direction executed at top speed to confuse any waiting predator. To the human observer it does appear that the animal has taken leave of its senses for it behaves this way with no visible cause.

**MAD AS A HATTER:** *Excessively insane or eccentric.*

It is widely suggested that this expression came to life as a result of a condition, similar to St Vitus Dance, which afflicted members of the hatting trade whose skin came into repeated contact with mercurious nitrates during the course of their work. However, the phrase was current long before such chemicals were used during the making of hats and originally appeared in the form 'mad as an atter', meaning as dangerous as an adder, 'mad' appearing in its older sense of violently enraged as indeed the term is still so understood in America. In its corrupted form, the expression was given a new lease of life through the popularity of Lewis Carroll's '*Alice's Adventures in Wonderland*' (1865) which featured the Mad Hatter's Tea Party and thus gave its support to the bogus theory.

**MAIN CHANCE, THE:** *A crucial time to profit and alter one's life.*

Taken from the once popular dice game of hazard – not dissimilar to the American game of craps – in which the first throw was called the main. Results of the main dictated following tactics and points objective. The game itself was extremely risky, hence the modern meaning of 'hazard', itself derived from the Arabic '*al azar*', the dice.

**MAKE A BEELINE FOR:** *To travel in a fixedly straight line.*

Folklore has it that having found a goodly supply of honey-making materials the industrious bee returns to the hive in a doggedly determined straight line to inform his companions of the find. Not so, bees return by a route that is equally circuitous as the out-going one. The same myth attached itself to the crow, hence 'as the crow flies' holding much the same meaning as the above. Whilst such birds rarely engage in the aerobatics indulged by starlings and the like, the crow is no more or less direct in its chosen flightpaths than any other bird.

**MAKE A CLEAN BREAST:** *To confess to all one's past transgressions.*

Unconfessed sins were believed to lie physically on the heart until cleansed by the Church.

**MAKE A PASS AT SOMEONE, TO:** *To make romantic overtures.*

Prior to engaging in battle the old ships of the line would make a run by the enemy to assess the cannon power and see how she was rigged in order to second-guess what her first move would be.

**MAKE BRICKS WITHOUT STRAW:** *To attempt the impossible.*

In Exodus 5, the Egyptians told the Jewish slaves that they would no longer be provided with the straw to make the bricks demanded of them by their taskmasters, and that they must go and gather it for themselves. Since they were also ordered to increase their production, their task became quite impossible.

**MAKE (BOTH) ENDS MEET:** *To conduct a balanced budget, especially a low one.*

This is an example of 'meet' in its all but redundant sense of fitting or right and proper. The 'ends' are the final figures on a balance sheet. If these are 'meet', or well-matched, then all is well.

**MAKE MONEY HAND OVER FIST, TO:** *To make considerable profits very rapidly.*

A rope is pulled in quickly by alternately passing one hand over the other, which is clenched, to grasp the rope further along.

**MAKE THE GRADE:** *Achieve your potential.*

Not examination results as so often asserted, for this was first used by nineteenth-century American railroad men to describe a locomotive that could take any hill, or gradient, thrown at it.

**MAKE HEAVY WEATHER:** *To make a task unnecessarily arduous.*

Originally descriptive of a ship's handling characteristics; if she rolled about alarmingly in normal conditions she was so described since the vessel was behaving as if in a severe storm.

**MAKE NO BONES ABOUT IT:** *To be straightforward of speech or action.*

Something of a mystery with all theories proving inconclusive and unconvincing. It has been suggested that 'making bones' refers to the undignified cavortings undertaken by gamblers about to throw the die, traditionally made from bones and called such. The more pragmatic gamester knew that all the rattling and intoning in the world would not influence the outcome so, without making any bones, he simply picked up the shaker and threw. That's all well and fine except the expression appears in Nicholas Udall's 1542 translation of Erasmus's 'Paraphrase of Luke', part of *Apophthegms from Erasmus*, when the author is discussing the command given to Abraham to sacrifice his son. Erasmus writes that 'he made no bones about it but went to offer up his son.' It is unlikely that a man like Erasmus would use a gaming expression when discussing such a subject. The expression could be simple allusion to someone wolfing down a stew, or whatever, bones and all, and so making short of the issue or, with 'bone' being a variant of 'bane' as meaning a cause of woe, we could be looking at an expression which orginally meant to do something without moaning and complaining.

**MAKE(-)DO AND MEND:** *Time spent catching up on various tasks.*

It was once the custom for the Navy to grant men at sea a half-day each week for *making* various little pieces of equipment, *doing* all the little things that invariably got left undone, and *mending* items of clothing and what have you. Increasingly the expression is heard as 'make-do and mend' when incorrectly used to mean doing the best you can with materials to hand.

**MAKE OUT, TO:** *To survive difficult circumstances; to visually identify something in poor conditions.*

At sea, 'make' carries a meaning of to increase or develop and a land promontory, island or any other obstacle looming out of mist or fog is said to be 'making out' towards the viewer as the distance closes. The first sense arose in allusion to the landmass being perceived as if extricating iself from the mist (poor conditions), and the second sense came into being from a straight reversal of application from the landmass to the observer.

**MAKESHIFT:** *Temporary or ill-made.*

A simple compound of 'make' and 'shift' as used to denote things constructed in the knowledge that they are temporary and like to be pulled down and moved at any moment.

**MAKE YOUR MARK:** *To establish one's presence or reputation.*

Dating from the days when even those who possessed writing skills would 'sign' a document with their own stylised symbol or mark, this originally denoted one who had established himself as one of a specific group by the placing of his mark on a petition, contract or whatever.

**MAKE YOUR NUMBER, TO:** *To establish presence in a group.*

Every ship in the Royal Navy has an identifying block of letters which, for some reason best known to the Admirality, is known as a number. In the days of sail a ship 'made her number' in flag-signal when entering port.

**MAKE YOUR PILE, TO:** *To amass your fortune.*

A contribution to English phraseology from the Californian Gold Rush. Having struck a workable deposit the miner took up lodging in his 'digs' and laboured long and hard to extract all the 'pay dirt' the claim had to offer. When he moved on to pastures new the only indication that he had been there was the pile of discarded material to the side of the dig. The bigger the pile, the more he had made.

**MALINGERER, A:** *An idler.*

Strangely enough, this is ultimately rooted in the French proper name of Malingre first noted in the thirteenth century. The name was formed from the words '*mal*', bad or ill, and '*haingre*', a term, possibly Germanic in origin, meaning weak or emaciated. By the eighteenth century 'malingerer' had entered British Forces jargon as a term for a genuinely sick or wounded applicant seeking to be excused from duty, but by the end of the same century 'malingerer' had shifted to describe a shirker.

**MALARKEY:** *Horseplay or verbal baloney.*

A relative newcomer which arose in 1920s America. Whilst the origin is unclear, much opinion favours the Greek '*malakia*' which has a similar meaning and will have invaded English through the influx of Greek immigrants to America.

**MAN BITES DOG:** *Real news.*

Taken from a speech made by John B. Bogart, city editor of *The Sun* newspaper in New York 1873–90. In an attempt to justify the publishing of some of the more prurient tales his organ favoured, Bogart said, 'When a dog bites a man, that is not news because it happen so often. But if a man bites a dog, that is news.'

**MAN OF STRAW:** *Person of no moral fortitude.*

At first glance the allusion could hardly be clearer, but there is a legal history to this. Throughout the seventeenth and eighteenth centuries this expression took on a quite specific meaning in legal circles and described a false witness. To indicate their willingness to be hired for perjury, vagrants and the like would hang around the Inns of Court and the grounds of Temple Church with a wisp of straw sticking out of their shoe as a badge of their availability.

**MAN OF THE CLOTH:** *A priest or other cleric.*

Prior to the seventeenth century various trades and callings were recognizable by the colour of the cloth of the livery of their adherents and so referred to as, for example, man of the blue cloth, a butcher, and so forth. By the 1800s the usage had been abandoned save for clerics so the stipulation of colour was no longer necessary.

**MAN OF THE WORLD:** *One who is knowledgeable on all matters of life.*

Recently this has taken on perjorative overtones through its smug and self-congratulatory use by men who in fact know nothing at all – i.e. 'speaking as a man of the world', or the weedling and conspiratorial 'come on, we're all men of the world here'. When first noted in the sixteenth century the expression meant only a married man and drew distinction between one who had taken such steps and thus placed himself beyond entry to the Church, and those who had taken orders and vowed celebacy. In short, it denoted a man who had plumped for the pleasures of the world rather those of the soul. Nor was such designation restricted to men; in *As You Like It* the opening lines of Act V, Scene III in response to Touchstone's reminder that on the morrow they will be married Audrey replies 'I do desire it with all my heart and I hope it is no dishonest desire to desire to be a woman of the world.'

**MAN ON THE CLAPHAM OMNIBUS:** *The epitome of 'the man in the street'.*

This 'person' was born of a notion put to the court by Lord Bowen while hearing a case of negligence in 1903. In an attempt to bring flesh and bones to the legal concept of 'the reasonable man', Bowen put to the court: 'We must ask ourselves what the man on the Clapham omnibus would think.' Whether this particular omnibus was picked at random for no good reason is unclear, for, then as now, route 77A to Clapham Junction does first pass through Westminster and Whitehall and had likely been seen countless times by Bowen though it is doubtful he ever availed himself of its service.

**MAN THE PUMPS:**

Cry for all to come to help. These are the bilge pumps in the hold of a ship which in the event of the hull being holed, would have to be operated to save the ship.

**MANKIE:** *Of unpleasing or filthy appearance.*

A corruption of the French '*manqué*' meaning lack, want, or deficiency.

**MANTLE OF ELIJAH:** *Symbol of power and authority.*

Most often used of the transfer of power – i.e. so-and-so has assumed the mantle of Elijah – unsurprisingly, this is a biblical reference taken from 1 Kings, 19:19 which tells how Elijah indicated his choice of Elisha as his successor by throwing his mantle about the other man's shoulders.

**MANY A MICKLE MAKES A MUCKLE:** *Gather the pennies and the pounds will follow.*

A tautology since both 'mickle' and 'muckle' mean a large or considerable amount. The original axiom was 'Many a pickle makes a mickle/muckle'. 'Pickle', an allied term of others such as 'peck' and 'peak', meant a small item and it seems that the similarity between this and 'mickle' created the modern form of the phrase.

**MARCH TO/HEAR A DIFFERENT DRUMMER, TO:** *To follow an individualistic way of life.*

A paraphrase of a passage from the writings of the American philosopher, Henry David Thoreau (1817–63), a leading light of a group often referred to as the Concorde Transcendentalists. An arch-individualist, he felt that each person should be self-determinating, and wrote: 'If a man does not keep pace with his companions, perhaps it is because he hears a different drummer . . . Let him step to the music which he hears, however measured or far away.'

**MARK OF CAIN:** *The stamp of a murderer.*

This is a somewhat erroneous usage since the mark God put upon Cain was intended as a defence and not a brand. When Cain murdered his brother, Abel, God condemned him to a life of empty, fugitive wandering, whereupon Cain, bemoaning his fate, pointed out that there would be those who would seek to kill him for his crime. God decreed [Genesis 4:15] that whosoever sought vengeance upon Cain would himself be the object of Divine vengeance, and 'set a mark upon Cain, lest any finding him should kill him.'

**MARK SOMEONE'S CARD:** *To give them good advice or warning.*

From the racetrack where most serious punters carry printed cards detailing the day's races and entered horses. To jot down a salient piece of inside information on another's card was to point them in the right direction.

**MARK TIME, TO:** *Fail to progress.*

Military term denoting men marching on the spot, marking the beat or time of the band with the right foot brought down smartly to the ground.

**MARTINET:** *A strict disciplinarian.*

In the reign of Louis XIV, Jean Martinet was appointed Commander in Chief of the king's own regiment which had attracted officers more interested in cutting a dash in Paris society than in military professionalism. In his drive toward the new model army of dedicated professionals Martinet included his officers in the new regime. Naturally this did little to endear him to them. There is no evidence at all to suggest he was anything other than a good soldier and commander but his unpopularity ensured his name took on derogatory overtones. Martinet died at the siege of Duisberg, killed by a salvo from his own artillery; it was rumoured that he was shot in the back by his own men. Killed at his side was a Swiss officer named Soury giving rise to the military pun that Duisberg cost the king but a martin and a mouse.

**MAUDLIN:** *Excessively melancholy.*

A variant of (Mary) Magdalene who is normally depicted weeping over the fate of Christ.

**MAVERICK:** *An unpredictable individual.*

The term is certainly based on the name of Samuel Augustus Maverick, a Texas cattle rancher of the mid 1800s. A lawyer by trade, it seems he accepted a ranch in 1846 in settlement of a bad debt but had little liking or aptitude for the life. Stories conflict as to whether he left his own stock unbranded or took everyone else's unbranded stock as his own, but, either way, he sold up in 1855 and moved east leaving behind his name in Texas ranching slang to denote any unbranded calf. The term did not appear in wider usage until the turn of the century when it had come to denote someone who was a truculent loner.

**MAZUMA:** *Money.*

This is directly borrowed from the Yiddish meaning 'that which is necessary'.

**MEAL TICKET, A:** *Anyone or anything seen a a source of freebies.*

This arose in early twentieth-century America to describe what is otherwise known as a luncheon voucher.

**MEALY MOUTHED:** *Obsequious or wheedling of speech.*

The reference is to the weak and crumbly nature of meal and no satisfactory connection to the Greek '*melimuthus*', honey speech, has been established although it could well have exerted some influence.

**MELTING POT:** *Any levelling or standardising influence.*

Direct reference to the jeweller's smelting pot into which all damaged items and shavings are consigned to be reduced to a block of metal of uniform purity. The expression now has a fairly specific application to the blending of all races and cultures after a play of this title opened in London in 1908. The piece was written by Israel Znagwill and dealt with the problems facing immigrants.

**MENDING FENCES:** *Patch up political differences.*

Misunderstanding of a statement made by American Secretary of State John Sherman who, in 1879, decided to run for the Senate, sure in the knowledge that he would shortly be losing his cabinet position as President Hyaes would not be seeking re-election. In that same year he returned to his farm in Ohio to be pestered by reporters anxious to know the reason for his appearance. Sherman later said that when he replied he had come back to mend his fences he was in no way being cryptic nor was the purpose of that visit to his home ground to drum up support for his run for the senate. He had, quite literally, returned to see to state business.

**MESS OF POTTAGE:** *Any paltry bribe for which one sells oneself.*

Although this refers to the well-known story in Genesis recounting how Esau sold his birthright to Jacob, the actual expression does not appear anywhere in the relevant text – nor elsewhere in the Bible, come to that. Esau foolishly sold out for 'bread and a pottage of lentils' (birthrights came cheap in those days!). The modern accepted form first appeared in 1526 and is a fine example of 'mess' in its old meaning of a meal – still surviving in the term officers 'mess'. Table manners of old brought 'mess' to its more popular meaning.

**MEXICAN STANDOFF:** *A stalemate.*

Wanted men in the nineteenth-century American West could elude their pursuers by making their way south and crossing the Rio Grande into Mexico where the posse could not follow. Once in Mexico the outlaws were safe in that they were of no interest to the Mexican authorities but it depended on how much money they had with them for the moment they committed a robbery for funds the Mexicans would be upon them and their only alternative means of getting their hands on money was by working which was not to their taste. On the other side of the border the authorities would be waiting for word that the men had re-crossed the river but until then everyone sat back and waited for the other chap to blink.

**MEXICAN WAVE:** *Crowd phenomenon.*

Most commonly seen at track events, this involves section of the crowd rising to their feet in excitement and then sitting down again, but doing so in sequence giving the distant observer the impression of a wave running through the terrace. Although not original to the 1986 World Cup final played in Mexico, this was the first time the action was seen on British television.

**MIDAS TOUCH:** *Incredible luck with money and investment.*

The tale of Midas, a legendary king of Phrygia, is the classic illustration of the Greco–Roman maxim: 'Never pray to the gods for what you think you want, lest they be in malicious humour and grant your request.' Midas beseeched the gods that everything he touched would be turned to gold, and to teach him a lesson, his wish was granted. His food, wine, wives, children all turned to metal before his eyes and, after the requisite grovelling to the heavens, the 'gift' was rescinded. Midas is not the only mythical figure of this tale is told, but only he has entered the realm of phraseology as a result.

**MILK RUN:** *Anything routine and devoid of risk; a first choice of that which is available.*

The term in its first application arose during WW2 to describe any patrol, be it infantry or airborne, which returned to base early in the morning. Normally this group would cover the hours when there was the least action, the next-out dawn patrol picking up on the first of the day's action. By the 1970s the second application had entered the arena having been coined in graduate recruitment circles to describe the crew who got to the universities first and gathered the 'cream' of the crop.

**MINCE, TO:** *To move in an effeminate manner.*

Derived from 'mince' as meaning to make small, this has been in use in this context since the sixteenth century alluding to the over-fastidious taking tiny, trotting steps and doing everything in small jerky movements.

**MINCE YOUR WORDS, TO:** *To be over-delicate of speech.*

Allusion to the mincing of meat to make less pleasant cuts more palatable.

**MIND YOUR Ps AND Qs:** *To pay attention to the finer points of etiquette.*

There are many fanciful theories attempting to link this to various aspects of social behaviour but the derivation lies in the similarity between the two letters so often confused by children learning to write. As for the best of the 'runner up' theories, the first maintains the expression to have been born in medieval drinking haunts wherein the cautious drinker minded how many pints or quarts he consumed, and the second forces a connection to French dancing instructors of the Royal Court admonishing their pupils '*Attention aux pieds et queues*!', look out for your feet and wigs, the latter being in danger of falling off if bows made during the dance were too low.

**MINGE:** *The vagina.*

This first entered English in the early seventeenth century as a verb meaning to pass urine, this is turn being based on the Latin '*mingere*', with the same meaning. By the opening of the nineteenth century 'minge' had attached itself exclusively to the vagina but its source has ensured that it has never been considered anything other than a disparaging term for the organ or for a woman seen solely as a sexual object. Inevitably, there have been attempts to link 'mingy', as meaning low or mean, to 'minge' but the terms developed separately. Mingy did not emerge until the early twentieth century and seems to have been a Forces slang word built on 'stingy and 'mangy'.

**MINX:** *A vindictive or Machiavellian woman.*

As have so many words – especially those applied to women – this has trod a downhill path from its inception as a term of endearment to one of contempt. Based on 'minnikin', based in turn on the Dutch '*minneken*', darling, minx first appeared in the mid sixteenth century as a term for a pet dog or plaything. Within fifty years the term became attached exclusively to kept mistresses or any 'wanton', pert hussy. From here on the word rapidly broadened to embrace connotations of avarice, self-interested cunning and petty viciousness. The degradation of the term will have been much aided by the fact that the separate and now obsolete 'minx' was a form of mink, an animal renowned for such traits.

**MISSING LINK, A:** *An especially thick-set and brutish male.*

A pseudo-scientific expression and notion alluding to the non-existant 'link' between man and ape which no one within the scientific community has ever searched for. The term is based on a total misunderstanding of Darwinian theories which never stated man to be descended from the apes, but imply that man and the apes – along with all other mammals – share a common progenitor and developed in parallel rather than in sequence.

**MISSIONARY POSITION:** *Standard face-to-face position for sexual intercourse.*

Known in Shakespeare's time as 'making the beast with two backs', this arose in the heyday of the nineteenth century missionary operation in the South Sea islands and the like. It is unclear whether these interlopers found the native's healthy approach to enthusiastic sex disturbing and recommended a less enjoyable, and therefore more godly, position, or, and doubtless this is the more likely, that the missionaries themselves were not averse to a bit of ungodly activity but always assumed the aforementioned position.

**MOANING MINNIE:** *A perpetual complainer.*

A product of WW2, this being the nickname bestowed on the German trench mortar by those on the receiving end of its attentions. The first element was inspired by the distinctive moaning sound made by the incoming shells and the second built squarely on the German '*Minenwerfer*', a mine-thrower.

**MOGGIE:** *A cat.*

Softening of 'Maggie', a traditional name given female cats in contrast to Tom. Such nomenclatory practice is widespread in the animal kingdom – Robin redbreasts, Mag the pie, Jack the daw and even Duncan as a pet name for a small ass, the diminutive of which, Dunkie, eventually transmuted to 'donkey'.

**MOJO WORKING, TO HAVE YOUR:** *To be on top form.*

American black slang meaning one's personal and internal 'magic'. First noted in the 1920s, it is likely based on the Gullah '*moco*', magic or a spell, or any one of a host of other similar African dialect terms. By the 1930s 'mojo' had come to mean any narcotic, as indeed it still does. It is not, however, clear whether this was a development from the notion that the drug enhanced one's 'mojo' or whether this is a wholly separate development from either the Mexica–Spanish 'mojar', to celebrate with much drink, or the Spanish '*mojo*', a spice or condiment.

**MOLLY-CODDLE:** *Excessively pamper.*

If not based on the Latin '*mollis*', soft, then the first element is probably the use of Moll as a generic name for any female servant expected to fuss round her employer. The second element appears in its cooking sense of gently warmed through.

**MOMENT OF TRUTH:** *The crunch, the decisive point in one's life.*

Popularised by Ernest Hemmingway and his obsession with Spain and bull-fighting this is an expression of the bullring denoting the moment when the weakened bull makes what the matador hopes will be its final charge. To receive the onslaught the matador must stand absolutely still with the sword held at exactly the right downwards angle so that the bull will run onto it, sever its own spinal cortex and drop dead at the matador's feet. Needless to say, one small error at this point and the bull will have its own moment of pleasure.

**MONEY FOR OLD ROPE:** *Easy money, but honestly made.*

It was common in the days of sail for crew members to retain all old rope ends and worn out lines, these were unpicked during their spare time so the threads and strips could be sold to the shipyards in the next port of call. Here it was hammered into the gaps between the decking prior to it being sealed with pitch.

**MONSTROUS CARBUNCLE:** *Anything hideous of aspect.*

First used by Prince Charles in June 1984 when speaking of the proposed design for the new wing of the National Gallery in London which the Prince dismissed as 'a monstrous carbuncle on the face of a much-loved and elegant friend'. The expression was immediately taken up by the media who worked it to death and so was introduced into general usage.

**MOONSHINE:** *Illicitly distilled liquor; verbal rubbish.*

The liquor comes first and takes its name from the most likely time of night for it to be made and transported whilst the Revenue Men were abed. The second meaning derives from the fact that those who drank moonshine usually ended up talking it as well.

**MOOT POINT:** *One under discussion; anything undecided.*

In Anglo–Saxon England a moot was a meeting, specifically the gathering of council for debate.

**MOTLEY CREW:** *Ill-matched assortment of people.*

An archaicism now only used tongue-in-cheek, this previously denoted the troupe of fools and jesters who traditionally dressed in patched clothing (CROSSPATCH) which gave them a 'mottled' appearance.

**MOVEABLE FEAST:** *Anything fluid of arrangement or fixture.*

This is taken from the Christian Calendar in which certain feasts, or festivals, are not pegged to a specific date. The major moveable feast is Easter Sunday which falls on the first Sunday after the full moon of the vernal equinox. This means that Easter can occur anywhere between 22 March and the 25 April.

**MOXIE:** *Courage or brash front.*

In 1927 Moxie was launched on the American fizzy-drink market with an advertising campaign centured on the slogan 'What this country needs is plenty of Moxie'. Follow-up posters tended to show exhausted children leaving the sportsfield only to be miraculously revived by a glass of said product. By the following year 'moxie' had entered the general swim with its present meaning.

**MUDLARKING:** *Indulging in shennanigans or foolish play.*

If not a straightforward compound meaning they who lark about in the mud, this could possibly be a corruption of 'mudlurk' since one of its earliest applications was to a common waterfront thief who specialised in hiding under ships at low tide to catch small packets of stolen goods dropped by members of the crew. A mudlark could also be a shoreline scavenger, an activity much undertaken by young children who mixed play with their collecting.

**MUFF:** *The vagina.*

Simply reference to the warm, furry muff as once worn by women and the more foppish men.

**MUFF IT, TO:** *To fail in grand manner.*

This first emerged in the mid 1800s and did so in public school slang to initially describe a bungled catch at cricket or any bad shot in any other activity – as if the player had his hands in a muff and had lost all dexterity. As for the ultimate origin of 'muff' itself, this could well rest on the French '*mouflon*', a type of wild sheep renowned for its high wool yield.

**MUFTI:** *Casual wear, especially instead of uniform.*

This was coined by British Army officers *c.* 1800 and its use of 'mufti' as the title of a Mohammedan priest. When relaxing in their quarters the fashion was for full-length smoking coats, complete with small circular hat with tassle. The overall appearance was not unlike the garb of the priest.

**MUG:** (1) *The face.*

A development of the eighteenth-century craze for jugs and drinking mugs sporting ugly and distorted faces. It has been suggested that a more respectable source is the Sanskrit '*mukha*', the face, but since this particular use of 'mug' did not emerge until the opening of the eighteenth century it does seem a mite too long a span for the term to have lain idle. (2) *An idiot or naive sucker.* Built on the foundations of (1) in reference to the demented demeanour of most of the characters depicted on drinking mugs.

**MUG, TO:** *To rob an individual with violence.*

Something of an oddity since 'to mug' has, on both sides of the Atlantic, held such meaning since the mid 1700s and described the selection of a victim who was plyed with several mugs of liquor until insensible enough to rob with impunity. The trouble with this is that the expression became largely obsolete by the turn of this century and the above 'reappeared' in post WW2 New York – everywhere else in America called the practice 'yoking'. Since no connection can be made between the old 'mug' and the new it does seem safer to regard this as born of the disdain held by the perpetrator for his victims who he sees as idiots.

**MUG UP, TO:** *To revise or* BONE UP.

This is almost certainly of theatrical origin and reference to the actors going over their lines one last time whilst being made up – or having their mug painted.

**MULL THINGS OVER, TO:** *To ponder them.*

Here, 'mull' is a variant of 'mill'

and the mind is likened to the millstone going over and over the grain.

**MUMBO-JUMBO:** *Convoluted speech or utter rubbish.*

One of the earliest mentions of 'mumbo-jumbo' appears in *Travels in the Interior of Africa*, 1795–97, published by Mungo Park, the Scottish explorer who opened up the Niger and other parts of the continent. In the Mandingo culture the spectre of Mama Dyambo, a name meaning 'Venerable Ancestor With Pom Pom', was used to keep any unruly or nagging wives in check. A husband who felt he had cause to complain along these lines would enter the village dressed up as the deity and assemble the inhabitants. He called out the alleged offender who was then stripped by the other women, tied to a stake and whipped to the accompaniment of undignified cavortings and jibbering undertaken by the spectators. Mumbo-Jumbo is a simple HOBSON-JOBSON of Mama Dyambo and gained its meaning from the nature of this ceremony.

**MURPHY'S LAW:** *Humorous rule of the iniquities of life.*

In essence this law states that if anything can possibly go wrong then it will; the bread will always hit the floor butter-side down, or if it is at all possible for an indiot-proof component to be fitted upside down or back to front then sooner or later someone will so install it. As to the identity of the much maligned Mr Murphy, while there have been several unsubstantiated nominees put forward, this is likely little more than a dig at the Irish reputation for convoluted reasoning and bizarre behaviour.

**MUTTON DRESSED AS LAMB:** *Anything or anyone disguising age, especially a woman.*

Whilst the allusion is quite straightforward, the source is not. The use of 'dressed' could be in the butchery sense of cutting and displaying, members of this trade still not beyond selling one cut of meat masquerading as another. Alternatively, from the sixteenth to the nineteenth century 'mutton' was a common term for a prostitute and 'lamb' denoted a young innocent virgin.

**MY OLD DUTCH:** *My wife.*

This is almost certainly Cockney rhyming slang, although it is unclear whether from 'Dutch plate' = mate, or 'Duchess of Fife' = wife – some even hold it to be a simple shortening of 'Duchess'. In any case, this London expression was given wide circulation in the closing years of the nineteenth century by Albert Chevalier (1861–1923), a British music hall performer acclaimed on both sides of the Atlantic; his most famous song was *My Old Dutch*.

# N

**NAFF:** *Unpleasant or thoroughly unfashionable.*

Despite the striking parallels in the paths followed by this and NAFF OFF, the two terms appear wholly unconnected. Not gaining general currency until the 1970s, this could well be ultimately rooted in the dialect 'naffhead', a simpleton. During WW2 'naff' was Naval officers' slang for an unpromiscuous Wren (not available for fucking) but immediately after the war – and this should not be taken as comment of the sexual proclivities of the officers of Her Majesty's Navy – the word remained the almost exclusive preserve of the homosexual community to describe an unattractive male or one who would not 'come across', a naff omi being the full designation. From here the term took the short step to the jargon of the Sloanes and the like before filtering down to general speech in the mid 1980s.

**NAFF OFF:** *Fuck off.*

A euphemism raised to drawing room respectability through its highly publicized use by Princess Anne in April 1982 when so dismissing intrusive photographers snapping at her during the Badminton Horse Trials. Having said that, its origins are less straightforward than the Princess' speech and the only thing for certain is that heavy sexual connotations have always been present in this 'naff'. Throughout the last century 'naf(f)' was a non-too vulgar term for the vagina and possibly nothing more than a back-slang based on FANNY. Alternatively, there is the separate 'naff', a now-obsolete variant of 'navel', itself a euphemism for the vagina in days gone by. Indeed, in earlier times, 'navel' was widely used to describe both male and female genitals as witnessed in the Bible at Job 40:15–17 which describes the power of the loins of the Behemoth 'his force is in the navel . . . and the sinews of his stones are wrapped together'. Perhaps 'navel' fell to such use for no other reason than its properly meaning the central part which, of course, the genitals are. By 1940 'naf(f)' had been adopted by prostitutes who used it of a lousy night's business – Not A Fuck. The writers of the 1970s television series 'Porridge' found themselves in need of a euphemism for 'fuck' to make the prisoners' turn of phrase more credible and they opted for 'naff', which really put the term on the map.

**NAIL A LIE TO THE COUNTER:** *To prove its falsehood to all.*

It used to be customary for traders who spotted counterfeit coins to nail the forgeries to their counters. This served as a warning to any would-be purveyor of dud coinage that they were dealing with an eagle-eyed expert. Nothing changes; much the same is now done with forged banknotes.

**NAIL YOUR COLOURS TO THE MAST:** *Take a resolute stand.*

The colours in question are the identification flags flown by the old ships of the line. To indicate surrender the vanquished ship only had to strike her colours down, something that couldn't be done if they were nailed to the masthead.

**NAKED TRUTH, THE:** *The absolute and unvarnished truth.*

Allusive to an old fable recounting how Truth and Falsehood went swimming together one day. Falsehood left the water first for the express purpose of stealing Truth's clothes in an attempt to pass himself off as his own opposite number. Truth left the pool and walked away naked, staying that way in perpetuity, thinking there be less shame in nakedness than dressed in the clothes of Falsehood.

**NAMBY-PAMBY:** *The affectedly dainty or the insipidly weak.*

The term was invented by Henry Carey (1687–1743) – best remembered for his ballad 'Sally in our Alley' – as a parody on the name of Ambrose Philips (1675–1749) a contemporary poet whose tendency to the wishy-washy did not endear him to many of his fellows. In a rare moment of insanity the *Guardian* (issue no. 30, 1713) hailed Philips as 'the only worthy successor to Spenser', a declaration which signalled the start of a protracted and malevolent exchange between Alexander Pope and Philips. *English Poets* (1725) contained two exceedingly mawkish poems by Philips eulogizing upon the cherubic qualities of the puling progeny of both Lord John Carteret and Daniel Pulteney – the tripe addressed 'To Mistress Charlotte Pulteney' opened: 'Timely blossom, infant fair, Fondling of a happy pair', and got rapidly worse. Amidst the derision this attracted Carey published a goad entitled 'Namby Pamby' and the nickname was readily taken up by many – most notably Pope, the Wasp of Twickenham.

**NARK:** *An informant.*

One of many Romany contributions, this being based on '*nak*', the nose, the connection between noses and informants is repeated in 'snitch'.

**NARKED:** *Angry.*

A spin off from NARK, in that those whose activities are reported to the police tend to get annoyed.

**NECKING:** *Amorous petting.*

Reference to a pre-mating ritual common to many creatures, especially horses, involving the intertwining of the neck or nibbling and biting of the same.

**NEED TO HAVE YOUR BUMPS FELT:** *In need of psychiatric attention.*

Around the turn of the nineteenth century, Franz Joseph Gall (1758–1828) began lecturing in Vienna on his theories of what he called cranioscopy, but his converts called phrenology. Gall and his disciples claimed to be able to read a person's entire character, identify his talents, criminal propensities and so forth, by running their fingertips over his head and 'reading' the bumps and nodules on his skull.

**NEITHER FISH NOR FOWL NOR FRESH RED HERRING:** *Neither one thing nor the other.*

Known since the sixteenth century this alludes to the typical fare consumed by the three divisions of society – fish for the clergy, fowl for the nobility and RED HERRING for the common herd. Sometimes 'flesh' as denoting venison or wild boar, replaced 'fowl'.

**NEITHER HIDE NOR HAIR:** *To find no trace at all.*

Early hunters divided game into two rough categories: 'hide' embraced deer, wild pig and the like, 'hair' included rabbit and other such small animals.

**NEITHER RHYME NOR REASON:** *Neither one thing or the other; useless.*

This usage is extremely old and relies on a long-redundant application of 'reason' which from the fourteenth to the seventeenth century could mean a narrative, written observation of a factual nature, or even a single sentence; 'parts of reason' then stood synonymous with 'parts of speech'. Basically the above means the subject is neither rhyme (capricious English for entertainment) nor is it factual text.

**NEST EGG:** *Special savings reserve.*

The china egg a farmer would place beneath a young hen reluctant to lay. It was thought that the egg's presence would encourage the hen to add to it.

**NEVER LOOK A GIFT HORSE IN THE MOUTH:** *Dither not when confronted by an opportunity.*

The state of a horse's teeth is a rough guide to its age; but if someone is prepared to give you the animal why worry about such details.

**NEVER SET THE THAMES ON FIRE, YOU'LL:** *You'll never be any great success at anything.*

Struck by the apparent illogicality of the expression scholars have attempted to force rationality upon it by hunting up homophones such as 'temse', an old word for a flour sieve. Thus, they reasoned, the phrase alluded to an ineffectual mill-worker who was never going to set his sieve on fire through frantic effort. Confronted with a parallel expression in French citing the Seine the theory was extended through the French '*seine*', a trawling net. Inventive as they are, these theories do not stand up to scrutiny; the Germans have an old saying referring to the Rhine and the Romans told the lazy that they would never set the Tiber on fire, so in all probability the phrase is a simple allusion to the amount of work required to set water alight.

**NIGHT OF THE LONG KNIVES:** *The purging of any organization.*

Actually a weekend of carnage spanning 29 June to 2 July 1934, this was organized by Hitler, Himmler and Goering who orchestrated the assassination of some 400 leading members of the S.A. (the Brownshirts) including the leader Rohm and his deputy Schleicher. '*Die Nacht der Lange Messer*' was used of the events during a speech of justification Hitler later made in the Reichstag on 13 July. He was quoting from a line in a popular Nazi drinking/marching song which in turn harked back to the heyday of the Germanic Saxons whose name means the long knives, in that '*sax*' is a short sword.

**NIGHT ON THE TILES:** *Nocturnal revelry.*

A direct reference to the carnal cavortings of cats on the rooftops.

**NINE DAY WONDER:** *Anything ephemeral.*

Although there are some plausible explanations for the above it is not beyond the realms of possibility that the number was chosen for no other reason than its mystical-religious associations, it being perceived as a trinity of trinities. Having said that, the expression is used in a derogatory way more fitting to one of the following origins. On sale to the robber barons and otherwise wealthy medievals was something called a novena, nine days of prayer uttered by the local monks to guarantee heavenly acceptance for the paymaster. To the cynical eye it seemed that as soon as the purchased piety ceased the payee was forgotten about as the monks performed similar service for another. It has been suggested that the source lies in 1600 when a gentleman by the name of William Kemp, a co-owner of the Globe Theatre, morris-danced his way from London to Norwich in nine days and published a pamphlet, 'A Nine Daies Wonder' recounting his adventures en route. The suggestion is that perhaps the more staid members of society thought his feat but folly and pilloried him with his own title. Unfortunately for this theory, the expression had already appeared in print in the previous century so Kemp's pamphlet must be discounted as the origin of the expression.

**NIP AND TUCK:** *To be neck and neck.*

Possibly a fencing expression of the nineteenth century when 'nip' was a common term for a light touch on the opponent and 'tuck', based on the Italian '*tocco*', a blow or strike, meant a heavier contact – so the duellers were matching each other point for point. It is also worth mentioning that yet another 'tuck' was a common term for a thrusting rapier, this being based on the French '*estock*'. Then again, the phrase might be one of seamstress' usage alluding to the closing of a seam, both hands moving together nipping and tucking the fabric under for sewing.

**NIP IN THE BUD:** *To arrest development early.*

Here, the 'nip' is the cold which, in the form of a late frost, will catch out and kill burgeoning growth.

**NIPPER:** *Small child.*

Perhaps no more complicated than street trader's cant for a young assistant who had to 'nip' here and there on errands, but the origin could be Naval. Anchor cable was far too thick to be wrapped round the capstan so it was laid out in parallel to a thinner line to which its first few feet were bound, this was used as a leader line to the capstan. Binding ropes in this way is called nipping and was always done by the ships' boys who were thus called nippers.

**NIT PICKING:** *Excessively finicky.*

Headlice were once removed by progressing across the scalp with a fine-tooth comb and methodically picking out the nits one by one. The nit-picker had to go over every square inch of scalp or the missed nits would simply reproduce and take over again.

**NO DICE!:** *No way; nothing doing.*

Taken from the American crap-dice tables whereon this is the cry when the dice either fall off the table or leap over the shoulder due to an over-enthusiastic throw. With this call the throw is made void and all bets are off.

**NO FLIES ON SOMEONE:** *They are astute.*

It is tempting to see this as a simple allusion to agile animals being too active to have flies settle on them but the true origin is more complicated. Its inspiration is the angler's fly and since the late nineteenth century a person was said to be 'no fly' if they failed to rise for the sucker-bait like a brainless fish (*see also:* TAKE A RISE). This generated the use of 'no flies' meaning 'no kidding' and by the turn of the century a 'no-flies' person was one who was honest and sincere. 'There are no flies on . . .' arose *c.* 1910 and was initially synonymous with 'no-flies' but later assumed its present connotations of shrewdness and cunning.

**NO GREAT SHAKES:** *Of no merit.*

It is generally suggested that this refers to a poor throw of dice made by a gambler after he has shaken the cup. It has also been mooted that when cannibalising old barrels, distorted and split shakes, the vertical sections, would be cast aside – but neither of these seems to be a satisfactory explanation. Since the 1700s 'shake' as a verb meant to coit and the nounal form served for a prostitute; SHAG is a variant thereof. It is quite likely that the above was initially an insult aimed at a woman unkeen on the transient pleasures of the bedroom or used of a harlot failing to attack her tasks with enthusiasm.

**NO HOLDS BARRED:** *No rules; anything goes.*

Every form of wrestling has its own rules, but for 'needle-matches' these were set aside.

**NO LOVE LOST BETWEEN THEM:** *They hate each other.*

A peculiar reversal of application

of this line from the ancient ballad 'The Children in the Wood': 'No love between the two was lost, each to the other was kind.' In other words, no love was wasted but lavished on the other.

**NO NAMES, NO PACK DRILL:** *A reason for not revealing sources of information.*

More twentieth-century Forces jargon, this time alluding to miscreants being force-marched in full kit as a punishment. But if the sergeant did not have the offenders' names, they could not be put through the hoops.

**NO ROYAL ROAD TO LEARNING:** *No easy course to success.*

The original form was supposedly 'There is no royal road to geometry', as uttered by Euclid to Ptolemy when the latter demanded a crash course in the subject. Some doubt the expression has such antiquity and point to the previous use of 'royal road' as synonymous with 'highway', these being straighter and easier to travel that their country cousins.

**NOD IS AS GOOD AS A WINK, A:** *Enough said; the meaning should be clear.*

The original and full expression was 'a nod is as good as a wink to a blind horse' and indicated stupidity on behalf of the listener who was failing to grasp the hints being put his way. If the 'horse' is blind then no amount of suggestive gestures is going to put the message across.

**NORKS:** *The female breast.*

An Australian word from a 1950s advertising campaign for Norco butter. Each advert featured dairy cows with massive udders.

**NOSEY PARKER:** *Any excessively intrusive person.*

First noted in 1851 all attempts to link this to persons named Parker are futile and the likelihood of this being eponymous are remote to say the least. In Londoners' parlance a parker was a rabbit living in one of the parks, especially Hyde Park. These 'parkers' tended to be quite tame, almost inquisitive; the permanent twitching of the creature's nose will no doubt have contributed greatly to the expression. In the year 1851 the Great Exhibition situated in Hyde Park caused London to be invaded by countless thousands of visitors gawping and craning at all and sundry, this almost certainly causing the designation to shift to humans.

**NOT A CAT IN HELL'S CHANCE:** *No chance at all.*

Originally appeared as 'not a cat's chance in hell' but it seems unlikely that the reference is feline as the cat's long-standing connection with the occult would make it the quadruped most likely to survive in this location. From the fifteenth century to the present, 'cat' has meant a prostitute since both cruise the night with sexual intent (*see also:* PUSSY) and it would seem more plausible that the reference is a sanctimonious one presupposing that all prostitutes will go to hell for a hard time while their customers ascend to another place.

**NOT A PATCH ON:** *Not in the same class.*

A reduced form of 'not fit to be a patch on' – a simple reference to one type of inferior cloth deemed unsuitable to mend a garment of a superior material.

**NOT A SAUSAGE:** *Nothing at all.*

Originally this denoted a paucity of money and is based on the rhyming slang sausage and mash = cash.

**NOT CARE ONE JOT:** *To be completely indifferent.*

The Greek letter 'iota', the smallest in the alphabet, was sometimes read in Latin as 'jota', hence 'jot' for something insignificant. The small pad for rough notes is named a 'jotter' from the same source. (*See also:* NOT ONE IOTA.)

**NOT ENOUGH ROOM TO SWING A CAT:** *Very cramped quarters.*

The cat here is the cat o' nine tails and the overall reference is to the cramped conditions endured by sailors of old.

**NOT FIT TO HOLD A CANDLE TO:** *So inferior as not to be comparable with.*

Based on a reference to link-boys, who formed the lowest stratum of seventeenth to nineteenth-century servants. They ran alongside carriages and sedan chairs carrying links, torches, to light the way and defend the occupants against robbers, who, as often as not, were off-duty link-boys themselves. They were also employed to stand about in places of public entertainment to light the way for their betters.

**NOT GIVE A FIG:** *To be completely unconcerned.*

The well-established use of 'fig' for the vagina, which the fruit in its dried form is supposed to resemble. To 'give the fig' means to make a sign by forcing the thumb into the clenched fist in a suggestive manner, a gesture comparable to the modern V sign, so 'not to give a fig' equates to a much more explicit expression. '*Fico*', the Italian for a fig, still enjoys similar usage but is less frequently heard. The antiquity of the link between sexuality and the fig can even be seen in the Bible for it is only after their transgression that Adam and Eve bedeck themselves in fig-leaves.

**NOT GIVING A HOOT:** *Totally indifferent.*

From the American dialect 'hoot', the smallest of particles or anything insignificant, which in turn derived from 'hooter', the American dialect corruption of 'iota'.

**NOT IN THE SAME STREET:** *Not in the same class.*

Each line of peg-holes on the cribbage scoreboard is called a street, hence also 'streets ahead'.

**NOT MAKE HEAD NOR TAIL:** *Unable to determine what is what.*

The reference here is to a hunter who spots game but at such a distance that he is unable to make out what it is and which way it is pointing. It has been in use in English since at least the seventeenth century.

**NOT MY BAG:** *Not appropriate for me.*

In drug addicts' jargon, a 'bag' is

the standard purchase unit of a specific drug bought from a street dealer. A 'bag' of the wrong drug is naturally unacceptable.

**NOT ON YOUR NELLIE:** *Most definitely not.*

An extended piece of rhyming slang based on Nellie Duff = puff, or the human breath and, by extension, life.

**NOT ONE IOTA:** *It is of no consequence.*

This is a straightforward reference to the smallest letter of the Greek alphabet, which also produced jot. There have been several attempts to link the source to specific events or disputes, but these are unnecessary embellishments. Most frequently mooted as the specific origin is the fourth-century Arian controversy; the orthodox view that God the Father and God the Son were one and the same was challenged by Arius (d. 336) who maintained that, while they were similar, they were not the same entity. The Greek term for the orthodox theory was 'Homo-ousion', whilst the Arian doctrine was 'Homoi-ousion'. To the man in the street, who was totally unconcerned with purist theological controversy, it all seemed a lot of fuss about nothing, the difference between the two terms consisting of but one letter – the iota.

**NOT OUT OF THE WOODS YET:** *Not yet clear of danger.*

Dating from the days when woods and forests held danger for travellers who were easy prey for brigands and outlaws.

**NOT TO BE SNEEZED AT:** *Of considerable merit.*

A survivor from the seventeenth and eighteenth-century fashion for taking snuff which the accomplished sniffer prided himself on inhaling without collapsing in a paroxysm of coughing and eye-watering. It became part of the social code for those bored by the company to permit themselves a sneeze or two and then withdraw to spare the company further interruption. By extension, things of merit were not to be sneezed at.

**NOT TO MISS A TRICK:** *To be alert to passing opportunity.*

The tricks are those won at the card table, these going to the player most aware of which cards have been played and which remain in play.

**NOT TONIGHT, JOSEPHINE:** *Humorous refusal of request, especially one of a sexual nature.*

Popular since the days of Wellington and Waterloo (1815), this piece of apocrypha laid at Napoleon's door made fun of the alleged gap between his own libido and that of his wife whose voracious appetites in that direction were supposedly a legend in her own bedtime.

**NOT TURN A HAIR:** *To accomplish with ease.*

A stables expression based on the rough appearance of a previously groomed mount which has been out for strenuous exercise so, by extension, any horse completing a course without turning a hair took all in its stride.

**NOT UP TO THE MARK:** *Substandard or bogus.*

The reference here is to the hallmark giving purity details of precious metals. Even today it is not unknown for purchased items not to assay out to the purity proclaimed by a hallmark which is then found to be forged.

**NOT WORTH A BRASS FARTHING:** *Completely worthless.*

Its name actually meaning a fourth part; the farthing was, until its withdrawal from circulation in 1960, a British coin representing one quarter of a penny. When first issued in the reign of Edward I (1239–1307) it was a silver coin of no little value, but, by the reign of Mary (1658–1718) it was being made of base metal. It was further devalued by the custom, in times of economic stricture, of striking low denomination coins from metal obtained from old, broken cannons, bells or any other brass scrap. People had little faith in such currency.

**NOT WORTH A CONTINENTAL:** *Valueless.*

Throughout the American War of Independence which started in 1775, the Continental Congress, set up in 1774, issued bank-notes which were not backed up by solid gold and were therefore regarded as less than useful, even by the Revolutionaries themselves. The Congress took its name from the literal meaning of 'continent' which, being allied to 'contain', is 'self-restraining or holding together'.

**NOT WORTH A PLUG NICKLE:** *Of no value whatsoever.*

Plugged coins were once widely distributed by bankrupt monarchs or governments and were not held in high regard by the end user. Instead of stamping coins entirely from a valuable metal gold or silver 'doughnuts' would be produced with a plug of base copper or brass in the middle. A nickle is not worth much at the best of times so a plug one would be refused if tendered.

**NOT WORTH A RAP:** *Of no value whatsoever.*

In early eighteenth-century Ireland there was a severe shortage of coins so illegal circulation of raps began. Although these coins held a face value of one half penny their acceptance value was more like half a farthing. How the coin itself acquired such name is obscure.

**NOT WORTH A RED CENT:** *Of no value whatsoever.*

The modern American cent coin is struck from an alloy of copper, tin and zinc. Older and no longer valid ones were made only of copper.

**NOT WORTH A TINKER'S DAM(N):** *Of no value whatsoever.*

The most widely postulated theory relating to the above cites the chewed-up piece of bread once used by itinerant tinkers to mend a pan or whatever. The wet bread serves as a dam to prevent migration of the solder from the site of the repair until it has a chance to harden. Of negligible value before use, the discarded dam is of no value at all after. Opponents of this theory point out, quite rightly, that 'damn' is now the only used form and that before 'not worth a tinker's cuss' was a frequently seen by-form which lends some support to the notion that the expression rests on the volubility of tinkers' profanities which, by overuse, no longer have any value or impact. Trouble is, that not only was the bread otherwise called a 'cuss' but the earliest appearance of the other form does proffer 'dam'. Another explanation points to a long-obsolete Irish coin of low value called a dam, but then why should a tinker's dam be worth less than a lord's? A fourth possibility is that 'dam' is used to mean a female companion or mate – i.e. not worth a tinker's drudge/whore.

**NOT WORTH THE CANDLE:** *Of no value whatsoever.*

An allusion to the days of candle lighting and an event, party, game or whatever, that was not even worth the cost of the candles to keep it illuminated.

**Nth DEGREE, TO THE:** *To the limit; into infinity.*

In mathematics the letter 'n' is used to represent any number, unlike 'x' which represents a specific number of an as yet unknown value.

**NURTURE A VIPER IN YOUR BOSOM, TO:** *To give another the key to your own downfall.*

An allusion to the old cautionary tale of the man who took pity on a frozen viper which he picked up and placed inside his shirt to warm it up whereupon it promptly bit him and he died.

**NUTTY AS A FRUITCAKE:** *Completely insane.*

Although occasionally dressed with a few, a fruitcake contains no nuts and this is an example of the older, nineteenth century use of 'nutty' as meaning spicy, piquant or intriguing. A fruitcake can be all these things and the expression is of course a play on the application of 'nuts' to the insane.

# O

**O.K.:** *Universal indication of approval or acceptance.* Without doubt the most successful coinage ever and one that has attracted more outlandish etymological speculation than any other expression. The unsubstantiated conjectures are abundant and range from suggested term-sources in Russian, Greek, Norwegian, Amerindian or any one of a dozen words supposedly brought in from Africa with the slave trade. The term was first noted in print in the Boston *Morning Post* of 23 March 1839: 'The Chairman of the Committee on Charity Lecture Bells is one of the Providence, and his train-band would have the "contribution box" et ceteras, o.k. – all correct – and cause the corks to fly, like sparks, upward.' This emerged amidst a plethora of other acronyms, some humorously misspelt as indeed is o.k. as it represents 'orl korrect' – this having been the vogue amongst Boston editors since mid 1838, a year in which the forerunner of o.k. – o.w. (orl wright) – was all the go. The fashion spread rapidly to New York where editorials were peppered with K.G. (no good); K.Y. (no use, as if spelt 'know yuse') and N.S.M.J. (nuff said 'mong gentlemen).

**ODD MAN OUT:** *The rogue of a group.*

Reference to the whittling down of a group to select one for a task or reward. Selection is achieved through the tossing of coins and when the group number but three, the winner is the one who, for example, reveals tails against the others' heads.

**ODDS AND ENDS:** *Any unstructured jumble.*

An expression from the haberdashers of old and reference to the one-off lengths of cloth and the ends of regular lines which would perhaps be a few feet or yards left on a bolt.

**ODDS AND SODS:** *Any unseemly mixture.*

Popular with British Army NCOs who used it *c.* 1915 to describe recruits who were either 'non-standard' in some way or were inept at soldiery. The Odds were 'Other Denominations' – i.e. neither Church of England nor Roman

Catholic – and the Sods were the ones who were living proof of 'sod's law'.

**OF THAT ILK:** *Popularly, of that kind.*

This expression is so widely misused that its proper application is never heard in general speech. Although it does derive from the Old English '*ilca*', the same, it is properly used only when referring to a noble who comes from an estate that bears the same name. For example, Lord Davenport of the Davenport Estate would be Lord Davenport of the ilk.

**OFF BEAM/ON BEAM:** *On the wrong/right course.*

Taken directly from the radar beam which plots the course of a ship or an aircraft.

**OFF-HAND:** *Casually rude.*

As did OUT OF HAND, this originally meant something done straightaway as if handed over on request, only in the nineteenth century did the above meaning take over.

**OFF THE WALL:** *Unpredictable.*

From the game of squash in which balls played off the side walls with top or side spin are unpredictable to say the least.

**OFF THE CUFF:** *Spontaneous.*

Allusion to the once popular habit of after-dinner speakers jotting down the odd reminder or pointer on their stiff, white shirt cuffs.

**OFF THE TOP OF YOUR HEAD:** *Ad lib.*

This has been in use since the late 1930s and originates in the world of radio and television programmes. The controller will pat his own head to indicate to those in front of camera that they are running ahead of schedule and will require material to fill in the rest of the time. Should the anticipated gap be three minutes, for example, the controller will hold up that number of fingers and pat their own head.

**OFF YOUR OWN BAT:** *Entirely of your own effort.*

Reference to the game of cricket in which the batsman can accrue points from incorrectly delivered balls which he does not even attempt to hit.

**OFF YOUR TROLLEY:** *Insane.*

A late nineteenth-century extension of 'to go off the rails', this alluding to a small cart or hopper jumping the tracks.

**OLD BILL, THE:** *The police, especially the London Metropolitan Division.*

The origin is unclear despite much conjecture, but some connection with the cartoon character of Old Bill, penned by Charles Bruce Bairnsfather (1888–1959) seems inescapable. Having said that, from the sixteenth to the eighteenth century the Constables of the Watch were known as the Bill for the bills they carried, this being a weapon not unlike a halberd with a concave blade. At first glance this does appear a neat explanation, except that the usage lapsed about 200 years ago which is a mite long for it to lie idle before being resurrected. Also, a prison sentence was previously known as 'the bill', i.e. payment for crimes done, and it is arrest by the police which leads there. It has further been suggested that the source is the Old Bailey Central Criminal Courts blended with the song 'Won't you come home Bill Bailey' but the link is tenuous to say the least. Throughout the WW1, Bairnsfather popularized his Old Bill series featuring a middle-aged Cockney infantryman with a walrus moustache and a handy line in homespun philosophy. The best remembered drawing showed Bill sharing a waterlogged fox-hole with a moaning recruit who was told 'If you know a better 'ole, go to it', this itself still being heard as a reproach to complainers. It has variously been suggested that the link was forged through so many ex-servicemen taking employment with the Metropolitan Force after the war, or that, during the conflict, posters showing Old Bill in a Special Constable's uniform were distributed in a recruiting drive to augment the regular force. Lastly there is the London taxi drivers' use of Old Bill for a good fare – i.e. a pleasant old duffer going a goodly distance and handing over a large tip at the end – and the drivers' use of 'The Bill' for the licence issued to them by the Metropolitan police as distinct from any council permit. If this were the main instigatory factor it would, if you will pardon the pun, FIT THE BILL in that any such modern usage for the police did originally have a strictly London-based circulation.

**OLD BOY NETWORK:** *Unofficial grapevine of favouritism and nepotism.*

A cynical and fairly accurate dig at the English Public School system, which encourages life-long loyalty to the ALMA MATER as well as a camaraderie amongst old pupils via yearly dinners for all the 'old boys' of any given year or decade. Almost like the Masons, membership to this 'club' can go a long way in later life. As a term of respectful affection or admiration, 'old boy' is itself frequently heard in general speech.

**OLD GUARD, THE:** *Any contingent of loyal, traditionalist supporters.*

So were known the veteran regiments of Napoleon's Imperial Guard, these being fanatically loyal and the mainstay of his powerbase. It was these regiments who made the last desperate cavalry charges at Waterloo but it is myth that when called upon to surrender the Commanding Officer, Baron de Cambronne (1770–1842) sent back the message 'The Guard dies but never surrenders.' The message sent back with a galloper actually read '*Merde!*'. As it turned out the Guard did surrender not long after. *See also:* LE MOT CAMBRONNE.

**OLD HAT:** *Very old-fashioned.*

By the mid 1500s the Italian city of Milan had established itself as the fashion centre of Europe, especially for hats, hence 'millinery'. Driven by much the same avarice that inspired modern fashion houses, the styles changed with almost indecent frequency, requiring those determined to be in the vanguard to constantly be buying hats. The modernity of a woman's hat was thus the prime indicator of the state of her wardrobe and of her husband's bank balance.

**OLD NICK:** *The Devil.*

In German mythology, Nickel was a subterranean demon. He also gave his name to the metal first isolated in 1751 by Axel Cronstedt who called it Kuppernickel, or demon-copper, because it looked like copper ore, yet yielded none.

**OLD SAW:** *One with wisdom built on experience.*

Use of the past tense of the verb 'to see', the original form was 'an old said-saw', this being the seventeenth-century version of 'been there, seen it, done it and worn the t-shirt'.

**OLD SCRATCH:** *The Devil.*

A term adopted from the old Scandinavian language of the Viking raiders to whom 'skratta' denoted any devil or monster.

**OLD SWEAT:** *Any experienced, old hand.*

Adopted during the WW1, this was based on the German militarism '*Alter Schwede*', old Swede, their term for an old campaigner. This had been in vogue in the German Army since the Thirty Years War (1618–48) and first used of the German soldiers who had stood against the victorious Swedish Army.

**ON A STICKY WICKET, TO BE:** *To be in a tight spot.*

Problems are created for the batsman on a soft cricket pitch which is of great advantage to the bowler who can produce more unpredictable deliveries using the increased friction.

**ON A WING AND A PRAYER, TO BE:** *Holding on but only just.*

Published in 1943, 'Comin' in on a Wing and a Prayer' was the title of a popular American WW2 song about a pilot desperately trying to make it home in a badly shot-up plane with part of one wing missing. It is unclear whether the song created the expression or such title was chosen as it was already an established saying amongst pilots.

**ON FORM/OFF FORM:** *Doing well/badly.*

This alluded originally to a horse's performance, called its form because its achievements are listed on a particular form or document. This gave rise also to the expression 'running true to form', meaning behaving as expected.

**ON TENTERHOOKS, TO BE:** *To be in a state of extreme agitation.*

In the textiles industry the tenter is the frame used to hold newly woven cloth taut by means of small hooks about its edge. The camping tent is a direct sister-word, this alluding to the canvas stretched tight over the frame.

**ON THE BACK BURNER:** *In a holding situation.*

The rear burners on domestic cookers were originally the lowest in output and were therefore used to keep a pot simmering.

**ON THE BALL:** *Alert.*

In any ball game the alert and vigilant player keeps his eye on the ball at all times and not just when in control of it.

**ON THE BREADLINE:** *In dire financial straits.*

In the late 1890s lines of poor people queued for free bread from charitable organizations, but the expression really came into prominence during the Great Depression of the 1930s when such queues were a common sight in America.

**ON THE CARDS:** *Likely to happen.*

The cards which gave rise to this expression are, of course, the tarot cards.

**ON THE CARPET:** *Up for a reprimand.*

This harks back to the days when a summons from the boss presaged a dressing-down in his office, which was the only room to boast a carpet.

**ON THE MAKE, TO BE:** *Acting out of self-interest.*

Originally seafaring jargon describing a sea that was showing all the indications of 'cutting up rough' and growing more and more angry. On land the expression first applied to avaricious people whose ambition demonstrated itself in a fairly ruthless and aggressive manner.

**ON THE NOD:** *Informal acceptance of terms.*

Reference to the auction rooms where deals of no little significance are sealed by the simple nod of a dealer's head.

**ON THE NOSE:** *Bang on time.*

One of the few contributions from the world of television wherein the placing of a finger on the end of the nose by a member of the floor crew tells those in front of the camera that all is running on schedule.

**ON THE SIDE OF THE ANGELS:** *Holding to traditional virtues.*

In 1864, at the height of the controversy caused by the theories of Darwin, Benjamin Disraeli made a speech at the Oxford Diocesan Conference in which he said, with uncharacteristic pomposity; 'The question is this. Is man an ape or an angel? Now I am on the side of the angels.'

**ON THE WAGGON:** *Abstaining from alcohol.*

An expression of the nineteenth-century American logging and mining camps, many of which were so remote that fresh drinking water had to be hauled in by waggon.

**ON THE WRONG TACK:** *An incorrect response or act.*

A sailing ship wishing to head upwind must do so in a series of zigzags, each known to the sailor as a tack; the overall course is described as tacking. If the helmsman holds any one tack too long he overshoots the point of turn and thus continues along the wrong tack away from his destination.

**ON WITH THE MOTLEY:** *Reluctantly, on with the show.*

Something of a catchphrase, this is taken from *I Pagliacci* (1892), an opera by Ruggiero Leoncavallo. The tried and tested storyline is that of the clown who must continue to play the fool despite his personal problems – 'Smile though your heart is breaking' and all that. The work centres on a group of strolling buffoons, one of whom, Canio, is betrayed by his wife, Nedda. In spite of his sure knowledge of her infidelity he launches into one of the most famous numbers of Italian opera, '*Vesti la Giubba*', On with the Motley. Needless to say, the piece ends in fine operatic style with general mayhem and heart-rending.

**ON YOUR BEAM ENDS:** *Almost ruined.*

This is the nautical equivalent of 'ON YOUR UPPERS' and referred to the heavy transverse timbers which ran at right angles to the keel of a wooden ship. If a vessel heeled over so far that her beam ends were in the water she was in dire trouble.

**ON YOUR JACK:** *Alone.*

From rhyming slang, 'on your Jack Jones'.

**ON YOUR UPPERS, TO BE:** *To be in financial difficulties.*

Reference to the shoes being so badly worn that the soles are no longer in existence, leaving the upper scraping on the ground.

**ON YOUR TOD:** *Alone.*

From the rhyming slang 'Tod Malone' = alone.

**ONCE IN A BLUE MOON:** *Rarely, if ever.*

On rare occasions the moon does appear to be blue due to minute dust particles in the upper atmosphere which block the light from the red end of the spectrum and scatter light from the blue end so that the reflected sunlight from the moon shines through to a terrestrial observer as blue.

**ONE DEGREE UNDER, TO BE:** *To be slightly unwell.*

It seems unlikely that this refers to degrees of body temperature as this usually rises if one is unwell. Perhaps the reference is to a navigator's course going slightly awry.

**ONE FOR THE BOOK:** *Anything of great merit or astonishment.*

Popular since the 1920s when every RAF mess kept a Lines Book – so named from TO SHOOT A LINE – to record the tall tales of the 'one that got away' genre. 'That's one for the book' was the standard none-too-serious reproach to the pilot exaggerating his skills or deeds.

**OPEN QUESTION:** *One inviting discussion.*

To quote Homersham *Cox's The Institutions of the English Government*: 'Certain questions brought before Parliament are treated as "open" questions, that is questions on which Ministers in Parliament are allowed to take opposite sides without resigning.'

**OPERA AIN'T OVER TILL THE FAT LADY SINGS, THE:** *Anything can happen in the last few minutes.*

An Americanism demonstrating a lamentable knowledge of opera in that the diva never sings last. This expression was given wide currency in English usage through its employment by the defence council in the *Spycatcher* trial in Australia and, more recently, American spokesmen commenting on the Gulf War. The first time the expression was used on American radio seems to have been in 1976, when Ralph Carpenter, sports information officer of Texas Technical College, observed 'The rodeo ain't over till the bull riders ride', in reference to a game that seemed all but won. Also present in the pressbox was San Antonio sports writer Dan Cook who gave support in the form of 'And the opera ain't over till the fat lady sings.' The popularity of the saying in sporting circles prompted the Baltimore Oriels to make use of it when dismissed by the sporting press in 1982 as being no-hopers in the Series, their track record having been less than inspiring. To boost flagging morale in both team and fans, they took advertising space on billboards showing a large Germanic lady – complete with horned helmet, spear et al. – who stood looking belligerent above the caption 'She ain't sung yet!'. The team were eliminated before the bill-posters' glue was dry.

**ORDER OF THE DAY, THE:** *That which is deemed necessary or proper.*

Originally of military usage denoting the specific orders issued daily by the commanding officer, these relating, for example, to which particular uniform would be worn or a variation in the ordinary routine on that particular day.

**OUT AND OUT:** *Completely, thoroughly.*

Rare surviving example of the fourteenth century adverbal use of 'out' as meaning to the conclusion or outcome. So, the out-and-out cad was the unredeemeable one destined to be an utter swine to the end of his days.

**OUT OF COMMISSION:** *Broken but repairable.*

The ships of the Royal Navy all sail under their own Commission which is suspended while the vessel goes into dry dock for repair or re-fitting.

**OUT OF HAND:** *Summarily.*

The original meaning was one of straightaway as something given or handed over on request. Since the nineteenth century the expression has assumed overtones of brusqueness and abruptness. (*See also:* OFF-HAND.)

**OUT OF KILTER:** *Not in proper working order.*

The root may be the Dutch '*kelter*', wine press, especially one not properly screwed down, or '*keelter*', stomach, especialy one out of sorts. It is possible too that 'kilt', to tuck up in neat pleats, derived from the Swedish '*kilta*', to wrap in swaddling bands, is the source.

**OUT OF SORTS, TO BE:** *To be unwell or upset.*

An early printers' expression referring to a fount of sorts with all the letters jumbled up and needing rearranging.

**OUT OF TOUCH, TO BE:** *Not* au fait *with developments.*

In precision marching the arm of each man should just be touching that of the man on either side. The pattern begins to break up if their arms become out of touch and the drill sergeant will demand that the troop 'keep in touch'.

**OUT OF THE CORNER:** *Eccentric or unpredictable.*

In the game of pool, a ball which is struck too hard jiggles in the mouth of the pocket, fails to drop, and comes back into play at a random angle.

**OUT ON A LIMB:** *Alone in a hazardous situation.*

It is not clear which 'limb' is responsible, but the most likely is that which derives from the Old Norse '*lim*', a tree's branch, since the expression then suggests a position from which a safe retreat is difficult, even if the bough itself does not break. The other 'limb' derives from the Latin '*limbus*', a border, thus being akin to LIMBO, so it too is a possible source.

**OVER THE TOP:** *Histrionics.*

Frequently seen as OTT, it is said that this derives from the trench fighting of the WW1 and all the yelling and screaming as men went over the top of the trench into enemy fire. The only trouble with this theory is that all such military use of 'going over the top', to mean doing something genuinely dangerous, was obsolete by 1919 and 'over the top' in the now accepted sense did not emerge until the late 1970s/early 1980s.

**OVERBEARING:** *Belligerent; intellectually bullying.*

As descriptive of the taller of two square-riggers either sailing side by side or grappled together with the taller heeled over and so shadowing the decks of the smaller with the sails and rigging.

**OVERREACH YOURSELF, TO:** *Bring about your own downfall through rash behaviour.*

There are two viable contenders for this, one Naval and the other equestrian. At sea, to reach can mean either to attempt to overtake another vessel or to make for an upwind destination by a series of tacking manoeuvres. Should those at the helm be too greedy and hold a tack that little bit too long, then they will over-shoot the proper point of turn and have to retrace their steps. (*See also:* ON THE WRONG TACK.) Alternatively, a horse is said to reach when lengthening its stride for speed. An animal that is too cocky will overreach resulting in its rear hooves clattering against the fore, the horse, quite literally, falling over its own feet.

# P

**PAD:** *Place of residence.*

Waning in use since the HEYDAY of the hippies, an invitation to come 'back to my pad' is nevertheless still heard. Originally this was low eighteenth/nineteenth-century cant for a straw-packed mattress and, by extension, the room where it was situated.

**PADDY, A:** *Violent temper.*

Little more than a reference to the Irish reputation for drunken irascibility.

**PADDY WAGGON:** *Police conveyance for miscreants.*

Otherwise nicknamed the BLACK MARIA, this arose in 1920s America due, like PADDY, to the fact that on pay-night a goodly proportion of the passengers were of Irish descent.

**PAINT THE TOWN RED:** *To indulge in drunken excesses.*

This certainly has its origin in mid nineteenth-century America and is likely tied to the antics of trailhands. Railhead towns of the west held ambivalent views of the big cattle drives; whilst they brought in much trade and cash, they also brought in drunken cowboys with too much money. It must be remembered that these towns were much smaller than most imagine so it would not take too many drunks, accompanied by the 'lady' of his choice, to spread red-light district behaviour to sectors where it was unwelcome.

**PALM OFF:** *To dispose of substandard goods by unfair means.*

A reference to the skilled card-sharp who can move low cards under his palm and place them at will about the table to keep himself winning.

**PALOOKA:** *Any stupid or clumsy.*

Introduced into American phraseology in 1925 by Jack Conway, baseball player turned vaudeville star who launched several successful coinages including 'scram', 'push-over', 'to click' (succeed) and allegedly, baloney. After his death in 1928, Walter Winchell's obituary hailed him as 'my tutor of the slanguage he helped me to perfect.' It is said that Conway's inspiration was the Spanish '*peluca*', a wig, in that 'to wig' then meant to annoy as a result of WIGGING being a telling off. Perhaps Conway's idea was that stupid and clumsy people are always getting told off.

**PAN, TO:** *To damn with harsh criticism.*

A turn of the century Americanism which seems to derive from 'roasting' in that roast meat was then known as panned meat. A good telling off has been known as a roasting for quite some time.

**PAN OUT, TO:** *To conclude successfully.*

An Americanism from the nineteenth-century gold-rush and a reference to the way gold-dust, or PAY-DIRT – was sifted out in the prospectors' wok-like pans. (*See also:* DISH THE DIRT.)

**PANDORA'S BOX:** *Any wonderful assortment or plethora of mixed blessings.*

Properly, this designates what the Americans call an ugly can of worms best left tightly shut. In mythology the arrival of a female on the scene always signals the end of peace and tranquility; she is the catalyst of all man's problems. In the Christian tradition women are vilified in the person of Eve and in classical mythology the parallel culprit was Pandora, sent to earth by Jupiter armed with a box as a dowry for her husband. This was Epimethius, the brother of Prometheus, a Titan who had angered Jupiter by stealing fire from heaven to give it to man. Although warned against opening Pandora's box, Epimethius did just that and out flew everything from sickness to the Inland Revenue.

**PANHANDLING:** *Scrounging or begging.*

Prior to the turn of the century this described the agitating motion of the gold sifting pan in the hands of the prospector. The shift in meaning was caused by the way beggars held out their mug, dishes or whatever and rattle them from side to side.

**PAPARAZZI:** *Freelance photographers specializing in 'celebrity' shots.*

An Italian term for an irritating fly that persistently buzzes round one's head, this first saw the light of day in the singular form of *paparazzo* as the name of the photographer constantly taking shots in *La Dolce Vita* (1960).

**PAPER TIGER:** *A hollow threat or wolf in sheep's clothing.*

The English rendering of the Chinese '*tsuh lao fu*' which describes the elongated paper tigers used in festivals and Chinese New Year Celebrations and so forth. It was introduced into Western phraseology by the speech of Mao Tse-Tung (1893–1976) who usually used the expression to describe the West or its industrial or military might.

**PARSON'S NOSE:** *The rump of a plucked fowl.*

Otherwise known as the Pope's nose, depending on one's religious persuasion, these designations have been in constant use since the early eighteenth century and are likely scathing analogy to the bloated features and pitted 'boozer's nose' sported by so many of the clerics of the time. With a little imagination, the pendulous fowl's rump can easily resemble a debauchee's nose.

**PARTHIAN SHOT/PARTING SHOT:** *A telling remark unleashed upon departure.*

Perhaps inevitably, the proper and original 'Parthian shot' has been corrupted to 'parting shot' if for no other reason than the timing and manner of delivery. The Parthians originated from an area now in Iran and were highly effective, if undisciplined, light mounted skirmishers. Their PARTY PIECE, for want of a better expression, was to feign full retreat and, having perfected the art of firing the bow to the rear at full gallop, cut to pieces any pursuers.

**PARTY PIECE:** *Anyone's speciality or particular knack.*

A product of the last century when parties were often staid and sober affairs where each guest would entertain the assembly with a specially prepared song or reading.

**PASS MUSTER, TO:** *To meet the required standard.*

Since the sixteenth century this has enjoyed such figurative use having first been applied to new troops passed as fit at the mustering of a force for war.

**PASS THE BUCK, TO:** *To shirk responsibility.*

In the poker games of the nineteenth-century American West it was common practice for the players to keep on the table a buck-horn knife or piece of heavy gauge buckshot to serve as a marker indicating whose turn it was to deal next. Without giving any reason, any player may abdicate this task and simply pass the deck and the marker to the next man. In the eastern states and on the Mississippi gambling boats poker chips were the norm and a silver dollar was allowed on the table to serve much the same purpose, it too being referred to as the buck, this rapidly becoming accepted slang for any dollar. 'Passing the buck', in its metaphorical sense, first appeared in print in the writings of Mark Twain but it was the poker-mad President Truman who gave the expression wide currency. (*See also:* BUCK STOPS HERE.)

**PAST-MASTER:** *One exceptionally skilled in any field.*

Certain confusion surrounds this phrase in that the earliest form found in 1563 is 'passed master'; the present form did not emerge until the 1760s. It is likely the original form applied to one who had cleared all the necessary tests to be considered a master but that the present form developed within the Freemasons as a term for an extremely wise and knowledgable lodge-member who had already held the office of Master and so had much grey-haired sagicity to impart. (*See also:* THIRD DEGREE.)

**PATSY:** *Dupe or fall guy.*

First seen in America at the opening of the 1900s, the most complicated theory points to the Italian use of Pasqualino – the diminutive of the proper name Pasquale – for any weak or runtish man or boy. It appears that Italians singled out this name through association with Pasqua, Easter, and the Pascal Lamb as once used to mean a weak and defenceless victim and, the notion is continued, the American–English diminutive of the same name is Patsy. It does seem rather unnecessary to formulate such a complicated theory when has the perfectly simple explanation that the Italian '*pazzo*' means a fool.

**PATTER:** *Coercive line in chat.*

Popular since the 1700s and likely built on the Paternoster as rattled off in Latin by clerics. The term was first seen as a verb in the 1400s.

**PAY DIRT:** *Money in abundance.*

A gold prospectors expression for the gold dust sifted out in the pan.

**PAY ON THE NAIL:** *Pay promptly, especially in cash.*

A popular phrase since the 1600s and one that has parallels in the French '*sur l'ongle*'; the Dutch '*up den nagel*' and the German '*auf den Nagel*' although none of these helps clear the mystery surrounding the origin. It is widely accepted that the origin lies with the stone pillars outside the Bristol Corn Exchange and other such establishments – these pillars were surmounted with brass dishes on trading days and served as counters. I myself used to accept this suggestion until more diligent research showed that the expression pre-dated any such custom – indeed, any such building. The only plausible explanation lies in the once common drinking custom of draining the glass prior to upending it over the left thumbnail with the intention of proving that the only fluid remaining will only form a droplet so small as to adhere to the nails. Anyone performing such task only to produce a drop large enough to run off the nail was required to refill his glass and those of the company. It was frequently employed as a dramatic – if not theatrical – gesture of unquestioning departure after which the tavern bill would have to be settled '*supernaculum*' as was then said. Since about 1640 this Latin equivalent has also served on its own as a term for fine wine which only a Philistine would leave in the glass. Modern French phraseology has embellished this old meaning with superb wines being said fit only to '*faire rubis sur l'ongle*', or make a ruby on the nail.

**PAY ON THE ROLL OF THE DRUM, TO:** *Not to pay at all.*

Synonymous with the sailors' 'pay on the first turn of the screw', this is the soldiers' version inspired by the fact that no soldier can be dunned for debt whilst on active service. The roll of the drum is the call to arms.

**PAY THROUGH THE NOSE:** *To pay reluctantly and excessively.*

Perhaps this is nothing more than an allusive expression hailing an extremely unpleasant and difficult place to extract coins from – things that annoy are still said to get 'right up your nose'. There are however two moderately plausible unsubstantiated theories. The first nominates the ninth-century Nose Tax which was little more than protection money extorted from Northern Britons and the Irish who paid Norse raiders to leave them in peace. Any defaulters endured their noses being cut as an inducement to cough up but there is no record of the above expression between that time and the early 1600s; 700 years seems too long for a sabbatical from general usage.

Without placing too much reliance on it himself Eric Partridge points to the contemporary seventeenth-century use of 'rhino' for money in general, this possibly occasioned by the highly lucrative trade in various parts of the rhinoceros' body regarded in China as aphrodisiacs by silly old mandarins. Whilst it is true that '*rhinos*' is the Greek for nose, it is hard to see how a connection with easy money and high profits spawned any such usage as the above.

**PAYOLA:** *Bribe money.*

First seen in the America of the 1930s – thirty years before its adoption here – this is based on a blend of 'pay' and 'ola', a Hispanic suffix indicating great quantity, itself likely inspired by the Spanish '*ola*', a wave. It has been suggested that the term was first applied to and inspired by the scandal of disc jockeys taking payment from the record companies named Victrola and Pianola, but the term was first applied to what H.L. Mencken calls 'monkey business' in the issue of prizes and money in the television quiz show world. The first time the music business came under the spotlight for the aforementioned pay-off to disc jockeys the term was transmuted to 'plugola' and, just as Watergate produced countless other 'gates', 'ola' was tagged onto any scandal of the day.

**PECKING ORDER:** *The established social stratas or status.*

Although to the human eye the barnyard fowls live a random existence they nevertheless have an ordered society and the more senior hens peck at any social inferior who gets in the way or tries to muscle in on the food.

**PEEPING TOM:** *Clandestine observer, especially with sexual motive.*

When Lady Godiva made her alleged naked ride through the streets of Coventry in a bizarre attempt to force her husband to lower the taxes, the suitably grateful masses spontaneously agreed to stay behind closed shutters to spare her any blushes – all except a tailor named Tom who was struck blind as soon as he peeked through a chink in his own shutters.

**PEG OUT:** *To die.*

Taken from the scoring method in many a game – notably cribbage – involving the moving of pegs along a series of holes in a perforated board, the winner is said to peg out and the game is over at this point.

**PELL MELL:** *Recklessly; helter-skelter.*

Originally the name of a game otherwise called pall mall, this being a fairly vigorous fore-runner of croquet taking its name from the Italian '*palla*', a ball, and '*maglio*', a mallet. The game took the British gentry by storm during the reign of Charles II and the more staid members of society stood aghast at the younger or more adventurous rushing around the pell mell alleys with such abandon. The fashionable London thoroughfare of Pall Mall took its name from the nearby location of one of the more up-market playing areas.

**PENNY-ANTE:** *Of low status or financial worth.*

The ante is the opening stake in a poker game which, if played for pennies, is of little interest to hardened gamblers.

**PETER OUT, TO:** *To come to nothing; to fizzle out.*

This certainly began life in the jargon on mid nineteenth-century American miners; there is a notion that the allusion is either a mine played out 'down to bedrock' ('*peter*' being the Latin for rock or stone) or a mine with all its wealth extracted with blasting powder nicknamed Peter for its high saltpetre content. Somewhat less likely is the French '*peter*', to fart; even less likely is any reference to St Peter and his repeated denial of knowledge of Christ before the cock crowed thrice.

**PETTIFOGGER:** *Petty-minded clerical type.*

Strictly speaking this denotes someone who undertakes minor legal tasks and the term is likely to be an alteration of 'pettyfactor' which appeared at around the same time at the end of the sixteenth century. Although the latter term ante-dates 'pettyfogger' in print it is a far more likely progenitor than the name of the German family of bankers called the Fuggers with whom no connection has been established.

**PHILADELPHIA LAWYER:** *Properly a canny lawyer but generally any sharp operator.*

The criminal libel trial of Peter Zenger in New York in 1735 is the probable source of this expression but it seems to have first enjoyed usage in Britain before its adoption in America. Zenger had long pilloried the grossly incompetent and corrupt British Governor Colonel William Cosby who finally had him arrested and jailed for seditious libel. The Governor's camp indulged in open jury rigging and hand-picked a tame judge leaving Zenger a seemingly doomed man until Andrew Hamilton, the most pre-eminent lawyer in Philadelphia, offered his services to Zenger free of charge. He won the day and did much for the freedom of the press in general which did little to endear him to the British who lost face over the whole affair. It seems that it was the disgruntled and ashamed vanquished litigants who coined the above usage since the earliest recorded incidence in print comes in 1788 in an American publication entitled *Colombian Magazine*: 'They have a proverb here [in London] which I do not know how to account for . . . when speaking of a difficult point they say "it would puzzle a Philadelphia lawyer",' so it seems fair to surmise the expression was unknown to the American public before then.

**PHILISTINE:** *Any uncultured male.*

Since the sixteenth century, and quite possibly earlier, 'Philistine' has been a blanket and jocular term for 'the enemy' – the Establishment, the tax-man, and what-have-you – and used in the sense of 'falling into the hands of' as meaning to get caught. The term has equally long-established use for any coarse drunkard, this being engendered by the Bible which repeatedly dismisses the Philistines as brutish barbarians. But the contemporary, rather intellectual-élitist, usage stems from violent town-and-gown battles between the students of Jena University in Germany and the locals. This situation came to a head in 1693 when a number of deaths occurred. A group of students were sleeping off the night's excesses slumped where they sat in the inn, when they were set upon and beaten to death in their sleep. The university chaplain chose Judges 16:12 for his opening text at the funeral service – in this reading Samson is alerted to impending attack by the words 'Samson, the Philistines be upon thee.' Almost immediately, 'Philistine' altered meaning in German academic circles; it lost all humorous overtones and became a decidedly sneering slur, aimed at uncultured boors. Its adoption by the general tongue came almost 200 years later through *Culture and Anarchy* (1869), Matthew Arnold's most widely read work in which he made repeated use of the German academic slang in such context as: 'The people who believe most that our greatness and welfare are proved by our being rich, and who most give their lives and thought to becoming rich, are just the people whom we call Philistines.' As stated above the original Philistines simply got a bad press. They were a highly civilized people, likely of Aegean origin, who inhabited the Gaza strip for over 1,000 years before the Israelites turned up looking for a fight. Their descendants are the Palestinians whose name is a modern variant of Philistine. So, it seems that things have not changed much in that neck of the woods over the millennia.

**PIE IN THE SKY:** *A vain hope or pipe-dream.*

Taken from a line in a song written by Joe Hill, an American Union activist who, at the turn of the century, was closely involved with the Workers of The World movement. In 1906 he published a song called 'The Preacher and The Slave' which had already been in use for some time as a taunt to non-sympathizers or the more traditionally minded worker who stopped short of strike action or sabotage. The thrust of the lyrics was that the Church and the Establishment generally tried to keep the labour force in its place by convincing them that it was the natural order of things and that they would get their reward in the next life whilst their 'betters' took rewards in this one. Words in the chorus: 'You will eat, bye and bye,/ In that glorious land in the sky;/ Work and pray, live on hay,/You'll get pie in the sky when you die.' and a good proportion of the other lyrics were a parody of the hymn 'In the sweet bye and bye'.

**PIECE DE RESISTANCE:** *The most significant or laudable item of a group.*

Originally this was a late eighteenth-century French culinary expression for the main course of a meal – the one which offered the most resistance to digestion. Since this tended to be the chef's showpiece and typically his speciality, the term shifted into general usage to describe any major effort in artistic endeavour.

**PIG IN A POKE:** *Substandard merchandise, a* WHITE ELEPHANT, *especially if bought sight-unseen.*

Like the phrases LET THE CAT OUT OF THE BAG and sold a pup, this derives from the old fairground trick of selling the customer a muted cat or puppy tied up in a sack instead of the plump sucking pig which they thought they were buying.

**PIGS, THE:** *The police.*

All attempts to link this to the Draconian rule instituted by the pigs in George Orwell's *Animal Farm* (1945) are doomed to failure since the term has enjoyed its current usage since about 1800; if anything, Orwell cast the pigs in his story *because* of such current slang. From the turn of the nineteenth century, a Bow Street Officer was known as a China Street pig for reasons that are now less than clear. It has been conjectured that Bow Street once boasted numerous china shops at a time when china pigs enjoyed even more popularity than they still do today. There is, of course, an allusion to pigs rooting for food and officer 'nosing' around for information.

**PIGGY IN THE MIDDLE:** *One trapped between two protagonists.*

In the game of tip-cat the wooden wedge as struck by the curved stick was commonly known as the pig and the game otherwise known as piggy or piggie. Sometimes opposing villages would line up at opposite ends of a field and take turns to knock the pig into the no man's land between and then nominate the number of strides it would take to reach the pig and retrieve it. Should they fail the other side took the pig and the game continued. In more recent times 'piggy-in-the-middle' has denoted a game played by three children; two throw the ball to each other whilst the third tries to intercept it.

**PIGGYBACK:** *One person or item carried on the back of another.*

No connection with pigs, this is a corruption of 'pick-a-back', a sixteenth-century expression for carrying a pack on the back. It has also been suggested that the French '*à pic*' exerted some influence.

**PILLOCK:** *A stupid person.*

Widely imagined to originally denote a testicle, the term is traceable back to the early fourteenth century form of 'pilkoc' or 'pillicock' which obviously denoted the penis. Perhaps the more modern development of round pills caused the slight shift.

**PIMP:** *Male procurer.*

Almost certainly of French origin, this has been in use since the early 1600s. Although some think that it was built on the Old French, '*pimpreneau*', a scoundrel, it is more likely that is derives from '*pimper*', to be seductively dressed. Interestingly, 'pimpish' is still used in America to mean stylishly dressed or ostentatiously elegant.

**PIN MONEY:** *Small change; petty cash.*

Originally this was a sizeable sum of money to be paid annually to a wife for the specific purpose of buying pins; there are countless examples of such agreed amounts being included in marriage contracts. Until the end of the fourteenth century English ladies made do with wooden pins and skewers until superior metal ones were imported from France. In 1483 legislation was passed banning imports of pins and they were produced in this country under a crown monopoly to keep prices high. As the monopoly relaxed and production costs tumbled, the wife's pin money fund was expended on various frivolities causing cost-conscious husbands to reduce the amount accordingly.

**PIN YOUR HOPES ON SOMEONE/THING :** *To invest heavily in something seen as total salvation.*

Prior to entering the lists for the joust, a knight would wrap a personal item, usually a scarf, belonging to the lady to whom he was champion for that day, around his arm. (*See also:* WEAR YOUR HEART ON YOUR SLEEVE.)

**PINCH-HITTER:** *One who steps into the breach in times of trouble.*

An American baseball expression for a batter called in when the team is in a pinch, or tight situation.

**PIP-SQUEAK:** *An insignificant individual.*

First noted in 1910, this would appear to be Army slang employed by the rank and file who had little liking or respect for lowly lieutenants, identified by just one pip on the shoulder. The variant form of 'one-pip-squeaker' is a clearer form of the insult.

**PIPE ABOARD:** *To welcome warmly and/or formally.*

A landlubber's equivalent of the maritime tradition 'piping the side'. All dignitaries visiting a sailing ship of old were hoisted aboard in the boatswain's chair to the call of the boatswain's whistle (pipe). The varying notes were signals to the man operating the yardarm whip (hoist).

**PIPE DOWN, TO:** *To cease belligerence.*

In Naval parlance, 'pipe down' was a particular call made on the boatswain's whistle last thing at night. This signalled all hands to turn in, all below-deck light to be extinguished and silence on the messdecks. The corresponding 'pipe up' in the morning has also moved into general speech meaning to join in a conversation or start talking.

**PIPE DREAM:** *A vain hope.*

Reference to the extravagant dreams experienced by users of the opium pipe.

**PIPING HOT:** *Extremely hot.*

The allusion is a simple one involving pies with steam hissing, or piping up through breaches in the pastry. It is safe to ignore all 'theories' citing meals hot from the kitchen being preceeded into the banqueting hall by a highland piper.

**PIPPED AT THE POST:** *To be defeated within sight of victory.*

The post here is obviously that making the finishing line on a track and the 'pip' is the old nickname for the small ball-shaped tokens cast in the voting in private members' clubs. In essence, the phrase means to be BLACKBALLED by one of the last voters.

**PISO'S JUSTICE:** *Anything technically correct yet morally absurd.*

Reference to the dictates of Lucius Calpurnius Piso, otherwise known as Frugi the Worthy, the Roman statesman and historian who served as tribune in 149 BC. He is best remembered for establishing regular courts under his Lex Calpurnia Repetundarum.

**PISS ON ICE, TO:** *To live in the lap of luxury.*

In the more expensive restaurants and exclusive clubs of America the troughs in the men's urinals are filled with ice-cubes to cut the miasma of uric acid.

**PITCHED BATTLE:** *One of great intensity.*

An expression born of the lack of communication which inhibited the armies of early medieval days when it was not uncommon for two forces to set out in search of each other only to spend days or weeks marching round in circles. For important battles the protagonists agreed a time and venue; in other words, they agreed the pitch on which it would take place – these did tend to be hard-fought and bloody affairs.

**PITS, THE:** *Anywhere or anything repulsive.*

Its origin is in the latter half of the twentieth century and it refers to nothing more complicated than the armpits as smelly places. It could be pure coincidence, but the usage arose with television breaking new ground with adverts mentioning the previously taboo subject of body odour. A night's viewing could not pass without millions of viewers being treated to the scene involving a person swooning through a sweaty armpit being shoved in their face.

**PIZZAZZ:** *Zip; verve; flashy activity.*

Popular in America since the beginning of the 1930s, this was not common in Britain until the 1960s when most domestic publications adopted the term with the incorrect spelling of 'bezzaz', or similar. However, unlike Britain where 'piss' always indicates perjorative overtones – piss-poor, piss-head, etc; in America the terms is used in the reverse – a piss-cutter is anything or anyone of excellence, and, unlike Britain where a piss-ass is a drunkard, in America anyone deemed a piss-ass is one of great elegance and in the vanguard of fashion. Polite American society opted for 'pizzazz' as an acceptable bowdlerization which had the added attraction of, to a certain degree, being onomatopeic suggesting speed and vim.

**PLACE YOURSELF ON A GOOD FOOTING:** *To ingratiate yourself.*

In the seventeenth and eighteenth centuries, any man joining a new group, trade association, or even just a new village, was expected to 'pay his footing' (pay his entrance, so to speak) and get everything off to a good start by throwing a party. When he made his entrance as host, he had to be careful to step in with the right foot first, thus ensuring a successful outcome to the new arrangement.

**PLAIN AS A PIKESTAFF:** *Abundantly plain.*

A corruption of the much older 'plain as a packstaff', this being the pole used by itinerant vendors and vagrants to tote their wares or possessions. Far from being ornate or carved, the staff would have been of ordinary wood and worn smooth with use.

**PLANE SAILING:** *Easy going.*

In 1569 Mercator produced the first navigational charts which showed the meridians as being parallel without distorting the navigational process. Prior to this navigators relied on plane charts drawn on the assumption that the earth was flat. Despite Mercator's efforts, navigators found it easier to use the old plane charts as no calculations were needed to convert departure into difference of latitude and the practice continued for over a century.

**PLAY BOTH ENDS AGAINST THE MIDDLE:** *To extract every possible advantage.*

The expression comes from the card tables of nineteenth-century America. It refers either to a faro player's double-betting or to the rigging of a pack of cards so that the dealer can issue a card from the top or the bottom to his own advantage.

**PLAY FAST AND LOOSE, TO:** *To behave erratically and immorally.*

At medieval fairs, 'fast and loose' was a cheating game played by tricksters. A long leather strap was doubled over, rolled up so that the loop was at the centre, and held *fast*; the crowd was challenged to arrest the loop with a skewer as the belt was allowed to unroll under its own steam after the cry of '*Loose!*'. This was an almost impossible feat in practice, but the gullible paid up for each try.

**PLAY FOR KEEPS, TO:** *To engage with deadly ernest.*

In a game of marbles, needle matches conclude with the winner pocketing the loser's taws.

**PLAY GOOSEBERRY:** *To be an unwelcome addition to a loving couple.*

Derived from the earlier 'gooseberry-picker' which denoted a chaperone who allowed her charges some time on their own by announcing her intention to go off and pick gooseberries, even if all three were fully aware that there were none to be had. Thus the term originally denoted one who made things sweeter for the lovers and perhaps the bitterness of the fruit combined with the traditional dislike of a chaperone created the change of meaning.

**PLAY HAVOC, TO:** *To wreak chaos and confusion.*

In earlier, less enlightened, times the cry of 'havoc!' prior to battle demanded the slaughter of the enemy without mercy or quarter; no prisoners were taken and all camp followers of women and children to be put to the sword. Needless to say, the issue of the order created uproar and chaos.

**PLAY HELL WITH SOMEONE/THING:** *To issue severe reprimand or damage beyond repair.*

This is an elliptic of the nineteenth-century 'play hell and Tommy' which is itself a corruption of the even earlier 'to play Hal and Tommy' as used of two warring parties, they being likened to the constant battles between Henry VIII and Thomas Cromwell.

**PLAY HOOKEY:** *To abscond temporarily, especially from school or college.*

Of mid nineteenth-century American origin, this appears to be an elliptic of the equally American 'hooky-crooky', as meaning not straightforward, dishonest or perverse. There could also be some influence from the gypsy '*hookai*', to lie or defraud.

**PLAY IN PEORIA, THAT WON'T:** *That won't work.*

A city in Illinois, Peoria has come to represent to Americans what perhaps Tunbridge Wells does to the British. As a benchmark of conservative opinion it was seen as the ideal testing ground for new plays which, if they would not go down well or 'play' in Peoria, never saw the lights of Broadway.

**PLAY IT CLOSE TO THE CHEST:** *To keep your own counsel.*

The cautious card-player will so hold their cards to prevent another spying their value.

**PLAY POSSUM, TO:** *To feign death; metaphorically, to maintain a low profile.*

An Americanism which actually manages to encapsulate not one but two misconceptions , for the creature of the New World is actually the opossum of the family Didepphidae (the possum is only found in Australia and is of the family Phalanger) and it never feigns death to elude death.

**PLAY THE FIELD:** *To keep options open especially romantically.*

Originally a gambling term to describe the backing of every horse in a race with the exceptions of the favourite.

**PLEASED AS PUNCH:** *Excessively smug.*

The hideous puppet was – and still is – inordinately self-satisfied at its own machinations and cruel ploys.

**PLONK:** *Any cheap wine.*

One of many terms brought back from the WW1 trenches in France; it is built on '*vin blanc*'.

**PLUG UGLY:** *Any thug or a belligerent person.*

First noted in mid nineteenth-century America – initially only in Baltimore – this is of obscure and much conjectured origin. The most straightforward notion suggest the term to allude to a thuggish person hit (plugged) so many times as to be terminally ugly, but it has also been suggested that the unseemly rows between the competing private and volunteer fire services of Baltimore lie at the root of the term. As explained under BUFF, the first fire services of the American cities were all staffed by volunteers who came to a deal with the insurance companies or the owner of the building and it was a case of first to secure a hose to the hydrant plug was the one that got to strike that deal. Whilst it is true that such a situation led to rival brigades brawling while the reason for their presence burned to the ground, this origin does smack of the apocryphal. There is an increasing tendency in British usage to apply the term as an adjective to excessively ugly people with no reference to their character.

**PLUMB CRAZY:** *Absolutely insane.*
This is a distortion of the meaning of 'plumb' as in the plumbline which is always absolutely vertical.

**PLUMB THE DEPTHS, TO:** *Attempt to fathom out a problem.*
An allusion to the old method of depth sounding explained in SWING THE LEAD.

**PO-FACED:** *Blank featured; stony faced.*
Built on the French pronunciation of 'pot' as in chamber-pot, one can only presume the analogy is to an empty po which is stony-white and featureless.

**PODUNK:** *Any one-horse town or out-of-the-way place.*
Originally this was the name of an Indian settlement in what is now Hartford, Connecticut. Etymologically, this is the Mohican for a small tract of land but the term fell so humorously on white ears that it was adopted for its present usage.

**POINT BLANK:** *Very close range.*
A corruption of the French '*point blanc*', the white spot, their term for the bull's eye on an archery target. The expression developed amongst military men to describe a gun aimed directly at target, pointed like a pistol, without any elevation, under which circumstances the range would be extremely limited.

**POKER-FACED:** *Inscrutable.*
An allusion to the impassive features of an experienced player of poker, a game where bluff becomes useless if the face betrays the lie.

**POLE POSITION:** *A position of advantage.*
Similar reference to 'HAVING THE INSIDE TRACK' and therefore the shortest distance to run, this is straightforward reference to the fencing poles about the inside perimeter of a racetrack.

**POMMIE:** *An Englishman.*
First used in the late 1800s this is almost certainly built on 'pomegranate' but the reason why is not as clear. It is possible that the inspiration was the red-blotched, sunburned skin of the new arrivals unaccustomed to the harsh sunlight and that this complexion resembled the skin of the fruit. Alternatively, it could be nothing more sophisticated than a child's street taunt to new arrivals who were goaded with 'Immigrant, Jimmygrant, Pommegrant' or 'Immigranate-pommegranate, immigranate-pommegranate'. There are countless recorded instances of such taunting recorded in print from 1900 onwards. Pommie does not appear in print until 1913 in memoirs of those who recalled the 1870s when the term was new, all of which demolishes acronymic flights of fancy

relying on transported convicts sporting P.O.H.M (Prisoner of His Majesty) or P.O.M.E. (Prisoner of Mother England).

**POMP AND CIRCUMSTANCE:** *Excessive ceremony.*

A line taken from *Othello*, Act 3, Scene 3, which refers to the: 'Pride, pomp and circumstance of glorious war'; in this sense the terms mean display and ceremony.

**PONCE:** *A* PIMP *or highly effeminate man.*

Popular since its emergence *c.* 1800 when it denoted a PIMP. It has been conjectured that this is a French import humorously based on either '*pensionaire*', a lodger, or the French use of the proper name, Alphonse, in much the same context. Come the end of the nineteenth century the term was generally understood to mean a man who lived off women within society, many of these being foppish dandies kept by rich women in need of entertainment and company. From here it was but a short step to the second application of the term.

**PONS ASINORUM:** *That which catches out the slow-witted in any field of endeavour.*

A nickname – Latin for 'the asses' bridge' – given to the fifth preposition found in Euclid's Book 1. It presents the first difficult theorum which less able students find problems in 'getting over'.

**PONY:** *Twenty-five pounds.*

This appears to be related to the much older phrase, 'pony up', pay up, which was noted in the sixteenth century. This, in turn, was inspired by the opening lines of the fifth division of Psalm 119 which began '*Legem pone mihi, Domine, viam justificationum tuarum*' – Teach me, O Lord, the way of thy statutes. So began the Psalms at Matins on the twenty-fifth day of every month, the final accounting day for all debts to be cleared. In certain circles, '*legem pone*' would still be understood to mean cash on the nail or due recompense.

**POOF or POOFTAH/POOFTER:** *Male homosexual, especially if effeminate.*

First seen in the early years of this century and still chiefly of British usage, this appears to be derived from the mid nineteenth-century 'puff' which held much the same meaning. This in turn was either based on effeminate ladies men hanging round the salons where the powderpuffs were frequently brandished – 'powderpuff' and 'creampuff' are still used as synonyms – or from the theatrical use of 'puff' as a verb denoting extreme flattery – advertisers' hype is still called a puff. If the latter meaning is the inspiration this would be a reference to the fact that with a few delightfully waspish exceptions, the more effeminate of those of alternative sexual persuasion tended to survive in earlier times by cultivating supreme affability, ensuring they ruffled no one's feathers, trod on no toes and were at all times the ideal weekend guest.

**POONTANG:** *Sexual intercourse, especially with a coloured woman; the vagina.*

Popular, if that be the right word, since the beginning of the twentieth century when it moved into widespread usage having being confined largely to the southern states of America – notably Louisiana – where it is first noted in the 1870s. Given the state of its apparent origin the most likely source is the French '*putain*' which in Creole and Cajun would be pronounced 'poo-tang', there sometimes arising a rogue 'g' on the end of words with similar endings. This is also common in the French Midi where '*matin*' becomes '*matang*' and '*maintenant*' becomes '*man-ten-ang*'. There may also be a Chinese or Pigin influence as variants such as 'poong tai' and 'poong kai' have also been noted.

**POOPED:** *Extremely tired.*

Taking its name from the Latin '*puppis*', the rear of a ship, the poop deck is that closest to the stern. In a heavy following sea a pooped ship is one with the sea breaking over her stern causing her to flounder.

**POOR AS JOB'S TURKEY:** *Totally impoverished.*

Although inspired by Job's descent into poverty, this expression is relatively modern. It was allegedly coined by Canadian humorist Thomas Chandler Haliburton (1796–1865) who is perhaps better known by his pen name, Sam Slick. He invented Job's turkey – a bird with strong North American associations – which was even poorer than its owner, had only one feather and was so weak with hunger that it had to lean against a fence to gobble.

**POPPYCOCK:** *A dismissal of verbal rubbish.*

An Americanism which only gained currency here in the mid 1800s through people's ignorance of that fact that it derives from the Dutch '*pappekak*', soft dung. Lady Thatcher was much quoted after using the term in 1991 in reference to a statement issued by the European Parliament.

**POSH:** *Smart; stylish, perhaps garishly so.*

About the only certainty is that this does not derive from Port Out, Starboard Home since P.O.S.H. was never once placed beside bookings for round trips to India. The story goes that the well heeled would travel to India in a portside cabin and return in a starboard one so they would have a shaded cabin for as much of the journey as possible. This falls down for many reasons. Firstly, P & O have no record of any such booking; the company archivist Mr Stuart Rabson revealed that the price of a specific size or class of cabin or stateroom was identical irrespective of the side of ship in relationship to the direction of travel, thus anyone with the price of a round trip could have so stipulated, so all connotations of wealth and superiority go straight out of the window, or rather the porthole. I was also informed by an aged and imperious ex-in-law, who spent most of her girlhood years making journeys to India, that no one stayed in their cabin because the 'action' was in the salon. Finally, and most telling of all, what happened to 'soph'? Just as many people were resident in India but visited home, so where are all the Starboard Out, Port Home bookings? With established terms such as 'sophisticated', surely this would be a more likely survivor. But as to the real origin, this must unfortunately remain a mystery. One likely source is the Romany '*posh*', half, which in the nineteenth century appeared in conjunctions such as 'posh-horri', a half-penny, and 'posh-koorona', a half-crown, these and others causing 'posh' on its own to indicate wealth or money, so a posh person was well-heeled, ergo well-dressed? The usage was established in general slang and cant by the turn of the century and perhaps became entangled with, and aided by, the pre-WW1 'posh' – a soldiers' elliptic of 'polish'. Additionally, the 1915 Oxbridge slang 'push' denoting anything in the vanguard of fashion was frequently elongated to 'poosh' for emphasis.

**POST HASTE:** *With the utmost urgency.*

This alludes to an old first-class mail service similar to the Pony Express. The courier changed horses every twenty-five miles and kept going until he delivered his charge. Another early postal designation was 'by return of post' which, whilst still used today, presents a nonsense in that there is no other way to send a letter. If a reply was required as quickly as possible, the outgoing letter would demand a reply to be made out and given the same rider who delivered – by return of the same post.

**POT:** *Marijuana.*

Taken from the Mexican 'potiguaya', marijuana leaves.

**POT BOILER:** *Any artistic work undertaken purely for the money.*

Originally said of any work that would keep the cooking pot boiling with something it it to keep body and soul together.

**POT LUCK:** *Random chance.*

An expression born in the days when the cooking in the average household was effected in a large pot heated over the main fire. Should a guest drop in unannounced and expect to be fed, then his luck depended on whatever was in the pot at the time and if there was enough to go round.

**POT SHOT:** *An unsporting jibe levelled at an easy target.*

When hunting for sport the quarry was given a fair chance but when stomachs and the cooking pot were empty no such nicety was involved – the hunter got as close as possible to ensure a kill.

**POTTERS' FIELD:** *A pauper's grave; an ignominious end.*

In common usage since the earliest recordings of print this is a reference to the plot of land supposedly bought by the priests with the money returned by Judas after the betrayal of Jesus (*See:* THIRTY PIECES OF SILVER). The Bible tells that this clay field was previously used by Jerusalem's potters as a reservoir of raw material, but that the priests bought it as a cemetery for strangers and the poor. Anyone who has ever tried to dig in clay will have good reason to doubt the plausibility of this account.

**POUND OF FLESH:** *Full and excessive restitution.*

In the *Merchant of Venice*, Shylock, the villain of the piece, lends money to Antonio but tricks him into signing an agreement stating that, should he default, Shylock will be entitled to a pound of his flesh. Antonio's merchant ship sinks, he is unable to repay his debt at the allotted time and, incredibly, Shylock sticks to the letter of the agreement, demanding his pound of flesh; this would, of course, result in Antonio's death – all that Shylock wanted in the first place. Fortunately for Antonio, his lover Portia is brighter than both of them, for she points out that the contract was untenable since it mentioned only flesh, making no mention of the blood that would inevitably be shed. Shylock, faced with the impossible task of cutting out exactly one pound of Antonio's flesh without spilling a single drop of his blood, is routed.

**POUR OIL ON TROUBLED WATER, TO:** *To calm a fraught situation.*

Ever superstitious, early sailors never put to sea without a small bottle of consecrated oil which, they believed, would calm an angry swell if poured overboard. It is recorded in Bede's *Ecclesiastical History* (731) that St Aidan presented such a bottle to a young priest charged with escorting King Osway's bride-to-be across the waters to her nuptials. Naturally, a storm cut up and the oil did the trick but quite why Christians – especially saints – should indulge in such pagan shenanigans is never explained.

**PRAISE THE LORD AND PASS THE AMMUNITION:** *Exhortation to maximum effort.*

Originally said to have been uttered by the US Navy Chaplain Howell Forgy whilst on board the cruiser *New Orleans* as she lay in Pearl Harbour under the infamous attack. Whether he did or didn't express such sentiments has been hotly debated and other contenders put forward, but either way the line became popularized in that same year of 1941 when used as the title of a music hall song by Frank Loesser.

**PRAT(T):** *The backside; the vagina; a stupid or unpleasant person.*

The origin is wholly obscure but seems separate from another 'prat', origin again obscure, dating from the early 1500s and meaning a piece of trickery or folly. The earliest meaning of the above 'prat' was the buttocks, this still used in America whilst the other two definitions are the norm in Britain. With other terms for the rear such as 'bum' from 'boom' – being echoic and alluding to the noise emanating therefrom – it is possible that 'prat' is derived from 'prattle', useless chatter or noise.

**PRIDE OF PLACE:** *In special prominence.*

Since medieval days falconers have so described a hawk which has reached its hunting height and is ready to stoop on anything that moves.

**PRIG:** *Overly and overtly moralistic.*

Probably based on the verb 'prig', to haggle, the noun emerged in the mid sixteenth century when it denoted a tinker who did not work from a fixed price list but bargained over every little detail. Later it was applied to anyone who nit-picked over each fine point of etiquette and probably developed from there to take on its modern meaning by the end of the seventeenth century.

**PRIME THE PUMP, TO:** *To get things moving.*

The old fashioned hand-lever water pump sometimes needed a small amount of water poured into the cylinder to create suction.

**PROOF OF THE PUDDING IS IN THE EATING:** *The acid test.*

One of the few remaining examples of 'proof' in its older and original meaning of test; tested spirits boast a proof rating and clothing found to be water-resistant is weather-proof.

**PUBLISH AND BE DAMNED:** *Reposte to any threat, especially one of blackmail or coercion.*

The famous reply made by the Duke of Wellington to a Paris-based publisher named Stockdale who intended publishing the 'memoirs' of one Harriette Wilson, a London based kiss-and-tell courtesan who numbered the Duke amongst her past lovers. In a letter dated 16 December 1824, Stockdale made it clear to Wellington that for a certain consideration all references to him would be expunged. Popular legend has it that the duke dashed the above words across Stockdale's own letter and sent it back, but the actual letter is still at Apsley House and has nothing on it but the original text.

**PUKKA:** *Proper or genuine.*

This was absorbed into English in the late 1700s and based on the Hindustani '*pakka*' meaning ripe, mature or cooked and, by extension, substantial. The shift to the above would have been occasioned by native usage such as 'pukka sahib' or 'pukka gentleman' which the English would have understood to mean demonstrably well-bred.

**PULL A FAST ONE, TO:** *To indulge in dubious but effective tactics.*

Popular since 1933, this was born of the infamous 'bodyline' or 'leg theory' bowling as employed by Douglas Jardine against the Australian cricket team in his determination to win the Ashes. Basically, he instructed his fast bowlers, Larwood and Voce, to eschew all gentlemanly ideas of bowling and just throw the ball at the batsman. Ungentlemanly it may have been but Jardine and his team triumphed.

**PULL A FLANKER, TO:** *To manoeuvre things to your advantage.*

Certainly of military origin, this refers either to the strategic advantage gained by moving in on the enemy from the side, flank, or to the advantage held by soldiers on the flank of the line, which is usually a less dangerous position than the middle.

**PULL A STROKE, TO:** *To succeed in a crafty gambit.*

Oxbridge rowing slang since the

1940s; a perfectly executed stroke of the skull would steal a march on those employing less effective ones.

**PULL THE WOOL OVER SOMEONE'S EYES, TO:** *To deceive someone.*

The use of 'wool' is an allusion to the powdered wigs of yesteryear when it was a common prank or insult to tug them forward to temporarily blind the owner.

**PULL OUT ALL THE STOPS, TO:** *To engage maximum effort.*

Direct reference to the stop-pegs on a church organ which, when pulled out, increase the volume.

**PULL SOMEONE'S CHESTNUTS OUT OF THE FIRE:** *To save them from downfall.*

A reference to an old fable involving a monkey and a cat, the former wishing to roast some chestnuts. Placing them in the fire was the easy part, but the monkey was less than keen to retrieve them so he grasped the cat's foreleg and used it as a rake. This has also led to 'cat's paw' being used of someone roped in as an unwilling or unwitting tool in some scheme or other.

**PULL SOMEONE'S LEG:** *To make jest of them.*

A survivor from the late eighteenth century when the streets of London or any other city were little more than mud-baths with running sewers at each side. It was then a popular street-prank to use a hooked stick or walking cane to trip up the unpopular or haughty to bring them face down in the mire.

**PULL THE OTHER ONE (ITS GOT BELLS ON):** *Expression of disbelief.*

A development from PULL SOMEONE'S LEG, this meaning 'I didn't fall for that trick, so you'd better pull the other leg if you wish to tumble me.'

**PULL STRINGS, TO:** *To exert unfair influence through personal contacts.*

Simple reference to the puppet master who achieves whatever he wants by such means.

**PULL YOUR WEIGHT, TO:** *To pay your way or justify your presence.*

An oarsman is less than useless if the amount of effort he exerts is not sufficient to propel his own weight through the water.

**PUNK:** *Any worthless individual; an adherent of the fashion of that name.*

This term has been in use since the late 1500s but the issue is clouded as there could well be two wholly separate 'punks' which have crossed and recrossed each others' paths. In sixteenth-century England 'punk' meant a prostitute and it has been conjectured that the origin of this usage lies in a play on the Latin '*puncta*', a woman who has been 'punctured' repeatedly. Throughout the nineteenth century and the early part of the twentieth this 'punk' had come to mean a catamite, this being the generally accepted meaning both here and in America. Then there is the other 'punk' not noted until 1705 when it emerged with the meaning of rotten wood or the white fungus growing on it. Chiefly of American usage it is further unclear as to whether the origin of this term lies in the Gaelic '*spong*', tinder, and therefore a term taken out with the settler, or, as the major body of American etymological opinion would have it, from a domestic native term. It is probably fair to say that both terms had a joint influence on producing 'punk' as applied to persons of no worth or merit – a meaning which emerged in the early part of the twentieth century. Punk in this sense was encapsulated in the 1970s fashion craze of the same name, characterized by talentless performance, gratuitous crudity and apparent lack of personal hygiene.

**PUNTER:** *A customer.*

When this phrase emerged at the opening of the eighteenth century, it denoted only a gambler, especially one playing against the bank. The source would appear to be French and the established used of '*ponte*', a gambler or player, this in turn inspired from the separate '*ponte*', the laying (of eggs). By the end of the nineteenth century the term had acquired the specific meaning of an auctioneer's plant in the crowd who needle-bid to jack up the prices. This development was no doubt helped by the separate verb 'punt' as meaning to kick a rugby ball before it hits the ground, and by the 1960s the term had come to describe any legitimate customer in any trade.

**PURLER, A:** *Anything of excellence or great force.*

Although the most commonly presented form involves the spelling 'pearler' through an obvious association with the pearl as a symbol of perfection and value, the proper form is 'purler' which, since the mid nineteenth century, has meant a powerful blow or anything of great force. Ultimately this is related to the 'purl' of knitting terminology which is in turn itself derived from the Italian '*pirlare*', to twirl (thread) about, and thus akin to 'pirouette'. In the 1500s purling was specifically understood to denote gold and silver embroidery of the finest quality and so something of high visual impact.

**PURPLE PROSE:** *Highly florid phraseology.*

A reference to the following observation in Horace's 'De Atre Poetica 14': 'Often to weighty enterprises and such as profess to great objects, one or two purple patches are sewn on to make a fine display in the distance.' Horace was making use of the allusion to the Tyrian Purple, a colour worn only by the élite in Greek or Roman society.

**PUSH COMES TO SHOVE, IF/WHEN:** *We will respond if things turn nasty.*

Born on the American football field and that which approximates the rugby scrum. As the protagonists take up the strain this is 'push' – the shoving comes soon after.

**PUSH OFF:** *Go away.*

Originally an instruction to a small craft or tender tied alongside a larger vessel.

**PUSH THE BOAT OUT, TO:** *To spend excessively, especially on others.*

Reference to a shore-party setting

back to the mother-ship – one of the group would always get wet whilst freeing the boat from the beach.

**PUSSY:** *The vagina; collectively, women as sexual objects.*

Since the late 1500s, both 'pussy' and 'puss' have served as synonyms for a harlot, the vagina or sexual activity and it is quite likely that this is a simple extension of 'cat' being used for a prostitute. Alternatively, this could be crude rhyming slang – pussy cat = TWAT. Other suggestions include the Old English '*pusa*', a bag and the Irish, '*pus*', a perjorative term for the lips or the mouth. Also, in pidgin English 'pus-pus' as derived from 'push-push' means sexual intercourse.

**PUT A NEW SLANT ON SOMETHING, TO:** *To impart a different perspective.*

At sea, 'slant' describes the angle of the wind in relation to the ship, any change of slant creating a new situation for helm and crew.

**PUT A SOCK IN IT:** *A call for noise reduction.*

This appears to have begun in the days of wind-up gramophones with large speaker horns but no volume control. The only way to play one quietly was to push a sock or similar item into the horn to muffle the music.

**PUT ON THE DOG, TO:** *To affect great style.*

Still popular since it appeared at the beginning of the century it is possible that this is an allusion to the fad for snappy lap dogs being sported in the crook of the arm by both men and women. Some even kept different dogs to go with different outfits or had the unfortunate animals dyed from week to week.

**PUT ON YOUR THINKING CAP, TO:** *To deliberate.*

Popular since the seventeenth century, this could refer to the cap of death put on by judges before delivering senstence. (*See also:* KIBOSH.)

**PUT PAID TO SOMEONE, TO:** *To settle a score with them.*

This is simply a reference to a tradesman's account when the word 'paid' is put next to the customer's name in the ledger.

**PUT SOMEONE'S NOSE OUT OF JOINT, TO:** *To make someone feel usurped, jealous and generally malcontent.*

In the folklore of yore it was believed that the nose swelled up or grew long as a result of jealousy. If someone was made excessively jealous their nose might grow to such size as to disjoint itself from the face under its own weight.

**PUT THE DAMPERS ON:** *To lessen enthusiasm.*

In mechanical devices, dampers reduce or depress the amplitude of cycles or vibrations. Perhaps the general application arose from the damper or SOFT PEDAL of a piano.

**PUT THE MOCKERS ON SOMETHING, TO:** *To ruin the occasion.*

From the Hebrew for bad luck and

in common use since the turn of the century. It is possible that '*mokardi*', the Romany word for a person or item blighted with a curse, had some influence on the phrase.

**PUT THROUGH YOUR FACINGS:** *Tested out.*

This reference to military drill depends on the commands 'left face', 'right face' and 'about face'; drill manoeuvres display the smartness of a good soldier.

**PUT YOUR ARSE ON THE LINE:** *To irrevocably commit yourself to a course of action.*

Distinctly American and derived from the habit of one small boy daring another to start a fight by inviting him to step over a line scratched in the dirt. Having taken such a step, the buttocks of the accepter of the challenge will be directly above the line.

**PUT YOUR BEST FOOT FORWARD:** *Do your best.*

This is a hand-me-down from the superstition that one must always start a journey with the right foot if it is to be successful.

**PUT IT IN A NUTSHELL, TO:** *To encapsulate succinctly.*

The 'it' in question is actually the *Iliad* which Pliny maintained could be copied out in a hand so small that the entire work could be fitted inside a walnut shell. Not content to take Pliny at his word, Bishop Huet of Avranches (d.1721) set about proving this experiment and satisfied himself that a parchment measuring twenty-seven by twenty-one centimetres would indeed contain the entire work and that this could be folded up and placed inside a nutshell. Nor is the passion for small books yet over; in 1985 the Gleniffer Press of Paisley, Strathclyde, produced eighty-five copies of the tale of Old King Cole in a book measuring a mere one miliimetre by one millimetre. With care, the pages can be turned with a needle.

**PUT SOMEONE ON, TO:** *To fool them.*

In early nineteenth-century street beggars' cant a put-on was anything assumed to invite pity and therefore money; this normally came in the form of a disguise 'put-on' to present a pathetic and injured appearance. This could also be called a 'have-on'; people still demanding 'are you having me on?'

**PUT THAT IN YOUR PIPE AND SMOKE IT:** *A verbal 'take that'.*

Really this is blunt advice for the other party to think on the words spoken and pipesmokers are almost invariably shown puffing away in meditative mood.

**PUT THROUGH YOUR PACES, TO BE:** *To be drilled or tested.*

When a horse is 'trotted out' before prospective purchasers, the animal is moved through the various paces from walk to gallop so the buyers can see how the animal moves.

**PUT TO BED:** *To complete a task.*

This expression originated in the

printing trade but was popularised by the newspaper industry. The 'bed' is the level surface of a printing press. When the forme is laid on this, everything is ready.

**PUT UP OR SHUT UP:** *Do something constructive and stop complaining.*

Reference to either a fighting situation when one party is required to put up their fists and back up their accusations or an allusion to the poker table where a vaunting bluffer reaches a point where he has to put money on the table.

**PUT YOUR FOOT DOWN, TO:** *To take up a definite position.*

An expression drawn from the fighting stance adopted by a boxer.

**PYRRHIC VICTORY:** *One obtained at crippling loass.*

Pyrrhus, King of Epirus, met with Roman forces at the Battle of Heraclea in 281 BC and although he defeated Valerius Laevinus he sustained heavy enough losses to prompt him to observe 'One more such victory and we are lost.' The battle in question is sometimes erroneously cited as Asculum which Pyrrhus won in 279 BC.

# Q

**QUEAN/QUEEN:** *Overtly effeminate homosexual.*

Opinion is divided as to whether 'quean' and 'queen' are even related, but the former has been in use since the early 1500s when it denoted a harlot or low woman. By the 1800s the term had largely shifted to passive male homosexuals, especially ones who plied their trade. This shift of application from female prostitutes to male one is quite an established trend; for more details see GAY.

**QUEENSBERRY RULES, TO PLAY BY:** *To be scrupulously fair and above board.*

The code of rules referred to are, of course, those covering the 'sport' of boxing. In reality the code was drawn up by one John Chambers (1843–83) who then sought out the sporting Marquis and asked him to sponsor their adoption. The Marquis' other claim to fame is that he was father to Lord Alfred Douglas, lover of Oscar Wilde, and subsequently co-litigant in the libel case that proved Wilde's downfall.

**QUID:** *A pound.*

Of obscure origin but possible from the Latin '*quid*', what (is needed).

# R

**RABBIT:** *Incessant prattle.*

An elliptic of the rhyming slang 'rabbit and pork' = talk, aided by the image of a rabbit with its incessantly twitching features.

**RACK AND RUIN:** *Total ruin.*

The first term is a variant of 'wrack' which is itself a variant of 'wreck'.

**RACKED OFF:** *Depressed or annoyed.*

An Australian expression entering the swim via the influx of Australian soap operas. This is the Antipodean equivalent of 'pissed off'. The reference is to the wine industry in which racking off describes the draining off of the primary fluid from the lees.

**RACKET:** *Any line in business, especially if illegal.*

Developed from the sense of an unholy noise or commotion, and possibly a spin-off from the much older sixteenth-century 'racket' as used in games, the association being with things battered together. If this be the case, then the ultimate source is the Arabic '*rahat*', the palm of the hand as employed long before any stringed item. The younger 'racket' is noted only from the turn of the nineteenth century and is possibly an elliptic of 'grab-racket' as previously used of a street robbery mounted under the confusion caused by some noisy diversion or other. Such ruses are long established; indeed, the entire plot of the classic con-film *The Sting* is but one long grab-racket. Every thief specialized in his own particular variant of the game and by the 1960s 'What's your racket?' could even be heard at cocktail parties between persons inquiring as to the profession of another.

**RAILROAD SOMEONE, TO:** *To coerce and bully them.*

An expression from nineteenth-century America when the railroad companies were fighting each other tooth and claw in the race to open up the West and link the coastlines. The tactics employed to acquire land in their path often boiled down to simple thuggery and murder.

**RAIN CATS AND DOGS, TO:** *To rain excessively hard.*

This was possibly inspired by the two animals having been long regarded as weather symbols and their behaviour interpreted as weather portents; should a cat indulge in excessive self-cleaning it heralded protracted rainfall or if a dog kept rolling on the ground then a thunder storm was close. There have been lofty theories pointed to the Greek '*catadupa*', a waterfall or '*kata*' and '*doxein*' meaning 'full' and 'receptacle' respectively but, unfortunately for all, mid seventeenth-century examples citing downpours of 'dogs and polecats' are well noted, so perhaps the expression is nothing more than a ludicrous exaggeration.

**RAIN CHECK:** *A metaphorical postponement.*

An expression from modern American baseball parks which issue replacement tickets to customers who have paid to see a game that gets rained off.

**RAISE CAIN:** *To make an angry fuss.*

This alludes to Adam's son and his apparently ungovernable temper, which led him to slay his brother. 'Raise' is here used in the sense of 'raise the spirit of'. Whilst it is true that, in early England, 'cain' meant a tax, there is no substance to the theory that the expression refers to the pandemonium caused by aggressive tax collection methods.

**RANDY:** *Excessively lecherous.*

First noted in the late seventeenth century this was always applied to beggars or other itinerants and appears to be a reference to their perambulatory existence. This lends support to the generally accepted notion maintaining the term derives from the old English '*rande*', itself akin to the German/Dutch '*Rand*', an edge or outer limit, and thus allusive to the far-flung travels of the tinkers. Come the 1700s the accepted meaning was that of unruly and boisterous, as were considered the tinkers; it was another century before the term took on its overtones of lust and lechery. By then it was likely that associations with the outer limits of acceptable behaviour had crept into the scene and were possibly given extra impetus by the Hindustani '*randi-baz*' – a lecher – then being heard and used by the colonial British. Other examples of this 'rand' exist in the South African currency unit first struck from gold mined at Witwatersrand, White Waters' Edge, and 'random' which initially meant with full force or at the outer limits of endurance but evolved to its generally accepted meaning through artillery jargon. A piece of ordnance on maximum elevation to achieve the limits of range also sacrificed accuracy leaving the load to fall at random.

**RANK AND FILE:** *The common herd.*

This refers to troops drawn up on the parade ground, the men forming lines across are the ranks and those forming depth lines are the files.

**RASPBERRY:** *Derisory noise made with the lips.*

Simple rhyming slang, raspberry tart = fart.

**RAT RACE, THE:** *The mainstream of stressful life.*

Since these rodents are never pitted against each other in contests of speed it seems likely that this is 'race' as in circular run of ballbearings, or whatever, and the phrase is an allusion to a rat running relentlessly in the wheel so often placed in hamster cages.

**READ BETWEEN THE LINES:** *To glean the unstated meaning.*

It has been suggested that this alludes to simple cryptography when trigger words appear in alternate lines, but this hardly sits well with the structure of the expression; any such tricks would have produced something more akin to reading every other line, or some such. If coded messages are involved at all here it is more likely the use of lemon juice as an 'invisible' ink so that a clandestine message could be sent written between the lines of a seemingly innocent communication to a recipient who then held the page over a candle to blacken the lemon and read between the lines. Perhaps all such thoughts are too clever by half and the phrase merely refers to the ability of the astute reader to gather information from what is not being written.

**READ THE RIOT ACT, TO:** *To lay down the law.*

The Riot Act of 1714 stipulated that any gathering of twelve or more people caused an affray and thus constituted a riot. Under these circumstances an order to disperse would be read out in the name of the Crown and all those failing to disperse within the hour could be deemed guilty of a felony and shot without further warning.

**REAL McCOY:** *The genuine article.*

All eponymous explanations of the above are fallacious – including that citing the American boxer Kid 'the Real' McCoy (1873–1940) whose chequered career long post-dated the appearance of the expression. The original form was most certainly 'the real Mackay' as first noted in 1883 and it has been suggested that the phrase dates from a schism within the Clan Mackay, two factions therof vying for recognition as the senior branch. One faction was seated in Reay and indeed there are some who maintain that the original form was 'the Reay Mackay!' Alternatively, the expression could involve the 'real' that means royal or elevated. In favour of the American boxer, it must be said that 'the Real McCoy' is recognized as an American corruption of the origin and one that emerged in the opening of the 1900s when the flamboyant ten times married fighter was much in the news, so perhaps he was at least responsible for the altered form.

**RED HERRING:** *Any deceptive ploy.*

Reference to the age-old trick of drawing smoked herrings across a trail to confuse the tracking hounds.

**RED LETTER DAY:** *One of great importance.*

An expression harking back to the days of illuminated script. Calendars prepared in the monasteries had saints' days and major religious festivals highlighted in red lead. The most important of the red letter days were granted the accolade of tiny but highly ornate pictorial artwork, these being the first miniature paintings – but the term has no connection with either the Latin '*minor*' or '*minimus*'. The term is derived instead from the Latin '*minimum*', red lead.

**RED LINE IT, TO:** *To push things to the limit.*

Allusion to the red line drawn on the tachometer monitoring a performance engine which can be damaged if over-revved.

**RED RAG TO A BULL, A:** *A goad guaranteed to infuriate another.*

The colour red has long been associated with violent temper and thus the ideal colour for the bullfighter's cape designed to lure and madden the bull. As is now common knowledge, bulls are colour-blind and will charge a cape of any colour.

**RED TAPE:** *Obdurate officialdom.*

The allusion is to the red tape used to tie up old parchments and legal documentation. Credit for the conception of the phrase is frequently given to Charles Dickens but examples of the phrase in his works are pre-dated by its appearance in the writings of Thomas Carlyle and Washington Irving.

**REDNECK:** *Bigoted, right-wing conservatism.*

Born in early nineteenth-century America, this first denoted poor Southern whites who generally typified this sort of fascist outlook. Amongst these folk the dietary deficiency known as pellagra was common – one of its symptoms is a reddening of the neck.

**REST ON YOUR LAURELS, TO:** *To trade on past glories.*

This is a reference to the laurel crowns handed to the victor in the ancient Greek games.

**RHUBARB:** *Verbal rubbish.*

A theatrical expression claimed by some to date back to Shakespearean times and certainly in use in the late eighteenth century. It denoted actors off-stage who had to drum up crowd noises by repeatedly muttering 'rhubarb'. Still used for crowd scenes in modern films, the repetition of the word does produce the desired effect.

**RIDE ROUGHSHOD OVER SOMEONE, TO:** *To browbeat or verbally steamroller them.*

The war-horses of old were invariably fitted with spiked shoes or ones with several nails left protruding. Not only did this afford the animal better grip but it ensured the death of any felled soldier over whom the animal was guided.

**RIGHT AS A TRIVET:** *In fine fettle.*

This is the three-legged trivet placed by the fireside to support kettles and pans for heating. Naturally, they had to be extremely stable, or 'right'.

**RIGHT AS NINEPENCE:** *In perfect health; neat and tidy.*

A corruption of the original 'right as nine-pins', as neatly placed on their markers before a game.

**RIGHT AS RAIN:** *Absolutely correct.*

A simple play on the use of 'right' – meaning straight or perpendicular. Heavy rain in particular does fall like this at times.

**RING DOWN THE CURTAIN, TO:** *To bring matters to a close.*

Reference to the backstage bell quietly rung to alert stage hands to close the curtains as required between acts and at the end of the performance.

**RING THE CHANGES, TO:** *To vary method of approach; to swindle.*

Both applications allude to church bells and the varying sequences in which they can be rung. On a major set of twelve bells there are over 479 million such change sequences; these are the basis of the expression. The alternative uses rests on the con-man changing his mind and the method of payment so many times that the buyer ends up paying more than they should.

**RING TRUE, TO:** *To prove valid.*

Surprisingly, this saying refers to coins not bells. It was once common to test coins by dropping them on a hard, cold surface. Coins of pure silver or gold had a distinctive ring to them but counterfeits or ones adulterated with base metal had a duller sound.

**RINGLEADER:** *The most culpable of a group.*

In a coven of witches the senior leads the ceremonial ring-dance and the abhorrent witch-hunts and trials made much use of terms such as 'leader of the ring' and 'ring-dance leader'. Incidentally, a coven may have thirteen members but only by coincidence. The monk-torturers were convinced that witches met in such numbers in parody of the Last Supper and countless witches were tortured until they agreed that this was the case.

**ROB BLIND, TO:** *To take every last penny.*

No longer the custom today, it was once common to place pennies on a corpse's eyes. This was reminiscent of older customs giving the dead the fare for the grim Ferryman but also served the practical purpose of keeping the eyes shut. Naturally only the lowest criminal would stoop to taking them.

**ROB PETER TO PAY PAUL:** *To shuffle funds in straitened circumstances.*

If these are not simply two common names picked for no other good reason then the phrase may be an allusion to 29 June – the Saint's day of both Peter and Paul. Any time spent in devotion to the one necessarily 'robbed' the other of adulation. Either way, the expression has been in use since the mid to late 1300s so there is no substance to the theory that it dates from the 1500s when the funds of the estates of St Peter's Church were plundered to effect repairs to St Paul's Cathedral.

**ROCK-BOTTOM:** *As low as you can get.*

A mining expression referring to the layers of bedrock struck when the mine is played out; 'down to bedrock' itself holds synonymous meaning.

**ROOK, TO:** *To rob or cheat.*

Simple reference to the thieving habits of rooks and their cousins, the magpies.

**ROOKIE/ROOKY:** *Raw recruit.*

First seen in the slang of the British Army of the late nineteenth century, its origin is unclear. It is possible that it could be based on the verb ROOK in that the new arrivals were unwary and easy pickings for more experienced hands. There is also the low cant 'rooky', rascally and scampish, which derives from the name of the bird. Finally, it could merely be a play on the word 'recruit'.

**ROOT FOR SOMEONE, TO:** *To cheer them on.*

From the Old English dialect 'route', to shout and roar.

**ROPEY:** *Inferior; in bad repair.*

This emerged from WW2 RAF slang and was basically a dig at older bi-planes held together by a network of wires and struts, these being likened to ropes.

**ROUGHNECK:** *A street-yob.*

First noted in the American carnival slang of the 1830s, this denoted any casual labourer hired for menial tasks. These tended to be local odd-job men used to outdoor work and had characteristic rough and red skin at the back of the neck.

**ROUND ROBIN:** *A knock-out system in sporting events.*

A corruption of '*rond ruban*', the French for round ribbon, this dates from the mid 1500s when it described a petition of grievance handed to a noble or ship's captain. It was the custom for the names of the petitioners to be inscribed on a loop of ribbon and attached to the document to disguise the order of signing – a necessary precaution since the recipient of the grievance had the right to hang the first signatory for inciting the others to mutiny should he consider the grievance unfounded. By the time the sporting application emerged in the nineteenth century the term had mellowed to denote any group of common cause or list of protagonists.

**RUB, THE:** *The major problem.*

An expression from the game of bowls where the rub is anything that impedes the smooth passage of the ball.

**RUB IT IN, TO:** *Harping on about faults and failures.*

After receiving a flogging with the cat o' nine tails the ship's cook would apply brine to inhibit infection and speed the healing process. Had the miscreant been caught stealing from shipmates then the disapproval of his peers would be forced home by the cook actually rubbing salt into the wounds, a far more painful way of achieving the same result.

**RUB SOMEONE'S NOSE IN IT, TO:** *To force them to face the ramifications of their wrong-doing.*

Developed from the once standard but now discredited method of house-training a puppy; a lot of pepper was added to every puddle and the animal's nose was rubbed into it.

**RUB UP THE WRONG WAY, TO:** *To address them without tact.*

An expression from horse-grooming where attempting to brush against the run of the animal's coat will produce a fairly violent reaction.

**RULE OF THUMB:** *Any rough guide.*

The middle joint of the average man's thumb is usually about an inch wide and was so used by carpenters for a rough measure.

**RULE THE ROOST, TO:** *To be in overall charge.*

This is the now-accepted form of the expression which began life in the 1600s as 'rule the roast', i.e. the kitchen or the banqueting table, to preside over the feasting in general. The modern form no doubt developed as the popular mind drew inspiration from the cockerel strutting vainly about the roost of hens under his control.

**RUMBLE A PLAN, TO:** *To uncover it.*

Possibly rooted in the Scottish '*romble*', to beat, the early seventeenth-century English '*romboyll*' meant to handle roughly or seize hold. The contemporary Watch were thus nicknamed the Romboyll and, in thieves' cant, to be romboyld was to be pursued and arrested under warrant.

**RUN AMOK/AMUCK, TO:** *To enter a deranged frenzy.*

This is the Malay version of a phenomenon common to many Eastern and Indian peoples who possess the ability to wind themselves up to a state of unbelievable hysteria prior to embarking on homocidal rampages. *Amok*, as the Malays call this state of mind, is not necessarily dependant on the use of drugs and is frequently used as a kind of honourable suicide in the face of overwhelming gambling debts. The drugless amok can take anything up to two or three days to induce but when the suitably deranged party takes to the streets he is assured of being shot down by the police or locals.

**RUN RINGS AROUND SOMEONE, TO:** *To outclass them.*

Reference to the more skilled boxer who nimbly moves about his opponent and delivers blows with impunity.

**RUN SOMETHING UP THE FLAGPOLE, TO:** *To test the validity of something.*

An elliptic of the military expression 'run it [a flag] up the flagpole and see how many salute it'.

**RUN THE GAUNTLET, TO:** *To take all life throws at you, and still triumph.*

One of the few examples of Swedish in English phraseology, this is a corruption of '*gatloppe*', the Swedish army's name for the military punishment requiring the miscreant to make as good a progress as he may between two lines of men intent on beating him to death. The English acquired both the term and the punishment during the Thirty Year War (1618–48) and well before the end of the seventeenth century the term had transmuted, no doubt through mental association with the gauntlets as thrown down in challenge.

**RUN THE GAMUT:** *To cover the entire range, especially of emotions.*

In the field of music 'gamut' denotes the range of notes attainable by an instrument or any one particular singer's voice. The term originated along with the medieval grand scale, a system of scales in which the semitone was always between the second and third of a tetrachord, as G, A, Bb and C. The Greek for the letter G is gamma and the French for the C at the beginning of the hexachord was 'ut'.

**RUN TO GROUND:** *To track down.*

Hunting dogs are trained to pursue a quarry right home to its earth and keep it holed up until the hunter arrives with terriers, a group of dogs which themselves take their name from the French '*terre*', ground.

**RUSSIAN ROULETTE:** *Any dangerous gamble.*

Although the Russians do appear to many to be a morbid and pessimistic people, there is no evidence that the officers of the Tsarist Court were much given to the habit of placing one round in a pistol, spinning the chamber and then placing it to their head to see if they drew a blank or no. Perhaps this is just one of many racist slurs in the genre of 'Welsh rabbit' and 'JEW'S HARP', which presumed a Russian to be so miserable and fatalistic that he would find such a pastime entertaining.

# S

**S.P., THE FULL:** *All the information.*

Bookmaker's slang deriving from 'starting price'.

**SACK, THE:** *Dismissal.*

The skilled labour of old was largely nomadic, moving from job to job and living on site. When they were no longer required or had otherwise displeased their employer, they were handed a sack in which to load their possessions and ship out. The modern equivalent is for the office worker to return from lunch to find a black bin-liner on his desk with the notice of dismissal.

**SACRED COW:** *Any hallowed institution or, rarely, a person.*

An expression developing not long after the British invasion of India where the Hindu treatment of cows was viewed as risible. The animals were allowed to roam the streets unchecked and damage done to crops was accepted by the owner as a compliment. Even in times of famine the cows will not be touched.

**SAD SACK:** *Any sorry, ineffectual individual.*

First seen in American student slang of the 1930s as a euphemistic elliptic of 'sad/sorry sack of shit' but was promoted to general speech by a WW2 cartoon strip of such title. Penned by one Sergeant George Baker it featured Sad Sack, a soldier whose uniform never fitted any more than he did into the military plan of things. In America there is a splinter group of WW2 and Korean War veterans called the Sad Sacks.

**SAIL TOO CLOSE TO THE WIND, TO:** *To flirt with illegality; to push things too far.*

Obviously no sailing vessel can sail directly into the wind, but they can come to within fifteen per cent of the wind since sailing vessels are in fact pulled along by a vacuum in front of the sail and not pushed along as most people imagine. If the crew in charge of the helm get too ambitious and exceed this point the sails collapse back against the mast and all drive is lost. When this occurs, the ship is said to have been TAKEN ABACK.

**SALAD DAYS:** *Youth.*

Nothing more than a direct reference to the green and raw nature of salad.

**SALT A BUSINESS, TO:** *To make it appear in better shape than it is.*

An expression from the early mining industry wherein it was not unknown for a vendor to scatter interesting looking rock samples in a played out mine like salt on a meal to titillate the 'taste' of prospective purchasers.

**SALT AWAY, TO:** *To save.*

In the days before fridges and freezers the storage of meat in salt was the only way to preserve it. Large corns of salt were layered with the meat, hence corned beef.

**SALT OF THE EARTH:** *The infrastructure of society; the trusty common people.*

Thus did Jesus described his persecuted yet still loyal followers at Matthew 5:13. The specific reference was to the Hill of Salt near the Dead Sea where most salt collection took place.

**SAMBO:** *Highly offensive term for any black male.*

As excessive christening of boys with popular monarch's names such as Charles and Richard produced the derogatory use of 'proper CHARLIE', and 'he's a right DICK', much the same happened to the above but with far more disastrous consequences. By the opening of the 1700s in America, Sambo was a well-established and extremely popular first name for black males, most likely based on a Hasua (Nigerian) word meaning second son or stepson, but by the close of the century the name had already assumed pejorative overtones and was being used of any black male of mixed European or Indian blood. The most likely cause of the term taking this path is plantation owners raping their female slaves to impregnate them and so breed more.

**SAP SOMEONE'S STRENGTH, TO:** *To steadily drain it.*

No connection with the vital fluid of plantlife but an example of 'sap' as meaning to dig trenches, especially those intended to undermine the walls of a fortification. This job was of old undertaken by the soldiers we now call the sappers, a fuller discussion of whom can be found in the discussion of 'zap' under ZANY.

**SAUSAGE, NOT A:** *Nothing at all.*

Originally this denoted a paucity of money and is based on the rhyming slang sausage and mash = cash.

**SAVE YOUR BACON:** *To escape unharmed from danger.*

Derived from the Old High German '*Bach*', which is akin to the Old English '*baec*', back, 'bacon' had, by the fourteenth century, come to mean the cleaned out carcass of a pig and also, by extension, the human body. To save one's bacon, then, simply meant to preserve one's safety. Conversely, people also spoke of 'selling their bacon' which meant putting themselves into the control or service of another. Different theories have been proposed including the one that, during the medieval mini ice-age, salted pork and smoked bacon alone preserved the lives of those isolated by snow, but these are fanciful.

**SAVING GRACE:** *The one positive aspect of an otherwise unacceptable person or situation.*

In the late Middle Ages this was used in a rather more literal sense by a Church considering a nomination for excommunication or a deceased party to be relegated to eternal damnation. These fates might be avoided should the persons under consideration have, amongst a sea of transgression, shown a tendency to good through one aspect of their character.

**SCALLYWAG:** *A mischievous person.*

First noted in America in the 1840s this word was first applied to under-sized or ill-conditioned cattle which lends some support to the notion that the term derives from the island name of Scallaway in the Shetlands, long famed for its dwarf ponies. Others point to the Scottish '*scurryvaig*', a vagabond. Whatever its origin, 'scallywag' was applied solely to people by 1848.

**SCAPEGOAT:** *A* PATSY *or a* FALL GUY.

Central to the rituals on the ancient Hebrew Day of Atonement was the bringing of two goats before the altar. One was consecrated to God and sacrificed whilst the other was anathematized and symbolically imbued with all the sins of the congregation before being turned out into the wilderness. Unlike the modern bearer of such title, the scapegoat of old most certainly got the better deal.

**SCARLET WOMAN, A:** *A* femme fatale *or dedicated seductress.*

Taken directly from Revelations 17:4 in which the unknown – rather mysogynistic – author claims to have visualized a woman 'arrayed in purple and scarlet colour . . . and having a golden cup in her hand full of abominations and the filthiness of her fornications; and on her forehead was written MYSTERY, BABYLON THE GREAT, THE MOTHER OF HARLOTS AND ABOMINATIONS OF THE EARTH.'

**SCARPER, TO:** *To decamp.*

Emerging in slang *c.* 1840 this came from the Italian '*scappare*', to escape, and arrived via LINGUA FRANCA. After 1918 it became fashionable to present the term as 'scapa' and claim it a cockney rhyming creation inspired by the scuttling of the capitulating German fleet which sank itself in Scapa Flow.

**SCOTCH A PLAN, TO:** *To render it useless.*

This 'scotch' is derived from the Anglo–French '*escocher*', to mark with a notch or cut into, and was first descriptive of serious but non-fatal wounding. Gradually the term came to mean to damage beyond repair but something closer to the original and proper meaning is still visible in the name of the game 'hopscotch' in which the participants hop over lines scored in the ground.

**SCRAPE, A:** *A problem.*

Extension of 'scrape' as slang for a shave – in this case a close one.

**SCRAPE ACQUAINTANCE, TO:** *To make social overtures.*

Ships riding at anchor in a crowded harbour are wont to scrape hulls now and again.

**SCRAPE THE BOTTOM OF THE BARREL, TO:** *To make the best of residual resource.*

The early form of meat provisions for a ship came packed in barrels lined and sealed with fat. In straitened circumstances a starving crew would check back through previously discarded barrels and scrape out the bottom layer of fat for any nourishment they could derive.

**SCREW:** (1) *A wage.*

Before the nineteenth century introduction of affordable paper bags or envelopes all commodities were weighed out and issued in what was known as a screw, a sheet of strong paper turned in the hand into a cone and then screwed shut on its contents. A workman's wages were issued in smaller versions thus the term is most often heard in the positive form of a desirable wage termed a good screw but usage is fading amongst those of delicate sensibilities who fear being misunderstood. (2) *Prison officer.* It is frequently suggested that the old style worm-drive locks driven by a screw-key are at the root of this, but such locks were long out of use by the opening of the nineteenth century when the above application is first noted. Having said that it is not impossible that keys are involved since 'screw' was then thieves' cant for a skeleton key and the warders did carry keys. Alternatively, it was common in the nineteenth century for the convicts to have to endure non-productive work in order to qualify for food and other petty privileges. The favourite was the crank which had to be turned so many times as would show on a gauge outside the cell on the landing where there was also a brake-screw which the warder could turn down to make the task all the more arduous; people placed in an invidious position still talk of being screwed down. Lastly, the term could be a play on 'scrutiny' in that the usual view the prisoner got of the warder was but his eye peering through the Judas trap on routine checks.

**SCREW YOUR COURAGE TO THE STICKING PLACE:** *To stand firm.*

The sticking point or place is one at which a screw can be turned no further.

**SCRUB SOMETHING, TO:** *To cancel it.*

In the Navy, orders and signals were written on a slate and scrubbed out when cancelled or executed.

**SCRUBBER:** *Woman of loose morals and rough demeanour.*

In both Britain and Australasia of the nineteenth century a scrubber was an animal or person who lived in the wilds or the scrublands. In these hard conditions women aged rapidly and probably would 'turn a trick' for a passing stranger for a dollar or two.

**SCUTTLE, TO:** *To destroy or defeat by unfair means.*

Synonymous with 'to scupper', both these expressions seem to rest on the allusion of a ship holed or sabotaged to sink until the water rushes in through the scupper or the scuttles and finishes her off. The scuppers are the drainage holes in the bulwarks intended to facilitate drainage from the decks and the scuttles are what the landlubber invariably called a porthole, this in turn being the hatchway through which the cannon of old protruded.

**SCUTTLEBUTT:** *Scurrilous gossip.*

The scuttlebutt, placed on the deck of every sailing ship, held the crew's daily allocation of fresh water. To prevent overfilling it had a scuttle, or hole, cut at its widest part. At specific times of the day the men gathered around the scuttlebutt for a drink and, inevitably, traded tittle-tattle.

**SEAMY SIDE, THE:** *The less acceptable aspect.*

Simple allusion to the reverse side of any garment showing all the seams and stitching.

**SECOND STRING:** *Relegated.*

Reference to the spare string kept in reserve by a bowman, the one on the bow seeing all the action.

**SEE NAPLES AND DIE:** *The best has been had so life might as well cease.*

Leaving aside other more fanciful theories for the moment, this is an Italian expression of no little antiquity which praises the beauty of the city to such extent that having seen it you might as well die for only heaven can hold anything more. This is most certainly the sense as seen in, for example, Goethe's *Italian Journey,* the following extract being dated 3 March 1787: 'I will not say another word about the beauty of the city and its situation, which have been described and praised so often As they say here, "Vedit Napoli e poi muori".' It has been mooted that the expression was born of young nobles on the Grand Tour who, falling for the charms of the city's brothels and, having picked up the local culture, so to speak, died of syphilis. Naples was indeed a filthy city and a noted centre of syphilis and typhoid, but why would the Italians invent an expression to denigrate their own tourist centre? One of the more ingenious notions hails the expression to be a pun on 'See Naples and Mori', a nearby town. Nice try.

**SEE WHICH WAY THE CAT JUMPS:** *Proceed with caution.*

There are two possible origins, the more gruesome comes from the old practice of hanging live cats from trees by their tails to use as archery targets; the archer needed to take his time and try to second guess the cat's movements. Alternatively, the phrase could derive from the game of tip-cat in which a wooden wedge is flipped up in the air by a downward stroke of a wooden bat prior to its being driven horizontally with full force. The wedge is known as the cat and it is highly unpredictable in its upward leap.

**SELL DOWN THE RIVER, TO:** *To betray.*

The usage certainly dates and derives from the era of the American slave trade and is an allusion to blacks being on the receiving end of the betrayal, but it is not clear as to who was the betrayer. One theory has it that when the laws were passed prohibiting the importing of any more slaves this drove up the price of those already there, especially the house-servants further north than the labour-hungry plantations in the south. Many northern owners found themselves accepting offers too good to refuse and their own slaves, not surprisingly, found themselves betrayed, having been sold down the Mississippi into a far harsher life. Alternatively, the phrase could have been born of escaped slaves making their way to the north only to fall pray to men posing as Abolitionists who simply sent them back whence they came and claimed the reward.

**SELL SHORT, TO:** *To cheat.*

It is tempting to see this as a simple reference to a tradesman giving short-measure or short-weight to a customer; it has been widely conjectured that it is, in fact, a stock-market expression. One method of trading is to purchase on another's behalf a certain amount of shares at a set price and then gamble on the value dropping before the accounting day so enabling the trader to pocket the difference. If this is the true origin, one can only assume that such practice was frowned upon by reputable dealers.

**SELL SOMEONE THE DUMMY, TO:** *To succeed in duping them.*

In rugby this describes the ploy of deflecting an attacker by making as if to pass the ball, then retaining it and continuing the run.

**SEND UP, TO:** *To deride.*

In late nineteenth-century British public school slang this described the sending of a boy to the headmaster for punishment. Most punishments involved a certain amount of humiliation before one's peers, so the term gradually shifted in meaning.

**SENT TO COVENTRY:** *Ostracized.*

The most convincing theory links the expression to the town of Coventry which, during the English Civil War, was a Parliamentary stronghold with a considerable garrison, the cost of which had to be borne by the citizens. In addition, it was a holding place for large numbers of Royalist prisoners, who also had to be fed and whose presence made the town the target of several attacks. Because of this, the locals resented the presence of any soldiers sent to Coventry, avoided them as much as possible, and shaved the head of any girl who associated with them.

**SEPARATE THE SHEEP FROM THE GOATS, TO:** *To sort out the good from the bad.*

Taken from Matthew 25:31–33 which talks of the coming of the Son of Man to sit in judgement of all nations which he will: 'separate them one from another, as a shepherd divideth his sheep from the goats; And he shall set the sheep on his right, but the goats on his left.' Not only is there at issue here the concept of the sheep/lamb as a symbol of divinity and the image of the goat as evil (*see also:* SCAPEGOAT) but also the use in biblical times of 'goat' as a blanket term for any wild goat or sheep, irrespective of sex, which had mingled in with the flock.

**SET YOUR CAP AT, TO:** *To set out to captivate.*

This expression originated in the early eighteenth century when sophisticated windmills were equipped with a dome, or cap, which could be rotated by pullies from within. Thus the cap, complete with sails attached, could be set to capture the wind at the best angle and gain the maximum advantage. Less plausible is the explanation centred on the fact that women of the same era always wore some sort of cap or bonnet, even indoors. The angle at which it was worn could indicate an interest in a potential beau, just as, later, a fan was used to send 'coded' signals. However, as this saying originally applied to either sex the link with womens' headwear seems tenuous.

**SEVENTH HEAVEN:** *Total ecstasy.*

The Mohammedans and certain mystical sects believe that there are seven separate heavens, the seventh being the most sublime and the home of the supreme being.

**SHAG, TO:** *To copulate.*

Attempts to link this modern-sounding term to the popular yet bizarre 1930s dance of the same name have proved fruitless. The term was certainly being used in its sexual sense as early as 1788 and had likely been understood in such context for many a year before that. The progenitor of the term is either 'shag' as meaning coarse hair – the female pubic variety – or the other 'shag' as meaning to shake violently. This 'shag' seems to have been interchangeable in the sexual application with 'shog' a variant of 'shock'. In *Henry V*, Act II, Scene 1 Corporal Nym demands of Pistol 'Will you shog off!' so that he, Nym, might be left alone with a woman. This is but one recorded early use of 'shog off' but it cannot be established with any certainty whether these are serving synonymous with the modern 'fuck off'. If Shakespeare was using the term it most probably was.

**SHAKE-DOWN, A:** *A robbery or con-trick.*

An American phrase originating in the 1940s, this first meant a street robbery but it is unclear whether the allusion is to the victim being turned upside down or shaken free of his money and possessions – this previously being known as a shake out – or because the victim was frisked down in a police-style search for any hidden valuables.

**SHAKE THE DUST FROM YOUR FEET, TO:** *To leave a place vowing never to return.*

There are references in the Bible at Matthew 10:14 and Acts 13:51 to the eastern custom of removing one's sandals and, by beating all the dust from them, indicating a resolve to eradicate every last vestige and memory of the place one has just left.

**SHAMBLES!, WHAT A:** *What a mess or confusion.*

Based on the Anglo-Saxon '*scamel*', a stool or a bench, a shambles was a fourteenth century slaughterhouse where beasts were chopped up on heavy working benches. The metaphorical use was quickly born of the allusion to the general disorder and gore. A person of ungainly gait is said to shamble as their awkwardness resembles the imagined movement of a stool or bench attempting locomotion.

**SHANGHAI A PERSON, TO:** *To kidnap and spirit them away.*

When the trade routes between Shanghai and America were opened up it did not take the sailors long to realize that the trip was long and dangerous, and that was just on the way there. On the return leg loaded with cargo, they had to RUN THE GAUNTLET of countless pirates. Consequently, more men were press-ganged for the Shanghai run than for any other.

**SHANKS' PONY, TO BE ON:** *On foot.*

First noted in the early 1700s this is still widely used and is a play on 'shank' as applied to the leg. This in turn in based on the Old English '*sceanca*', the tibia or shin area in general.

**SHANTY TOWN:** *A ramshackle collection of temporary dwellings or the rough side of town.*

An Americanism of the early 1800s, this first described the ramshackle collection of huts in which logging crews and similar workers lived. Irish immigrants formed a large part of this working population and, before long, the still common term 'shanty-Irish' meaning poor, illiterate Irish, developed. In American academic circles, the ultimate source of 'shanty' is still a matter for debate; it may derive from the French '*chantier*', a hut or log cabin, or from the Irish '*sean-tig*', an old derelict house.

**SHAPE UP!:** *A call for concentrated effort.*

At sea, a navigator is said to 'shape' a course for the ship to follow, the term means much the same as 'plot'. Should an inattentive helmsman allow the ship to drift off course, the cry of 'Shape up!' demanded he buck up his ideas and bring the ship back to shape.

**SHAPE UP OR SHIP OUT:** *Toe the line or leave.*

Another use of 'shape' as explained in SHAPE UP, this alludes to a meandering vessel which should either resume the plotted course so everyone else knows where they are up to, or 'ship' right out of the area and stop causing doubt and confusion.

**SHAPE YOURSELF! :** *Start acting properly; get working.*

At sea a course set for a specific purpose other than pure destination – i.e. to avoid a newly announced storm – was said to be shaped so, by extension, a person who shaped themselves responded properly to circumstances.

**SHAVER:** *A boy or young man.*

In permanent use since the sixteenth century, all attempts to link this to the activity of shaving the face are wholly unconvincing and there seems little need to look beyond the gypsy '*chavvie*', a boy.

**SHAVETAIL:** *Any novice.*

Borrowed from late nineteenth-century American Army slang wherein the term denoted a new pack mule which had its tail shaved as a warning to all that the animal might be unpredictable and prone to lashing out.

**SHEILA:** *A woman, especially one regarded as a sex object.*

A term most popular in Australia yet one which has its origin in the semi-pagan, rural Ireland of the eighteenth/nineteenth centuries and the statues of Sheila-na-gig as seen all over Ireland, especially in churchyards, since the sixteenth century. Basically the term translates as perhaps 'vulva-woman' for the statue represented a crouching crone-like woman holding open and wide a gaping vagina, so it is little wonder that the Irish settlers in the new colony took with them the name Sheil with much the same overtones it carries today. When first noted in print in 1828 the term did apply quite specifically to an Irish girl. As for the statue itself this was meant to represent the eternal cycle of life and death in that the crone is the devourer of the dead and the gaping vagina the route back to life again. The origins of the concept lie in India where similar statues of Kali can still be seen at temple doors with deep depressions at the top of the vagina from centuries of worshippers licking a finger and then touching the statue for luck. Kali is also reflected in the ancient Irish 'Caillech' – Old Woman, the goddess giving life to all humanity. It is the second part of the statue's name that meant 'vagina', 'up your giggy' still a commonly heard insult. It is also possible that the danced 'jig' is related term in that the French for a violin – the descendant of instruments likely played at pre-Christian orgiastic revels – is '*gigue*'. Perhaps significantly this also means leg, and there is a long and internationally well-established link between 'leg' and sexual innuendo or activity. Although no firm linkage can be established there is a constant crossing of 'gig' in the sense of music and dance and promiscuous or professionally tendered sexual activity. The first to bear the title '*gigolo*' was any prostitute – a bit of leg – who frequented the dance halls of nineteenth-century Paris and Venice. To go back even further, in Ancient Mesopotamia the sacred prostitutes of the temples were called *nu-gig*. Still throughout much of Africa, especially in the North, '*jig-a-jig*' is the generally accepted term for sexual intercourse.

**SHELL OUT, TO:** *To pay.*

First recorded in the nineteenth century it is unclear whether this is a reference to shells still then serving as currency in many parts of the world or to the use of large shells employed as scoops to measure out grain or whatever. It has also been suggested that the allusion is to money being shelled out of the wallet like peas from a pod or nuts from the shells.

**SHENANIGANS:** *High jinks or deceit.*

First noted in mid nineteenth-century America and most likely an Anglicized form of the Irish '*sion-nachuighhim*', to play tricks or be foxy – quite literally the word means 'I play the fox.' There is also a possible influence from the Spanish '*chanada*', a trick.

**SHINDIG, A:** *A riotous party or celebration.*

There have been attempts to present this as a spin-off from 'shindy' or 'shinty', a somewhat riotous Irish game best described as a blend of hockey and GBH. However, there is plenty of evidence to support the theory that it is a straightforward blend of 'shin' and 'dig'. First noted in mid nineteenth-century America where it denoted an unruly 'hoe down' or country dance, the expression might be no more than a humorous allusion to over-enthusiastic dancers kicking up their heel so far as to bark the shins of their neighbours. Similar in style to Lancashire clog-fighting was a custom common amongst lumberjacks who sorted out their differences with the protagonists facing each other, hands tied behind their backs. Shod with offensive footwear, they tried to kick chunks out of each others' legs. The agitated movements of the fighters would not be much different from those enacted by participants in a jig or other peasantish cavortings.

**SHIRTY:** *Extremely irritable.*

A nineteenth century development from KEEP YOUR SHIRT ON, as said to one about to remove same for a fight.

**SHOOT A LINE, TO:** *To lie or exaggerate.*

Likely from early twentieth-century theatrical jargon in which a line that was shot was one proclaimed with too much volume and exaggerated gesture. By the 1920s 'line-shooter' is noted in the sense of 'liar' and by the outbreak of WW2 'to shoot a line' was in general use.

**SHOOT YOUR BOLT, TO:** *To expend all resources in one ill-advised venture.*

Whilst the longbow in the right hands had a comparatively high rate of fire – a good archer should be able to keep three arrows in the air at any one time – the crossbow was long and laborious to load. Once the crossbow man had discharged his bolt he was defenceless or a spent force until he managed to load it again.

**SHORT COMMONS:** *Restricted funds or resources.*

A surviving example of a sixteenth-century meaning of 'common' as denoting a meal served to a group at a common table.

**SHOT:** *Ruined.*

Said of a pheasant too peppered with shotgun pellets to be any use for the table.

**SHOUT THE ODDS, TO:** *To argue on.*

The expression originally meant to talk too loudly or boastfully and derives from the early twentieth-century racetrack and the bookies on the tote trying to shout each other down with better odds to attract the punters.

**SHOW A CLEAN PAIR OF HEELS:** *To escape completely.*

'Clean' in this context means free from all obstruction.

**SHOW A LEG!:** *Get a move on.*

From the fifteenth to the eighteenth century the scandal of prostitutes living full time on serving ships of the line was rarely out of the public eye and the practice was not finally abolished by the Navy until 1840. The custom arose through so many of the crew having been pressed into service leaving captains reluctant to allow them ashore in case they never came back. Cries of 'show a leg' became the traditional cry of the boatswain turning out the crew in the morning as he called on those still a-hammock to show a leg over the side. Any hammock showing a woman's leg was left alone whereas any man sleeping in was unceremoniously turfed out to work. (*See also:* SON OF A GUN.)

**SHOW DOWN:** *The final confrontation.*

When all the betting and bluffing is done in poker, there always comes the time for the cards to be lain down for all to see.

**SHOWER, A:** *An unruly mob.*

Widely employed in the forces by unimpressed NCOs surveying the new influx of recruits, this is the polite elliptic of the original 'shower of shit'. This is turn is the progeny of a crude saga entitled 'A Shower of Shit over Shropshire' which tells of the effect of exploding cesspits and manure stores.

**SHOW THE WHITE FEATHER, TO:** *To show cowardice.*

In cock-fighting circles the appearance of a white tail feather is indicative of poor breeding and therefore poor spirit.

**SHYSTER:** *A corrupt person, especially a lawyer.*

Of the many false etymologies proposed for this term the least plausible hails it to be eponym born of the machinations of dazzlingly unscrupulous New York lawyer named Schuster or Scheuster – how could such a noble name as this fall to such use? Although the OED cites the first appearance in print in 1844, the slightly earlier example which appeared on 29 July 1843 in a New York underground magazine called the *Subterranean* points to the true origin being the German '*Scheisse*'. The editor, Mike Walsh, did much to popularize the term with his cultish readers, he having first heard it from a lawyer named Cornelius Terhune who frequented the Tombs Prison, New York, touting for business. The quote read as follows: 'The Counsellor [Terhune] expressed the utmost surprise at our ignorance of the true meaning of that expressive appellation "shiseter" [note the spelling] after which, by special request, he gave us a definition, which we would now give our readers, were it not that it would certainly subject us to prosecution for libel and obscenity.' The term had been coined by the inmates of the Tombs who perceived the visiting lawyers as continually taking fees but performing little valid service in return. So what else is new?

**SICK AS A PARROT:** *Extremely upset or disappointed.*

Now made something of a cliché through its constant use by footballers, it has been suggested that this rests on the effects of psittacosis, a disease of parrots brought about by the stress of captivity. Some trace the origin of the phrase to a 1970 outbreak of the disease and the attendant scare stories in the tabloid press. However, birds have been caged for centuries and in the seventeenth century people were sometimes said to be 'as melancholy as a parrot' because psittacotic birds do become rather dejected and inactive.

**SIDE-KICK:** *Close and trusted partner.*

In eighteenth and nineteenth century pickpockets' jargon a pocket was called a kick as it was a target that kicked about as their victim moved along. The side trouser pocket, or side-kick, was the most difficult to dip so those aware of the activities of pickpockets put their money and trust in their side-kicks.

**SIGN OFF, TO:** *To leave.*

Although letter writing would seem the obvious source this phrase actually refers to the legal requirement of radio stations to issue their station call-sign when ceasing transmission.

**SING FOR YOUR SUPPER, TO:** *To work for what you get.*

A hang-over from the days when musicians were less well paid than today and would frequently have to play all night in a noble's house just to get a meal and a bed.

**SING LIKE A CANARY:** *Willingly to give away damning information, especially about others.*

'Sing' used to be a grim euphemism of the torture chamber to describe how agonised victims screamed out their 'confessions'. In the mid-late sixteenth century, when the canary became the most popular caged song-bird, its name was tacked on to produce this simile. It was reinforced and nourished by the fact that, within a decade or so, a 'canary' had become thieves' cant for a caged criminal who is often quick to plea bargain or turn King's (Queen's) Evidence.

**SIT ON YOUR DUFF:** *To idle.*

'Duff' here signifies the human posterior which, in the case of troops lazing about awaiting transport, is usually to be found resting on duffel kit bags.

**SIT TIGHT, TO:** *To hold station.*

A poker expression to describe a player who plays a cover on the kitty; this means he no longer wishes to keep on betting but he is not willing to throw in his hand. Those wishing to continue begin another pot but even if the player sitting tight eventually proves to hold the best hand of all he may not claim any of this second kitty which goes to the holder of the second-best hand. Any superior hand from the second kitty would take all of the first pile too.

**SIXTH SENSE:** *Intuition.*

Numerically incorrect in that all humans are already possessed of six senses – sight, touch, hearing, smell, taste and kinaesthesis, the sense of one's position in space and the relationship of the limbs to one another. Properly, therefore, intuition should be called the seventh sense.

**SIXTY FOUR THOUSAND DOLLAR QUESTION, THE:** *The ultimate question whose answer reveals all.*

This is an elaboration of the original American 'sixty-four dollar question', this being the highest value question on a CBS Radio quiz *Take It Or Leave It* which ran from 1941 to 1948. The show collapsed after it was revealed that the producer, in an attempt to revive the show's flagging fortunes, had fed the contestants all the answers but coached them in the art of appearing to hesitate and ponder whilst the value of the questions progressed up the dollar scale 1-2-4-8-16-32-64. Perhaps inspired by the inflated-value expression, in 1955 there was indeed an American TV version where the prize did indeed go up to sixty-four thousand dollars but no one ever won the jackpot. The show came to Britain in 1956 as *The 64,000 Question*, the zeros in the title showing as sixpences leaving the maximum prize at £1,600. Lady Cynthia Asquith, daughter-in-law of the WW1 Prime Minister, was the first winner of the prize.

**SKEDADDLE, TO:** *To decamp in a hurry.*

The earliest appearance in print of this phrase was in America in 1861 when it was used to refer to the unruly retreat of vanquished troops quitting the battlefield. It is possible that this developed from the Scottish term with the same spelling meaning to spill milk, potatoes or any foodstuff. It was used in this sense in domestic print in 1862 and the casual manner of its inclusion implies that the word was familiar to readers. Alternatively, and far more academic, is the Greek '*skedannumi*', to disperse, especially in disarray; it is mooted that 'skedaddle' was a humorous word built on the Greek by, perhaps, Harvard students who later introduced it into the Union Officer Corps where it was first applied in the military sense to the Confederate foe. Self-interested businessmen who quit New England at the outbreak of the Civil War and fled across the Canadian border, just in case, were also labelled Skedaddlers by the press. There is even a Canadian town called Skedaddlers' Ridge.

**SKELETON AT THE FEAST:** *That which ruins a festive occasion.*

Relating to an ancient custom of the Egyptians who, prior to the beginning of a sumptuous banquet, would parade a human skeleton round the table whilst the guests were called up to 'Look on this! Eat, drink and be merry, for tomorrow you die.' Both Plutarch and Herodotus mention the grim little ritual and relate how small wooden replicas were sometimes substituted or that the real skeleton was occasionally seated at the head of the table. The purpose, of course, was to remind all present of the transitory nature of life and its earthly pleasures.

**SKELETON IN THE CLOSET/ CUPBOARD:** *The dark shame peculiar to every family.*

The phrase alludes to an old morality tale which recounts the search for the one person without a single care in the world and one with no shame. When the likely candidate was interviewed she took them upstairs and opened a cupboard in her bedroom to reveal a skeleton which her husband forced her to kiss each night before retiring. The bones were those of her one-time adulterous lover killed by her husband in a duel. In more modern times this has produced the spin-off, 'to COME OUT of the closet', meaning to proclaim one's homosexuality, previously regarded as a 'skeleton' by so many families.

**SKID ROW/ROAD:** *The degraded side of town.*

In general use on both sides of the Atlantic since the early–mid 1800s, the original skid road was the chute of greased logs down which felled trees were shot to the lumber mill or river. This dirty, unskilled work was only undertaken by derelicts, drunks and drifters who, in the eyes of the jacks, were the scum of the camp and forced to live apart.

**SKIVE OFF, TO:** *To evade work.*

Likely from the French '*esquiver*', to dodge or avoid, this emerged in Forces slang *c.* 1915 doubtless through contact with French terminology in the battlefield. It is unclear whether the lowly 'skivvy' is an allied term for this is first noted in the late nineteenth century. If this too is taken from the French it is either because the girl had to dodge round doing all sorts of menial tasks, or for her employers deeming her lazy and idle no matter how hard she worked.

**SKULDUGGERY:** *Devious tactics.*

Something of a mystery, the only surety is that human skulls are not involved at all. The most likely source is the Scottish 'sculdudrie', obscene or bawdy behaviour; indeed in the eighteenth century this is the spelling of the first noted example of the term. All variants hinting at the digging up of skulls are later American distortions.

**SKYLARKING:** *Wasting time or playing when work should be done.*

A term of Naval origin, this was used to describe the play of the ships' boys who would engage in a dangerous game of tag high up in the rigging after the day's work was done.

**SLAG OFF, TO:** *To reprimand or denigrate another's reputation.*

Inspired by perhaps the Swedish '*slagg*', sleet, or the Norwegian term of the same spelling meaning 'slaver', the Scottish '*slag*' has long been in existence meaning to moisten or besmirch with filth. Scottish migrants to Australia took the term with them and by the early part of this century 'slag' meant to spit and they who were slagged off had their reputations metaphorically spat on in public. The derogatory use of 'slag' for an unattractive or loose woman first appeared in the mid sixteenth century and derives from the separate 'slag' as meaning refuse or rubbish as dumped on a slag-heap.

**SLAP HAPPY:** *Cheerfully reckless.*

Originally imported from America in the 1940s with a meaning of insane or mentally impaired and synonymous with 'punch-drunk'.

**SLAP-BANG:** *Absolutely or immediately.*

When this emerged in the 1780s it denoted a cheap eating house with but one item on the 'menu' and cash up front. The customers slapped down their money and a plate of food was banged down in exchange.

**SLEEP LIKE A TOP, TO:** *To sleep soundly.*

There is no foundation to the notion that the above is a pun on the French idiom '*dormir comme une taupe*', to sleep like a mole. The top involved here is the child's spinning toy and the use of 'sleep' is that applied to items spinning at such a velocity that all rotary movement becomes indiscernible. Should the item be spun at any higher r.p.m. the top will appear to slowly reverse its direction of turn, as do waggon-wheels in films.

**SLEEP ON A CLOTHESLINE, TO:** *To be in penury.*

In the 1800s, the cheapest flop-houses in London offered nothing more elaborate than two rows of benches either side of a rope strung the length of the room. In the morning the 'host' would untie one end of the rope to wake up his clients.

**SLING YOUR HOOK! :** *Go away.*

The hook is the ship's anchor which must be secured properly in its sling at the bow before the ship can get under way.

**SLIPSHOD:** *Untidy or inefficiently.*

A compression of the word 'slip-pershod' more generally seen in the sixteenth century when it denoted the poor and needy who, when given a pair of shoes too small, did not baulk at breaking down the heels to wear them as slippers. By extension, people of such station were also called 'down at heel'.

**SLOPE OFF, TO:** *To sneak away.*

From the Dutch '*sloop*', to steal away in the night.

**SLUSH FUND:** *Hidden account for illicit funds.*

When the British Navy was under sail the cooks would make a bit of money on the side by collecting and storing all the fat derived from the boiling down of meat. This slush would be made into candles for sale at the next port of call and the money would be spent on frivolities.

**SMACKER:** *A pound sterling.*

First used in nineteenth-century America in reference to the silver dollar which made a smacking sound when slapped manfully down on the bar. It appears that smacker arrived in the UK and became associated with the pound in the late 1920s.

**SMOKE FILLED ROOM, THE:** *Any* ÉMINENCE GRIS *or hidden power-base.*

In the above form the designation is attributed to Harry Micajah Dougherty (1860–1941), the American lawyer/politician who secured the Republican Presidential nomination in 1920 for his close friend Senator Warren Harding. Dougherty predicted a deadlock which would be broken by 'a group of men who will sit down about two o'clock in the morning around a table in a smoke filled room'. Dougherty later stated he never said 'smoke filled'. Even if this is true whoever added the term was not original. Long famous in American political circles was the description of the infamously powerful Boston Caucus Club as found in the diary of John Adams, obsessive diarist and second President of the United States. In February of 1763 he recorded 'The Caucus Club meets at certain times in the garrett of Tom Daws, the adjutant of the Boston Regiment. He has a large house and moveable partition is his garrett which is taken down and the whole club meets in the one room. They smoke tobacco until you cannot see from one end of the garrett to the other. There they chose a moderator who puts questions to the vote regularly and Selectmen, Collectors, Wardens, Fire Wards and representatives are regularly chosen [here] before they are chosen in town.'

**SMOKE SOMEONE, TO:** *To kill them.*

On America's death rows this is the convicts' slang for execution in the gas chamber.

**SNATCH:** *The vagina or women in general as sex objects.*

Widely regarded in Britain as a recent American import, 'snatch' is, in fact, of sixteenth-century British origin as perhaps alludes to the hurried and casual copulation snatched as a transitory pleasure. Some commentators however, see the term as an especially derogatory one in that it further derides the vagina to the image of the supposed concept of '*vagina dentata*', an alleged male phobia of the snapping vagina waiting to emasculate them.

**SOD:** *Any unpleasant person.*

Properly the term denoted one engaging in buggery and, etymologically, is a quite unjustified slur on the residents of the city of Sodom, supposedly destroyed by God for such sin. All rests on the interpretation of 'know' as it appears in Genesis 19:5. Lot, although resident in the city of Sodom, is generally regarded as a stranger, which indeed he was. Next two other strangers start hanging round the city gates and Lot invites them to stay at this place. Everybody was then pretty xenophobic and the suspicious Sodomites – every last one of them according to the Bible – foregathered outside Lot's house and demanded: 'Where are the men who came in to thee this night? Bring them out unto us, that we may know them.' Now it is beyond dispute that in certain instances 'know' in the Bible means to have carnal knowledge of, but then so too does 'to go in to', so are we to assume that the strangers had both first buggered Lot? A far more logical interpretation is that the Sodomites simply want to 'know' who is hanging around their city; are they pre-invasion spies for example? Had there been a town so debauched and depraved that their idea of a good time was the gang-buggery of two strangers while the rest of the town looked on and cheered, then surely the city would have warranted mention by some other contemporary historian. It is true that Lot refuses to hand over the strangers, offering his two daughters for rape instead – the Bible doesn't record what the daughters thought of this wizard wheeze – but this would not have been a sexual alternative to homosexual activity but an attempt to save the strangers from a doubtlessly violent interrogation. The laws of hospitality then decreed that no price was too high to pay to keep one's guests from harm. It was a matter of honour, and Lot was quite prepared to let his daughters pay the price of diverting the mob's attention from his guests who in any event turn out to be angels and so save the day. Lot, this 'good and holy' man, himself later takes both his daughters' virginity for himself, so perhaps Mrs Lot was better off in her salty fate. Either way, the Sodom/buggery association is now so strong that the New International Version of the Bible interprets the line as: 'Bring them out to us so that we can have sex with them.'

**SOFT PEDAL, TO:** *To proceed with caution.*

This is a reference to the foot-operated damper pedal on a piano which mutes the volume.

**SOFT SOAP, TO:** *To flatter.*

Prior to the recent fad for pump dispensers of liquid soap, most mid-late nineteenth-century soaps of quality came in scented and liquid form. To those left scrubbing themselves with the thin lather of hard basic bar-soap the more fortunate bathers would seem to be pampering themselves.

**SOMETHING ROTTEN IN THE STATE OF DENMARK:** *A distinct whiff of corruption and double-dealing.*

From *Hamlet* Act 1, Scene iv, in which Marcellus makes the observation to Hamlet that 'Something is rotten in the State of Denmark' when the ghost has made his appearance. Denmark was renowned for its strong cheeses even in Shakespeare's time, and there is more than a passing likelihood that he was making a light play on the fact.

**SON OF A GUN:** *A rascal, a term of surprise or affection.*

Although this is now almost a title of honour bestowed on one who is considered 'a bit of a lad', the epithet was already well established in the late 1600s and applied to ship-born bastards. As explained in SHOW A LEG common prostitutes were frequent residents of a man-of-war and it was not unknown for them to fall pregnant. The only place for these women to give birth with privacy and, importantly, not block the gangway, was behind a makeshift canvas screen suspended between two mid-ship guns. Female births were not considered worthy of mention in the ship's log but male offspring were in case they were to stay on as ship's boy. Actual paternity was at best a matter of conjecture so the birth was entered as 'son of a gun'. Long standing is the self-description so beloved of bluff seafaring types – 'Begotten in the galley and born under a gun. Every hair a rope yarn, every tooth a marlin spike, every finger a fish-hook and blood of good Stockholm tar.'

**SOP TO CERBERUS:** *A pacifying gesture.*

Cerberus was the three-headed dog that guarded the gates to the underworld of ancient mythology. When a Roman died, it was customary to place in his hand a piece of cake or biscuit with which to bribe the animal to let him pass unhindered. The Greek had much the same custom.

**SOUND OFF, TO:** *To boast or complain.*

Troops on the parade ground are sometimes required to 'Sound off!' by calling out their name and number so the above came to mean talking about oneself in one form or another.

**SOUPED UP:** *Greatly enhanced.*

This most certainly first applied in the 1940s to cars with blown engines but it is unclear whether the inspiration was the 'supercharger' or the dangerously volatile fuels that were the inspiration. The favourite mixture was one of petrol and nitromethane which was, like nitro-glycerine, known as soup.

**SOUR GRAPES:** *Jealous dismissal of that which you really desire.*

An allusion to one of the so-called Aesop's fables, none of which were written by this legendary figure. The tale tells of a fox desperately trying to leap up and pick some fresh grapes; his repeated failure causes him to stalk off in disgust announcing to observers that the grapes were sour anyway and that he did not really want them.

**SOUTHPAW:** *Left handed, especially a sportsperson.*

First applied to left-handed baseball pitchers, credit for the coinage is frequently yet erroneously laid at the feet of American sports writer journalist and humorist, Finley Peter Dunne. Unfortunately, the chronology of this phrase robs Dunne of the honour as it was extant nearly twenty-seven years before he was born. It was, and still is, the custom to construct ballparks to run east-west so that the batsman will not have the afternoon sun shining in his eyes. Similar consideration was thus afforded the pitcher who, under such conditions, faced east and if left-handed, threw with his 'southside' hand or paw.

**SOW YOUR WILD OATS, TO:** *To give free reign to youthful excess.*

The wild oat, *avena fatua*, is a largely useless plant that invades fields of more cultured strains and causes problems. The reference is to the harvest of problems which come in later life when too many metaphorical wild oats have been sown, for only a foolish farmer would deliberately introduce such into his crops.

**SPARE, TO GO:** *To become enraged or distraught.*

This was 1930s Force's slang for a soldier who went absent without leave; such men were usually at the end of their tether about some or all aspects of service life.

**SPEAK OF THE DEVIL:** *Here comes the very person under discussion.*

Ancient superstition held that those who had the temerity to use the name of an evil deity invited his presence; the original expression was: 'Speak of the Devil and he will appear.' This is why the person doing the catching in a game of tag, supposedly the Devil, is always called 'it'.

**SPEAKEASY:** *Low club or* DIVE*:* A development from the early nineteenth-century British thieves' and smugglers' 'speak-softly shop', a place where contraband and stolen goods were traded or ordered. In such establishments it was advisable to conduct one's business in as hushed tones as possible to prevent others hearing and betraying. Some thirty years before the Prohibition era the term is noted in the 'dry' state of Kansas where it described an illegal drinking haunt or shebeen. Within sixteen days of the Volstead Act being passed on 16 January 1920, the first club was raided in Chicago. The federal raid on the Red Lantern basement bar – described as a 'speakeasy' – received huge publicity and the word, not to mention the bootlegged booze, was soon on everyone's lips. Incidentally, film scenes showing the customers being rounded up are largely fiction; it was not illegal to drink during Prohibition, only illegal to manufacture, transport or sell alcohol.

**SPEND A PENNY, TO:** *Politely, to urinate.*

In the pre-decimal era one old penny was required to activate the lock on the cubicle door of public lavatories, hence also, 'HAS THE PENNY DROPPED?' as inquired of those pondering a problem.

**SPICK AND SPAN:** *Extremely neat and tidy.*

In the ship-building yards of old a spick was a nail and a span was a wood-chip or a shaving. Spick and span was a shipyard phrase applied to a newly completed ship with every nail still shiny and the cuts in her timbers still well defined and unsmoothed with wear.

**SPIKE A DRINK, TO:** *To load it with spirits or drugs.*

Possibly dating from early nineteenth-century America this could allude to the spiking of artillery guns, an operation which involved driving metal spikes into the touch-holes to render them useless – as useless as extra alcohol or drugs leave the drinker.

**SPILL THE BEANS, TO:** *To divulge information.*

This was adopted from America around the turn of the century when its prime meaning was to vomit – 'beans' being a blanket term for basic foods. This would place the expression on a par with 'cough it up', 'spit it out', 'he spilled his guts to the police', and a host of other parallels. It has also been suggested that the origins lie in the ancient voting method – still favoured by private members' clubs – involving coloured beans or small balls as ballot tokens. As explained under BLACKBALL, to be passed, votes had to be unanimously white, just one black token would scotch the motion. If a clumsy voter knocked over the open vase containing the cast votes, then the result is there for all to see as the beans spill out onto the committee table.

**SPIN A YARN, TO:** *To lie or exaggerate.*

In seafaring parlance a yarn is one of the threads making up the individual strands of a rope and 'spinning a yarn' was the recounting of a long and involved tale of one's own experiences at sea – stretching it out like a rope with complicated interlocking side issues. Sailors, like anglers, are wont to exaggerated their deeds and victories.

**SPIN DOCTOR:** *One who conducts damage limitation or presents unpleasant facts to the public in the most acceptable form.*

Born in the American political arenas, spin doctors have always been around but not so called until recently. At the root lies American pool/snooker terminology and baseball pitcher's jargon relating to a ball struck by the cue or pitched in such a way as to behave deceptively in travel due to what is known in British sporting circles as 'side', or spin. The original spin doctor was a wily pool shooter or ball pitcher who could make the ball appear to travel true but in reality behave unpredictably.

**SPIN-OFF:** *A subsidiary product or benefit.*

Reference to the lumps of clay flaying from the main lump on a potter's wheel.

**SPIN OUT, TO:** *To extend unnecessarily.*

An allusion to the flax being drawn out on the spinning wheel.

**SPITTING IMAGE, THE:** *The exact replica.*

Attempts to hail this as a corruption of 'the very spirit and image of' lack substantiation for the earliest noted forms of this phrase were seen in the early nineteenth century and took the form of 'the very spit of' so it seems that the allusion is to one person or item having been spat out by another – people still hail a likeness to be the 'dead' spit of the original.

**SPLICE THE MAINBRACE, TO:** *To take a drink.*

Whilst this is a well-established term of the British Navy the origin itself is a complete mystery. The main brace is a rope attached to the lower yard of a square-rigged sail and is hauled to brace the canvas round to the wind. One of the most important ropes on such a ship, the mainbrace would never be spliced but replaced at the first signs of wear and tear. The order 'to splice the main brace' in the drinking sense called for the issue of an extra tot of rum to the crew after coping with inordinately bad weather and perhaps it is nothing more than a humorous allusion to their having hauled so hard on the main brace as to break it and render it in need of splicing.

**SPOIL THE SHIP FOR A HA'PORTH OF TAR:** *To ruin a job for the want of some minor effort or expense.*

Although the allusion seems quite straightforward in that ships are sealed with tar, however, the original form of the expression was 'to spoil the sheep for a ha'porth of tar'. Before vetinary skills were a formalized profession the farmers tended their own stock with crude but effective balms – like a dab of tar to a badly cut sheep which might otherwise develop septicaemia and die. Tar was routinely applied to the stumps of field amputations and 'creosote' derives its name from the Greek '*kreasote*', the flesh saver.

**SPONDULIX:** *Money, especially in abundance.*

First noted in America in 1856 and the UK in 1885, it has been conjectured that this is a play on the Greek '*spondulikos*', the adjectival form of '*spondulos*', the recognized name of a type of sea-shell once much used in trade and still serving as currency today in some parts of Asia. It must be remembered that the use of shells, or wampum – an elliptic of the Algonquin '*wampumpeak*', a string of white shall-beads – was wide spread in nineteenth-century America, even amongst whites in the remoter areas. The last factory producing wampum artifacts for fur traders to deal with Indians ceased production in 1899 with the death of owner Alexander Campbell of Pascack, New Jersey, so the sight of seashells as currency would not have been rare even in twentieth-century America. Accepting that 'spondulix' is an invention of the alumni of Harvard and Yale, (*see also:* SKEDADDLE) it is also possible the the construction was influenced heavily by another Greek term, '*spondein*', to pour out a libation. This was used of the pouring out of sacred wine at a Greek temple while solemn vows were taken before the gods, hence the 'sponsor' who promised funds aplenty for a venture.

**SPOON, TO:** *To engage in mawkish romantics.*

Allusive to the once common habit of amorous young men carving intricate wooden spoons to present to their sweethearts, this symbol of the girl's forthcoming domestic servitude serving much as does an engagement ring today.

**SPRUCE UP, TO:** *To put in fine order.*

A late Middle English adaptation of the French 'Pruce' which denoted anything Prussian, particularly fine Prussian leather clothing of horsetack. With the long-abiding Germanic reputation for smartness and precision, the verb was not long in developing. The tree of the same name is native to that area.

**SQUARE, A:** *An excessively conventional person.*

Early twentieth-century American jazz musicians' terminology likely allusive to a conductor's hand movements describing a square in the air to an orchestra required to play a piece in regular, unsynchopated 4/4 time.

**SQUARE AWAY, TO:** *To tidy or regulate affairs.*

Since the late sixteenth century 'square' alone held such meaning and is most likely of Naval origin alluding to the regulating of the yardarms of a docked square-rigger, all sails neatly furled and arms struck at right-angles to the masts. It is also possible that calling a messy situation a 'cock-up' is a reference to badly struck yards and is not a crude allusion.

**SQUARE THE CIRCLE, TO:** *To attempt the impossible.*

An allusion to the mathematical dilemma of drawing a square with exactly the same area as a given circle. The value of pi is approximately 3.14 but the figures after the point go on into infinity so it is impossible to be absolutely precise.

**STACKED AGAINST YOU:** *You are destined to lose.*

When a deck of cards is placed in advantageous order by a skilled cheat the cards are said to be stacked.

**STAKE, TO:** *To place in bet or to fund another.*

The use of 'stake' or 'at stake', in the gambling sense is anything but new as shown by *Twelfth Night*, Act III, Scene 1: 'Have you not set mine honour at the stake and baited it with all the unmuzzled thoughts that a tyrannous heart can think?', that last pointing in the origins of such usage deriving from the hunter staking out live bait to draw in the quarry. By the early 1880s 'to stake someone' was to supply risk-capital for a business venture, the Americans extending this to 'grubstake' which denoted the funding of a prospector's supplies and food while he grubbed round for a strike; by the end of the century 'grub' on its own had come to stand for food in general. The most recent development in this chain is the surveillance 'stake-out' which yet again alludes to the staked-out bait and the ever-vigilant hunters waiting on the predator to enter the trap.

**STALKING HORSE:** *A pretext to conceal real intentions.*

The hunters of old trained their horses to amble slowly towards the deer or whatever, until, within easy bowshot, the hunter emerged from behind the horse to let lose.

**STAMPING GROUND:** *Your home turf.*

An early nineteenth-century import from America where it referred to the habitual breeding ground of wild horses to which herds would return year after year. Here the stallions would rear and stamp in shows of strength as they vied for females.

**STAND ALOOF:** *To stand distant and reserved.*

Originally a Dutch naval command '*a loef*' which called for the vessel's head to be turned into the wind. In sailing parlance to 'luff' still means to sail close to the wind, and, in yacht racing, to move to the windward side of an opponent. In the seventeenth century the word acquired the wider meaning of steering clear of the coast, a significant step towards its present usage.

**STAND ON CEREMONY, TO:** *Incorrectly, to observe formalities.*

From its use in *Julius Caesar,* it is clear that the proper meaning is to believe in prophecies and portents. In Act II, Scene 2, Calpurnia is warning Caesar against venturing out of the house on the Ides of March; she has heard of hideous sights seen by the watch; a lioness whelping in the street; the graves yielding up the dead, and blood drizzled on the Capitol; 'Caesar, I never stood on ceremonies before, yet now they fright me.'

**STAND PAT, TO:** *To hold true to choice.*

From the American poker tables of the late nineteenth century and an expression used of a player who was content with the first five cards dealt and refused the option of exchange. The non-verbal indicator to the dealer was to place the cards in a neat pile and pat them two or three times in rapid succession; the noise also indicated to the other players that someone might have a very good hand indeed.

**STAND SOMEONE UP, TO:** *To ignore a rendezvous, especially a date.*

Initially, this referred specifically to a girl failing to turn up for her own wedding so leaving the groom 'standing up' at the altar.

**STAND THE GAFF:** *To withstand the iniquities of life.*

The gaff in question was the spike fitted to the legs of fighting cocks with which the birds gouged each other.

**STAND-OFFISH:** *Remote; aloof.* The ship that stands off is one holding a course well clear of the shore or anchoring outside the harbour.

**STARK NAKED:** *Absolutely naked.*

A corruption of the sixteenth-century 'start naked' as derived from the German '*Start*', the tail or buttocks, hence bird names such as redstart and whitestart.

**START FROM SCRATCH, TO:** *To begin with no resources or advantage.*

On the racetrack handicapped runners always have to start at the baseline or 'scratch' line whilst others are granted several yards advantage.

**STATE-OF-THE-ART:** *The very latest developments in a particular field of endeavour.*

As in 'state of play', this shows 'state' in the sense of the point at which matters currently lie, so the above denotes anything produced by the cutting-edge technology of any particular field of expertise.

**STAVE OFF, TO:** *To fend off unpleasantness.*

In the bearpit there were men armed with staves whose job it was to beat the dogs back from the bear every now and again so as to drag out the 'sport' and postpone the inevitable end of the bear.

**STAY DOWN FOR THE COUNT:** *To make the most of a respite from a difficult situation; to conserve one's assets.*

An exhausted boxer who is knocked down but not out can profit from some rest by staying down on the canvas until the count is nearly finished.

**STEAL A MARCH ON SOMEONE, TO:** *To make a sudden gain on them.*

An old military expression used of a forced march through the night to place an army far closer to the enemy than they might realize.

**STEAL SOMEONE'S THUNDER, TO:** *To grab their glory.*

*Appius and Virginia* was not the greatest success in the career of English playwright and critic John Dennis (1657–1734); the abortive production folded after a few nights in 1709. The only positive thing the critics had to say about the fiasco was that a device designed by Dennis to produce thunder noises was by far the most realistic they had ever heard. The Drury Lane Theatre hung on to the machine against uncleared debts and when Dennis attended a production of *Macbeth* a short time later he realized that his machine was being used for the opening sequence. This brought him to his feet to cause a commotion by yelling out that whilst they would not let his play run they nevertheless stole his thunder.

**STICK IN YOUR CRAW:** *To go against the grain.*

'Craw' is a variant of 'crop', the dilation in a bird's oesophagus where, usually with the aid of stones deliberately swallowed to act as grinders, primary digestion takes place prior to assimilation into the stomach proper. Anything that stuck in the craw would be extremely unpalatable.

**STICK YOUR NECK OUT, TO:** *To take risks.*

From the boxing ring where such action places your head within range of your opponent.

**STICK YOUR OAR IN, TO:** *To interrupt.*

The surviving elliptic of 'to stick your oar in another man's boat'. When shore leave was granted the parties would row ashore in the ship's boats and set to their pleasures. Should one member of a party wish to remain he would remove his oar from his departing transport and place it in one of the remaining shuttles as a sign that they should not leave without him. When that party returned they might have to wait for the reveller and so be inconvenienced.

**STICKLER:** *One obsessed with the observance of form.*

This was the old title of the umpires overseeing judicial combat between knights. Fully versed in the rules and rituals of chivalry, they insisted on the observance of every little nicety and point of etiquette.

**STICKS, THE:** *The rural outback.*

Originally this was a nineteenth-century North American loggers' term for the regions where they worked, the trees being 'the big sticks'.

**STIFF SOMEONE, TO:** *To treat harshly or* ROOK *them completely.*

From the field of contact sports, such as rugby, in which the aggressive player fends off an opponent on the run with the arm held rigid so as to inflict serious damage.

**STIFF UPPER LIP:** *Staunch demeanour.*

The upper lip of those about to dissolve in tears tends to tremble but those of sterner stuff fight off such display by clamping their lips together.

**STITCH SOMEONE UP, TO:** *To set up for a* ROOKING.

It could be that this alludes to the traditional method of burial at sea when the deceased is sewn up in a canvas shroud with the last stitch passed through the divide of the nostrils as a hangover from earlier times when this was thought the best way to make a last-minute check that the person really was dead and not just unconscious.

**STOOL PIGEON:** *An informer.*

Originally a hunting term for a pigeon cruelly nailed to a stool and then placed out in the open so it emitted distress calls to lure others of its species down and under the hunters' guns. From this the term was adopted into criminal slang for a man who, acting as an agent of entrapment, would set up a job and then inform the police for the reward paid after they had swooped and arrested the gang wholesale. Gradually the term broadened to encompass any pedlar of information to the authorities.

**STOOGE:** FALL-GUY *or dupe.*

A variant of 'student' this is first noted in early twentieth-century America vaudeville slang as descriptive of a comic's foil or straight-man who tended to be a novice in the business and so served as the butt of all the others' jokes and stunts.

**STRAIGHT AND NARROW, THE:** *The path of virtue and righteousness.*

The widely accepted yet erroneous form of 'the strait and narrow' as taken from Matthew 7:14 'Because strait is thought, and narrow is the way, which leadeth unto life, and few there be that find it.'

**STRAIGHT AS A DIE:** *Physically or morally upright.*

The reference here is to the engineer's die which is used to cut the thread down the outside of a metal rod to turn it into a fixing device and which must of necessity be straight-running and true if the thread is to engage properly with the groove cut by the tap into the female receiver.

**STRAIGHT FROM THE HORSE'S MOUTH:** *Information direct from source.*

The rule-of-thumb gauge of a horse's age is to look at its teeth and not trust to the dealer's word on the matter.

**STRAIGHT FROM THE SHOULDER:** *Direct and unvarnished speech.*

The most telling punch from a boxer is one delivered by the arm fully extended from the shoulder.

**STRAIT-LACED:** HIDEBOUND, *excessively conservative.*

Correct form, though 'straight-laced' is also used, alluding to the constraints of a tightly laced corset.

**STRAPPED:** *In penury.*

Certainly of nineteenth-century origin but it is unclear as to whether the source is the dialect 'strap', a variant of 'strip' or the tightening of a belt in times of hunger.

**STRETCH A POINT, TO:** *To exaggerate or exceed normality.*

Known since the mid sixteenth century, this expression has taken the variant forms of 'strain a point' and 'stretch a string', both giving support to the notion that the point in question was that used to tie up garments and corsets. A woman could exaggerate her own charms by hauling in her points here and there, and men who had exceeded an elegant sufficiency at table found themselves stretching their own points through gluttony.

**STRICTLY FOR THE BIRDS:** *Anything outlandish or unacceptable.*

An American Forces expression of the early part of this century and one that rests on that which emanated from their horses in great quantities. This matter in turn attracted countless maggots and similar creatures which in turn enticed the birds onto the small mound where, to the untrained eye, they appeared to consume that upon which they stood not that which infested it. Basically then, the term is a convoluted euphemism for 'horse-shit', a phrase which has enjoyed much longer usage as a synonym for lies and tall stories.

**STRIKE IT LUCKY, TO:** *To secure good fortune.*

To the American gold miner/prospector, a strike was a line of ore shining in a rock-face.

**STRIKE OUT, TO:** *To fail completely.*

In baseball the batsman attracts a scorer's mark, or strike, against his name of the sheet for each ball he fails to hit; three strikes and he is out. In general terms in America it is understood to denote a batsman who misses the first three balls in succession and quits the pitch having achieved nothing at all.

**STRIKE WHILE THE IRON IS HOT, TO:** *To press home advantage.*

The blacksmith's job is made all the easier by his hammering the iron as soon as it comes from the fire for it becomes less malleable as it cools.

**STRING ALONG, TO:** *To lead another into a dubious course of action.*

A late nineteenth-century American development alluding to pack-mules tied together in trains.

**STRINGER:** *An independant or* FREELANCE, *especially a journalist.*

Of journalistic origin in late nineteenth century America, this was born of the method by which independent correspondents were paid. At the end of the month they cut out all their articles from the relevant papers and pasted them together in single column length so as to resemble a piece of string. This was then sent into the editor who sanctioned payment at a rate of so much per column inch.

**STRIKE ME PINK!:** *Exclamation of surprise.*

A 'softening' of the nineteenth-century Cockney 'strike me perpendicular' as meaning 'I was so surprised it knocked me bolt upright.' In time this was truncated to 'strike me perp' which others imagined to be an elliptic of 'purple', so lesser surprises warranted 'pink'.

**STUFFED SHIRT, A:** *A pompous and vain man.*

One of the main window displays of menswear shops of the previous century was an array of dress-shirts stuffed to appear occupied. The human stuffed shirt was seen as not only puffed up but of no real substance and brainless to boot.

**STUMP UP, TO:** *To pay promptly in cash.*

Likely a reference to the use of old tree stumps as trading counters at open markets and fairs.

**STUMPED:** *Puzzled.*

This phrase is either taken from the game of cricket or is a reference to a plough striking the just-hidden remnants of a felled tree.

**STYMIED:** *Completely blocked in a desired course of action.*

Synonymous with 'snookered' and BEHIND THE EIGHT BALL, this phrase came from the game of golf where a stymie was a ball which fell on the green more than six inches away from an opponent's ball but in direct line of the hole. Thus a direct shot was denied the other player leaving only the unattractive option of a chip-shot over the top.

**SUB, TO:** *To borrow.*

Properly the term should only be used of a loan secured against wages owed. Such a loan was once generally known as subsistence money to see the worker through to their first payday.

**SUCKER:** *A dupe or gullible person.*

Not, as you might imagine, allusive to the naivety of suckling infants, but to the lead miners of early nineteenth-century Illinois. At the root of the insult lies the cerebally challenged sucker-fish of the genus Catostomus found in profusion in the waters of Illinois. The fish's nickname was based on its mouth movements as it seemed to suck up any bait presented to it, even tiny bits of coloured cloth would guarantee a catch. These fish swam up the western rivers in the spring and then retreated south in the autumn, a migratory pattern adopted by prospectors and itinerant miners come to exploit the lead deposits found in the Northern reaches of the state in the 1820s. The overtones of stupidity were reinforced by the number of these rather unworldly types who fell prey to dishonest land agents and claim-filings. Gradually, the term came to denote any Illinoisian and that state is still known as the the Sucker State.

**SUN IS OVER THE YARDARM, THE:** *It is time for a drink.*

In the northern latitudes the sun generally shows over the foreyard – the foremost and uppermost yardarm struck across the leading mast – by 11.00a.m. which co-incided with the mid-morning stand-easy when officers went below for the first drink of the day. The phrase is essentially a landlubbers' distortion of the original form citing the foreyard; properly the cross-spars are called yards and 'yardarm' denoted only the outer tips thereof.

**SURE FIRE PLAN, A:** *One destined for success.*

Taken from the early twentieth-century American advertising of more reliable rim-fire ammunition.

**SURVIVAL OF THE FITTEST:** *Incorrectly, only the toughest win through.*

Borrowed from the writings of Darwin – although he was not the first to use such expression – this does not in fact mean that the strongest will survive but rather that survival will be attained by those best 'fitted' to their environment be they tough and intelligent or weak and stupid.

**SUSS OUT, TO:** *To figure out or unravel a mystery.*

The above has been the accepted spelling since the 1940s, prior to which 'sus' was the standard form. The reference is to Section 4 of the Vagrancy Act which was invoked by the police in the early twentieth century and used as a blanket reason for arrest without any hard evidence that any specific crime had been committed. 'Every suspected person or reputed thief frequenting or loitering about in any place of public resort . . . with intent to commit an arrestable offence . . . shall be deemed a rogue and a vagabond.' Thus, the criminals arrested purely on general suspicion and subsequently linked to specific crimes spoke of having been 'sussed out'.

**SWAN AROUND, TO:** *To meander aimlessly.*

First used in army slang of the 1940s when it described tanks and other vehicles on training manoeuvres when they resembled swans parading the waters in circles and meandering in convoy.

**SWAN SONG:** *A farewell performance.*

Ancient indeed is the belief that the swan sings but once in its life, this being just prior to its death when it sends forth a hauntingly melancholic air. Like many pieces of folklore this idea is erroneous as is the notion that a swan can break a man's arm with one sweep of its mighty wings.

**SWAP HORSES IN MID-STREAM:** *To alter course half-way through a plan.*

An American maxim of the mid 1800s which may or may not be original to Abraham Lincoln who, when making light of his own re-nomination for the Presidency by the Republicans, used the expression in public. The president was thinking of himself as the horse and the Civil War as the stream.

**SWEET FANNY ADAMS/F.A.:** *Euphemistic 'sweet fuck all' – nothing.*

On 24 August 1867 the pathetic remains of eight-year-old Francis – pet name Fanny – Adams were found in a hop-field at Alton in Hampshire; she had likely been raped before being completely hacked up with an axe. The find caused national outrage and a solicitor's clerk, twenty-one year old Frederick Baker, was tried soon after and hanged at Winchester. Among the grimmer humoured sectors of society the sympathetic press's epithet of

'Sweet Fanny Adams' was put to its now-common use because, to put it bluntly, that neatly summed up what was left of her. Not long after the case was concluded the Navy received the first issues of tinned mutton which was promptly christened Fanny Adams, as it was composed of random pieces reconstituted into long blocks. It became the practice to open the tins down one side for, when empty, they made an ideal mess tin which is to this day called a fanny in the Navy.

**SWEET ODOUR OF SANCTITY:** *The stench of hypocrisy.*

But one of the many pagan ideas held dear by the Church in earlier times was the incorruptibility of the corpses of their holy men – those destined for sainthood. Countless are the medieval accounts of the opening of various saints' tombs immediately resulting in the whole city/country being enveloped in a perfumed cloud lasting for years. The bodies, of course, were just as they were when interred years before. A growing fear of their saints becoming confused with or accused of being vampires caused the Church to abandon the foolish notion.

**SWEETNESS AND LIGHT:** *Sarcastically, very friendly.*

Popularized by Matthew Arnold's *Culture and Anarchy* (1869), the current application is a long way removed from the original meaning of intellectual harmony and balance. The usage is first noted in the writings of Philo Judaeus, a philosopher born some time around 10 BC in Alexandria. As were many others, Philo was much influenced by Plato, nicknamed The Athenian Bee for the sweetness of his speech and reasoning, and the two benefits afforded mankind by that creature are sweetness, honey and light from wax candles. There is however also a subtle pun at work here with 'sweetness' representing the sublime and 'light' in its older sense of intellectual perception – enlightenment in other words. Long before Arnold made so much of the expression Swift had made cryptic allusion to its older sense in his *Battle of the Books* (1609) which presented itself as an imaginary work of Aesop discussing the relative merits of the bee and spider – the former representing the Ancients and the latter more modern thinkers and writers. 'The difference is that instead of dirt and poison, we have rather chosen to fill our hives with honey and wax, thus furnishing mankind with the two noblest of things, which are sweetness and light.'

**SWING THE LEAD, TO:** *To malinger.*

When moving through unknown shallows a man would always be posted at the prow of a ship to take constant depth readings whilst the rest of the crew charged about the deck and rigging making alterations in accordance with his readings and the commands from the bridge.

**SWORD OF DAMOCLES:** *An ever-present danger.*

Damocles was a courtier at the palace of Dionysius the Elder, Tyrant of Syracuse, who envied the ruler's position, power and wealth.

To teach Damocles a lesson, the king invited him to a sumptuous banquet over which he, Damocles, would preside. The envious courtier was having a whale of a time until it was pointed out that above his head and hanging by a single thread was a heavy sword suspended point downwards. If the thread broke the sword would skewer him to the seat he so coveted. This, so the story goes, had been done to teach Damocles the lesson that along with the power and position he desired there also came the ever-present danger of assassination from those who would wrest it from him. It is this message which proves the tale apocryphal; any courtier foolish enough to show open jealousy of tyrants like Dionysius met a violent death; they were not regarded as one would a wayward child who needs putting in the picture.

# T

**T, TO FIT TO A:** *An exact fit.*

Whilst the origin is popularly ascribed to the draughtsman's T square, the above usage is noted in the early 1600s which is long before the advent of the item concerned. The term at the source of this phrase is 'tittle' which most usually denoted the cross on a 't' but could also indicate other minor strokes in writing. Basically, the expression alludes to something perfect to use right down to all the 'i's dotted and the 't's crossed.

**TAKE A BATH:** *To be cheated.*

The Yiddish expression '*er haut mikh in bod arayn*', he led me to the bath, was born in the days of mass immigration to the USA when arrivals were deloused and decontaminated after their long, cramped, unhygienic voyage, and many of them complained that their possessions had been rifled the while. The saying must have received an unwelcome boost in the Nazi death camps where Jews were tricked into the gas chambers by being told they were going for decontamination.

**TAKE A DIVE:** *To feign illness or to lose deliberately.*

In the world of boxing, a contender intent on throwing away the fight goes down after a blow which does not really knock him out.

**TAKE A GANDER:** *Take a look.*

Originating in British Forces slang in the early–mid twentieth century, this drew on the frequent neck-craning that typified a goose or gander, and originally described the neck-craning involved in reading over someone's shoulder.

**TAKE A RISE, TO:** *To ridicule someone.*

An expression from angling in which the hunter encourages the quarry to 'rise to the bait' on or near the surface.

**TAKE DOWN A PEG OR TWO, TO:** *To humiliate or teach someone a lesson.*

At the base of the main mast on the old ships of the line were a series of pegs determining the height at which the vessel's colours would fly. The etiquette of the sea demanded that, in the presence of a senior ship, a ship's captain would order his colours to be flown lower down the mast than those of the senior vessel.

**TAKE THE CAKE:** *To carry off the honours.*

This expression, now sometimes used ironically of something that beggars description, was born in America and is an extension from 'take the biscuit'; 'cake' and 'biscuit' were originally interchangeable, (compare the Scottish thin oat biscuits, still called 'oatcakes'). Since the earliest records, cakes and biscuits have been awarded as prizes, the ingredients sometimes indicating the field of excellence, e.g. in Ancient Greece, a biscuit of roast wheat and honey was awarded to the most vigilant of the night watch. The usage itself goes back a long time. Wilfred Blunt's (1840–1922) *Sebastiano* mentions a famous inn-keeper's beautiful daughter who attended the 1610 International Inn-keepers' Conference at Rothenburg-am-Tauber. Her charms were such that the hosting Secretary wrote beside her name on the attendance list: *'Ista capit biscottum* ', That one takes the biscuit.

**TAKE THE GILT OFF THE GINGERBREAD, TO:** *To diminish a pleasure.*

Since 1600 'gingerbread' has been used metaphorically of anything flashy or a person given to show, and it could be that the above alludes to the veneer or 'show' being but the thickness of gold leaf as used to dress dull or base metals. It has also been asserted by some food historians that gingerbread delicacies were quite literally dressed in gold leaf before delivery to the tables of the rich and there is, perhaps inevitably, a suggested origin from the sea where 'gingerbread' described the ornate scrollwork at the prow of a ship. Cast in iron it was painted gold; without such covering it became uninteresting and bland.

**TAKE THE HUMP, TO:** *To take offence.*

Those in ill-humour tend to hunch the shoulders.

**TAKE THINGS IN YOUR STRIDE, TO:** *To accomplish them in unhurried manner.*

Originally said of a good cross-country horse or jumper which remained unfazed by hedges and gates, clearing them without breaking or altering pace, something a horse does by lengthening its stride.

**TAKE TIME BY THE FORELOCK:** *To seize an opportunity.*

One who seizes a forelock of hair on the head of another has him at his mercy, and this expression could have its source in a creation by Lysippus (*c*.360–16 BC), the prolific Greek sculptor, whose statue 'Opportunity' was a figure sporting a head that was bald save for a lock of hair at the front; this is also how Time is personified, indicating that the past (the back of the head) is useless and that only the future can be exploited. The expression is, however, seen by others to lie in the writings of Pittacus of Mitylene (*c*.650–570 BC), whose best-known aphorism is 'Know thine opportunity', or in like statements from the collective fables of Phaedrus, a translator in the employ of Aesop during the first century AD.

**TAKE TO TASK, TO:** *To interrogate or reprimand.*

All but redundant, save in the above, this is an example of 'task' in its very old verbal form meaning to examine for soundness – especially a ship's timbers. In the sixteenth century this phrase meant to assume responsibility for a job – to take the task unto oneself. By extension, a superior could also take on the responsibility of knocking a wayward underling into shape.

**TAKE UMBRAGE, TO:** *To take offence.*

A sister-word of umbrella, the keyword is derived from the Latin '*umbra*', shadow, and alludes to the darkening of the face with rage.

**TAKE WITH A PINCH OF SALT:** *Treat with suspicion.*

A sentiment of great antiquity, the Romans issued a similar caution in the form of '*cum grano salis*', and it is not beyond the realms of possibility that this encapsulates an erudite pun. Even the Romans acknowledged the culture of the Greeks to be on a par with their own and, with the ancient name of Athens being Attica, coined the term Attic salt to describe pithy comment; sharp wit or ponderous sagacity, all add piquancy to conversation as does salt to food. Perhaps the original admonition cautioned the listener to use their wits to assess what they were being told. It is perhaps worth mentioning here that 'attic' fell to its architectural usage after the revival of the neo-classical style for civic buildings and the like. The triangular wall above the colonnade was invariably decorated with classical Grecian figures and came to be called the Attic wall, the term later shifted to the roof-void behind.

**TAKE THE WIND OUT OF SOMEONE'S SAILS, TO:** *To render them as a spent force.*

Still regarded as a legitimate move in yacht racing, the old ships of the line would attempt to attack the enemy from the windward side and use her own sails to block the wind from the other ship which, deprived of drive and manoeuvrability, could be pounded at will.

**TAKEN ABACK:** *To be taken by surprise.*

If the helmsman's attention strays and he does not notice a dramatic change in the wind direction, the ship can start to SAIL TOO CLOSE TO THE WIND. If this happens the sails are knocked flat back against the mast and the ship is stopped in her tracks.

**TAKEN TO THE CLEANERS:** *Robbed of everything.*

One who is taken to the cleaners is led, unsuspecting, into a trap, so there are obvious connections here with CLEAN OUT, and the mastery of the hunter over the quarry. This expression, however, arose fairly recently; it is most likely that the cleaners are the abattoir workers who clean out the slaughtered carcass. However, it is also possible (but less likely) that it is a reference to the commercial cleaning services that came within the reach of ordinary people this century; in the nineteenth century, clothes were laundered in the home.

**TAKES THE BISCUIT:** *That beats everything.*

Biscuits and special cakes containing ingredients such as cinnamon were anciently held to be symbolic of certain virtues or attributes and were given as prizes in a variety of competitions.

**TALK THE HIND LEGS OFF A DONKEY, TO:** *To chatter incessantly.*

When the expression first appeared it did so with the sense of to wheedle or employ a coercive line in talk, and the hind legs of a donkey are the reservoir of its strength, so the above is properly a parallel of 'to charm the birds out of the trees'.

**TALK THROUGH YOUR HAT, TO:** *To waffle, speak rubbish.*

When this emerged in late nineteenth-century America, it held a meaning more akin to 'bull' or hypocrisy and is said to allude to the deliberately projected image of piety feigned by men in church who hold their hats in front of their faces and appear to be deep in prayer.

**TALK TURKEY, TO:** *Hard factual discussion.*

This expression has been noted in American usage from the early part of the nineteenth century when its prime meaning was one of to sweet-talk or wheedle another into a course of action or to get them to do exactly what you wanted. The most likely suggestion is that this derives from the earlier turkey-hunters making gobbling noises to induce the incredibly stupid birds to emerge to respond or divulge their position by returning the call. In business circles the meaning altered slightly to describe the drawing in of a moneyed sucker to be fleeced in a one-sided deal but by the opening of the twentieth century the modern meaning was generally accepted.

**TEACH YOUR GRANDMOTHER TO SUCK EGGS, (DON'T TRY) TO:** *Don't try to teach those older and wiser than yourself.*

Eggs used to be perforated and sucked or blown empty so that the shells could be preserved for a number of uses; Fabergé elevated the craft of decorating them into an art form. A grandmother, apart from being more experienced, would probably also be, in the days when this expression originated, toothless, and therefore more suited to the delicate task of sucking an egg than any young upstart.

**TEAR A STRIP OFF SOMEONE, TO:** *To reprimand them in no uncertain manner.*

RAF slang developed in the 1920 and 30s as an extension of a reprimand being previously known as a rasper for its metaphorical abrasion of the skin. If you tear a strip of cloth from a sheet, or whatever, the resultant noise is not unlike the raspberry as blown in derision.

**TEETOTAL:** *Complete abstinence from alcohol.*

The term is almost certainly of American coinage but seems to have been first applied without specific reference to alcohol or abstinence therefrom. In the form of 'teetotally' the word is noted in the 1807 writing of Parson Mason Locke Weems, the American historian responsible for inventing the cherry-tree yarn for inclusion in his biography of Washington, but doesn't appear in print in Britain until 1834. To quote H.L. Mencken's *The American Language* 'The use of intensifying prefixes and suffixes, often set down as characteristically American, may have been borrowed from the Irish. Examples of such stretch forms are "yes, indeedy" and "teetotal".' This use of 'teetotally' was certainly used in early–mid nineteenth-century Britain and it could well be that the shift to its specific application could have been occasioned by the temperance speeches of one Richard Turner of Preston in Lancashire who was a vehement advocate of total abstinence as opposed to those calling for the shunning of only wines and spirits, so perhaps the Americans may claim the accolade of coinage only in the general sense. There seems to be no hard evidence to support the notion that those taking the Pledge as advocated by Turner placed a 'T' beside their signatures but, either way, his gravestone boasts the legend 'Beneath this stone are deposited the remains of Richard Turner, author of the word 'teetotal' as applied to the abstinence from all intoxicating liquor, [it is interesting in itself that the monumental mason felt the need to indicate application] who departed this life on the 27th day of October, 1846, aged 56 years.'

**TELL IT TO THE MARINES:** *I do not believe it.*

Doubtless all made up by marines, there have been several tales attempting to explain the origin by linking it to events in court wherein the marines' knowledge is validated and praised by the monarch. Most commonly reported as the origin is the following: When regaling Charles II with tales of the wonders of the world, Samuel Pepys mentioned flying fish and was promptly riduculed by the assembled courtiers. A marine officer present announced that he too had seen such creatures, this was a spur for Charles to launch himself on the full seas of a rambling speech hailing the marines as the most widely travelled and knowledgeable of his subjects and solidly announcing that, if anything else was called into doubt, he would give it the acid test by 'telling it to the marines', if they believed it then so would he. Unfortunately, this is hardly in keeping with the sentiment of the phrase which was coined instead by sailors in their disdain for the military, especially the marines whom they had to transport and live with from time to time. The thrust of the expression jibes at the supposed gullibility of the marines, not their worldly wisdom.

**TENDER MERCIES:** *Cruelty.*

Proverb 12:10 advises that: 'The righteous man regardeth the life of his beast, but [even] the tender mercies of the wicked are cruel.'

**TENDERFOOT:** *A novice.*

Coined in the Californian gold-rush to describe new arrivals at the diggings whose feet were soon raw from the effort of breaking in their new boots.

**TERMINOLOGICAL INEXACTITUDE:** *Popularly, a lie.*

Churchill never used this phrase as a circumlocution for a lie; he used the expression in complete seriousness. In 1906 the plight of the Chinese workers in the Transvaal was mentioned and their condition described as one of slavery. Replying as Under Secretary at the Colonial Office, Churchill refuted the allegation as follows: 'The conditions of the Transvaal ordinance under which Chinese Labour is now being carried on do not, in my opinion, constitute a state of slavery. A labour contract into which men enter voluntarily for a limited and brief period, under which they are paid wages which they consider adequate, under which they are not bought or sold and from which they can obtain relief on payment of seventeen pounds ten shillings, the cost of their passage, may not be a healthy or proper contract, but it cannot in the opinion of His Majesty's government be classified as slavery in the extreme acceptance of the word without some risk of terminological inexactitude.'

**THAT RINGS A BELL:** *That connects in the memory.*

Argument over which type of bell is here at issue is largely pointless in that the meaning is pretty clear. If a guess must be made then perhaps it is the bell at the top of the fairground equipment requiring the punter to thump the base with a mallet to drive the shuttle up to ring the bell at the top.

**THAT WON'T WASH:** *That will not do.*

It is unclear whether this is a reference to a poorly dyed garment which will run or a prospector's expression in that 'washing' was synonymous with 'panning', so the expression could allude to a sample of dirt that reveals nothing of value.

**THAT'LL BE THE DAY:** *That day will never come.*

In the early stages of WW1 this was used by British troops as a sceptical comment on a rather unpleasant German rallying song '*Song of Hate*', which included repeated references to '*der Tag*' (the day), in this case *the* day when the Germans would really come to the fore and smash Britain. Its continued usage was considerably helped by the 1957 hit single of the same title by Buddy Holly, and the incorporation of that hit as the theme music of the 1973 film of the same title, starring Ringo Starr and David Essex.

**THAT'S THE TICKET:** *Exactly what is required.*

Opinion is divided as to whether this is an altered form of 'etiquette' or simple reference to a winning lottery ticket or some such similar analogy. The roots of 'ticket' lie in the French '*estiquette*' as taken from '*estiquer*', to stick, since the do's and don'ts of the day were once posted or stuck up in a royal court for all to read and observe. Since manners usually get one what is desired, perhaps 'that's etiquette' (in the sense of that is what is required of you) became 'that's the ticket'. The diplomats' 'protocol' has similar origin in the Greek '*protos*', first, and '*kolla*', glue. Ambassadors visiting courts were given booklets of information to help them avoid *faux pas* and glued in the front was a page informing them of the seating arrangements of forthcoming discussions and formal banquets.

**THICK AND FAST:** *Anything arriving in abundance, especially aggressively.*

If there is one specific origin for this it could well be a reference to archery fire dispatched at a maximum rate. The sixteenth-century version was 'thick and threefold' and a competent archer was supposed to be able to maintain a rate of fire which would keep three arrows in flight at any one time.

**THICK AND THIN, TO FOLLOW SOMEONE THROUGH:** *To remain loyal no matter what.*

The most ardent competitor in a WILD GOOSE CHASE would follow the leader through 'thick', forested or wooded areas, and through 'thin', the open countryside.

**THIMBLE-RIGGING:** *Cheating.*

Before the prevalence of playing cards enabling the cheats to dupe the public with endless rounds of 'find the lady', something similar was done with three thimbles and a pea which were furiously moved around leaving the dupe to guess which one concealed the pea.

**THIN END OF THE WEDGE, THE:** *The first introduction of weakness.*

A simple reference to the loggers' wedge as used to split log and rails.

**THIN ON THE GROUND:** *Scarce.*

Originally a hunting expression referring to the strength of the quarry's scent on the trail.

**THINK THAT THE MOON IS MADE OF GREEN CHEESE, TO:** *To be foolish and gullible.*

Green cheese is used here to mean unmatured cheese, or what is now called fromage frais.

**THIRD DEGREE, THE:** *Intensive even brutal interrogation.*

The highest order of Freemasonry is that of Master Mason, otherwise known as the Third Degree. Those aspiring to this estate are subjected to the most stringent tests and gruelling interviews.

**THIRD RATE:** *Very substandard.*

Although the term is quite expressive there is a specific origin in the old ships of the line, classified in three rates according to their cannon power. First Rate carried up to 110; Second Rate about ninety, and Third Rate about seventy cannon. Although there were other and lower ratings, Third Rate was the smallest ship allowed into line engagement.

**THIRD WORLD:** *Poverty-ridden countries, primarily those in Africa and Asia.*

Coined in 1956, some say by the American State Department, others by the French National Assembly, this did not at first carry any connotations of poverty as the designation applied in general to any minor country which had not yet aligned itself with either the Western or Communist power bloc. Whether of French or American coinage the expression was doubtlessly of Western origin so that is the First World, the Communist bloc the Second World, and the 'undecideds', the Third World.

**THIRTY PIECES OF SILVER:** *To betray another.*

This is an allusion to the money supposedly paid Judas for his alleged betrayal. That any such event occurred is unlikely in the extreme since Jesus was moving openly about the city claiming to be in conversation with angels and proclaiming himself the Bridegroom of Zion, the title anciently afforded the human sacrifice, treated like a king, but also guarded by his twelve zodiacal companions who ensured he went through with the whole business. If the Sanhedrin wanted Jesus arrested they would simply have issued the order, not paid out the modern equivalent of £2,500 for an identifying kiss when everyone knew who he was. The sum alleged has a special significance in that this was the price demanded by Aramaic law for the accidental killing of another's slave. The significantly flawed gospel allegedly written by Matthew is attempting to further debase the alleged betrayal by stating Judas to value Jesus on a par with a dead slave. (*See also*: POTTERS FIELD.)

**THREE SHEETS IN THE WIND:** *Very drunk.*

At sea, only ropes over one inch in diameter are called ropes; anything less is a sheet and the ones in question here are those attached to a square sail and used to trim. When a sheet is slackened off to such degree that it no longer exercises any control it is said to be 'in the wind' and should both controlling sheets be so slackened the craft would be deprived of most, if not all, driver and steerage and lurch about drunkenly at the mercy of the prevailing seas. As stated a square sail has but two sheets so the above is an overstatement.

**THROW A CURVE:** *To disconcert with unexpected action.*

In American baseball, a curve-ball is spun and executes a parabolic deviation on its way to the batter.

**THROW DOWN THE GAUNTLET:** *Issue a challenge.*

In medieval days, a knight challenged a rival to battle by simply throwing down a gauntlet at his feet; when the gauntlet was picked up, the challenge was accepted.

**THROW IN THE TOWEL/ SPONGE:** *To capitulate.*

Long established in boxing circles is the tradition of a vanquished fighter's second or trainer throwing either sponge or towel into the ring to call a halt to the fight.

**THROW THE BOOK AT:** *To punish every possible misdemeanour.*

The book is the police Charge Book or, possibly, some imagined book listing all crimes and their punishments.

**THROW YOUR HAT INTO THE RING:** *To make an open challenge.*

After a nineteenth-century bare-knuckle fight it was generally the rule that any spectator who fancied their chance at defeating the champion could throw his hat into the ring and try for the purse.

**THUMBS UP:** *Approval or encouragement.*

This, and the popular explanation of the gesture on which it is based, is a classic example of Hollywood rewriting history so well that the celluloid version becomes more accepted than the truth. Indeed, several writings have been reinterpreted to fit the falsehood. The story goes that the bloodthirsty crowd in the Roman arena held their thumbs upright if they wished a vanquished gladiator to be allowed to live and fight another day, but turned them down if he was to die. The presiding emperor read the signal and then himself gave such sign to the victor as he saw fit. This is all very neat and tidy, but how was the emperor meant to be able to conduct a thumb-count between such similar signals made by the crowd opposite? In truth the crowd held their thumbs out in any old direction, most often moved in a stabbing movement to the chest if they craved blood or kept their hand in their laps if they wished mercy. This way there could be little confusion and the emperor could gauge the mood by the number of waving arms.

**TICK OFF, TO:** *To reprimand.*

When the time comes to parade a miscreant before the commanding officer a senior NCO will stand by with a list of the names and place a tick beside each as their punishment is decided.

**TICK, ON:** *On credit.*

Noted as early as the 1600s, this is an elliptic of the ticket kept as a record of debts incurred.

**TIDE OVER, TO:** *To give just sufficient help.*

Sometimes a vessel is blocked in a particular course by sand-bars too high for her draught and must wait for the rising tide to lift her over.

**TIE/HANG ONE ON, TO:** *To drink to excess.*

An Americanism alluding to a horse with its nose-bag tied permanently to his face like the drinker with a glass. The expression first appeared as 'to tie a bag on'.

**TIE THE KNOT, TO:** *To marry.*

Although countless cultures feature a knot-tying ritual in the marriage ceremony as symbolic of the two life-thread of fate intertwining, the above seems to derive from the sixteenth century 'To tie with the tongue the knot that may not be undone with the teeth'.

**TIED TO THE APRON STRINGS:** *Said of any man dominated by a woman, especially a wife or mother.*

Although the allusion is fairly plain it was much reinforced in the 1600s by the legal concept of apron-string tenure by which a man held an estate only as long as he remained married to the woman concerned; upon her death all rights were lost. Thus many families protected their daughters by making such dowry and the men they married had to TOE THE LINE or cease to play lord of the manor.

**TILL KINGDOM COME:** *For ever.*

In the Bible much is made of the establishing of the kingdom of God here on earth which is supposed to happen at some unspecified point in the future. The above was doubtlessly coined by the less convinced who applied it in the sense of 'never'.

**TILT AT WINDMILLS, TO:** *To assail non-existent difficulties.*

Don Quixote, the eponymous hero of Cervantes' novel, was prone to attacking windmills under the misapprehension they were giants of evil intent.

**TINHORN:** *Anyone or anything inferior or corrupt.*

An Americanism for any huckster or carpetbagger, this originally denoted an itinerant gambler moving from saloon to saloon ripping off the locals. The reference is to his tin-mug serving as a dice-shaker; the more sophisticated gamester employed one made of horn.

**TO THE MANNER BORN:** *Accustomed to the fashion.*

Still frequently seen in the incorrect form of 'to the manor born' used to mean native to the district, this is taken from Shakespeare's *Hamlet.* The scene is the castle at Elsinore wherein is taking place a fearful drunken racket off-stage. Haratio asks Hamlet just what the Devil is going on, to be told that every time the King empties his goblet, drums and trumpets are sounded. Hamlet goes on to say: 'But to my mind, though I am native here and to the manner born, it is a CUSTOM MORE HONOURED IN THE BREACH THAN THE OBSERVANCE.'

**TOADY, TO:** *To behave in an obsequious manner.*

An early nineteenth-century corruption of the seventeenth-century 'toadeat', the 'title' given to a travelling charlatan's assistant who had the unenviable job of swallowing or pretending to swallow a small toad. This done, his master could then 'prove' the value of his bogus medicines to the gullible crowd who believed toads to be lethal. The toady would take some of the patent nostrum and miraculously survive. Other assistants of more reputable traders earned their keep by holding up the goods for the crowd to see. As shops evolved these upholders or upholderers specialized in displaying goods against pleasing backdrops of cloth. In time they specialized even more with cloth and their name changed to upholsterers.

**TOE THE LINE, TO:** *To follow the rules.*

Common in military circles since the turn of the century this alludes to troops drawing themselves up on the parade ground and making sure their boots make a nice neat line in front of the sergeant.

**TOE-RAG:** *Any despicable individual.*

Racist attempts to hail this as a corruption of Tuareg are groundless and the term was already well established in the mid 1800s as a pejorative term for a tramp or any so impoverished that instead of shoes their feet were bound with strips of rag. Interestingly enough, the parallel 'toe-ragger' is common in Australasia but wholly unconnected as it derives instead from the Maori '*tua rika rika*', a slave or dishonoured person.

**TOMMY-ROT:** *Rubbish of any description.*

Until its abolition in 1831 the Truck System was a scandal by which employers paid the work-force largely in tokens that could only be spent at the company stores. Needless to say, this led to sub-standard goods being sold at inflated prices to a captive market forced to buy all their food at these outlets. A likely corruption of 'tummy', the name 'Tommy' was given to basics such as bread and the workers' regard for the standard of tommy they received for their labours eventually produced tommy-rot.

**TONGUE-IN-CHEEK:** *Not seriously.*

At the opening of the nineteenth century the forcing of the tongue into the left cheek served as a clandestine signal of disbelief or disregard for the one talking at the time. This would place the above parallel with other gestures associated with the left, or sinister, side, such as a jerking of the thumb over the left shoulder in a hitch-hiking motion, but the above had the advantage of secrecy in that it could be made whilst appearing to turn to another to nod in approval. From use such as this overtones of taking the mickey crept in through the assembled company encouraging the talker to continue merely to be laughed at later.

**TOP DRAWER:** *Of the best quality.*

In the typical Victorian chest of drawers the top two were the smallest and used to store items of jewellery and the like.

**TOSH:** *Verbal rubbish.*

In the nineteenth century a tosher was a man who walked the sewers of London and used a pole to retrieve any items blocking the central channel. His title came, possibly, from the gypsy '*tov*', to wash, either because the items retrieved were those washed in by flooding or because they were later washed and cleaned up for sale. Either way, the merchandise was not held in high regard. The use of 'tash' amongst a certain type of man is likely from the same source as is the Gypsy or dialect '*tosh*' meaning neat and dandy, as is a person after being washed and smartened up.

**TOUCH AND GO:** *Treading the line between success and failure.*

As does the keel of a ship moving across submerged reefs and sandbars that exactly match her draught.

**TOUCH SOMEONE ON THE RAW, TO:** *To insult or offend them.*

An expression from the stable and the reaction of a horse when the brush or curry-comb hits broken skin.

**TOUCH WOOD:** *Exclamation to ensure luck.*

A very old custom and expression dating back to the days when trees were believed to be the dwelling-place of assorted deities whose help in any venture could be enlisted by the laying of one's hands on to the tree of the relevant god or goddess.

**TOUCHED, A BIT:** *Subnormal; a bit simple-minded.*

The notion that all the world's fools are specially chosen for the role by God is both ancient and bizarre. Those he selects he simply touches with his celestial hand. This idea is reflected in the use of 'CRETIN'.

**TRIP THE LIGHT FANTASTIC, TO:** *To move with agility, physically or metaphorically.*

A great peculiarity indeed which for some reason has been saved from obscurity in John Milton's 'L'Allegro' (1632) which includes the lines: 'Come and trip it as you go/On the light fantastic toe.' Whilst there never has been a specific dance called the Fantastic, it has been conjectured that Milton substituted the term for 'dance' itself, in that fantastic steps are undertaken.

**TROJAN HORSE:** *A device to mask true intent.*

It is said that the Greeks laid siege to the city of Troy but found it impossible to take and so feigned retreat leaving behind a massive wooden horse which the foolish Trojans dragged into the city presuming it to be a tribute to their fortitude. As every schoolboy knows, a number of Greek soldiers were hiding inside and they crept out at night, bumped off the guard and opened the gates to admit the entire Greek army. Unfortunately, the Greeks did not lay siege to the city but made camp quite some distance away on the shore since they did not conduct siege warfare, knew nothing of its technique nor were they possessed of any attendant equipment. The yarn collapses entirely with the knowledge that the city was a mere 200 yards at its widest point and surrounded by walls twenty feet high and fifteen feet thick which allowed gateways to be no more than six or eight feet. Any wooden horse built in proportion to such a height might have accommodated one rather small chap but that would be all.

**TROT SOMETHING OUT, TO:** *To re-issue something already hackneyed.*

An expression of horse-trading circles alluding to prospective sales being trotted out before the buyers and the same old nags being brought out time after time.

**TROUBLE SHOOTER, A:** *Brutish type brought in to resolve matters.*

An expression from the range wars of the American West and descriptive of hired guns brought in as required.

**TRUMP UP CHARGES, TO:** *To invent allegations.*

Adopted from the French in the fifteenth century when their verb '*tromper*', to play the trumpet, held a slang meaning of to boast, lie or cheat. Although it can no longer be ascertained, it is likely this meaning arose from the vaunting blowing of trumpets to announce the arrival of dignitaries.

**TUMBLE A PLAN, TO:** *To figure it out.*

An elliptic of 'understumble', a humorous play on 'understand'.

**TURKEY:** *An abject failure.*

A relatively modern Americanism first noted in theatrical jargon of the 1920s denoting any show that flopped. The turkey came to stand for failure through its monumental stupidity; these birds have even been known to drown in rainstorms through looking upwards with their beaks open to see where the water is coming from.

**TURN A BLIND EYE:** *Studiously to ignore.*

At the Battle of Copenhagen in 1801, Horatio Nelson (1758–1805) reputedly disregarded an order to disengage by putting his telescope to his blind eye and averring that he saw no such flag signal from Admiral Sir Hyde Parker's ship. In reality, Parker had previously arranged with Nelson that he could use his own discretion if such a signal was hoisted. The farce with the telescope was to wind up Colonel Stewart who was standing nearby and was unaware of the over-rider. Whilst on the subject of Nelson's eyes it is worth mention that though one did receive serious injury from a powder flash and was thereby grossly impaired, he never actually lost an eye nor wore an eye patch.

**TURN CAT IN PAN:** *Skilfully to reverse everything or change sides.*

Although the derivation remains obscure, the best suggestion is the French '*tourner ôte en peine*', to change sides when danger threatens.

**TURN OVER NEW LEAF, TO:** *To begin afresh.*

A reference to the long-abandoned copybook once used in schools which, if messed up, required the pupil to turn over a page, or leaf, and start the writing exercise all over again.

**TURN THE CORNER:** *To get through the worst part.*

This is probably from the game of cribbage in which a player scores his points by moving a peg along one line of perforations in a board, then back down another to the end. When the corner is turned, the player is on the home stretch.

**TURN THE TABLES, TO:** *To reverse the situation to advantage.*

In the fourteenth century 'table' held a specific meaning of a gaming board as might be used for chess or draughts; the above phrase rests on the notion of one player falling to disadvantage and reversing the board to change sides.

**TURN UP FOR THE BOOKS:** *A surprise event.*

An old bookmakers' expression for an unexpected showing of a last-minute contestant who turns up at an event and must therefore be included on the books.

**TURNCOAT:** *A traitor.*

Widely used since the sixteenth century this alludes to one of shallow principles who might keep a reversible coat so as to quickly change his colours to suit the standard of the winning side.

**TWAT:** *The vagina or an unpleasant person.*

A word which has been in general use since the 1600s and derived either from the Old Norse '*thveit*' or the English '*twachylle*', a passage. Interestingly, the word occupies a special place in literary lore in that it serves as a salutory reminder to all never to use a word until sure of its proper meaning. In 'Vanity of Vanities', a poem of 1660, there appear the lines 'They talk't of his having a Cardinal's hat/They'd sent him as soon an Old Nun's Twat.'. Here, 'nun' is the old synonym for a prostitute, so Shakespeare's 'get thee to a nunnery' does not instruct the lady to take holy vows. Having read this work Robert Browning was left with the impression that 'twat' was an alternative term for a nun's wimple and so included the word in his *Pippa Passes* (1841) – 'The owls and bats/Cowls and Twats/Monks and nuns/In a cloister's mood.' Needless to say, he was mortified when he discovered the actual meaning.

**TWERP:** *Any idiot.*

An unlikely eponym but none the less based on the name of T.W. Earp of Exeter College, Oxford, who matriculated in the Michaelmas term of 1911. To his admirers he was the last of the great decadents but he also seems to have inspired the extreme hatred and derision from the rugby and rowing fraternity who used his name to create 'twerp'. The author Tolkien (whose name incidentally means 'foolhardy'), who was up at Oxford not long after Earp, and indeed remained to assume certain professorships, recalls the man in the following extract taken from one of his letters: 'He lived in Oxford at the time we lived in Pusey Street, rooming with Walton, the composer, and going about with T.W. Earp, the original twerp.'

**TWIG, TO:** *To fathom out.*

An English rendition of the Irish '*tuigim*', I understand.

**TWO-TIME LOSER:** *Someone with nothing more to lose.*

In the American penal code any felon going down for the third offence stays down for life. Equally common is 'three-time loser' denoting one who has had their lot. Both designations are most frequently heard in Britain denoting failures.

# U

**UGLY DUCKLING:** *Anything seemingly ugly but full of latent beauty or potential.*

Allusive to the old fable of a swan's egg inadvertently hatched out by a duck who did not like the look of the product of such labour. The rest of her brood gave the interloper a hard time until the tatty down fell away to reveal splendid white plumage.

**UMPTEEN:** *Any unknown but great number.*

WW1 signals' parlance based on the earlier 'umty' as formed from 'ummm' used as a pondering sound.

**UNCLE SAM:** *America.*

Inspired by the characteristics of one Samuel Wilson (1766–1854), a well-established and respected meat-packer of Troy, New York. A prominent citizen of the state, he was appointed Government Inspector of provisions for the Army at the onset of the War of 1812 with Britain, and on 2 October 1812 a delegation visited his own plant in Troy. The group included Governor Daniel D. Tomkins of New York; when he inquired of their guide what the 'EA-US' stamped on every barrel stood for, he was informed in joke that this represented 'Elbert Anderson – Uncle Sam'. Anderson was the contractor for whom Wilson worked and Wilson himself was known to one and all as Uncle Sam by dint of his easy going and avuncular manner. The story was repeated round every barrel of provisions sent out from Troy and by the close of the war 'Uncle Sam' was well-established as the embodiment of the national character. In 1961 Congress passed a resolution to finally adopt Sam Wilson as a symbol of the country and everything it stood for.

**UNDER THE AEGIS:** *Patronage.*

The Greek '*aegis*' means goatskin. Mythology has it that Zeus was suckled by a goat named Amalthaea. When the animal died, Hephaestos used its skin as a covering for Zeus's shield which later became the symbol of his umbrella of power under which the lesser gods operated.

**UNDER THE AUSPICES:** *Patronage.*

Built on the Latin '*avis*', a bird and '*specere*', to observe, this originally referred to the prediction of events by interpreting the presence and flight directions of birds. In a war, only the commander-in-chief was allowed to foretell the outcome of impending battle by 'taking the auspices', the advantage of which was two-fold; firstly, it prevented anyone deliberately taking the edge off the troops' morale by forecasting defeat and secondly, it ensured all glory to the commander. If a junior officer won honour in the battle, he was held to have achieved it 'under the auspices' of his superior.

**UNDER THE COUNTER:** *Clandestine, illicit.*

Used today mainly of pornographic material, this was born in WW2 Britain where unscrupulous traders kept rationed or extremely scarce goods hidden under the counter, reserved for customers who were willing to pay black-market prices for them.

**UNDER THE ROSE:** *In confidence.*

This is based in ancient mythology and the story of Venus who was discovered in a compromising situation by Harpocrates, the god of silence. Cupid, the progeny of Venus and Mercury, managed to buy the silence of Harpocrates with a rose that never faded; later Harpocrates was always identified by this rose. Because of this story, the ceilings of the rooms set aside for diplomatic discussions in the palaces of old were traditionally decorated with roses as a constant reminder that what was said in the chamber was, quite literally, under the rose.

**UNDER THE THUMB:** *Dominated.*

When the angler has hooked his fish, the thumb is used as a brake on the line to allow the quarry to run as required.

**UNDER THE WEATHER:** *Slightly ill or indisposed.*

In all likelihood this is a maritime expression built on the destination of those unused to the motion of a ship at sea who disappear below, quite literally under the weather.

**UNDERGROUND MOVEMENTS:** *Clandestine organizations.*

This began during the slave-era of America as the Abolitionists were setting up a rescue system for escaped slaves. Because the railroads were then new and opening up the country, the Abolitionists called their organization the Underground Railroad, extending this jargon with safe-houses being called stations and guides named conductors. The term resurfaced during WW2 to describe the networks helping Allied military personnel escape from Occupied Europe.

**UNTIL THE COWS COME HOME:** *A very long wait indeed.*

This has been in general use since the sixteenth century when dairy herds worked on a far more natural cycle than today when cows are milked daily. Under normal conditions the herd would be allowed a dry spell and would thus not come in from pasture for quite some time.

**UP AND DOWNER:** *A really good row.*

This originally seems to have been ships' signals officers parlance in the days of semaphore when the rapid exchange of information between two ships called for the constant raising and lowering of flags.

**UP THE POLE:** *Insane or eccentric.*

This is certainly noted in Army slang of the late nineteenth century when it then meant of high repute and doubtless alluded to the regimental colours flying from the flag-pole. As to the now accepted usage it has been suggested that the pole at issue here is the mast on a ship and the Army's long-standing suspicion regarding the sanity of sailors, especially those who climb high up the mast and into the tops. Perhaps the insane-looking grimaces on the faces carved onto a totem pole have some influence.

**UP THE SPOUT:** *Pregnant; lost; damaged.*

In the Army a rifle is so described when fully loaded with one round in the breech ready to fire, as is the pregnant woman perceived as 'loaded'. The other senses derive from the world of pawnbroking and items taken in pledge being sent up the dumb waiter – the spout – to the depository.

**UPPER CRUST, THE:** *The upper echelons of society.*

At the formal banqueting table of bygone days the loaves were torn lengthwise and the crisp, more tasty upper sections went to the head of the table.

**UPSHOT OF A MATTER, THE:** *The essence thereof.*

At the opening of the sixteenth century 'upshot' denoted the final arrow fired in a competition but later came to mean the highest scoring arrow in each round and no matter how many arrows fired, that closest to the actual centre settled the matter.

**UPSTAGE SOMEONE, TO:** *To show them in a poor light.*

This denoted the part of a theatrical stage furthest from the audience to where a vain actor could move forcing all others on stage to turn their backs to the audience to deliver their lines.

**USE YOUR LOAF:** *Employ common sense.*

Comes from rhyming slang – loaf of bread = head.

# W

**WAISTER:** *An idler.*

Through associations with the wasting of time this is frequently seen as and understood to be 'waster' but the term arose on board ships where the injured and sick were allowed to remain in the waist of the ship, that part of the upper deck between the forecastle and quarter-deck, and concentrate on light duties such as rope-mending and the like. It was a malingerer's objective to spend as much time in the waist as he could.

**WALLY:** *An idiot.*

The countless eponymous claims put forward for the above are all groundless and spurious – if any specific name is involved here then this would be Walter employed in much the same way as CHARLIE or DICK. Many favour Scottish origin and if this be the case then '*peerie-wallie*', pale, wan, and vapid, is a likely contender. But is there any need to look past 'wallie', 'wally', or 'wally-o' in use in the United States since the 1920s; 'Some wally tried to horn in on our gang' – *Philadelphia Evening Bulletin* 8 March 1920. Originally this applied to a dandy or foppish Italian and seems based on the Italian dialect '*uaglio*' meaning something like a pipsqueak or runt. By the 1960s, when 'wally' was establishing itself over here, the American usage had lost all racial overtones and denoted any ineffectual male or abject failure.

**WARM THE COCKLES OF THE HEART:** *To warm to the very core.*

The marine cockle is similar in shape and function to the heart. It sits on the ocean floor, pumping like a heart, processing water through its body to extract the microscopic life-forms on which it feeds. Significantly, the zoological name for the cockle is 'cardium'.

**WARTS AND ALL:** *Fair portrayal, including faults.*

When Sir Peter Lely was commissioned to paint Oliver Cromwell the subject was all too aware that portraits of the rich and powerful tended to be overkind in that the artist wished not only to be paid but also to survive long enough to spend his money. In his letter to Lely Cromwell wrote: 'I desire you would use all your skill to paint my picture truly like me, and not to flatter me at all; but remark all the roughnesses, pimples, warts and everything as you see me, otherwise I will not pay a farthing for it.'

**WASH YOUR HANDS OF A MATTER, TO:** *To shed all responsibility.*

As Pilate did of the fate of Jesus, the public washing of one's hands was a common ritual throughout the ancient world when someone wished to publicly distance themselves from some situation or other.

**WASH-OUT, A:** *A complete failure.*

Since WW1, and possibly before, wash-out was Army slang for a shot taken on the range that missed the target completely. The marker in the bunker below the targets indicated this by waving his disk-topped pointer from side to side across the face of the target which was likened to his washing its face.

**WAX SOMEONE, TO:** *To defeat them soundly.*

A simple extension of 'to polish them off'.

**WAY OUT IN THE LEFT FIELD, TO BE:** *To have grossly misinterpreted the situation.*

In both cricket and baseball the fielders on the left of the pitch are positioned well back from play and as such are further out of touch than other team members.

**WE ARE NOT AMUSED:**

Queen Victoria is alleged to have made this remark when she caught one of her grooms-in-waiting, the Hon. Alexander Grantham Yorke, in the act of imitating her in a bad mood, but Princess Alice recalled in 1978 that she had asked her grandmother about it and the Queen replied that she had never said anything of the kind.

**WEAR IT, WILL OR WILL NOT:** *Whether or not equipment will take the strain or a person accept a situation.*

If a square-rigger found herself in extremely rough seas and unable to tack the helmsman would be ordered to 'wear' the ship by putting her stern-up to the wind. This 'wear' appears to be a variant of 'veer'. If this solved the problem then 'she would wear it' but if the seas were too rough and began breaking over the stern then she wouldn't wear it.

**WEAR SACKCLOTH AND ASHES, TO:** *To be abjectly penitent.*

Throughout the Bible reference is made to the ancient Hebrew custom of donning sackcloth garments and covering the head with ashes to indicate total humility when attending major religious festivals of cleansing and penitence. The use of sackcloth is similar to the use of hair-shirts worn by later religious fundamentalists who were unhappy when comfortable. The ashes had a double significance in that they symbolized purity for their use in filtration beds and their association with fire was perceived as the great purger of all things mortal.

**WEAR YOUR HEART ON YOUR SLEEVE, TO:** *To make open show of one's affections.*

In the days of chivalry, it was the custom for a knight's inamorata to give him something she herself wore, a 'favour' which was often a scarf which he tied around his elbow before taking the field or entering the joust. This showed he fought as her champion and was tantamount to a public admission of a romantic liaison.

**WEATHER/RIDE THE STORM, TO:** *To endure iniquities.*

Any ship caught by a storm will strike all sail and try to ride the waves until respite. A gambler leaving winnings on the table for a repeat bet will likewise tell the croupier to 'let it ride'.

**WELL HEELED:** *Rich.*

Another example of a person's situation being judged by the state of their footwear. Conversely, the poor are DOWN AT HEEL, SLIPSHOD or ON THEIR UPPERS.

**WELSH ON A BET, TO:** *To not pay.*

A legacy from the nineteenth century when relationships with the Welsh were not what they are today. This stands alongside other racial slurs – FRENCH leaves, DUTCH treat – the only other example mocking the Welsh being 'welsh rabbit' to describe cheese on toast. Rabbit was pauper's fare and the implication was that the Welsh were so poor that they could not even afford this. Perhaps prompted by either ignorance or delicate sensibilities, some menus present the incorrect form of 'Welsh rarebit'.

**WET BEHIND THE EARS:** *Extremely immature.*

The last places to dry on a new-born calf are the deep indentations behind the ears.

**WETBACK:** *Any Mexican.*

Properly this only applies to those entering America illegally having swum the Rio Grande.

**WHAT THE DICKENS!:** *Exclamation of surprise or anger.*

The name was chosen simply as a suitable euphemism for the Devil, and attempts to present it as a contraction of 'devilkins' are to no avail. As for any associations with the celebrated author, the OED records the expression in use as early as 1598 in Shakespeare's *The Merry Wives of Windsor* Act 3, Scene 2.

**WHEELER-DEALER:** *Entrepreneur with various interests.*

From gambling circles wherein it described a player as game for the roulette wheel as for the cards.

**WHEELS WITHIN WHEELS:** *Convoluted machinations; petty politics.*

A misunderstanding of the passage at Ezekiel 1:15–17 which talks of a vision of four wheels set one inside each other and pointing in various directions so the structure could move where it willed. The vision was intended to portray the omnipresence of God not earthly cunning.

**WHEN IN ROME:** *To observe local tradition.*

Reference to an apocryphal conversation which supposedly took place between Saints Monica, Augustine and Ambrose, the latter being asked advice on points of religious etiquette in that Rome observed a fast ignored in Milan. Ambrose replied 'When I am at Milan, I do as they do at Milan; but when I go to Rome, I do as Rome does.'

**WHERE'S THE BEEF? :** *There is no substance in what you say.*

In 1983, Wendy's, one of America's leading hamburger chains, mounted a TV commercial in which an outraged old lady, ill-advisedly patronizing a non-Wendy establishment which served buns with salad and little else, furiously demanded of the manager: 'Where's the beef?' and the expression became a by-word. Walter Mondale used it during a televised political debate to ridicule the ideas of his opponent, Gary Hart, and when Clara Peller, who had played the part of the old lady, died in 1987, Alistair Cooke devoted his 'Letter from America' to her and to the expression.

**WHIPPING BOY:** *One punished for another's sins.*

From ancient Greece until the reign of Charles I, the sons of royalty all had a commoner sit beside them in class so the teacher had someone to beat for the transgressions of the prince whom he could only touch under pain of death. This seemingly fruitless practice was of far more benefit to the commoner than the prince in that the former gained an education open to but a few. If it matters, Charles I's surrogate was called Mungo Murray.

**WHISTLE-STOP TOUR:** *Lightening tour of minor venues after major ones have been covered.*

In the jargon of nineteenth-century America railroad men a whistle-stop was any small town where the train did not make scheduled stops. Anyone wishing to board the train had to flag it down, such signal being acknowledged by the engineer's whistle, and anyone wishing to get off at such a place had to tell the conductor who pulled the communication cord attached to the engineer's whistle to let him know to stop.

**WHITE ELEPHANT:** *Anything monumentally useless.*

It is said that, when offended by a courtier, the old kings of Siam would make them a present of one of his sacred white elephants, the cost of upkeep being ruinous. The royal gift could not be refused and the present was worse than useless, but this yarn does not hold water for three reasons; first, the kings of Siam were not the most subtle of chaps – if you offended them they killed you; secondly there is no record of any such incident taking place, and thirdly there is no such thing as a white elephant. The designation is likely born of a blending of a European's general amazement at the pampering of the sacred elephants of Siam and the Siamese Order of the Knights of the White Elephant. Even albino elephants show grey and the so-called white rhino is a distortion of the Afrikaans '*wijd*', broad or wide, reference to the animals broad lips used for grazing; both the white and black rhino are in fact a dirty grey-brown.

**WHITED SEPULCHRE:** *A hypocrite.*

In the book of Matthew 23–27, an analogy is drawn by Jesus between the hypocrisy of the Pharisees and nearby burial chambers and tombs which were beautifully whitewashed on the outside but charnel houses within. 'Ye are like unto whited sepulchres, which indeed appear beautiful outward, but are full of dead men's bones, and of all uncleanness.' To the ancient Hebrew any contact with the dead or that which housed them was strictly taboo so sepulchres were painted white to stand out as a warning to travellers who, strange to the area, might inadvertently lean up against the wall of a sepulchre or settle down to eat in its shade.

**WHO PAYS THE FERRYMAN?:** *Who has to bear the ultimate cost?*

The final payment in Greek mythology was that demanded by Charon, the ghostly ferryman who carried the souls of the departed across the rivers Styx and Acheron to the Elysian fields.

**WHOLE BALL OF WAX, THE:** *Everything.*

Definitely something of a mystery with only two plausible explanations. It could be a corruption of 'the whole bailiwick', a district under the charge of a bailie or bailiff or it could derive from a long established legal ritual involved in the dividing up of parcels of land between qualifying heirs. The details of each lot are written on pieces of paper which are then screwed up into little balls and coated in wax to prevent their being read by those who lined up to take pot luck selecting one each from a hat. Whatever their choice turned out to be, that was the matter settled.

**WHOLE KIT AND CABOODLE:** *The whole collection.*

Commonly perceived as a blend of 'kit' as meaning personal possessions and the Dutch '*boedel*', household goods and furniture, as describing a family on the move LOCK, STOCK AND BARREL.

**WHOLE SHEBANG, THE:** *Everything.*

An early–mid nineteenth-century term for a crude shed or shelter and possibly a dialect distortion of the Irish '*shebeen*' since 'shebang' would also denote an illegal drinking haunt.

**WHOLE SHOOTING MATCH, THE:** *Everything.*

A nineteenth-century American frontier shooting contest was a mobile affair moving from venue to venue for different types of target. When the shooters moved so too did the officials, along with all observers and interested parties.

**WIDOW'S PEAK:** *Sharply pointed and descending hairline at centre-forehead.*

So named for its being reminiscent of the profile of a rather tight-fitting hat worn by widows in Tudor times, this intended to indicate their status to one and all.

**WIGGING:** *A severe reprimand.*
Reminiscent of the days when all officials wore wigs as did the aristocracy.

**WILD AND WOOLLY WEST, THE:** *The American West.*
A reference to the sheepskin jackets and chaps worn by cattlemen wishing protection from the thorny shrubbery.

**WILD GOOSE CHASE:** *Any fruitless exercise.*
Unlike a steeplechase run from one church spire to another, a wild goose chase was a dangerous exercise designed to unseat as many riders as possible. One rider set and led the course with his fellows spread out in chevron formation behind thus resembling a skein of geese in flight. Others of more same disposition took the above to its present meaning.

**WIMP:** *Any man of weak character.*
First used in 1909 at Cambridge University where it denoted any female student and was based on 'whimperer'. It was not long before the usage embraced ineffectual males or those more inclined to the academic than the sporting.

**WIN HANDS DOWN:** *To win easily.*
When a jockey has established such a good lead that he no longer needs to drive his horse along, he holds the reins gently and his hands fall to the side of his horse's neck.

**WIN, PLACE OR SHOW:** *However things turn out.*
This is the American equivalent of 'each way', or horse-players' jargon for a bet that pays differing amounts whether the animals *wins*, takes second *place* or comes in third, which means that its name nevertheless *shows* on the announcement board.

**WIN THE UPPER HAND, TO:** *To gain advantage.*
This is most likely taken from the sport of arm-wrestling in which he with the hand uppermost is the winner. Attempts to link this to the alternate placing of hands up a stick are unconvincing.

**WINDFALL:** *Surprise benefit.*
In all likelihood this refers to the gathering rights afforded the peasants of old who were permitted to gather from their lord's land only such firewood and fruit that fell through natural causes.

**WING IT, TO:** *To improvise.*
Despite the decidedly aeronautical sound, this is of earlier nineteenth-century theatrical origin and descriptive of an actor having to suddenly stand in at the last minute, snatch-learning the lines as best he can in the wings before he enters for each appearance. Naturally, this could only be done with bit-parts, lead roles being underpinned by understudies.

**WITH BRASS KNOBS ON:** *More so, with interest.*
In the nineteenth century, furniture was available with a choice of fittings ranging from wood to solid brass – which was the most expensive. The expression is now normally reduced to 'with knobs on'.

**WITH FLYING COLOURS:** *Triumphant in success.*

When a fighting ship of old came out of battle victorious, her colours (flags) still flew proudly at her masthead. On the other hand, a ship indicated capitulation by lowering her colours.

**WITHIN AN ACE:** *Very close.*

Although the ace is now generally the highest card, in the past it more frequently denoted only 'one' and, since the single spot on gaming dice was also called the ace, a player at cards or dice who was one point away from winning – or losing – was within an ace of it.

**WOOLGATHER, TO:** *To allow the mind to wander.*

Children used to be sent out to collect any clumps of wool they could find in the hedges and take it home to be spun. Naturally, children on such an errand made the most of the perambulatory nature of their task.

**WOP:** *Any Italian.*

Like so many racist slurs, this began life as a term amongst those it is now used to offend. In the Neapolitan dialect '*guappo*' means a fine, handsome man and was a common form of greeting between male friends. In the immigrant-crowded New York of the early twentieth century the much used greeting became a label eventually acquiring derogatory overtones.

**WORD TO THE WISE:** *Good advice.*

This has altered quite significantly over the centuries for in Roman times the full expression was 'a word to the wise is enough'. In other words, the intelligent need only a hint to grasp the drift of good advice, they do not need it spelling out at length.

**WORK BOTH SIDES OF THE STREET, TO:** *To be deceitful or to cover all the options.*

Beggars' jargon for knocking on all the doors in the one street which becomes counterproductive in that the second side has likely observed the beggar's progress along the other. Two beggars moving up in tandem achieve more, this division of labour producing 'don't work my side of the street'.

**WORK LIKE A TROJAN:** *To work extremely hard.*

In much of his work, Virgil made great mention of the diligence and tenacity of the Trojans.

**WORK LIKE A TURK, TO:** *To work extremely hard.*

A likely contribution from the Irish '*torc*', literally a wild boar, but metaphorically any large and powerful man.

**WORLD IS YOUR OYSTER, THE:** *All opportunity is there.*

Allusion to its pearls to be plundered at will.

**WORN TO A FRAZZLE:** *Exhausted.*

This literally means 'worn to a shred'. The word 'frazzle' is ultimately allied to 'fray' and probably changed its form via some dialect word like 'frayze'.

**WRITING IS ON THE WALL, THE:** *All the portents of failure are there.*

At Daniel 5 is found the account of the imminent fall of Babylon due to the sins and excesses of Nebuchadrezzar (sic – nezzar is erroneous). At one point during an orgiastic feast a mysterious hand appeared and wrote on the wall words that heralded the collapse of the kingdom.

# Y

**YANK:** *Any American.*

Whilst this is the accepted meaning in Britain, in America the application has always depended on who is using the term and where. The origin has been much speculated but is almost certainly from the Dutch 'Jan Kaas', Johnny Cheese, which appeared as early as 1683, in the form of Yankey – but for many a year before that the term had served in Germany and Flanders as an insult for any Hollander. Thus it was the natural epithet for the settlers of New Amsterdam – later New York – who began arriving in 1624. It is most likely that it was the Indians who first applied the term in the blanket form for any white man – they being supremely indifferent as to the various countries of origin of their invaders. The Dutch themselves soon took to employing the term to insult their adversaries, the English settlers further north in Connecticut and did so with hefty tones of perfidy – a quality for which the British have rightly long been famed – and general cunning. These settlers so became the original Connecticut Yankees, too clever by half, as personified by the late Bing Crosby in the Hollywood classic *A Connecticut Yankee at the Court of King Arthur.* The association of the term with a northerly direction was perpetuated by the Confederate use of the term in the Civil War and the understood implication of cunning still survives in the ingenious Yankee jib, Yankee screwdriver and the multiple bet, Yankee, placed at the bookmakers.

**YELLOW:** *Cowardly.*

Before the colour green (*see*: GREEN-EYED-MONSTER) became the sign of jealousy this unworthy emotion was symbolized by yellow. By extension it also represented treachery in that the jealous attempt the downfall of those of whom they are jealous; Judas is traditionally portrayed in yellow and victims of the Inquisition *en route* to the stake were always so arrayed. In addition to this comes the very ancient idea of the bodily fluids being responsible for moods and characteristics – 'humour' is the Greek for a fluid. Too much blood and one become 'sanguine'; excess of black bile and 'melancholy' is the result, and the liver, once believed the seat of courage, functions with yellow bile.

In the case of the coward this was imagined to 'flee' the liver and leave the coward visibly yellow as a result, hence the more pointed 'yellow-bellied' and the parallel 'LILY-LIVERED'. The ancient physicians believed the complex interaction of the five major humours could be read in the face, hence 'complexion'.

**YELLOW PRESS, THE:** *The less scrupulous sector of the Press.*

The term first appeared in America in the run-up to the Spanish–American War of 1898, American involvement being largely instigated by Press Baron William Hearst, determined to force President McKinley into a war he passionately wished to avoid. In a circulation war with the protagonists reaching new depths of tasteless sabre-rattling, Hearst's *New York Journal* and Joseph Pulitzer's *New York World* attracted the above epithet which had been previously reserved for cheap, scurrilous magazines and books produced with cheap yellow covers. Such use of 'yellow' as early as 1846 scotches the theory that the epithet arose solely from the aforementioned papers fighting earlier in 1895 over the rights to a strip cartoon penned by Richard F. Outcault and properly entitled 'Shantytown' but destined to become known to the readership of both organs as 'The Yellow Kid'. When Hearst bought up the *New York Journal* he enticed Outcault away from the *New York World* which continued to run the strip by paying one George B. Luks to take over the artwork under the new title of 'Hogan's Alley'. Having pioneered the use of colour in 1893, the *World* in February 1896 imparted a yellow tinge to the sack-like garment worn by the central ragamuffin character and the so-called Yellow-kid War began when the *Journal* followed suit. It would be naive in the extreme to presume that all of this merrily coloured coincidence did not greatly help the transfer of the already extant use of 'yellow' in such context, but it was not the only factor.

**YID, A:** *Any Jew.*

Perhaps one of the least offensive of such terms in that it is but a shortening of 'Yiddish', itself an anglicized form of 'Judish–Deutsch', Jewish–German.

**YOB:** *Uncouth young man.*

A fine example of Cockney BACKCHAT in which all major words are reversed; the above is a reversal of 'boy' as in 'barrow-boy', not the most civilized denizens of mid-nineteenth-century London.

**YOMPING:** *To move over rough terrain.*

Brought to prominence by the Falklands War, this piece of marine/paratrooper slang almost certainly has its origins in the Scandinavian countries where such troops do much training. It has been suggested that prior to military use rally-drivers used the term for crossing rough sectors, but either way, the term is but a mimic of the way a Scandinavian would pronounce 'jumping'.

**YONKS:** *Inordinately long time.*

Of unclear origins and first surfacing in the 1960s this has been conjectured as either a humorous play on DONKEY'S YEARS or a fanciful acronym of Years, mONths, weeKS.

**YOU CAN WHISTLE FOR IT:** *You have no hope of achieving your objective.*

Ever a superstitious lot, sailors believed that when the ship was becalmed they could raise the wind if they all sat about the deck whistling. The normal rate of success of such a ploy brought the above to its present meaning.

**YOUR NAME IS MUD(D):** *To have a terrible reputation.*

This expression was given a considerable shot in the arm after the complicity trial of Doctor Samuel Mudd who had treated John Wilkes Booth for the injuries sustained during his assassination of President Lincoln on the night of 14 April 1865. However, it was in general American usage for at least forty years before the Civil War. The most likely inspiration is the adage 'throw enough mud and some of it is bound to stick', and indeed it was also from this that the less fastidious sector of the mid-nineteenth century American press was known as the Mud Press. The phrase may also have been influenced by the earlier seventeenth-century use of 'mud' for a fool, dope or unpopular person. As for the unfortunately named and fated Dr Mudd, it was never satisfactorily proved that he was involved in the assassination plot and he was eventually pardoned.

**YOUR NUMBER IS UP:** *You are in trouble.*

A twentieth-century British Army expression referring to the queue of men sent for punishment who are summoned to the commanding officers' presence by the calling out of their service number. The use of the phrase was also reinforced by talk of the 'bullet with your number on it', i.e., the one that fate has in mind for you. The notion is that when that bullet flies, no matter where you are it is going to kill you.

**YUPPIE:** *Anyone moderately moneyed and image conscious.*

One of the few words that really *is* derived from an acronym, this is from Young Upwardly mobile Professional Person. Whilst it is true the term was given great currency by the American publication *The Yuppie Handbook* by Piesman and Hartley (1984) there have been so many claims of origination that the matter is best left unsettled.

# Z

**ZANY:** *Amusingly eccentric.*

Despite the term's decidedly modern feel and its adoption into the hippy jargon of the 1960s the term has actually been in use since the early 1500s. In the form of Zanni, this is the diminutive of Giovanni and was the name of the stock buffoon in the *Commedia dell' Arte.* This may not be the only example of early Italian masquerading as a modernism. The OED carries a quote from 1600 exhorting that the ramparts be either 'beaten or zapped', this based on the Italian '*zappere*', to inflict damage with explosives as dug in with a hoe by the man we now called the 'sapper'. The Italians have thus being talking about zapping things for centuries and with the initial meaning in 1920s America being 'kill with a gun' it is perhaps not too hard to think of which particular Italian influence was responsible for imparting the term to general use.